ELIZABETH SEVERN

Elizabeth Severn: The "Evil Genius" of Psychoanalysis chronicles the life and work of Elizabeth Severn, both as one of the most controversial analysands in the history of psychoanalysis and as a psychoanalyst in her own right. Condemning her as "an evil genius", Freud disapproved of Severn's work and had her influence expelled from the psychoanalytic mainstream. In this book, Arnold William Rachman draws on years of research into Severn to present a much-needed reappraisal of her life and work, as well as her contribution to modern psychoanalysis.

Rachman's re-discovery, restoration, and analysis of The Elizabeth Severn Papers – including previously unpublished interviews, papers, books, brochures, and photographs – suggests that, far from a failure, the analysis of Severn by Sándor Ferenczi constitutes one of the great cases in psychoanalysis, one that was responsible for a new theory and methodology for the study and treatment of trauma disorder, in which Severn played a pioneering role.

Elizabeth Severn should be of interest to any psychoanalyst looking to shed fresh light on Severn's progressive views on clinical empathy, self-disclosure, countertransference analysis, intersubjectivity, and the origins of relational analysis.

Arnold William Rachman is a licensed psychologist, trained psychoanalyst, and Fellow of the American Group Psychotherapy Association.

PSYCHOANALYTIC INQUIRY BOOK SERIES

JOSEPH D. LICHTENBERG

Series Editor

Like its counterpart, Psychoanalytic Inquiry: A Topical Journal for Mental Health Professionals, the Psychoanalytic Inquiry Book Series presents a diversity of subjects within a diversity of approaches to those subjects. Under the editorship of Joseph Lichtenberg, in collaboration with Melvin Bornstein and the editorial board of Psychoanalytic Inquiry, the volumes in this series strike a balance between research, theory, and clinical application. We are honored to have published the works of various innovators in psychoanalysis, including Frank Lachmann, James Fosshage, Robert Stolorow, Donna Orange, Louis Sander, Léon Wurmser, James Grotstein, Joseph Jones, Doris Brothers, Fredric Busch, and Joseph Lichtenberg, among others.

The series includes books and monographs on mainline psychoanalytic topics, such as sexuality, narcissism, trauma, homosexuality, jealousy, envy, and varied aspects of analytic process and technique. In our efforts to broaden the field of analytic interest, the series has incorporated and embraced innovative discoveries in infant research, Self Psychology, intersubjectivity, motivational systems, affects as process, responses to cancer, borderline states, contextualism, postmodernism, attachment research and theory, medication, and mentalization. As further investigations in psychoanalysis come to fruition, we seek to present them in readable, easily comprehensible writing.

After more than 25 years, the core vision of this series remains the investigation, analysis and discussion of developments on the cutting edge of the psychoanalytic field, inspired by a boundless spirit of inquiry. A full list of all the titles available in the Psychoanalytic Inquiry Book Series is available at https://www.routledge.com/Psychoanalytic-Inquiry-Book-Series/book-series/LEAPIBS.

ELIZABETH SEVERN

THE "EVIL GENIUS" OF PSYCHOANALYSIS

Arnold William Rachman

Routledge
Taylor & Francis Group

LONDON AND NEW YORK

First published 2018
by Routledge
2 Park Square, Milton Park, Abingdon, Oxon OX14 4RN

and by Routledge
711 Third Avenue, New York, NY 10017

Routledge is an imprint of the Taylor & Francis Group, an informa business

British Library Cataloguing-in-Publication Data
A catalogue record for this book is available from the British Library

Library of Congress Cataloging-in-Publication Data
A catalog record for this book has been requested

ISBN: 978-1-138-12286-4 (hbk)
ISBN: 978-1-138-12287-1 (pbk)
ISBN: 978-1-315-64922-1 (ebk)

Typeset in Bembo
by Deanta Global Publishing Services, Chennai, India

IMAGE 1 Picture of Sándor Ferenczi, 1925, given to Elizabeth Severn with the inscription: "To Dr. Elizabeth Severn as a token of high consideration. Budapest, December 1925. S. Ferenczi"

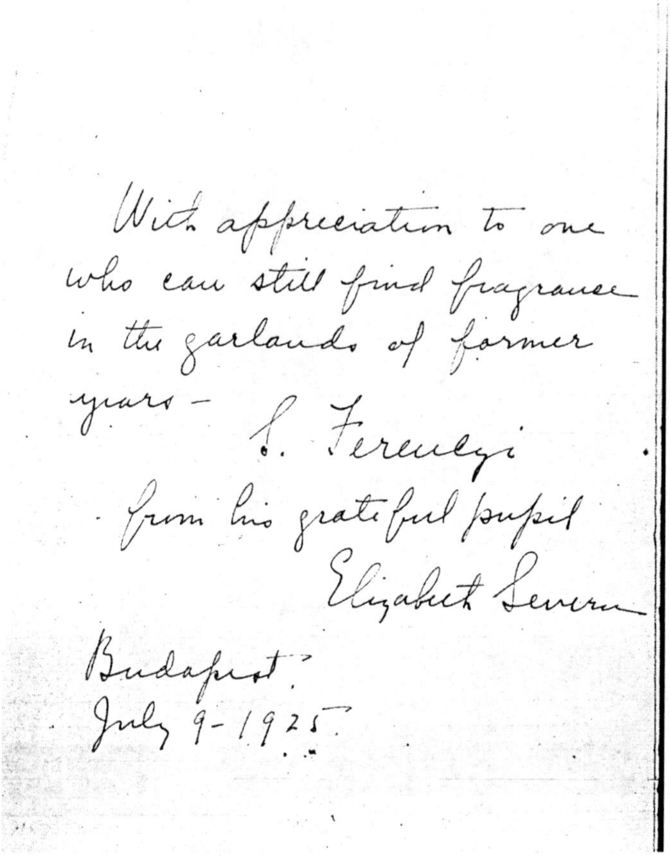

With appreciation to one
who can still find fragrance
in the garlands of former
years – S. Ferenczi
from his grateful pupil
Elizabeth Severn
Budapest.
July 9 - 1925.

IMAGE 2 Severn's dedication from her 1920 book, *The Psychology of Behavior*, which she gave to Sándor Ferenczi in July 1925, written in her own handwriting with the inscription: "With appreciation to one who can still find fragrance in the garlands of former years, S. Ferenczi. From his grateful pupil, Elizabeth Severn, Budapest July 9, 1925"

CONTENTS

LIST OF FIGURES

These are the 19 images used in the book, *Elizabeth Severn: "The Evil Genius" of Psychoanalysis*, taken from The Elizabeth Severn Papers, which are the literary property of Arnold William Rachman.

FOREWORD

As a mother comforts her son, so will I comfort you. (Isiah 66:13)

Laws which prescribe that everyone must believe and forbid men to say or write against this or that opinion, are often passed to gratify, or rather to appease the anger of those who cannot abide independent minds. (Baruch Spinoza)

When people come to you for help, do not turn them off with pious words, saying Have faith and take your troubles to God! Act instead as though there were no God, as though there were only one person in the world who could help – only yourself. (Martin Buber)

I do not know of any analyst whose analysis I could declare, theoretically, as concluded (least of all my own). Thus we have, in every single analysis, quite enough to learn about ourselves. (Sándor Ferenczi)

I wish here to emphasize the difference between the accepted psycho-analytic mode of treatment which is purely dissecting in nature ... and a method [that] does not scorn to 'play mother' ... to the injured one and which encourages the full reproduction of the emotions and feeling-tone of the traumatic period ... *under different and better communications* ... it takes above all an emotional capacity or 'gift' on the part of the analyst, who unless he can do this, is not a true physician to the soul. (Elizabeth Severn)

ABOUT THE AUTHOR

Arnold William Rachman, PhD, FAGPA:

Member, Board of Directors, The Sándor Ferenczi Center NYC
The New School for Social Research, NYC
Honorary Member – The Sándor Ferenczi Society, Budapest, Hungary
Donor – The Elizabeth Severn Papers, the Library of Congress, Washington, DC

Author –

(1997) *Sándor Ferenczi: the Psychotherapist of Tenderness and Passion*
(2003) *The Psychotherapy of Difficult Cases: Flexibility and Responsiveness in Contemporary Practice*
(2015) (with Susanne Klett) *Analysis of the Incest Trauma: Retrieval, Recovery, Renewal*
(2016) *The Budapest School of Psychoanalysis*
(2018) *Elizabeth Severn: The "Evil Genius" of Psychoanalysis*

ACKNOWLEDGMENTS

The late Hannah Kapit, PhD, a colleague at the Postgraduate Psychoanalytic Institute, began the process that led to the writing of this book about 15 years ago. She was a best friend of the late Margaret Severn, the daughter of Elizabeth Severn, Sándor Ferenczi's most controversial and famous analysand. When Margaret died, Hannah maintained contact with Peter Lipskis, a personal friend of Margaret and the literary executor of her estate, which included The Elizabeth Severn Papers. Peter contacted Hannah to find a party interested in acquiring Elizabeth Severn's personal and professional documents. I continue to be grateful to Hannah for putting me in contact with Peter to help rescue this lost legacy of psychoanalytic history. In my contacts with Peter, it became clear that Margaret believed her mother was a significant figure in the history of psychoanalysis and was dedicated to preserving her legacy. The documents were left to Peter after Margaret's death.

We also need to acknowledge Peter Lipskis's contribution to preserving The Elizabeth Severn Papers so that the analytic community would have the opportunity to discover one of the lost voices in analytic history. Psychoanalysis owes a debt of gratitude to Margaret Severn and Peter Lipskis, who had the foresight to preserve this legacy.

Once Peter Lipskis began sending me The Elizabeth Severn Papers from Vancouver to New York City, it was essential to find a safe and meaningful place to store these valuable documents. I was a member of the A.A. Brill Library at The New York Psychoanalytic Institute and had developed a relationship with Nellie Thompson, PhD, the library's archivist. I shared with Nellie that I had discovered the previously unknown papers of Ferenczi's most famous analysand, Elizabeth Severn. Her interest and responsiveness encouraged me to ask her if there was any possibility of storing the papers in the A.A. Brill Library archives. She explained that there was both a lack of funds and no longer room in the archives. But, in her dedication to analytic history and her personal generosity, she offered me a temporary solution: The Elizabeth Severn Papers would be stored in the anti-room to the archives until a permanent location was found. Nellie was also part of the permanent solution. In the spring of 2008, it became paramount that a permanent home be found for The Elizabeth Severn Papers. Nellie suggested that I contact Leonard Bruno, PhD, of the Library of Congress.

Leonard Bruno, the former chief of the Scientific Manuscript Division at the Library of Congress, gladly accepted The Elizabeth Severn Papers. He believed in the importance of these papers and Severn's significance for the history of psychoanalysis. We began to discuss the establishment of an Elizabeth Severn Section of the Freud Archives. Len Bruno's involvement became an important avenue for believing that Severn could be rescued as a lost figure of psychoanalysis. When Leonard Bruno retired, I worked with Jim Hutson, director of the Manuscript Division of the Library of Congress, who became the individual who helped finalize the establishment of The Elizabeth Severn Archives. He was a thoughtful and knowledgeable individual who helped plan and execute the Elizabeth Severn Symposium that celebrated the establishment of The Elizabeth Severn Archives. The Elizabeth Severn Symposium occurred on Friday, June 20, 2014, and consisted of a presentation by Arnold William Rachman, PhD, with Lewis Aron, PhD, and Joe Lichtenberg, MD, as discussants. It is believed this event was the first scheduled psychoanalytic symposium to focus on Elizabeth Severn as a meaningful figure in psychoanalysis.

In 2016, the remaining five boxes of The Elizabeth Severn Papers were sent to the Library of Congress, adding to the five originally sent in 2008. In December of 2016, Xerox copies of The Elizabeth Severn Papers were sent to Judit Mészaros, President of The Sándor Ferenczi Society, Budapest, Hungary. We now have an Elizabeth Severn archive at The Library of Congress and The Ferenczi House in Budapest, Hungary.

It was a highlight of writing this book that I was able to review the manuscript with my dear friend of 54 years, Harold Kooden, PhD, who I first met while we were graduate students at the University of Chicago in The Committee on Human Development. For over half a century we have been best friends, sharing our personal and professional lives. As we went over this manuscript we both became aware that, although we took different paths to becoming clinicians, our education and training at the University of Chicago, The Committee on Human Development, and the Counseling Center had been so influential in our thinking and functioning, that his comments were invaluable in both improving and expanding the form and content of the manuscript.

Herb Westphalen contributed his artistic ability to producing the images for the manuscript.

Mabel Mapp did a masterful job in translating my handwriting into a typed manuscript.

I am very grateful to Joe Lictenberg, MD, Editor-in-Chief for encouraging me to submit the manuscript to Routledge Press. I am also grateful to Kate Hawes, the publisher, who helped shepherd the manuscript through the submission process, and Charles Bath, Editor, who patiently guided the manuscript through the editorial process. I am very grateful to Lisa Keating for her editorial help in bringing together the final edition of this book.

1

FINDING PSYCHOANALYSIS

A personal journey

Personal motivation

It has been said that the motivation to become a psychoanalyst is derived from the individual's desire to solve his/her own personal problems. Although I was not conscious of this motivation when I began my academic and, later, clinical studies to become a psychoanalyst, I can now see personal motivation informed my desire to become a clinician. It also informed my attraction to phenomenology, humanistic psychotherapy, Sándor Ferenczi and the Budapest School of psychoanalysis, and finally, relational psychoanalysis (Rachman, 2006). My childhood contributed emotional issues. Two major emotional issues lingered from childhood into adulthood: feelings of maternal coldness and emotional distance, and feelings of domination and control. My longings in a relationship were for empathy and equality, and responsivity and flexibility. What was missing with my mother, I experienced with my grandmother. For nine years of my childhood, prior to my father's death, I also experienced interest and warmth.

During my pre-college years I was most responsive to teachers who showed an interest in me and affirmed that I was a student with some ability. This kind of attention was a marked contrast to my mother's response to me, which I clearly felt lacked affirmation and affection. I felt she did not like me. My *lifesaving experience*, the one that kept me from becoming dysfunctional, was the ongoing loving relationship my grandmother provided. I knew and felt that she loved me. What is more, she showed her affection directly toward me by referring to me, in her native German, as "*mein Gellebter*" ("my beloved"). She also had a dream for me, which she shared: "*Mein Gellebter*," she would say, "you would make such a fine teacher. You are tall, good looking, like your father. You are smart!" This affirmation of me by my grandmother became part of my internal psychological structure. In my career,

I have published 100 papers, seven books, and given hundreds of presentations. I was also appointed a professor, fulfilling my grandmother's dream for me.

My development as a humanistic psychotherapist

I did not come to psychoanalysis easily. In fact, I was involved in a protracted and difficult struggle to find a home in the field of psychoanalysis. The struggle was intellectual, interpersonal, and emotional. In truth, I did not have an ambition to become a psychoanalyst. My original aim in pursuing postgraduate training was to improve my capacity to be a psychotherapist. I had first been trained as a humanistic psychotherapist at the University of Chicago. But, I chose an analytic institute in New York City because I wanted to return to New York and my family for postgraduate training, after finishing my education and training at the University of Chicago. If I had not been interested in returning home, I would have pursued a postdoctoral program at the University of Wisconsin where Carl Rogers and Eugene Gendlin had gone after Chicago to establish a client-centered psychotherapy training program with the more disturbed clients. In other words, at that time, after graduating with a doctorate in human development and clinical psychology in the 1960s, I was interested in further developing my understanding and functioning as a humanistic psychotherapist. At the beginning of my postgraduate training, my theoretical orientation was informed by a group of scholars who were termed "the third force" in psychology and psychotherapy (Bugenthal, 1964; Fromm, 1956; Maslow, 1962; May, 1958; Rank, 1996; Rogers, 1961). I developed an orientation as a humanistic psychotherapist that was intellectually and emotionally compatible with my personal needs and my personality.

My academic training as an undergraduate at the University of Buffalo in the late 1950s and at the University of Chicago in the early 1960s emphasized phenomenology, humanistic psychology and psychotherapy, and the American philosophical traditions of democratic and liberal thought of G.H. Mead and John Dewey (Farber, 2006; Hickman & Alexander, 1998; Mead, 1934). I had combined these intellectual and clinical ideas with my clinical training in client-centered psychotherapy at the University of Chicago. The Counseling Center at the University of Chicago, founded by Carl Rogers, focused on a clinical approach of accurate empathic understanding, responsiveness, clinical flexibility, and unconditional positive regard. In the 1960s, many clinical psychologists felt like second-class citizens in contrast to the elevated and superior status automatically given to psychiatrists. Social workers, in that era, had status because they were viewed positively as being a psychiatrist's *right hand*. Psychologists, however, were greeted with criticism and hostility by many psychiatrists and psychoanalysts, who viewed them as a direct financial and competitive threat. It was not until the American Psychological Association successfully sued the American Psychoanalytic Association and International Psychoanalytic Association for *constraint of trade* for refusing to accept psychologists in their approved analytic training institute that the so-called *lay analyst* could receive equal status with medical analysts. This prejudice toward non-medical analysts developed in the United States, in spite of the fact that non-medical analysts, such as Anna Freud, Melanie Klein, and Otto Rank, were approved by Freud and the orthodox analytic community. I was very fortunate to train at the Counseling Center, where academic clinicians such as Rosalind Cartwright, Eugene Gendlin, Laura Rice, John Shlien, and Fred Zimring affirmed and helped solidify my identity as a psychologist/psychotherapist. It was with this positive identity as a therapist that I left the University of Chicago and looked forward to my experience of postgraduate training in psychoanalysis in New York City. The Counseling Center and Rogers' humanistic psychotherapy perspective provided me with an emphatic approach, which I brought to my analytic training.

A Confusion of Tongues trauma in analytic training

Almost immediately after entering analytic training at the Institute in New York City I was thrown into a Confusion of Tongues trauma (Rachman & Klett, 2015). The trauma was created by the Dean of the Institute in a series of disturbing experiences (Rachman, 2004b). These experiences interfered with my enjoying a positive introduction to psychoanalysis and caused me to question my desire to pursue analytic training. In my opinion, the Dean was a hyper-aggressive, dominating, intellectual, and emotional bully. In a series of emotionally damaging experiences, early in my training, I found him to be unempathic, overpowering, and severely critical. These experiences were completely different from my academic and training experiences at the universities of Buffalo and Chicago, where I felt affirmed and prized (Rachman, 2006). The trauma began on the first day of orientation for new analytic candidates. Each director of a department at the Institute spent five-to-ten minutes in some form of a welcoming address. In his address, the Dean said the following, which made me question whether I had made a serious mistake in coming to the Institute: "If you believe that Eric Fromm is a psychoanalyst that you will study here, you are in the wrong church and wrong pew."

This declaration against Eric Fromm as a dissident whose ideas were not welcomed in the Institute was shocking to me. Eric Fromm was viewed at the University of Chicago as a psychoanalyst who was compatible with humanistic psychotherapy. When I discovered Ferenczi (see Chapter 2), I found one of Fromm's works to be extremely important for my Ferenczi research (Fromm, 1959). He, as I later found out, valued Ferenczi's work. In those first moments at the Institute I felt alone and unwanted, as none of the candidates raised an objection to the Dean's condemnation of Fromm. I was too frightened and confused to speak up.

A still more disturbing event occurred during the same first week of training and contributed further to the Confusion of Tongues trauma. I had finished my course of study for my doctorate in clinical psychology and human development in the spring of 1964. I was interviewed, prior to finishing my PhD, at the American Psychological Association meeting in Chicago by the late Ted Reiss,

PhD, the Director of Research at the Institute. After interviewing me, Ted Reiss told me it was not necessary for me to see anyone else from the Institute because he accepted me for training, right then and there. A feeling of elation lingered after the Ted Reiss interview. He made it clear he found me a potentially worthwhile analytical candidate. I found him a responsive and likeable person. This positive interview helped me look forward to my new training experience. But a problem arose in scheduling my doctoral exam before I could leave Chicago and come to New York City. None of my doctoral committee was available for the oral exam during the summer. I was to begin analytical training in September.

My analytical training began in September of 1964. Before leaving Chicago I called the director of the Psychology Department, the late Tao Abel, PhD, and asked her if I could begin my analytical training without completing my doctoral orals before I left Chicago. I said I had arranged to take my oral examination in the fall. She completely agreed with my plans and told me to come to study at the Institute without any reservation.

At that time, I thought that passing the oral examination was just a formality, not a necessary final step to having earned your doctorate and being referred to as doctor. This discrepancy exploded in my face in that first day of contact with the Dean of the Institute. In my attempt at honesty and full disclosure, I revealed to him that I had not taken my orals and was planning to take them in the fall. Furthermore, I told him this arrangement was approved by the director of the Psychology Department. I was under the impression he had been informed of this arrangement. No sooner had I told him about the oral exam dilemma than he blurted out:

> *You are a psychopath, young man!* You'd better fix this, right away. I can't have you ruining my post-doctoral program with your high jinks. You are going to get your orals done as soon as possible or you are out of here!

I deeply felt his rage towards me. He was so emotionally out of control that he could not hear me clearly say that I had checked with the head of the Psychology Department, gotten permission to enter the analytic training program without the orals, and made preparations to take my orals in the fall. His rage prevented him from hearing me.

Prior to the Dean becoming enraged with my postponing the oral examination, the dissertation committee had given me approval to schedule my oral examinations in the fall of 1964. As the Dean was screaming at me and calling me a psychopath, I was trying to tell him I had taken care of scheduling the formal requirements for the doctorate. Both the doctoral committee members at the University of Chicago and the director of psychology at the Institute raised no objection to my plan and were totally positive and cooperative with me. They affirmed the positive feeling as a person and clinician I had enjoyed during my experiences at the universities of Buffalo and Chicago. The Dean's extremely negative reaction to my disclosure about the doctoral orals intensified and expanded the Confusion of Tongues trauma that had been activated the first day of orientation at the Institute. Anxiety, confusion, and anger predominated my experience during the next week. I felt I had been honest and forthright but the Dean said I was a psychopath, manipulating the Institute and him to satisfy my need to challenge authority. Just as I began to seriously entertain dropping out of the training program, I found an empathic presence at the Institute. This presence was to allow me to continue and begin a positive journey on the road to becoming a psychoanalyst.

I began my personal analysis shortly after the beginning of my Confusion of Tongues trauma, as the Dean continued to create emotional difficulties for me (Rachman, 2004b). The late Betty Feldman, MSW, became the empathic presence that I needed in the next four years of my analytic training (Rachman, 2014c). In our first week of sessions I unloaded my trauma on her shoulders. Her empathic response demonstrated to me how psychoanalysis can integrate phenomenology and humanistic psychotherapy. She listened to me and then, as her first response, self-disclosed her experience with the Dean. She told of her perception of him as an overly aggressive individual who had a decided tendency to create emotional crises with male candidates when he felt threatened by them or felt they were questioning his authority. It is impossible to fully describe in words how emotionally embraced I felt at that moment in my analysis. Betty's response was important to me in several ways: it helped me own my experience of the trauma; it wasn't all me, it was also him; I may have done something neurotic, but I wasn't a psychopath. Then I was able to express my anger toward the Dean with my family, friends, and fellow candidates. Betty provided me with the empathy I badly needed at a moment of emotional crisis, the kind of empathy to which I was accustomed at the Counseling Center. I felt affirmed, prized, and given unconditional positive regard. Betty Feldman's therapeutic behavior showed me the value of an analyst who can embrace empathy within the analytic encounter, a way of being that I embraced in my later thinking and functioning as a psychoanalyst (Rachman, 1997a, 2003a; Rachman & Klett, 2015). In my later research on the Freud/Ferenczi relationship, I realized this kind of empathy was what Ferenczi wanted from Freud.

Although I did receive some affirmation from my fellow candidates, their relationship to the Dean prevented them from fully responding to my need. The Dean was considered one of the foremost role models as a psychoanalyst at the Institute. He was considered a powerful, successful clinician who was the right-hand man of the Institute's founder and one of its most prestigious members. The Dean's status as an analyst, teacher, and supervisor was elevated by the fact he rarely accepted any candidates for analysis and even less often for supervision. He held himself aloof as a very desirable but unattainable analyst. Finally, almost all candidates were afraid of him. They were willing to put up with what I would now term emotional abuse (Rachman, 2004b) so that they could graduate from the analytic training program. I believe it is a part of the psychodynamic of analytic training institutes that the candidate's desire to graduate and become a practicing psychoanalyst suppresses the confrontation with the emotional abuse of authority. This psychodynamic was clearly illustrated in the comments of a second-year candidate when I told him, as a first-year candidate, about my difficulties with the Dean. He offered the following response, with a smile on his face:

> Listen, Arnold! I know the Dean can be a son-of-a-bitch, sometimes. But, I am only interested in graduating and starting a practice. I am not interested in locking horns with him.

My intense difficulties with the Dean can illuminate the question as to how I decided to train at the Institute. When choosing a postdoctoral training program in New York City, I was acquainted with two programs, New York University's postdoctoral program in psychoanalysis and the Postgraduate Center for Mental Health. For some reason, the William Alanson White Institute, which was in NYC, was not on my radar. I was not interested in a traditional analytical program, which focused on a Freudian orientation of psychology and psychoanalysis as I have discussed. I wanted an analytic experience which believed in clinical empathy, responsiveness, flexibility, and creativity. My interview for the NYU postdoctoral program did not go well. The interviewing analyst focused on my interest and acquaintance with psychoanalysis. I did have some knowledge of analytic authors, such as Fromm, who were compatible with the third force in psychology and psychotherapy. The NYU analyst who interviewed me seemed critical that I had not sought out personal analysis as a graduate student. He gave me the distinct impression that he did not view me as someone who was dedicated to psychoanalysis (which, of course, at that point in time, was true). Consequently, I was not accepted at NYU's postdoctoral program. There is some irony in that some 20 years later I became part of NYU's postdoctoral program as a member of the Relational Track. As I have outlined, I had an excellent interview with the late Ted Reiss who seemed to feel my phenomenological and humanistic psychology background was an asset. He never questioned my not having been in personal analysis. The Institute also had the reputation as having an eclectic/liberal analytic approach.

When I began to question whether I should continue my analytic training at the Institute, another experience, in addition to my analysis, helped me realize becoming an analyst was a reasonable goal. At the time of my anxiety and self-doubt, a senior supervisor at the Institute, the late Alice Hampshire, MD, took a special interest in me. After working with me for a couple of weeks, as a senior supervisor, she offered the following dramatic statement:

> Arnold, you are too intelligent, too interested in empathy and being clinically responsive to be at the Institute. You should enroll at the William Alanson White Institute. That's the place for you.

Where did this "angel of empathy" come from in my great moment of need? Alice Hampshire's reaction to me was the complete opposite of the Dean's reaction. I now felt elated, supported, understood, and affirmed. I could not wait to tell my analyst what Alice Hampshire had said to me. She had provided me with what seemed like a very positive way out of my trauma. No sooner had I told my analyst of my desire to transfer to the William Alanson White Institute than I was faced with another layer of the trauma. Without hesitating for a moment, and speaking in a decisive and focused manner, Betty Feldman responded to my plan to transfer with a statement that took the air out of the room and replaced it with a dark cloud. I became silent and sullen as I heard her say the following:

> Arnold, the Dean *will not let you transfer* from our Institute to William Alanson White. *He will blackball you*, by calling all institutes you contact and telling them not to take you. *He can do this, and he will.* He will be angry and will not let you publically embarrass him and his training program.

Her response enraged me. I also felt defenseless and totally defeated. I could hardly speak. After a long silence, I reacted with anger at her, for delivering this vile message. Betty Feldman accepted my anger. She made it clear that she was trying to protect me from a professional and, subsequent, personal disaster. In this difficult message, she was conveying to me a dark side of the Dean, which she knew personally. My anger toward my analyst gradually dissipated, realizing she was trying to help, not hurt me. However, my anger toward the Dean did not diminish. Faced with a decision to leave the Institute and face threats to my career, I swallowed the bitter pill of being blackballed from entering a new institute. I found a creative way to deal with my anger and disappointment through my analysis and decided to stay at the Institute. Do I regret the decision to stay? I have questioned whether I should have left. The irony is that I have been able to develop my own intellectual and emotional proclivities, which may indicate that the Institute has been more than a reflection of the Dean's need to dominate the candidates. My experiences with Betty Feldman and Alice Hampshire showed me the humanistic side of psychoanalysis.

When I wrote my first Ferenczi book (Rachman, 1997a), I traced my kinship with Ferenczi to the members of the Institute in the following way:

> I was analyzed by Betty Feldman, who was analyzed by the director of the Institute, who was analyzed by Clara Thompson, who in turn, was analyzed by Ferenczi.
>
> *(Rachman, 1997a)*

Tracing this analytic lineage makes me a fifth generation analysand of Ferenczi. (If I continued this lineage, Ferenczi was analyzed by Freud, which would make me a sixth generation analysand of Freud.) The director of the Institute developed his non-traditional orientation to psychoanalysis from his work with Clara Thompson (Wolberg, 1967). My analyst Betty Feldman was in turn influenced in her analytic thinking and clinical behavior by Lewis Wolberg, MD, the founder of the Institute, which was indicated in her active and empathic interaction with me.

There are some regrets about not exposing the Dean's abusive behavior during my training period. Then, I did not have the emotional courage to initiate such a confrontation. I also did not have the support of fellow candidates. I felt like an unknown, insignificant individual in the analytic community. I did not believe anyone would come forward publicly to support me. I have found that psychoanalysts generally do not speak out about the abuses in their profession. In fact, I have found that psychoanalysis has institutionalized not speaking out, and, what is more, developing a methodology to prevent its members from confronting abuses in the profession. The late Esther Menaker, PhD, and I developed a concept for this phenomenon. Menaker became a mentor for me after graduation from analytic training, when colleagues introduced us to each other, feeling we were dissidents who shared similar views. Menaker and I met regularly, exchanging ideas and planning to write a book on her analyst, Anna Freud. Although Menaker was analyzed by Anna Freud and graduated from the Vienna Psychoanalytic Institute run by the Freuds, she developed an interest in non-Freudian perspectives, which led to a journey from Otto Rank to Self Psychology (Menaker, 1989). We talked often about the institutionalized way traditional psychoanalysis suppressed any critique of Freud. Menaker suggested we use the German term *Todschweigen* (death by silence) (Rachman, 1999) to denote this process. We believed psychoanalysis institutionalized the silencing of dissident voices, like Ferenczi and Rank, by suppressing and neglecting their ideas and publications (Rachman, 1997b). This idea will be discussed in Chapter 7.

My struggles with the Dean of the Institute reached a bizarre crescendo in my last year of training. By then, I was able to settle down into a comfortable place in thinking and practice where I found a place for my interest in activity and empathy in work with adolescents (Rachman, 1975) and group interaction (Rachman, 1981). I began to experience myself as a psychoanalyst. Wanting to move toward greater analytic understanding and functioning, I asked my analyst, Betty Feldman, with whom should I have supervision before leaving the Institute. Without a moment of hesitation, she said:

> There is only one person with whom you should work before you leave. You should contact the Dean for supervision. He has the most to offer you.

I was incredulous! I thought to myself, "Is she crazy? Is she sadistic?" Betty, who I loved and viewed as a kind person also had the capacity to be assertive. She stood her ground, emphasizing that the Dean had the most to offer. Furthermore, it was up to me to convince him to take me on for supervision. As I previously mentioned, the Dean rarely saw anyone for supervision, which elevated him to the status of an unavailable guru.

Betty Feldman's suggestion forced me to be torn between wanting to self-actualize my capacity to be an analyst and entering into a masochistic relationship with the *Demon Dean*. I decided to trust my analyst and arranged a consultation for supervision with the Dean. My only explanation for this strange move on my part was that it was a counter-phobic maneuver. I was trying to work through my Confusion of Tongues trauma by directly confronting it with a good dose of masochism. Looking back, I believe that my willingness to see the Dean for supervision, after having such negative interaction with him, suggests that I was willing to tolerate potential emotional abuse in order to gain greater understanding and enhanced clinical functioning. There are many stories in the public consciousness of tyrannical teachers who help students/victims develop their gifts. A recent academy award-winning film, *Whiplash* (Carter, 2015), depicts such an abusive teacher/student relationship.

Much to my surprise, the Dean was enthusiastic to see me for a consultation about supervision. But, he said he would see me for supervision "with one condition." I would have to present case material to him as part of the supervisory training course, behind a one-way mirror, while advanced candidates could view the supervision. Should I have been more cautious or questioning of this offer? Was I being emotionally seduced? My anxieties were diminished by his convincing statement, which, at the time seemed sincere:

> You have nothing to worry about. All the attention will be on me. The class will want to see how I supervise you, not how you do therapy.

I do not really know why I accepted his declaration of protection so readily. My analyst also seemed to be fine with the arrangement. I would say he emotionally seduced me. Also, I had not worked through my Confusion of Tongues trauma with him (Rachman & Klett, 2015). Unfortunately, I now moved into a full-blown Confusion of Tongues experience in supervision.

The Confusion of Tongues experience in supervision intensified while I was presenting a therapy case of a young man exploring his homosexual feelings. This young man and I believed we enjoyed a very good working relationship. He felt he was making satisfactory progress and was analyzing his fundamental emotional issues. I felt he was working well with me. Not asking me to review my assessment of the case's progress, the Dean quickly intervened during my presentation and asked me if I had seen the film *Reflection in a Golden Eye* (Ebert, 1967). I said I had not seen this film. Pressing forward he asked me why I had not seen it. I became emotionally uncomfortable, realizing he was not keeping the promise he made during our consultation session. He seemed dissatisfied with something in my case presentation and was about to confront me about it. I felt myself beginning to dissociate to protect myself from the disturbance that was coming. I gathered my emotional resources and answered him:

> I don't have time to go to the movies. I am in the training program, I work part-time and I have to spend time with my wife and two young children.

He jumped on my response, implying that I gave the wrong answer. He said that I should make the time to see such a movie, whose theme of *repressed homosexuality* would help me understand my case. In front of a class of about 15 analysts taking the supervisory course, he suggested that I was not in touch with my repressed homosexuality and needed to become so. He declared that before I could understand and help the individual I was presenting for supervision, I needed to see this film. I did not say anything in response to this accusation because I felt shamed and criticized. My silence was my defense against the abuse. Actually, the Dean was not interested in any response from me. His aim, as I experienced it, was to demonstrate to the supervision training class how acute his capacities were in discussing a personal issue of mine, and how creative he was in using a projective device to help me confront my own issue. He was directing me to see a movie that he felt addressed my repressed homosexuality, which was interfering with my emotional capacity to help the individual struggling with homosexual feelings. I felt at that moment that he had broken his promise that the supervisory relationship would focus on him, not me. In fact, in this abusive interaction, as well as in others, the Dean showed no interest in my reaction to his *abusive interpretations*. It was a demonstration of his narcissism; he was showing off, demonstrating his prowess as a supervisor, in front of a captive audience of candidates, as if he was in show business.

There was another abusive interaction with the Dean that could be called "The Arab-Woman Interpretation." This encounter reinforced the Dean's interpretation that I was a passive, effeminate therapist, who lacked the required masculine, assertive characteristics to be a Freudian analyst and adequately help an individual who was struggling with homosexuality. As I was presenting case material, exploring the analysand's childhood experience with his mother when she dressed him up in girl's clothing, he suddenly turned to me and questioned my idea of therapeutic interaction. He asked me what was my idea of the analyst's role in the clinical interaction. Then, the following exchange ensued. First, I answered:

> I believe the analyst should allow the analysand to take the lead and say where, how, and when they want to explore issues in their functioning that concern them. The analyst walks, side-by-side, with the analysand, sharing the experience and being available to help.

I was basically outlining a humanistic, client-centered perspective that I brought with me from Chicago and in which I truly believed. At the time of the supervisory encounter in the mid-1960s, the analytic approaches such as Self Psychology and relational analysis had not been developed. In addition, the Object Relations and Cultural School approaches were not fully integrated into the Institute's perspective. No sooner had I expressed my humanistic idea of a therapeutic relationship than the Dean told me in a sarcastic and accusing way:

> You sound like you are describing an Arab woman, who walks behind her husband. She defers to him.

It was another accusation that I was not a good-enough analyst because I lacked the aggressive, masculine, dominant qualities he valued for an analyst. I wondered if there was any room in psychoanalysis for an empathic, compassionate, unobtrusive analyst?

A final incident in the Confusion of Tongues trauma of supervision occurred toward the end of the training year. In the last week of the one-way mirror supervision, the Dean, without warning, initiated a session by telling me that he had asked the advanced analytic candidates of the supervision course to rate my readiness to graduate from the individual analytic program. I was devastated by his request of the class. Once again, I could feel myself emotionally drifting away. (Ferenczi described this experience of psychological numbing in the Confusion of Tongues trauma [Ferenczi 1980k].) I numbed myself from what I experienced as abusive behavior by the Dean. I was outraged that he would subject me to an evaluation by the class, without my knowledge and permission. The Dean again, broke what I, as an analytic candidate, considered a sacred promise, to maintain the *focus of the supervision on his functioning.* Without asking me if I wanted to hear the results, he proceeded to tell me the finding of the class survey. I barely heard what he said because I was in a dissociative state. I believe the Dean indicated that 70 % of the class said I was ready to graduate, 20% said I was not, and 10% were unsure. The Dean looked at me after he presented this so-called evidence and saw my sullen and distant face. At some level he finally sensed that I was injured and offered me the following:

> Arnold, you are very good. I want to help you be the best. In fact, you could be as great as I am!

As I write these words, I am as incredulous. If there ever was a left-handed compliment, he had offered it. But, it was not the narcissistically oriented compliment that disturbed me. After all, in his half-assed way, the Dean was saying I could be as great an analyst as he was. The real disturbing fact was that the Dean did not seem to have any awareness that his intrusive interpretations and his non-emphatic and aggressive, and perhaps sadistic, manner of relating were tramatogenic. He never responded to my face or body posture after he offered his devastating interventions. If he had done so, he would have seen an emotionally injured individual. I was too traumatized and afraid to really confront him because I felt criticized and shamed in front of a class of analysts. The class was told by the Dean not to talk to me during the course of the class, which almost left me with no support. Fortunately, two brave individuals, the late Charles Smith, PhD, and Herbert Rabin, PhD, made sure to tell me that I was doing fine as a clinician and the Dean was too hard on me.

The Confusion of Tongues experience with the Dean was one of the most significant experiences in my analytic training. After the one-way mirror supervision, I had finished all my requirements for graduation. I was ready to graduate, but I was frustrated, angry, and confused. I was not only angry with the Dean for subjecting me to abusive treatment, but, also angry with my analyst for suggesting I see the Dean for supervision. Didn't she know she was sending me into an abusive experience? The Dean created a Confusion of Tongues dynamic where you could not express your true feelings for fear he would retaliate against you, preventing you from graduating. I also believe his sense of self could not tolerate anger or criticism by a candidate. He created an experience where the abuser could not be confronted. In this situation, where the abused is not allowed to speak of his experience, I lost my voice to speak of the trauma, as Ferenczi has said (Ferenczi, 1980k). The Dean never asked me to voice any feelings about what was transpiring in our relationship. An awareness of a two-person psychology in a relationship was not part of the Dean's analytic perspective. I could not speak of the trauma the Dean had created. *I suffered the trauma.* Since becoming a practicing analyst, I have been able to deal more therapeutically with this kind of traumatic experience. Insight about these experiences came through two measures. Writing about trauma and The Confusion of Tongues became a way to gain an understanding of the psychodynamics of the interaction between the Dean and myself. It provided an avenue for finding a voice to fully speak of the trauma and to be able to continue to express my feelings associated with the trauma and to gain an understanding of the Dean's functioning. I was also able to use my understanding of Ferenczi and The Budapest School of Psychoanalysis (Rachman, 2016) to formulate the trauma experience as a Confusion of Tongues experience. Writing about the trauma has been therapeutic (Rachman, 2004b, 2006, 2007b, 2016). As we shall see in Chapter 7, Elizabeth Severn was an early proponent of using writing as a therapeutic tool.

A second measure that was helpful in expressing my feelings and understanding the trauma was talking to my colleagues, some of whom were graduates of the Institute. These colleagues were now no longer fearful of the Dean, since they had graduated and established themselves as peers within the analytic community. The responses of these peers was enormously helpful, because they had been witnesses to my experience as well as having their own negative encounters with the Dean. There was one such interaction with a colleague and dear friend, Harriet Pappenheim, CSW, who at a presentation I was giving about my analytic journey (Rachman, 2006), said the following to me:

> Arnold, have you ever considered that the Dean was jealous of you, and that precipitated his anger toward you. He was small, fat, unattractive, not well liked. You are tall, attractive, well liked.

Harriett gave her assessment of a psychodynamic formulation of the Dean's behavior toward me as envy, jealously, and anger on the basis of my positive attributes. I felt so prized at that moment that it felt like a loving statement that my grandmother had made to me. Harriet's response also made me realize that I was so encased in my Confusion of Tongues trauma I could never formulate that the abuser was deficient. I had been discussing the supervisory experience as the victim so it never dawned on me that the Dean envied me. What a wonderful insight, I thought, like the child/victim realizing that the parent/abuser is causing the trauma (Rachman, 1997a, 2000a, 2003a; Rachman & Klett, 2015).

These disturbing experiences I have outlined were completely contrary to my emotional sensibilities and therapeutic aims. They gave me an impression that traditional psychoanalysis, which I identified with the Dean's orientation, did not value empathy as a necessary and sufficient condition of a therapeutic interaction. As I have mentioned, empathy was an essential part of my clinical education at the University of Chicago Counseling Center. The Dean's approach, as I experienced it, was in severe contrast to an empathic and experiential perspective. His approach seemed to represent clinical psychoanalysis as providing intellectually correct interpretations in an aggressive manner, so that the analysand was forced to face their unconscious issues. In the example of my interactions with him, especially the "Arab-Woman Interpretation," being empathic and showing compassion and tender heartedness was equivalent to being passive, effeminate, submissive, and impotent as an analyst. In the Dean's approach, there was no idea about a two-person analytic relationship, where both analyst and analysand were involved in an examination and understanding of the transaction that was occurring between them. There was no idea of an ever-hovering attention to the relationship, attending to the disruptions and their repair. In addition, what was absent was the use of an *empathic compass* to modulate the analyst's responsiveness in the relationship. My experiences at Chicago helped me realize there was another way. The challenge was to find someone in psychoanalysis with whom I could identify and integrate my cherished beliefs, which I brought to my analytic training. I needed to search for what William James described as a *tender-minded* person (Putnam, 1999). I needed to find an analyst who believed in empathy, compassion, responsiveness, and relationship.

I learned a great deal from this traumatic experience with the Dean. It crystalized for me that the empathy I had learned at the Counseling Center was an important part of being a clinician. The Dean, I believe, did not value empathy in his interaction with students, and perhaps, by analogy, with his analysands. He valued being smart, right, aggressive, and dominant. He did not concern himself with the feelings of others. In our interactions, he was not aware of my suffering. He concentrated on his diagnosis of my emotional behavior. He left me with a very negative view of psychoanalysis. I thought to myself: "I could not be, and do not want to be, an analyst like him. If this is what psychoanalysis is, I do not want to be an analyst."

The Dean's version of psychoanalysis, as I came to conceptualize it, through his behavior with me and the comments he made in class and supervision, was what I would call *a minimal human experience*. In the classroom, he once told us: "It is possible to conduct an analysis where the analyst responds minimally." In other words, if you had an ideal patient and a classically trained analyst, you could create a clinical interaction where *the analyst would only respond minimally* with a few interpretations to keep the individual exploring their unconscious. He referred to Karl Menninger's work as his inspiration for this analytic perspective (Menniger, 1958). I remember feeling he was describing a cold and distant experience, which, for me, felt like repeating my childhood disturbance with my mother (Rachman, 1997a). The minimalist form of therapy seemed to come to a crescendo in psychoanalysis in the 1970s with Robert Langs, who emphasized *not breaking the frame*

(1973, 1974). Langs, as legend has it, would not offer a box of tissues to a crying patient, because by doing so he would be encouraging a dependency upon the therapist to satisfy the patient's unfulfilled needs. It seemed as if Langs was outdoing Freud by creating an emotionally pure, transference-free atmosphere. In this analyst-free interaction, anything that emerged in the analytic encounter would be a function of the patient. As an analytic candidate and young analyst, I felt repelled by this attitude. I was looking for a way to integrate the caring, empathic attitude of the humanism I learned and believed in at Chicago with psychoanalysis. Fortunately, during this same time period, while I was suffering from a Confusion of Tongues trauma, I had begun an analysis with Betty Feldman. As mentioned, she made an important contribution to my recovery from my trauma by being human with me. Her sharing with me of her emotional experience with the Dean helped me experience that empathy and a two-person psychology existed in psychoanalysis, a perspective which later defined my work (Rachman, 2016).

2

FINDING FERENCZI

My struggle to build a bridge from
phenomenology and humanistic
psychotherapy to relational analysis

My discovery of Sándor Ferenczi

After graduation from analytic training in 1968, I carried around an empty feeling
that, unlike my colleagues who had identified with Freud, I was not emotionally
connected to any psychoanalytic hero. Existential analysis, which had a presence in
the 1960s was of interest to me (May, 1958; Tillich, 1952) but, at that time, there
was no psychoanalyst with whom I could identify. I had maintained my identification with members of the client–centered community, such as Carl Rogers (1959)
and Eugene Gendlin (1962). What I needed was a bridge from phenomenology and
humanistic psychotherapy to psychoanalysis. In the 1960s and 1970s, I was able to
channel my search into the encounter and marathon group psychotherapy moment
(Rachman, 1977, 1978, 1981a, b). These new forms of therapeutic intervention
provided an opportunity for me to express my clinical interest in active and experimental psychotherapy. Then, in or about the spring of 1976, while I was searching
the literature for any analytic precursors to the encounter and human potentiality
movement (Lieberman, Morton, Miles & Yalom, 1973; Rogers, 1970; Schutz, 1973),
I ran across an issue of the *American Journal of Psychotherapy*, which had an article
on active psychotherapy (Rachman, 1997a). Someone called Sándor Ferenczi was
referenced as an early advocate of active techniques. Listed in the bibliography was
one of his papers: "The further development of the active therapy in psychoanalysis"
(Ferenczi, 1980b). I thought this reference had some promise, but I could not say
there was any initial excitement in stumbling over this reference to Ferenczi. What
happened next brought excitement and changed my professional and personal life.
On a beautiful autumn morning of the same year, I went to the Institute's library
for the purpose of looking up the Ferenczi reference. I remember this experience
today as if it happened yesterday. When I asked the librarian if there was any material on Ferenczi, she pointed to the first stacks to my right, just a step away from the

entrance. About halfway up the stacks I found Ferenczi's work. I found the original Hogarth Press three-volume Ferenczi series (Ferenczi, 1950, 1952, 1955).

Before I looked up the aforementioned 1920 reference to Ferenczi on active therapy I looked over Volume I (Ferenczi, 1950). As I looked through these pages I began to realize I was discovering material to which I had not been exposed. I was becoming acquainted with what seemed like an analyst, as reflected in Ferenczi's writings, who was a creative, flexible, and responsive clinician. When I reached Volume II, (Ferenczi, 1952), where the 1920 active-therapy paper was located, my excitement continued to mount. I read paper after paper by an analyst who was a pioneer in introducing activity into psychoanalysis, experimented with the analytic method, was approved of by Freud for his dissident functioning, and seemed to share with my humanistic psychotherapy role models *a belief in the relationship*. There was no way I was leaving the library until I read Volume III.

Reading Volume III, entitled *Final Contributions*, created a revolution for me. Ferenczi's papers in the years 1927–33, were completely new to me. I loved everything he was describing: the necessary role of clinical empathy in the analytic process (Ferenczi, 1980k); the active role of the analyst in the analytic encounter (Ferenczi, 1980b); the use of non-interpretative measures in the treatment of difficult cases (Ferenczi, 1980i); analyst self-disclosure (Ferenczi, 1980k); a belief in a two-person experience in psychoanalysis (Ferenczi, 1980k); and a theory of trauma (Ferenczi, 1988). Why hadn't anyone at the University of Chicago or the Institute ever mentioned Ferenczi to me? *No one had ever placed Ferenczi's name on a reference list or uttered it in class, supervision, or a lecture.* This omission is particularly puzzling since both Carl Rogers, the founder of client-centered therapy, and the founder of the Institute where I received my analytic training were influenced by The Budapest School and Ferenczi. Rogers was influenced by Otto Rank (de Carvalho; 1999; Rogers, 1975). Rank was not only a colleague of Ferenczi but a collaborator (Ferenczi and Rank, 1925). So, why was there no mention of Ferenczi at The Counseling and Psychotherapy Research Center that Rogers founded at the University of Chicago, where I did my clinical internship and later became a staff member? At the Counseling and Psychotherapy Research Center I was taught, supervised, and became friends with Robert Butler, Eugene Gendlin, and John Shlien; all had been taught by Rogers and had become his close associates. They never once mentioned Ferenczi. At the University of Chicago, I was also a student of Erika Fromm, PhD, the cousin of Eric Fromm who was herself a psychoanalyst. Fromm had an extensive knowledge of Freud's work and, in our interactions, *referred to herself as* a psychoanalyst (French & Fromm, 1986). Fromm was chairperson of my doctoral research paper in clinical psychology. In these professional and personal contacts with me, Fromm never mentioned Ferenczi.

Still more puzzling was the total absence of Ferenczi's presence at the analytic institute where I trained. The founder of the Institute was analyzed by Clara Thompson, who was in turn analyzed by Ferenczi (Rachman, 1997a). In fact, Thompson became one of Ferenczi's most important followers, especially in the United States. She helped found the William Alonson White Institute, which became one of the few analytic training institutes where Ferenczi was revered. In the William Alonson White Institute auditorium four pictures of analysts which are displayed are Ferenczi, Fromm, Thompson, and Harry Stack Sullivan. Thompson sought out Ferenczi as her second analyst on the advice of Sullivan. She also became a conduit for Ferenczi's ideas and clinical thinking (Thompson, 1942, 1943, 1944, 1950, 1964). Although Thompson had some reservations about Ferenczi's dramatic and experimental clinical functioning (Thompson, 1943), she was strongly influenced by him. How does one explain Thompson's analysis of the Institute's director without believing she functioned under Ferenczi's influence? Isn't it likely she mentioned Ferenczi in their interactions? Furthermore, how does one explain the director not passing on the mention of Ferenczi to his student and analysand, Betty Feldman, who was my analyst? In fact, the director was a creative force in introducing a psychodynamic psychotherapy (Wolberg, 1967). In all the lectures I attended and the supervisory sessions the director conducted behind the one-way mirror, he never mentioned Ferenczi. This was borne out by my analyst's experience at the Institute where she also trained in the 1950s. She reported that she had never heard about Ferenczi from any analyst at the Institute. This included Franz Alexander (Alexander & French, 1980). According to Betty Feldman, Alexander had done a clinical demonstration at the Institute in the 1950s. Alexander had close ties to Ferenczi. His invitation to give a clinical demonstration at the Institute must have been issued by the director, who knew his work and connection to Ferenczi. There was some recognition of Ferenczi's ideas at my training institute through the flexible thinking and clinical functioning of the director, but there was no formal mention made of Ferenczi as a psychoanalytic ancestor.

When I first checked out the three volumes of Ferenczi from the Institute's library, I glanced at the card that indicated who had taken out the Ferenczi volumes in the past. I was the only person who had taken out these books in ten years. I felt all alone in my admiration of Ferenczi in those early days of 1976, since none of my colleagues had ever heard of him. I was eager to put my new knowledge to use. In 1977, I discovered that Sándor Lorand, MD, an analysand of Ferenczi, was living in New York City. In 1927, Lorand was the first European analyst to immigrate to the United States. He was the founder of the analytic training program at the Downstate Medical Center of the State University of New York. Lorand was a student of Ferenczi (Lorand, 1946). I found his number in the New York City phone book and gave him a call. He graciously agreed to see me. In the fall and winter of 1977, I interviewed him over two sessions (Rachman, 1977). Lorand was a gracious host, meeting with me in his office as well as taking me out to lunch. His office was a replica of Freud's Vienna consultation room, filled from floor to ceiling with books and with a Persian rug on the traditional analytic couch. As he requested, I presented my case of Oedipus from Brooklyn (Rachman, 1981). The case was based upon a liberal use of non-interpretative measures integrated into the analysis of trauma (Rachman & Klett, 2015). I wanted to hear if Lorand thought my active, non-interpretative approach was in the Ferenczi mode. Lorand's response was very important to me at that early period of my Ferenczi research and development as a psychoanalyst. He affirmed me as an analyst when he told me that my use of non-interpretive measures with Oedipus from Brooklyn was in the Ferenczian mode. In his thick Hungarian accent he bellowed:

> Arnold, when you used your new techniques, what happened to the patient! Did he accept your intervention? Had it helped him! *That's the issue, did it help him!* If it did, that's the end of it!
>
> *(Rachman, 1977, p. 10)*

It was a wonderful moment for me. My dissident analytic behavior was acceptable. What is more, as a living representative of Ferenczi, Sándor Lorand believed my non-traditional clinical behavior was in the tradition of Ferenczi's work. This experience with Lorand was a landmark for me. His acceptance of me and my work helped me feel I was going in a direction that would lead to an integration of my phenomenology and humanistic psychotherapy orientation with psychoanalysis. What is more, my work was being verified by a student, analysand, and personal friend of Ferenczi.

A second contact with the legacy of Ferenczi occurred about ten years later, which also was very important to me in solidifying my connection to Ferenczi and my identity as a psychoanalyst. At the 1988 Conference of the American Psychoanalytic Association, Anna Ornstein, MD, and I were on the same panel on empathy. Anna and Paul Ornstein, MD, introduced themselves to me. They were gracious, showing interest in me and my work, congratulating me on my thesis that Ferenczi should be credited with introducing clinical empathy into psychoanalysis (Rachman, 1988). I experienced Paul Ornstein as being a "living Ferenczi" by virtue of his acceptance, warmth, responsiveness, and friendliness. The Ornsteins had had ongoing professional and personal contact with Michael Balint, Ferenczi's successor to The Budapest School of Psychoanalysis (Ornstein, 1992/1968). They integrated their thinking with the Self Psychology perspective. Paul Ornstein told me he felt that Heinz Kohut, the originator of Self Psychology, provided a more comprehensive theoretical framework than Balint.

Ferenczi as the bridge between phenomenology and humanistic psychotherapy and relational analysis

My professional and interpersonal experiences with the Hungarian psychoanalysts Sándor Lorand and Anna and Paul Ornstein helped confirm and solidify my professional journey towards Ferenczi. From about 1976 to the present time I am continuing a journey researching Ferenczi's life and work, giving presentations at conferences in the United States, Europe, and South America. My first paper using Ferenczi as a frame of reference appeared in 1977, one year after discovering him. I had the audacity to write a paper entitled "The First Encounter Session: Ferenczi's case of the Female Croatian Musician" (Rachman, 1978). Ferenczi's 1920 paper "The Further Development of the Active Therapy in Psychoanalysis" (Ferenczi, 1980b), which brought me to discover his work, was so impressive that I thought it contained the origins of an active approach that could be seen as a precursor to the marathon and encounter movement. When I first heard about the human potentiality and encounter movement in the 1960s, this 1920 paper was never mentioned. I thought I had discovered a link between Ferenczi and my phenomenology and humanistic psychotherapy background. A prominent group psychotherapist, to whom I had sent my encounter paper, took time to write back to say I had "chutzpah" (Yiddish for unmitigated gall) to link Ferenczi with the encounter movement. I thought he was gently criticizing me for confabulating the connection between the encounter movement and Ferenczi. Actually, I was surprised that he did not make the connection himself, because he was trained as an analyst and had become a group therapist who was comfortable with being active. I still think Ferenczi's work was overlooked in the encounter and human potentiality movement. Perhaps, in some way that neglect was a good thing because many of the clinical abuses of that movement may have been blamed on Ferenczi's dissident ideas and practices. The 1978 paper on the first encounter session started my writing career about Ferenczi and The Budapest School of Psychoanalysis, which has continued to this day (Rachman, 1978).

My first presentation about Ferenczi took place at the Institute at which I did my analytic training, after colleagues became aware of my research. When I made my first Ferenczi presentation in the winter of 1977, I was the only person I knew who was interested in Ferenczi. It is a special and weird feeling to think you are devoted to a subject about which no one else you know cares. The invitation to speak at an Institute class was very appreciated and helped me feel special, since I believe it was the first Ferenczi presentation at the Institute. The class gave me a friendly and enthusiastic response. In fact, much to my surprise, I have always gotten a positive response to my presentations about Ferenczi, whether in the United States or abroad. In the U.S., audiences have appreciated the presentation of material that has been missing in their training. Another special step occurred when I was able to offer a Ferenczi course at the Institute. The first was a senior seminar offered in the late 1980s for fourth-year candidates. There was minor interest expressed then, as four candidates registered for the semester-long seminar. In the 1990s, under the leadership of Louise de Costa, PhD, an Object Relations Sequence was instituted as a required course. The study of Ferenczi and Balint began the sequence. It was a milestone for the Institute to include The Budapest School of Psychoanalysis as part of the required curriculum. I was thrilled to be asked to teach Ferenczi and Balint to analytic candidates. The silencing of Ferenczi had been shattered at the Institute. I had gone from not knowing who Ferenczi was to helping contemporary analytic candidates discover him. It was an honor to be part of helping to remove the wall of silence that surrounded Ferenczi's ideas from mainstream psychoanalysis (Rachman, 1999).

By 1990, I had been researching and talking about Ferenczi for 14 years in my quiet way to a select group in the analytic community of New York City. I spoke before candidates in institutes where colleagues were interested in hearing about

Ferenczi. My access to a greater part of the analytic community was fostered by several colleagues/friends in the greater analytic community in the New York City area. Bob Marshall, PhD, invited me to present lectures on Ferenczi at the Modern Psychoanalytic Institute (Rachman, 1988). Further, through the efforts of Clemens Lowe, PhD, I gave an elective senior seminar on Ferenczi at the National Institute for the Psychotherapies. When Aryeh Maidenbaum, PhD, was director of The New York Jungian Institute in the 1990s, he broadened the scope of analytic thinking and invited me to give lectures using Ferenczi as a frame of reference (Rachman, 1993). Through these contacts with colleagues and training candidates at different institutes I began to widen the scope of awareness of Ferenczi's importance for psychoanalysis.

A further expansion of my contact within the analytic community occurred through the efforts of Beatrice Beebe (Beebe, 2014). Beatrice was a member of the Relational Track at the NYU postdoctoral program. She told me she was going to pave the way for me to join the Relational Track at NYU. First, she told Lewis Aron and Adrienne Harris about my Ferenczi studies and urged them to make me a part of their upcoming conference on Ferenczi. Aron and Harris organized the International Ferenczi Conference in 1991 at the Mt. Sinai Medical School in New York City. Their book, *The Legacy of Sándor Ferenczi*, which is based upon the conference, became instrumental as a significant contribution to developing awareness about Ferenczi (Aron and Harris, 1993). My contribution to the conference was entitled "Ferenczi and Sexuality," which also appeared in their book (Rachman, 1993). In this paper I examined the rumors that many analysts accepted as fact that Ferenczi sexually acted out with his analysands. In the 1990s for example, a respected psychiatrist/psychoanalyst asked me, as soon as he found out that I was interested in Ferenczi: "Isn't Ferenczi the one who slept with his patients?" This paper about Ferenczi and sexuality began research into his actual clinical behavior with analysands. I broadened my investigation of psychoanalytic history to include Ferenczi's clinical interaction theory with two of his most famous analysands, Elizabeth Severn and Clara Thompson. According to my research on this subject, the rumors of sexual acting out were fueled by a romantic infatuation between Ferenczi and his future wife's daughter, Elma Palos. It was a romance that was maintained at a fantasy level, ending in their going their separate ways. I could find no evidence then, or subsequently, in the Freud/Ferenczi Correspondence, Ferenczi's *Clinical Diary*, or my correspondence with André Haynal, the chief editor of the Freud/Ferenczi Correspondence, of Ferenczi's acting out sexually with any analysand. In fact, Ferenczi's groundbreaking theory the Confusion of Tongues (Ferenczi, 1980k) explicitly stated that psychoanalysis should be performed in a *passion-free clinical encounter* to prevent the re-traumatization of a sexual trauma survivor (Rachman & Klett, 2015). I believe there were two incidents in psychoanalytic history that fueled the sexual acting out rumors. They involved Ferenczi's analysands Elizabeth Severn and Clara Thompson. Elizabeth Severn's professional relationship with Ferenczi will be fully discussed in an upcoming chapter. For now, it can be said that there is no evidence that Ferenczi had a sexual relationship with Severn. The clinical interventions with Severn were developed to treat her trauma disorder (Rachman, 2012a, 2014a, b) 2015a, b). Ferenczi's non-interpretive behavior was conceived as a clinical measure to cure her Confusion of Tongues childhood trauma, not to create a more intimate, passionate relationship. Clara Thompson was in analysis with Ferenczi at the same time as Severn. The rumor attributed to Thompson was that she bragged she could kiss Ferenczi any time she desired (Ferenczi, 1988). Thompson's statement about Ferenczi's so-called sexual behavior with her circulated in the analytic community at a time when Ferenczi was gradually moving away from Freud's influence as he devoted himself to the analysis of trauma. In this growing professional distance between Freud and Ferenczi, and criticisms by Freud of Ferenczi, the rumor of Thompson's dramatic statements gained a foothold (Rachman, 1997b). This kissing statement by Thompson was reported by Ferenczi in the first entry in his *Clinical Diary*:

> The case of (Dm/Clara Thompson) ... who ... had allowed herself to take more and more liberties, and occasionally even kissed me ... she remarked quite casually in the company of other patients, who were undergoing analysis elsewhere:
> 'I am allowed to kiss Papa Ferenczi as often as I like.'
> *(Ferenczi, 1988, p. 2 – Clinical Entry January 7, 1932)*

Ferenczi said that he did allow Thompson to kiss him out of sexual interest. He was responding to Thompson's eroticizing of the transference by creating a holding environment for her to *act in* her childhood incest trauma with a father figure; Ferenczi did this with the awareness of Thompson's incest trauma:

> As a child, Dm had been grossly abused sexually by her father, who was out of control ...
> *(Ferenczi, 1988, p. 3 – Entry January 7, 1932)*

We must remember there is an important issue in clinical behavior illustrated in Ferenczi's kissing interaction with Thompson. Ferenczi *did not initiate* the kissing interaction with Thompson. In addition, *he did not respond* to Thompson's invitation by *kissing her back*. Ferenczi *accepted her acting in* of her erotic father transference (Rachman, 2012a, 2014b, 2015a, b). Thompson's behavior was an integral part of the analysis. Ferenczi allowed the kiss because it was part of his relaxation principle (Ferenczi, 1980b), becoming accepting, empathic, and allowing the expression of all thoughts, feelings, and behaviors in the analytic situations without judgment, criticism, or need to interpret them (Ferenczi, 1980i). But, Ferenczi also was aware that his relaxation therapy could lead to difficulties.

> I had to acknowledge that the principle of relaxation ... could similarly lead
> to experiences [where] ... . The patients begin to abuse my patience, they
> permit themselves more and more, create very embarrassing situations for us.
> *(Ferenczi, 1988, p. 2 – Entry January 7, 1932)*

Ferenczi was talking about Thompson misusing his empathic behavior:

> But then the patient began to make herself ridiculous, ostentatiously as it
> were, in her sexual conduct (for example at social gatherings, while dancing).
> *(Ferenczi, 1988, p. 2 – Entry January 7, 1932)*

This entry from his *Clinical Diary* indicates that *Thompson misinterpreted Ferenczi's kindness, affection, and empathic behavior for sexuality*, a classic Confusion of Tongues reaction. Ferenczi offered her a reparative therapeutic experience with a non-sexual, affectionate father. *Thompson misinterpreted or confused Ferenczi's affection for sexuality*. Her Confusion of Tongues with Ferenczi had its origins in Thompson's experience with her abusive father, in which he gave her sexuality and asked her to accept it as love.

When Thompson's declaration of being able to "kiss Papa Ferenczi as often as I like" (Ferenczi, 1988, p. 2) reached Freud, he became alarmed that his once-favorite pupil was encouraging *sexual acting out with analysands*. He wrote the infamous "kissing letter" to Ferenczi (Freud to Ferenczi Letter – December 13, 1933), in which he accused Ferenczi of the following:

> You have made no secret of the fact that you kiss your patients and let them
> kiss you. I had heard the same thing from my patients (via Clara Thompson).
> *(Falzeder, Brabant & Giampieri-Deutsch, 2000, p. 422)*

Freud accepted Thompson's version of the event, ignoring that its so-called sexual content may have been a part of the erotic transferences she had expressed to Ferenczi. Was Thompson "flirting" with Freud by revealing her so-called erotic contact with Ferenczi? Freud became angry at Ferenczi, rather than try to understand why Thompson, who was Ferenczi's most ardent and important follower in North America, would spread such damaging rumors. Why didn't Freud contact Ferenczi before condemning him for acting out sexually with an analysand rather than suggest he always had a problem with sexual behavior with analysands (referring to Elma Palos)? Freud's words in this letter lack understanding, empathy, and affection for his once-favorite follower; Freud's condemnation comes up in the following manner:

> Now, I am certainly not one to condemn such little erotic gratifications out
> of prudishness or consideration for bourgeois convention ... Now, picture to
> yourself what will be the consequence of making your technique public ...
> Why stop with a kiss? Certainly, one will achieve still more if one adds

'pawing' … and then bolder ones will come along who will take the first step of peeping and showing, and soon we will have accepted into the technique of psychoanalysis … petting parties … and Godfather Ferenczi, looking at the busy scenery that he has created, will possibly say to himself: Perhaps I should have stopped in my technique of maternal tenderness *before* the kiss.

(Falzeder, Brabant & Giampieri-Deutsch 2000, p. 422 –
Letter from Freud to Ferenczi, December 13, 1931)

The kissing letter demonstrates the darker side of Freud's personality: his capacity to be very critical and condemning of a once-cherished colleague (this may have been why Freud was not able to maintain enduring close relationships with colleagues); an exaggerated reaction to a suggestion of sexuality, which led to a confabulation that Ferenczi was encouraging analysands to have sexual contact; his personal discomfort with negotiating a maternal transference (which Freud did acknowledge); and his intense anger toward Ferenczi for developing an alternate perspective, e.g. the Confusion of Tongues theory and trauma analysis method. This kissing letter seemed to have been an indication of Freud's anger and condemnation of Ferenczi without investigating Clara Thompson's declarations of what appeared, on the surface, to be so-called sexual acting out by Ferenczi. Freud accepted Thompson's declarations without contacting Ferenczi for an explanation as to whether his pupil had a theoretical or clinical rationale for his method with Thompson.

3

FINDING "R.N." AS ELIZABETH SEVERN

Identifying Ferenczi's case of "R.N." in the *Clinical Diary* as Elizabeth Severn

"R.N." as Elizabeth Severn

There is a history to the discovery of the identity of Ferenczi's Case of "R.N.," as he called Elizabeth Severn in his *Clinical Diary* (Ferenczi, 1988). This diary was written from January 7, 1932 until October 2, 1932 unbeknownst to Freud or his traditional analytic community. It was intended to be a "[s]cientific diary written during his 'grand experiment' [the analysis of Elizabeth Severn]. The notes were intended only for his own use" (Balint, 1992/1968, p. 114). Balint, Ferenczi's student was a witness to the Ferenczi/Severn analysis, which he called the "grand experiment." The *Clinical Diary* was preserved by passing the document from Mrs. Ferenczi to Michael Balint and then to Judith Dupont, which allowed the case of Elizabeth Severn to now be considered a significant part of analytic history. Balint felt that publishing the analysis of Ferenczi's most difficult case during the period of 1950 through the 1960s would produce a split in the analytic community and reinforce the negative perception of Ferenczi in traditional circles. Balint was also *expressing the reality of the neglectful reception his own work had received* in the 1960s–1970s (Balint 1992/1968).

Ferenczi was the first to mention Elizabeth Severn in two publications, but did not connect her identity as R.N. in the *Clinical Diary*.

1. "I am partly indebted to discoveries made by our colleague; Elizabeth Severn, which she personally communicated to me" (Ferenczi 1980i, p. 122).
2. "Our colleague, Elizabeth Severn, who is doing a training analysis with me. ... [said] that I sometimes disturbed the spontaneity of the fantasy of production with my questions and answers" (Ferenczi, 1980j, p. 133).

Balint did not refer to R.N. as Severn in his discussion of the "grand experiment" (Balint, 1992/1968). Ferenczi was hinting at an analysis with Severn that was unusual and perhaps groundbreaking. In the two quotations cited he hints at an analysand who was making a significant contribution to her own analysis and from which Ferenczi was learning how to best treat her. In an unprecedented statement, Ferenczi called his analysand "our colleague."

It was in the *Clinical Diary*, during the last years of their analysis, that Ferenczi brought R.N. out of the closet and into analytic history. The case of R.N. became one of the major themes of Ferenczi's attempt to inform psychoanalysis about how this case became a clinical experiment for understanding and treating an area neglected by Freud and his orthodox followers, namely, trauma disorder. It is the analysis between Ferenczi and Severn that gave birth to his pioneering ideas about trauma (Rachman, 2014c). At the beginning of the *Clinical Diary*, Ferenczi began his discussion of Severn's analysis under the heading of "Case of Schizophrenia progressive (R.N.)" (Ferenczi, 1988, p. 80 – Clinical entry January 12, 1932). Although Ferenczi discussed the case of R.N. in more pages of the diary than any other case (Ferenczi, 1988, pp. 8–18, 25–26, 43–45, 60–63, 96–100, 106–107, 117, 119–121, 129, 139, 155, 157, 167, 193, 206–207, 214), he did not indicate in these discussions that R.N. was Elizabeth Severn.

More than 50 years later, the connection between R.N. and Elizabeth Severn was finally revealed by Jeffrey Moussaieff Masson in the book *Assault on Truth* (Mason, 1984). In his research on Ferenczi's Confusion of Tongues paper, Masson was able, at that time, when the *Clinical Diary* had not yet been published, to get permission from the Sigmund Freud Archives to quote from Ferenczi's *Clinical Diary*. He contacted Judith Dupont, Ferenczi's literary executor and she sent him a copy of the diary. Masson made the first connection between R.N. and Elizabeth Severn: "One patient ... seems to have played a major role in Ferenczi's developing ideas ... that patient was Elizabeth Severn, a name not previously known in the analytic literature" (Masson, 1984, p. 161). Masson has suggested that he became aware of this connection in his research at the Freud home in London, when he went through one of Freud's desks. In the desk, he found unpublished material about Ferenczi. Masson also suggested he verified the connection with Judith Dupont, who, after Balint's death, had become Ferenczi's literary executor (Masson, 1984). We owe a debt to Masson, whose research and publications while secretary of the Freud Archives, although controversial, helped revive interest in Ferenczi and Severn. Masson also understood and respected Ferenczi's ideas about sexual abuse as a factor in emotional disorder (Rachman, 1997a, 2012).

Returning to Ferenczi's citations of Severn in his *Final Contributions to the Theory and Technique of Psychoanalysis*, Volume III (Ferenczi, 1980), we can begin to elaborate on the analysis. In 1929, during the fourth year of their analysis, Ferenczi said the following about Severn:

> In every case of neurotic amnesia, and possibly also in ordinary childhood-amnesia, it seems likely that a *psychotic splitting off* of a part of the personality

occurs under the influence of shock. The dissociated part, however, lives on hidden, ceaselessly endeavoring to make itself felt without finding any outlet except in neurotic symptoms. For this finding I am partly indebted to discoveries made by our colleague, Elizabeth Severn, which she personally communicated to me.

(Ferenczi, 1980i, pp. 121–22)

In this reference to Severn, Ferenczi is clearly acknowledging her contribution to his theoretical formulations about trauma, particularly the role of splitting off the experience and memory of the abuse. This idea will be further developed in the concept of trauma analysis, which was co-developed by Ferenczi and Severn in their analyses (see Chapter 11).

As has been mentioned, Ferenczi also identified Severn as being in a training analysis with him. These references solidified the idea that Severn was not just an analysand but in training to be an analyst under the influence of Ferenczi's dissident frame of reference (see Chapter 10 and Chapters 12–16).

Christopher Fortune, an analytic researcher, has contributed data on the life and work of Elizabeth Severn by virtue of his interviews with her daughter, Margaret. In the 1980s Margaret and her personal friend Peter Lipskis heard about Fortune giving a lecture on psychoanalysis in Vancouver, British Columbia, where they were living. They contacted Fortune, initially wanting help in reaching Jeffrey Masson. Margaret had a dissatisfaction about the photograph in Masson's 1984 book about Freud (Masson, 1984), which incorrectly identified a photograph of her as her mother. Their contact began a ten-year relationship where Fortune interviewed Margaret about her mother, Elizabeth, Ferenczi, and her own dancing career (Fortune, 2015). Fortune's papers provided the analytic community with the first material about Elizabeth Severn's life and relationships (Fortune, 1993, 1996).

Collaboration between Severn and Ferenczi

Severn's influence on Ferenczi, and his influence on her functioning became clearer when the *Clinical Diary* was published in English (Ferenczi, 1988). In an entry in 1932, when Severn and Ferenczi were deep into the analysis, there are two notations under the heading "on the acceptance of un-pleasure ..." (Ferenczi, 1988, p. 31), which illustrate their reciprocal exchange of ideas:

The difference between the suffering person and the philosopher would then be that the sufferer is in total revolt against the specific painful reality; perhaps what we call pain is after all nothing but such a revolt ... the revolt against the disturbance, might rather be an obstacle to adaptation. (Coué's phrase— there is no illness; every day in every way, I am better and better—the same as Baker Eddy's negation of illness is perhaps effective, if it works at all because behind it is hidden a kind of *friendly acceptance of illness*.) ... I have sometimes found quite helpful the advice not to fight the pain but to allow it to run its full course.

(Ferenczi, 1988, p. 33)

In Ferenczi's reference to Coué and Baker Eddy, he is reflecting Severn's thinking. Although, Ferenczi does not specifically mention Severn in this context, Severn was influenced in her self-taught clinical studies by both Coué and Baker Eddy. Severn first studied Baker Eddy's Christian science philosophy, popular in the early part of the twentieth century, which provided her with a non-medical framework for working with psychological issues as a therapist. Later she also became interested in Coué's ideas as a positive, person-centered approach to therapy (see Chapter 11). Apparently, in the theoretical exchanges between Severn and Ferenczi, she presented her view of clinically dealing with pain, to which he paid attention.

Masson (1984) pointed out that Ferenczi had introduced a pioneering method of dream interpretation, which may have been influenced by his clinical interaction with Severn. In what we can now consider Ferenczi's last paper, "Trauma in psychoanalysis" (Ferenczi, 1934), which was published posthumously, he interpreted a dream as being a re-enactment of an early seduction with a father (or father figure). Ferenczi reported the patient's dream as a re-enactment of an early seduction where a child was seduced by a man, while, perhaps, a father figure does not intervene to help the child. The interpretation of the dream introduced the dream data as authentic images of actual events. The patient had stored away the damage of childhood sexual abuse, which was too painful to face in consciousness but could be more safely confronted in a dream. Masson realized the importance of Ferenczi and Severn's work on trauma:

> This is an original and revolutionary use of dream technique, one anticipated by Freud in 1899 in *The Interpretation of Dreams*, but never further elaborated (possibly because it belonged to the period of his faith in the seduction theory).
>
> *(Masson, 1984, p. 164)*

It is likely that Severn was instrumental in helping Ferenczi in formulating this trauma-influenced theory of dream interpretation. Severn was determined to both cure her own trauma-based illness as well as teach Ferenczi to help her accomplish this goal. In this way, there was a unique marriage of psychoanalytic forces. A well-motivated analysand, Severn, was in great need, possessed psychic wisdom about her emotional illness, and had knowledge and experience about therapeutic encounters. She also dared to experiment within the analytic encounter. Tethered to this extraordinary analysand, there was a brilliant, daring, and exceptionally empathic analyst whose identity was embedded in being a healer. Clearly, Severn would not have been able to expand the analytic method to treat trauma disorder without someone like Ferenczi. They mutually influenced each other. Whatever may be the value of mutual analysis (see Chapter 13), I believe the process of sharing subjectivities and the openness to analyze these subjectivities was one of the greatest values of their work together (Rachman, 2010a).

Perhaps, the next indication of the reciprocal influence between Severn and Ferenczi is found in her last book, *The Discovery of the Self: A Study in Psychological Cure* (Severn, 1933). Masson (1984), who is one of the few analysts to mention Severn's book, felt it was:

> a curious work, written in a pious, mystical manner, unprofessional and unscholarly, but nevertheless with a certain admirable ability to recognize the suffering of a child.
>
> *(pp. 164–165)*

I am inclined to review this book by Severn in a more positive way for several reasons. It was published in 1933, less than a year after Severn was prematurely terminated from the analysis with Ferenczi due to his incapacitation with pernicious anemia (Rachman, 1997a). Severn was in a state of malignant regression when she left analysis with Ferenczi to live with her daughter Margaret in London (Rachman, 2016b). It seems remarkable that she was able to publish this book under these circumstances. But, I do not, on the other hand, view it as a work reflecting a seriously disturbed individual's idiosyncratic view of a treatment process. Rather, it is a meaningful summary of an alternative psychoanalytic process of treatment, free of jargon and over-intellectualized conceptualizations. It also formulates a psychoanalysis of trauma, both in theory and treatment. In fact, I look at this book as the first book of trauma. It was authored by Severn, but can be seen as joint publication by her and Ferenczi, the book they had planned to write together (Eissler, 1952). The book reflects the perspective of an analysand who participated actively, from a theoretical and clinical point of view, in her analysis with Ferenczi, (Rachman, 2010a, 2012a, b, 2014a, b, 2015a, b). We can see in Severn's 1933 book the partnership between Severn and Ferenczi, specifically in Severn's discussion of the analysis of trauma:

> How much sympathy and tact and up building do these damaged psyches require! To deal in the delicate psychic issues which have been stretched and distorted and torn requires not only a specific facility of identification with the sufferer, but a plastic technique capable of galvanizing them into new life and reality. It was to do this that I devised a 'Direct Method' for entrance into the unconscious, introducing a temporary trance state, etc., to induce recollection. [f1: This addition to, or alteration in, psychoanalytic technique has since been adopted by Ferenczi, and is the basis of his so-called "Relaxation–principle."]
>
> *(Severn, 1933, p. 95)*

In this passage, Severn verified that Ferenczi's clinical experiments in the analysis of trauma was co-created, a hallmark of the Relational Perspective. Severn was referring to the general principle of relaxation, which Ferenczi introduced (Ferenczi 1980j) to reduce the authoritarian attitude of traditional psychoanalysis developed to analyze the Oedipal trauma. The traditional method focused on analyzing resistance, transference, etc., by using interpretation to develop insight. As a result of the controversial Ferenczi/Severn analysis of trauma it became clear to both of them that analytic technique needed to be changed toward an emphasis upon empathy, flexibility, and responsiveness in order to analyze trauma (Rachman, 2000, 2003a).

Severn also acknowledged Ferenczi's influence on a psychoanalytic theory of trauma:

> He thus resurrected and gave new value to an idea which had once, much earlier, been entertained by Freud, but which was discarded by him in favor of 'phantasy', as the explanation of the strange tales or manifestations given by his patients.
>
> *(Severn, 1933, pp. 125–126)*

Severn contributed her own thinking, her clinical experience as a therapist, her cumulative experience as a patient over her adult life to treat her severe emotional disturbances (Rachman, 2016b) and, most importantly, her analysis with Ferenczi:

> Experience has convinced me, however, that, the patient does not 'invent'; but *always tells the truth*, even though in a distracted form … That the patient, when a child, might have been the innocent victim of unrestrained passion of various sorts from certain adults in his immediate environment was never considered seriously, and has only very recently been stated by Ferenczi as his opinion in a published paper. [f2: The Emotions of Adult and their Influence on the Development of the Sexual Life and Character of Children. Paper read at the 12th International Psycho-Analytic Congress, Wiesbaden, Sept. 1932 (The famous Confusion of Tongues paper).].
>
> *(Severn, 1933, p. 126)*

Severn was the first of several female analysts who maintained Ferenczi's importance for psychoanalysis. In the decade following Ferenczi's death, Clara Thompson joined Severn in sustaining Ferenczi's ideas. She helped integrate Ferenczi's ideas in the post-pioneering psychoanalysis period into interpersonal psychoanalysis. (Thompson, 1943, 1944, 1950, 1964). Following Thompson, Izette De Forest helped integrate Ferenczi's ideas into American humanistic psychotherapy (De Forest, 1942, 1954). It seems worth noting that, as in the case of Freud, women analysands first helped shape psychoanalysis. What is more, Severn, Thompson, and De Forest joined Balint, and later Fromm, Dupont, Haynal, Hidas, Masson, Meszáros, and Roazen to maintain that there was a legitimate alternative to Freudianism called The Budapest School of Psychoanalysis (Rachman, 2016).

4

FINDING THE ELIZABETH SEVERN PAPERS

An unknown legacy of psychoanalysis

Ever since I discovered the existence of Sándor Ferenczi as an analyst that I could use as a role model (Rachman, 2014d), I began to develop a fantasy that I would, one day, discover some lost or unknown legacy of Ferenczi. This romantic notion of discovery was fueled by an early interest in history, archeology, and biography. Since my grammar school days, I was fascinated by these subjects and the stories of discovery that scholars had made through the years. In high school I wanted to be an archeologist. I have been fascinated with the discovery of the Pithecanthropus Erectus, the Java Man (Swisher, Curtis & Lewen, 2000b), the Dead Sea Scrolls (Abegg & Virich, 2002), and Tutankhamun (Edwards, 1976). I developed a fantasy of being a scholar who someday would discover something of value that had been unknown. Since high school, when I began to experience myself as someone who had some intellectual capacities, I began to collect ideas in a manila folder. In the folder there was a collection of single-lined notations, titles, and ideas for research or publications. I was expressing a need for recognition and affirmation (Rachman, 2003a). Becoming a scholar and discovering something of intellectual significance was the road toward self-esteem, personal and professional recognition, and feeling prized by peers and authority.

Of course, my finding Ferenczi was the key to finding Severn. From 1976, when I first discovered Ferenczi (1997a, also see Chapter 2), until 2003, I harbored the fantasy of discovering an unknown or lost legacy of Ferenczi's life or work. In the 1990s I thought I had discovered something of significance in one of Ferenczi's earliest publications. I became acquainted with a French psychologist, Claude Lorin, whose book, *Le Jeune Ferenczi: Premiers Ecrits* (*Young Ferenczi's First Writings*) (Lorin, 1983), contained references and discussions of Ferenczi's first publications in the Hungarian medical journal, *Gyogydszat*. Lorin had gone from his place of study in Paris to Hungary in the hope he could find a Ferenczi treasure in Budapest. Searching through the back streets and out-of-the-way bookstores in Budapest,

Lorin found a cash of old magazines, which included the early issues of *Gyogydszat*, which contained Ferenczi's earliest publications as a psychiatrist. Lorin renewed my hope for the discovery of a lost Ferenczi treasure. With the help of a French-speaking colleague, Michael Larivrére of Strasbourg, France, I contacted Lorin and asked him to contribute to a Ferenczi issue of *Psychoanalytic Inquiry*, which I edited. His material about Ferenczi's earliest work was published in English for the first time (Lorin, 1997) in this Ferenczi issue.

In his book, *Young Ferenczi's First Writings*, Lorin discussed one of Ferenczi's first clinical cases, the Case of Rosa K. (Ferenczi, 1902). Lorin's description of Rosa K.'s case was in French. It was translated into English for me by Sylvie Teicher-Kamens. Inspecting the English version of this case made me realize that this early Ferenczi case should become known to the analytic community. Rosa K. was described as a female homosexual, who dressed up in men's clothing. I thought the case was a historically important case of a psychiatrist treating a lesbian, who cross-dressed, with humanism and empathy at a time in the nineteenth century when such individuals were subject to arrest.

In order to further research this case, I contacted Judith Dupont, MD, the literary executor of the Sándor Ferenczi estate and one of the world's leading Ferenczi scholars, asking her if she knew about Rosa K. I also asked her if she could get me a copy of the case. She graciously sent me a Xerox copy of the original 1902 article from the Hungarian medical journal. Sylvie Teicher-Kamens helped with my research by enlisting Gabor Kalman to translate the case of Rosa K. into English. I published the English translation of the case of Rosa K. in my first Ferenczi book (Rachman, 1997a, pp. 15–18). Rosa K. also assumed the name Robert. In the early 1900s, assuming the role of the opposite gender, i.e. a woman assuming the look and behavior of a man, was considered a criminal act in Hungary, as well as in the United States. Rosa K. was harassed by the police for her cross-dressing. Ferenczi was one of the pioneers of treating homosexual and cross-dressing individuals with empathy and humanism. Ferenczi wrote a letter for Rosa K. stating that she was an individual who should not be treated as a criminal but rather as someone who had emotional problems. As her doctor, he granted her permission to dress as a man. The letter told the police she should not be arrested or placed in any institution.

He translated his humanistic beliefs and clinical creativity into his clinical practice with Rosa K. Besides writing a letter on her behalf, he also asked her to write her autobiography so he could better understand her psychologically. She responded and gave him an informative and insightful document. I was hoping that I could locate Rosa K.'s autobiography as the Ferenczi discovery for which I had been searching. Unfortunately, in my inquiries to the Hungarian Ferenczi scholars – Drs. Dupont, Haynal, Hidas, and Lorin – Rosa K.'s autobiography could not be located. I believe that Ferenczi's case of Rosa K. should be better known. I am hoping to publish the case in a contemporary journal.

Then, one day, out of the blue, I received a phone call from a senior analyst from my training institute, the late Hannah Kapit, PhD, who asked me if I was interested in purchasing the materials that Elizabeth Severn had left to her daughter, Margaret, when she died. To myself, I said:

> Are you kidding! I have been waiting for this moment for about thirty years.

I collected myself and said to Hanna Kapit: "This is a dream come true."

I was very surprised to hear from Kapit at all, and especially with such positive news about Ferenczi. Prior to this landmark phone call, I was witness to a negative experience that Kapit had created at a professional meeting of the Institute, the focus of which was Ferenczi's ideas and work. Kapit was severely critical of Ferenczi at this meeting (see Chapter 7). I was puzzled to understand why Kapit contacted me about my acquiring Elizabeth Severn's materials when I had the negative experience of her dismissing Ferenczi. I brought my confusion to a colleague who told me that Kapit had been best friends with Elizabeth Severn's daughter, Margaret. What is more, Kapit was also acquainted with Peter Lipskis, who was Margaret Severn's literary executor and was offering me The Elizabeth Severn Papers. Although I had lingering negative feelings about Kapit's previous critical tirade against Ferenczi, she was trying to make a positive gesture for her late friend Margaret Severn and her literary executor, Peter Lipskis, who both wanted the psychoanalytic community to become aware of Elizabeth Severn's legacy. When Kapit introduced me to Lipskis, she presented me with an enormous opportunity to be next the custodian of The Elizabeth Severn Papers (Rachman, 2016b) for which I will always be grateful (see Acknowledgments).

In the week following the Kapit's phone call and communicating my desire to acquire The Elizabeth Severn Papers, I received a phone call from Lipskis. He explained that he had in storage, in Vancouver, B.C., Canada, the Elizabeth Severn materials, which had been given to her daughter Margaret when Elizabeth Severn died in 1959. In turn, Margaret Severn left these materials to Peter Lipskis when she died in 1997. From 1997 until my acquiring these materials in 2003, the papers were housed in a storage facility in Vancouver. Lipskis and I agreed to a purchase price and a legal document was drawn up and signed (Rachman, 2003c). The materials were later established as The Elizabeth Severn Papers (Rachman, 2016b). The literary rights of The Elizabeth Severn Papers were transferred to me (Rachman, 2003c).

Over a period of several years, Peter Lipskis sent me The Elizabeth Severn Papers. The Elizabeth Severn Papers were a treasure trove of materials, which included the following:

1. The letters Margaret Severn sent to her mother Elizabeth from the 1920s to the 1940s.
2. Margaret Severn's autobiography *Spotlight* (M. Severn, 1989).
3. Materials related to Elizabeth Severn's clinical practice, such as announcements and pamphlets.
4. Unpublished papers and books.

5. Out-of-print copies of Elizabeth Severn's three published books (Severn, 1913, 1920, 1933).
6. Unpublished photographs of Ferenczi, Severn, and her family and friends.
7. Severn's telephone directory with personal notes.
8. Information about Margaret Severn's life and career.

All in all, The Elizabeth Severn Papers provided a picture of Elizabeth Severn's life and work that was not previously known in the analytic community. As we shall see in the upcoming chapters, because of Freud's negative assessment of Severn, the analytic community dismissed her as a person whose life and work were not worth studying. Therefore, psychoanalysts were not interested in researching Severn as a person or clinician. Also, the materials relevant to her life and work were not known. I feel privileged to be in possession of this previously unknown treasure of psychoanalytic history and have made it a mission to share it with the analytic community. I also want to rehabilitate Elizabeth Severn's reputation as an "evil genius" who is alleged to have ruined Ferenczi's personal and professional life. The analytic community owes a great deal of gratitude to Margaret Severn and Peter Lipskis for saving The Elizabeth Severn Papers. Margaret Severn, as we shall see, was a devoted daughter, who appreciated and valued her mother's contribution to psychoanalysis. Peter Lipskis was a devoted personal friend of Margaret Severn, who took great pains to save these historical documents. Peter Lipskis continues to contribute by consulting with me about the Severns.

As I began to receive The Elizabeth Severn Papers, it became clear I needed to find an appropriate place to store these valuable materials while they were being preserved and researched. I approached Nellie Thompson, PhD, the archivist at the A.A. Brill Library of the New York Psychoanalytic Institute. Nellie Thompson was very generous and helpful with preserving these documents. First, she offered to store them in the New York Psychoanalytic Institute Archives, which had the correct temperature control for preservation. Once the storage issue of the papers was settled, I began consulting with Thompson about how to handle and preserve the documents so they could be researched. She said it was necessary to take all of the letters out of their original envelopes and very carefully unfold them. I wore document gloves, so that the materials would not be soiled with any body oil. After each letter was unfolded, they were stacked under books, so that the paper creases could be straightened. After the sheets were evened out, they were placed in acid free, three-hole plastic sleeves. Each sleeve, which contained a letter and its envelope, was placed in a binder; the letters were arranged by year.

Most of the documents in The Elizabeth Severn Papers were Xeroxed in duplicate. One copy was retained by me, until I finished my research and writing about Severn. The originals were donated to The Library of Congress, Washington, D.C. The connection with the Library of Congress was also developed with the help of Thompson. In April of 2008, the first installment of the original copies of Margaret Severn's letters to Elizabeth Severn were sent to Leonard Bruno, PhD, the former chief of scientific manuscripts at The Library of Congress, Washington, D.C. When

I contacted Dr. Bruno, he immediately accepted The Elizabeth Severn Papers. When Bruno retired from The Library of Congress in 2012, I began working with Jim Hutson, PhD, chief of the Manuscript Division at The Library of Congress. With Jim's help, two important events were established. Upon my suggestion, Hutson approved the establishment of an Elizabeth Severn section of The Freud Archives at The Library of Congress. This section was established in the late spring of 2014 and celebrated by a Severn symposium in June of 2014 (Rachman, 2014a). The Library of Congress will continue to have the task of preserving, documenting, and cataloguing the material so that all scholars will have access to the archive. There are no restrictions on the availability of The Elizabeth Severn Papers.

Judit Mészáros, president of The Sándor Ferenczi Society, Budapest, Hungary, has agreed to establish an Elizabeth Severn section of The Ferenczi Archives at The Sándor Ferenczi House. Ferenczi's apartment in Budapest was recently purchased by the Sándor Ferenczi Society of Budapest and is now designated as The Sándor Ferenczi House. A second copy of The Elizabeth Severn Papers has been donated to The Sándor Ferenczi House and is stored in the room where Ferenczi analyzed Severn and wrote his *Clinical Diary* about her.

A second event accomplished with the help of Jim Hutson of The Library of Congress was the Severn Symposium held at The Library of Congress on Friday, June 20, 2014 (Rachman, 2014a) to celebrate the establishment of the Severn section of The Freud Archives. I gave a lecture entitled "Elizabeth Severn, The Evil Genius of Psychoanalysis: Sándor Ferenczi's Analysand and Collaborator in the Study and Treatment of Trauma." Lewis Aron, PhD, and Joseph Lichtenberg, MD, were the discussants for the paper. For the first time, a portion of the documents from The Elizabeth Severn Papers (Rachman, 2016b) was presented to help re-evaluate Severn as a person, clinician, and analysand of Ferenczi.

The presentation of the previously unknown data from Severn's life and work was intended to help rehabilitate the view of her as a disturbed patient who was discarded by Freud and considered by traditional psychoanalysis as a disturbing influence on Ferenczi.

5

EISSLER FINDS SEVERN

Discovering the 1952 Eissler/Severn interview

Although the discovery of The Elizabeth Severn Papers (Rachman, 2016b) was a major recovery of unknown materials as part of the Ferenczi legacy, the discovery of Kurt Eissler's interview of Elizabeth Severn in 1952, seven years before her death in 1959, was also a significant event. I first heard of the possibility of the Eissler/Severn Interview (Eissler, 1952) in August of 2011 when I made direct contact with Peter Lipskis, the former literary executor of The Elizabeth Severn Papers in Vancouver, B.C., Canada. During a week of consultation sessions with Lipskis as well as a visit to the storage site of The Elizabeth Severn Papers in Vancouver, he said there was a source of potentially rich information about Elizabeth Severn that was unknown in the analytic community. Lipskis said the late Kurt Eissler, MD, the first secretary of The Freud Archives, had found Severn living in New York City and interviewed her in 1952. He also said that the tape-recorded transcript as well as a typed version of the interview were stored at the Library of Congress in Washington, D.C. When I got back to New York City, I contacted Leonard Bruno, PhD, the head of the Science Manuscript Division of the Library of Congress. Bruno verified there were typed manuscript copies of the Eissler/ Severn Interview in the Ferenczi folder of The Freud Archives. The delight I experienced on discovering these materials was equivalent to what I had experienced upon discovering The Elizabeth Severn Papers. What added another dimension of joy for me was that the Eissler/Severn Interview had occurred almost 20 years after Severn's analysis was terminated with Ferenczi. I anticipated I might find some helpful information about Severn's life and career after she left Ferenczi in February of 1933. No one to my knowledge had ever written about Severn's life after Ferenczi.

Kurt Eissler: the keeper of the keys to Freudian psychoanalysis

Kurt Eissler, MD, came to America in 1938 never having had any direct contact with Freud (Eissler, 1952). Escaping Hitler, he not only found a home in the United

States but became the keeper of the keys to Freud's reputation and the orthodox version of psychoanalysis. He vehemently defended Freud and the orthodox position, sometimes in an obsessive and irrational way. He made significant contributions to psychoanalysis in his clinical papers. The most famous paper, "The Effect of the Structure of the Ego on Psychoanalytic Technique" (Eissler, 1953), was an attempt to integrate Ferenczi's original work on non-interpretative measures (Ferenczi, 1980h–k) into traditional psychoanalytic clinical thinking. It was an important step in reintroducing Ferenczi's idea that difficult cases need new clinical measures and the analyst's flexibility in order to be successfully analyzed. Eissler introduced the concept of *parameters*, which was an attempt to introduce guidelines within traditional psychoanalysis, for non-interpretative clinical activity with difficult cases. Eissler stipulated that one could use a parameter as long as it was removed before the analysis was completed. Stone (1954, 1981) wanted to expand the integration of non-interpretative measures into traditional psychoanalysis. Stone believed that difficult cases may need parameters throughout their analysis. It is unrealistic and clinically unsound, he felt, for parameters to be removed in certain very difficult cases. Stone's idea was that it was necessary to widen the scope of clinical psychoanalysis by integrating parameters as a part of an analysis with particular difficult cases.

Eissler was described as thorny and passionate: he always spoke his mind; he revered genius; his extraordinary kindness was well known (Malcolm, 2000). My own contact with Eissler came in the 1980s when I was researching Ferenczi's Confusion of Tongues paper, which was delivered in September of 1932 in Wiesbaden, Germany. Eissler was in the conversation in the analysis community in those days because of The Freud Archives controversy. I wondered if Eissler, who was from Vienna and was 25 years old in 1933, could have attended Ferenczi's Confusion of Tongues presentation at the 12th International Psychoanalytic Congress. To my surprise, his name and address were listed in the New York City telephone directory. When I wrote to him, he graciously sent me a handwritten response. Eissler responded to my inquiry about Ferenczi by referring me to someone who he believed had attended the Confusion of Tongues presentation. Unfortunately, I could not locate that person. In his note, Eissler also wrote about the issue of childhood trauma of which I had inquired. His response indicated great sensitivity to the experience of a child in family life. He wrote that all children suffer from the experience of family interaction. He believed that childhood was an emotionally difficult, if not traumatic, experience. It was a touching moment in my Ferenczi research that such a significant figure of psychoanalysis responded to my inquiry in such a moving way.

The Sigmund Freud Archives

Eissler's most significant and lasting contribution to psychoanalysis, was his creative idea of establishing The Freud Archives. Officially founded in 1951, Eissler and a group of psychoanalysts who knew Freud personally decided to preserve his letters and papers. The original members of the group who worked with Eissler were Heinz Hartmann, Ernst Kris, Bertram Levin, and Herman Nunberg. By the 1950s,

Eissler was clearly the driving force behind the archives project. By then, The Freud Archives were established at the Library of Congress in Washington, D.C. and at The Freud Museum, 20 Mansfield Gardens in Northwest London, where Freud had lived after leaving Vienna. In the 1980s, with the help of Anna Freud, Eissler had collected thousands of tapes, letters, and papers. Eissler then became known as the *keeper of the keys*, viewing himself as Jones had originally seen himself, as Freud's champion and protector, the keeper of Freud's legacy.

A dramatic example of Eissler's protectiveness of Freud, was evident in a controversy that developed around one of Freud's students, Victor Tausk, MD. On the morning of July 3, 1919 Tausk committed suicide. Paul Roazen, PhD, the founder of the Critical Freud Studies Movement, said that Freud bore some responsibility for Tausk's suicide, because Tausk's analyst, Helene Deutsch, MD, stopped her analysis with Tausk because Freud demanded it (Roazen, 1969). After a complicated relationship with Freud and Lou Andreas-Salomé, Tausk committed suicide by tying a curtain braid around his neck and then firing a pistol to his right temple, hanging himself as he fell (Richards, 2010, p. 170). Freud wrote to Lou Andreas-Salomé:

> I confess that I had long realized that he could be of no further service; indeed that he constituted a threat.
>
> *(Clark, 1980, p. 399)*

In response to Roazen's accusation of Freud's responsibility in Tausk suicide, Eissler wrote two books, defending Freud (Eissler, 1971, 1983). Eissler's writing of these books seems to indicate he felt Roazen was attempting to destroy Freud's personal and professional reputation. Although, Roazen is seen as a critic of Freud, he was a scholar who contributed to a revisionist history of psychoanalysis (Roazen, 1975). He was not trying to destroy Freud. My contact and conversations with Roazen (Roazen, 1988) indicated a scholar who wished to set the record straight, attempting to *see the truth* in his investigations of orthodox psychoanalytic thinking (Pearce, 2009).

For a generation of analysts who identified with new analytic role models, such as Balint, Ferenczi, Kohut, Rank, Searles, Winnicott, and others, Roazen was a beacon of light, providing an alternative to the orthodox history of Freud's life and work and the development of psychoanalysis as it was written by Ernest Jones (Jones, 1953–1957). Roazen's landmark book, *Freud and his Followers* (Roazen, 1975), provided a revisionist history of psychoanalysis, which introduced the positive contributions of psychoanalytic dissidents, such as Ferenczi and Rank. Though orthodox psychoanalysis was highly critical of Roazen, members of contemporary non-Freudian perspectives view him as a hero (Dufrense, 2007). Roazen was the first scholar to reveal, in print, that Freud analyzed his daughter Anna (Roazen, 1969). This revelation could have initiated a new dialogue about this issue and its relation to psychoanalytic theory and technique. Unfortunately, Roazen's revelation was ignored by the orthodox analytic community. In the 1980s I organized a symposium about Freud's analysis of his daughter, Anna, for New York University's postdoctoral program in psychoanalysis with me, Esther Menaker, and Paul Roazen as the panel members. Although, the postdoctoral program was receptive to the idea of the symposium, there was not a vivid response to our presentations or in the discussion to follow.

Another dimension of Eissler's stewardship of The Freud Archives was the lack of availability of these archives to interested scholars. Peter Swales, the historian of the first 50 years of Freud's life, wrote in 1985 of these restrictions:

> work has been severely hampered, however, because data crucial to the pursuit of such urgent fact finding is being obstinately withheld by The Freud Archives and monopolized by certain of its officers (none of whom are competent as historians) at cost to free investigative enterprise. Not only does such a policy of restriction inhibit further research and the consequent preservation of history – it also has the effect of crippling democratic scholarship.
>
> *(Swales, 1985, p. 1)*

Crisis in the archives: Masson contra Eissler

It was perhaps inevitable that Eissler, as the keeper of the keys to analytic orthodoxy, would be involved in a still more traumatic controversy as psychoanalysis was being examined and criticized by scholars like Roazen in the post-pioneering period of the 1950s–70s. The Critical Freud Studies Movement (Dufrense, 1997), which challenged some of the ideas of Freudian psychology, also began to take root. Before the crises in The Freud Archives I am about to describe, Eissler was not known beyond the circle of traditional analysts. But in the 1970s, Eissler met Jeffrey Moussaieff Masson PhD, and a perfect storm in analytic history was created. Masson was academically trained as a Sanskrit and Indian studies scholar at Harvard University. He was encouraged to study Sanskrit by his parents' guru, Paul Brunton, who was a British mystic who lived with the Massons. At one point, Brunton lived with Jeffrey Moussaieff Masson and was interested in passing on his mystic legacy to him (Brunton, 1952; Masson, 1993). Masson eventually became disillusioned with Brunton. While a professor of Sanskrit and Indian studies at the University of Toronto, Masson trained to be a psychoanalyst in the Freudian tradition. Did Masson become enamored with Freud, as a new and better guru whose genius he could appreciate and ideas he could follow? Eventually, just as he became disillusioned with his father's guru, he became disillusioned by Freud. In addition to rejecting Freud and psychoanalysis, he became disillusioned with his analyst, Irvine Schiffer, MD (Masson, 1990).

The process of disillusionment unfolded when Masson met Eissler at a meeting of the American Psychoanalyst Association in 1974. Masson was considered charming, brilliant, and devoted to Freudian psychology. Malcolm (2000) suggested a dynamic in the rapid and intense relationship that was formed by Eissler and Masson:

> He [Eissler] and his wife were childless, and he was given to forming fatherly friendships with younger men and women.
>
> *(Malcolm, 2000, p. 1)*

Masson's enthusiasm for meeting Eissler was great. Eissler has hundreds of hours of tape recordings of Freud's patients. For Masson, Eissler represented the connection between Freud, Vienna, and psychoanalysis (Malcolm, 2000). Masson and Eissler became fast friends and valued colleagues. Masson learned German and studied the history of psychoanalysis. In 1980, Eissler decided that Masson would be his successor as director of The Freud Archives. In the meantime, Masson was named as projects director of the archives, with Anna Freud's approval, and was given complete access to the treasure trove that was The Freud Archives, which included material unknown and unpublished. No doubt, Eissler let Masson loose in the archives so that he would enhance Freud's reputation. What happened next was completely unforeseen and caused a seismic shock to the archives, psychoanalysis, and the world's intellectual community. The more Masson researched Freud's papers, the more he became disillusioned and began to develop the idea that Freud was not a hero but a man who lost his emotional courage to defend his original theory of neurosis, the seduction hypothesis (Rachman, 2012a).

Freud's original theory of neurosis was that hysteria/neurosis was caused by parental childhood sexual abuse. Masson was asserting that psychoanalysis should return to the seduction theory because Freud abandoned it as a result of the hostile reception he received when he originally presented it to the Vienna Medical Society. The abandonment was due to a personal matter for Freud: maintaining his reputation, prestige, and intellectual status. The theory was not invalidated by any new clinical formulation or observation about a connection between actual parental behavior and psychopathology in children (Masson, 1984). Freud built a new psychoanalytic theory, the Oedipal Complex Theory of Neuroses. This second formulation changed the focus from actual pathologic behavior within family interaction to a symbolic, unconscious conflict in an individual's mind (Rachman, 2012a). This new focus changed traditional psychoanalysis forever, concentrating on a one-person psychology.

Masson uncovered documents in his research of The Freud Archives and The Freud Museum that indicated Ferenczi's Confusion of Tongues paradigm, an alternative to The Oedipal Theory, presented three profound issues:

1. Freud was ambivalent about abandoning the seduction theory.
2. When Ferenczi attempted to expand, reformulate and reintroduce the seduction theory in his Confusion of Tongues paradigm, Freud, Jones, and the orthodox analytic community made a deliberate attempt to suppress it.
3. The Confusion of Tongues actually supported Freud's original seduction hypothesis (Masson, 1984).

Ferenczi scholars owe a great debt to Masson who made a significant contribution to reviving interest in Ferenczi as an abandoned, yet significant, contributor to psychoanalysis. Masson also noted that Ferenczi was the analyst who focused on the role of real trauma. His landmark book, *The Assault on Truth: Freud's Suppression of the Seduction Theory* (Masson, 1984), outlined these issues and arguments. Three years earlier, in 1981, Masson was dismissed from his position as projects director of The

Freud Archives and stripped of his membership in the International Psychoanalytic Society. Prior to the publication of the book, Masson gave several presentations that were very critical of Freud. Eissler, who thought he had created a successor to save the Freudian legacy, now felt Masson would destroy it. Almost everyone in the analytic community, whether orthodox or liberal, became critical of Masson. He became a pariah. Just as psychoanalysis had rejected Ferenczi when he dared to deviate from Freud, it now rejected Masson, feeling he was trying to destroy Freud. They killed the messenger and could not listen to the message. I would paraphrase the message Masson wanted to deliver as follows:

> Freud was right the first time. One of the origins of psychological disorder is the real sexual abuse of children by their parents. Ferenczi tried to inform Freud and the analytic community that his clinical work with difficult cases were individuals who were victims of childhood sexual abuse, thereby, verifying Freud's original findings of the seduction hypothesis.

I would like to add my own version of the message:

> Ever since the suppression of Ferenczi's Confusion of Tongues idea and the silencing of dissident voices like Roazen and Masson, psychoanalysis has neglected Ferenczi, The Confusion of Tongues paradigm and the incest trauma.
>
> *(Rachman, 1997a, 2012c; Rachman & Klett, 2015)*

Eissler discovered Severn

As part of his continued contribution to The Freud Archives, Eissler sought out individuals connected to the history of psychoanalysis to interview. By the time Eissler interviewed Severn, he had conducted 42 interviews, which are part of The Freud Archives (Hutson, 2014). Eissler's interview of Severn is a significant contribution to psychoanalytic history and the psychohistory of Ferenczi's and Severn's ideas and lives. First, let me describe the events that led to Eissler's interview with Severn, and then I will outline my discovery of the interview, which very people knew existed.

Peter Swales' response to Eissler

Peter Swales is an amateur historian of psychoanalysis whose specialty is the first 50 years of Freud's life. In *The New York Review of Books* dated October 24, 1985, Swales replied to a request by Eissler asking for biographical data about Elizabeth Severn. Swales said he knew "that a tape-recorded interview, with this woman some years ago, is to be found in the Sigmund Freud Archives in the Library of Congress in Washington" (Swales, 1985, p. 1). He goes on to describe the difficulty he and other researchers had in obtaining materials from The Freud Archives, because the materials were sequestered. In the case of the Severn material he reported it was sealed until 2017. In my 35 years of research on Ferenczi, as well as in consultation with Ferenczi scholars in the United States, Europe, and South America, no one mentioned the Eissler interview with Severn until that day in 2011.

As mentioned, in August of 2011, while I was consulting with Peter Lipskis, the former literary executor of The Elizabeth Severn Papers, in Vancouver, B.C., Canada, about any information he had not yet communicated to me about Severn, he said there was an interview conducted by Kurt Eissler of Elizabeth Severn that was sequestered in The Freud Archives of the Library of Congress. There was a typed version of the interview and an original tape recording that Eissler had made, from which the typed interview was developed. On my return from Vancouver, I arranged to visit The Freud Archives. Leonard Bruno, PhD, former chief of the Scientific Manuscript Division of the Library of Congress, met me at the library when I visited it in November of 2012, in order to research the Eissler/Severn Interview. Bruno told me the Eissler/Severn Interview was not allowed to be Xeroxed until 2017. This verified Swales statement in *The New York Review of Books*. Bruno said I could take notes using the paper and pencils the library supplied. You cannot bring any of your own materials into the library. You are assigned a desk and seat number for the time you are researching the documents. Before I decided to go to the Library of Congress, on Bruno's advice, I contacted Harold Blum, MD, the present secretary of The Freud Archives to see if the prohibition on reproducing the Eissler/Severn Interview could be lifted. Blum was very gracious, explaining that the restriction was placed by the Eissler family. When he checked to see if the prohibition on reproducing the interview could be lifted, he revealed that the family wanted to maintain the restriction. When I inspected the Eissler interview of Severn, I saw there were two typed versions. One was a typed version corrected by Severn herself. In inspecting the two versions, I found the Severn-corrected version superior. At that time, I took copious notes and put them away, expecting to use them when I was ready to write a book about Severn. After I received the contract from Routledge to write the present volume about Severn, I decided to contact Blum again, to see, this time in the winter of 2013, whether there could be a lifting of the restrictions on the Eissler/Severn Interview. I had gone over my notes, several times, realizing that Severn's response formed significant material about psychoanalytic history. In particular, the material illuminates Severn's life and work and contribution to psychoanalysis. To my surprise, in the winter of 2013, following my request, Blum lifted the restrictions on this material (Blum, 2013). When I asked Blum why the ban was lifted, he said it seemed like the right time to do so. Jim Hutson, the chief of the Manuscript Division of the Library of Congress sent me a Xeroxed copy of the interview. I was also given permission to quote from the Eissler/Severn Interview (Hutson, 2013).

Eissler's interview with Severn

On December 20, 1952, in New York City, the late Kurt Eissler, MD, the founder and director of The Freud Archives, interviewed Elizabeth Severn, Sándor

Ferenczi's most famous and controversial analysand. The analytic community owes a great debt to Eissler for tracking down and interviewing Severn and thereby preserving a neglected part of analytic history. By the time Eissler interviewed Severn, she had been settled on the Upper East Side of New York for many years. She had established a psychoanalytic clinical practice. She lived with her daughter, Margaret, who, by the 1940s was retired from being a pioneering figure in modern dance. It must be said, that if one views the Eissler/Severn Interview overall, Severn comes across as a very intelligent, thoughtful, articulate, and emotionally intact human being. In 1952, the year of the interview, it was 19 years after Severn had been prematurely terminated by Ferenczi from continuing their analysis.

There is some irony in saying this, but traditional psychoanalysis probably paid tribute to Elizabeth Severn in the interview Eissler conducted in 1952. The irony is that it is not clear if Eissler was interested in Severn as a figure in psychoanalysis or, more likely, as a conduit to gaining information about Freud and Ferenczi. Eissler, although clearly focused on retrieving data about Freud and Ferenczi, allowed Severn to demonstrate her considerable intellect, assertiveness, and knowledge of psychoanalysis, as well as her emotional strength and interpersonal capacity. Severn was Eissler's equal in this interview. She showed herself to be the same thoughtful and well-functioning psychoanalyst as was Eissler. In some instances, Eissler tried to focus Severn on giving him information he wanted, e.g., anything about Ferenczi's personal functioning and their relationship. Severn was completely cooperative, but she would not let Eissler push her into a response. The same assertiveness was demonstrated in her analysis with Ferenczi. At no time in the interview, did Severn appear to be a severely disturbed individual who was having trouble coping with life, work, or relationships. In the opinion of this writer, there was no evidence in the interview that Severn was hampered intellectually, interpersonally, or emotionally.

The content of the interview provides valuable, previously unknown information about Ferenczi, Freud, and Severn. The interview can be seen as *Severn finding her voice about her trauma and recovery*. As Ferenczi discussed in his Confusion of Tongues paradigm, the individual loses his/her voice in the experience of the incest trauma. Severn lost her voice at least twice: the first time as a child who was sexually abused, and again as an adult when she tried to communicate to the analytic community about trauma as an important factor in psychological disorder and treatment. In the Eissler/Severn Interview, Severn had the opportunity to give voice to her own thoughts, feelings, and conclusions about her psychological disorder, her analysis with Ferenczi, her recovery, and her functioning as a human being and a clinician. In finding her voice, Severn continued to work through her own Confusion of Tongues trauma. In this way, she became a meaningful spokesperson for herself and Ferenczi. The fact that Eissler chose Severn to be interviewed and that Severn responded in such a rational, relevant, and analytically informed way makes this interview an important document in the history of psychoanalysis.

Six categories of information that Severn provided in the Eissler/Severn Interview have been integrated into the body of the present volume:

1. Severn's psychoanalysis before the analysis with Ferenczi, which was previously unknown.
2. Details of the techniques of trauma analysis developed by the collaboration of Ferenczi and Severn that are not found in the description of the clinical experience detailed in Ferenczi's *Clinical Diary*.
3. Some details of the mutual analysis between Severn and Ferenczi not found in the *Clinical Diary*.
4. Details of actual interactions between Severn and Ferenczi, as well as Severn's own perspective of the clinical experience, which are not available in other sources.
5. Severn, in an open and emotionally honest way described the idea that she had developed, and Ferenczi put into clinical practice in the development of their trauma analysis. She developed the idea of the necessity of a trauma survivor to go through a process of returning to the sources of the original trauma of childhood and reliving them in the psychoanalytic situation. Ferenczi's student, Michael Balint, further developed this important advance into the concept of Therapeutic Regression (Balint, 1992/1968; see Chapter 22).
6. During her analysis with Ferenczi, and afterwards, Severn arranged for three consultations with Sigmund Freud, in the winters of 1925, 1928 and 1938. In the Eissler/Severn Interview, she discussed her experience of Freud and her idea of Ferenczi's basic transference to Freud.

During the course of writing this volume, I had the idea to contact the present secretary of The Freud Archives to gain permission to have the 1952 Eissler/ Severn Interview published in a portion of the Severn volume. This was an attempt to encourage greater transparency between The Freud Archives and the analytic scholarly community. Unfortunately, this request was turned down. How much more unknown material is housed in The Freud Archives, yet to be discovered? In my research on the Wolf Man, Sergei Pankejeff, I found that Masson reported that he had run across an unpublished paper by Ruth Mark Brunswick, which said that Pankejeff was anally seduced by a member of his family (see Chapter 8, Masson, 1984). Freud, it was said, was unaware of this while he was treating him. So far, in my preliminary research, in contracting Masson and The Freud Archives, the location of the Brunswick paper has not been established. Is the unpublished Brunswick paper and its unknown location part of the *Todschweigen* (death by silence) experience that became part of the traditional psychoanalysis's method of silencing dissidence (see Chapter 7)?

6

FREUD'S CONDEMNATION OF SEVERN AS AN "EVIL GENIUS"

It is difficult to know if Freud has such antipathy for any other individual as he had for Severn. In an obscure passage, toward the end of the third volume of Jones's approved biography of Freud, the condemnation of Severn was communicated:

> ... an ex-patient of his – *a woman Freud called 'Ferenczi's evil genius'*
> *(Jones, 1957, p. 407, italics added)*

In a famous letter written to Jones, Freud described Severn as a seriously disturbed analysand who was outside the mainstream of psychoanalysis:

> So he himself [Ferenczi] became a better mother, even found the children he needed, *among these a suspect American woman* to whom he often devoted 4–5 hours a day [Mrs. Severn?].
> *(Paskauskas, 1993, pp. 721–722, letter from Freud to Jones,*
> *May 29, 1933, italics added)*

During the period 1925–1933, when she was in analysis with Ferenczi, there were several issues that disturbed Freud about Ferenczi's analysis with Severn: (1) Ferenczi's relaxation therapy and the use of non-interpretive measures, particularly the so-called kissing technique. (2) The tender-Mother transference. (3) Mutual analysis. (4) Extra mural contact. (5) Trauma analysis and therapeutic regression. (6) Countertransference analysis and analyst self-disclosure. (6) Triangular relationship between Freud, Ferenczi, and Severn. (7) Freud's negative feelings about patients and psychotics.

The drama of the difficult analysand: Clara Thompson and the so-called kissing technique

During the time Severn was in analysis with Ferenczi, he produced his most controversial work. Severn was an integral part of this controversy. In fact, one could say, Severn instigated these controversies. Ferenczi knew Severn was an especially difficult analysand when he began their analysis. He knew she had a history of several unsuccessful analyses; she had very serious psychological problems, such as severe depression with suicidal ideation and personal features to which Ferenczi had antipathy. She had her own ideas about clinical interaction and how she wanted to be treated. With these difficulties, Ferenczi not only decided to see her, but dedicated himself to the analysis until Severn was fully analyzed and functioning free of her crippling psychopathology.

Although Ferenczi and Severn both knew their analysis would be different, perhaps even especially difficult, neither could have predicted the tumultuous and controversial clinical experience that they would create. As I have outlined in previous work, (Rachman, 2010a, 2012b, 2014a, b, 2015a, b, c), the Ferenczi/Severn analysis became the talk of the analytic world in the early 1930s. This period was the time Ferenczi withdrew from intimate contact with Freud because he knew his mentor would not approve of his ideas and clinical work with Severn and others (Rachman, 1997a, b, 2003a, 2015a). Freud did not know of Ferenczi's work first hand. The *Clinical Diary* that discussed this work (Ferenczi, 1988) was not shared with Freud or with colleagues in Vienna, Berlin, England, or the United States. The diary was shared with Ferenczi's inner circle of Hungarian psychoanalysts, such as Michael Balint.

The analytic community surrounding Freud in the crucial period for the *drama of the difficult patient*, roughly 1930–33, was small and intimate. Freud, of course, was the matrix of analytic politics and gossip. Everyone was geared to report deviations in personal and professional functioning either directly or indirectly to Freud. He was the arbitrator of all things analytic, e.g. intellectual, political, interpersonal, emotional, etc. Jones, for example, was in competition with Ferenczi for Freud's attention and love (Rachman, 1997a). Jones assumed the role of Freud's primary defender. In actuality, he became the designated "political assassin" of dissidents (Rachman, 1997a, b).

Clara Thompson, another analysand of Ferenczi, who was in analysis at the same time as Severn, spread rumors within the analytic community about Ferenczi's clinical behavior. Thompson was a difficult analysand in many ways besides spreading rumors and gossip. She misused Ferenczi's empathic method, as he noted in the *Clinical Diary*:

> The patients begin to abuse my patience [Thompson], they permit themselves more and more, create very embarrassing situations for us, and cause us not insignificant trouble. Only when we recognize this trend and openly admit it to the patient does the artificial obstacle, which is of

our own creation, disappear. However, such mistakes and their subsequent correction often provide the motive and opportunity to dig deeply into similar conflicts.

(Ferenczi, 1988, p. 2)

Ferenczi is pointing to difficult cases such as Thompson, who abused his empathic method:

> See the case of Dm [Clara Thompson–Dupont, 1988, f3. p. 3] lady who, 'complying' with my passivity, had allowed herself to take more and more liberties and *occasionally kissed me* … she remarked quite casually in the company of other patients … *I am allowed to kiss Papa Ferenczi, as I like.*
>
> *(Ferenczi, 1988, p. 2, italics added)*

What is so significant, is that Freud did not check with Ferenczi about the rumor but used it as an opportunity to develop a *Tödschweigen* campaign against Ferenczi's alternative mode of trauma analysis with trauma disorder. Freud misinterpreted the so-called kissing technique as an example of sexual acting out. What is more, he labeled it as a technique, as if Ferenczi was using it with all his trauma analysands. The irony is that there is no evidence that in Ferenczi's analysis with Severn any sexual acting out occurred (Ferenczi, 1988; Rachman, 2012b). We now know that Thompson was the one acting out, not Severn:

> From Ferenczi we know that Thompson was a difficult treatment. Thompson tested the boundaries repeatedly—moving from distancing, to the sexualized affection, to humiliating disclosure and distortion of her analyst's behavior and frequent acting out on her transference through triangulation with other patients. Reading the diaries, I wondered how Thompson unconsciously reacted to the intensity of Ferenczi's relationship with his patient RN [Elizabeth Severn]. Could envy or competition have contributed to her more drastic efforts to get Ferenczi's attention?
>
> *(Shapiro, 1993, p. 167)*

Freud and Ferenczi exchanged two significant letters relating to the issue of the so-called kissing technique generated by Thompson. The first letter is Freud's admonition of Ferenczi, referred to as *The Kissing Letter*, Rachman (1999). Freud began the letter by accusing Ferenczi of using a kissing technique as part of his new methodology of trauma analysis:

> … *You have* made *no secret of the fact that you kissed your patients and let them kiss you*, I had also heard the same thing from my patients. I am certainly not one to condemn such little erotic gratification … [In earlier times] a kiss was only a *harmless* greeting, which was bestowed on every guest. Up to now in technique *we have held fast … that erotic gratifications should be denied the patient* ….

Now, picture to yourself what will be the consequence of making your technique public ... why stop with a kiss? ... one will achieve still more if one adds 'pawing', bolder ones ... will take the further step of peeping and showing ... soon we will have accepted into the technique of psychoanalysis the whole repertoire of demiviergerie [seductions] and petting parties, with the result being a great increase in analysis on the part of analysts and those who are being analyzed ... and Godfather Ferenczi, looking at the busy scenery that he has created, will possibly say to himself, perhaps I should have stopped in my technique of maternal tenderness before the kiss, but since you like *to play the tender mother role with others*, then perhaps [you will do so] with yourself ... you should hear *the warning from the brutal father side*. To the best of my recollection – the inclination toward sexual games [Spielerei] with patients was not alien to you in the pre-analytic times, *so that one could put the new technique into context with the old misdemeanor*. The need for defiant self-assertion seems to me to be more powerful in you than you recognize.

> *(Letter from Freud to Ferenczi, December 5, 1931 – Falzeder, Brabant and Giamperi-Deutsch, 2000, pp. 421–422, italics added)*

Almost a month later, Ferenczi sent his, *Sin of Youth Letter* response to Freud. It must have been a terrible blow to Ferenczi that Freud not only severely criticized his evolving method of relaxation therapy, which he had developed with Severn's help to treat trauma, but that Freud attacked him personally, as if he were a sexually preoccupied adolescent. The discussion of the meaning of this historic exchange of letters will follow. For now, let us hear what Ferenczi was able to say to Freud in his defense:

> it is happening for the first time that factors of not being in agreement are mixing into our relationship ... I have allowed the affective current to run its course, I believe I am in a position to reply to you in a reassuring sense ... it was I who declared it to be necessary ....To communicate now you think it would be dishonorable to keep silent, ...
>
> I consider your fear that I will turn into another Stekel unfounded. *'Youthful misdemeanors' when they have been overcome and analytically worked through, can even make one wiser and more careful than people who did not go through such trauma.* My extremely ascetic active therapy was surely a precautionary measure against tendencies of this kind ... When I gained insight into this, I relaxed the stiffness of the prohibitions and avoidances to which I condemn myself (and others). *Now, I believe I am capable of creating a mild passionless atmosphere, ...* But, since I fear the dangers just as much as you do ... I must and will, as before, keep in mind the warnings that you reproach me with, and strive to criticize myself harshly.
>
> Since I overcame the sorrow about the tone of our correspondence, I can't help expressing the hope that the amicable personal and scientific harmony

between us will not be disrupted by these developments, or, that it will soon
be restored!!

*(Letter from Ferenczi to Freud, December 27, 1931 – Falzeder, Brabant and
Giamperi-Deutsch, 2000, pp. 424–25, italics added)*

One could write a book about this exchange of letters, but I will confine myself
to the issues relevant to Freud's criticisms and anger toward Ferenczi and Severn:

1. Tender-mother transference: cherishing love.
2. Relaxation therapy and non-interpretive measures.
3. Analysand as therapist to the analyst: mutual analysis.
4. Therapeutic regression and trauma analysis.
5. Countertransference analysis: from opaque to transparent.
6. Freud's negative feelings about analysands.
7. Freud, Ferenczi and Severn: three's a crowd in a two-person relationship.

Tender-mother transference: cherishing love as empathy

It is a tribute to Ferenczi as a thinker and clinician that his students have been
the messengers of his theory and clinical methods. Izette De Forest (1942, 1954),
Elizabeth Severn (1933), and Clara Thompson (1950) have conveyed to the analytic community their clinical interactions with Ferenczi in their analyses. We have
thereby a theory and method that is informed by analysands. This is fitting since
it verified Ferenczi's idea that analysis is a two-person experience, which involves
the intersection of the subjectivities of both analyst and analysand (Rachman,
1997a, 2003a; Rachman and Klett, 2015). It is toward De Forest and Severn as
messengers that we need to turn to understand the idea of Ferenczi's concept of
the tender-mother transference and why Freud and Jones became so critical of
Ferenczi and Severn.

De Forest was the messenger of Ferenczi's ideas about the role of the analyst
in his relaxation therapy. It must be emphasized that Ferenczi's relaxation therapy
is basically built on the concept of clinical empathy, which he introduced into
psychoanalysis (Rachman, 1989). For Ferenczi, the analyst is a warm, responsive,
affectionate clinician and human being. In cases where trauma is the cause of
the psychological disorder, empathy can be more important than interpretation.
De Forest, Severn, and Thompson experienced this new form of psychoanalysis
with Ferenczi. These analysands were also his students, so these ideas were discussed
in their analyses (Ferenczi, 1988).

De Forest became the messenger for his ideas about the notion of cherishing
love, which was based upon her experience in analysis with him and the theoretical
discussions they had. First, De Forest (1954) summarized Ferenczi's ideas:

> Psychoanalytic 'cure' is in direct proportion to the cherishing love by the
> psychoanalyst ... *the patient really needed at the early age—a loving care and*

nurture which would have allowed his self-confidence, his self-enjoyment to develop wholesomely. *Each patient needs a different experience of tender, supporting care. This process ... must be pursued ... with all skill and tact and loving-kindness,* and fearlessly. It must be absolutely honest and genuine.

(Fromm, 1959, f.3, p. 65 – Personal communication from Izette De Forest, italics added)

Ferenczi gave two descriptions of the tender-mother transference of cherishing love:

> It is important for the analysis that the analyst should be able to meet the patient as far as possible with almost in-exhaustible patience, understanding, goodwill and kindliness ... the patient will then feel the contrast between our behavior and that which he experienced in the real family and knowing himself safe from the repetition of such situations .... *The analyst's behavior is thus rather like that of an affectionate mother,* who will not go to bed at night until she has talked over with the child all his current troubles, large and small, fears, bad intentions and scruples of conscience, and has set them at rest.
>
> *(Ferenczi, 1980k, pp. 132 and 137, italics added)*

Ferenczi's idea of a tender-mother transference seems to have been taken up by Winnicott in the post-pioneering era in the Object Relations perspective, with his concept of *good enough mothering* (Winnicott, 1958, 1960).

De Forest, as did Severn, attempted to report on Ferenczi's clinical work from the perspective of the analysand (they were also therapists). They believed in Ferenczi's clinical work and ideas because they were being helped by Ferenczi's empathic psychoanalysis. As students of psychoanalysis, they were also intellectually interested in Ferenczi besides being analysands. They also knew they were involved in a unique, groundbreaking experience, and they were excited to be part of a new form of psychoanalysis. As Americans, De Forest, Severn, and Thompson helped convey Ferenczi's ideas to the therapeutic community in the United States, influencing the development of the American humanistic and interpersonal perspectives.

Unfortunately, this idea became known to Freud and the orthodox analytic community through rumors spread by analysands. Freud cherished neutrality and emotional control. He was critical and demeaning of the tender-mother transference, which seemed to ignore or challenge the father transference and focus on the importance of the empathic method in psychoanalysis (Rachman, 1989). Ferenczi's seminal work on empathy (Ferenczi, 1980k) has not been recognized because the *Todschweigen* experience (see Chapter 7) resulted in his ideas being suppressed and ignored. Mainstream psychoanalysis seems to credit Kohut with originating clinical empathy, thereby demonstrating how successful the attempt to silence Ferenczi has been. In actuality, Ferenczi's recognition that cherishing love is an essential ingredient in the therapeutic experience, as it is in human interaction, is echoed in Kohut's theory (Kohut, 1984) but without any reference to Ferenczi as a progenitor.

Ferenczi and Severn were able to clarify the essential meaning of cherishing love for personality development and human behavior.

> In addition to the capacity to integrate the fragments intellectually, *there must also be kindness, as this alone makes the integration permanent. Analysis on its own is intellectual anatomical dissection.* A child cannot be healed with understanding alone. It must be helped first in real terms and then with comfort and the awakening of hope. We must stop dispensing suggestion when faced with the needs of purely infantile neurotics. *Kindness alone would not help much either, but only both together.*
>
> *(Ferenczi, 1988, p. 209, italics added)*

Severn's understanding of Ferenczi's empathic methods

In 1952, Severn clarified the idea of Ferenczi's cherishing love, which clearly was a passionless (non-erotic) contact:

> ... he developed the idea, and I think it came in part from me, certainly, that *the analyst must have more than mere good will for the patient, and he adopted the word love. It all did not mean being in love,* of course, *but a sensitiveness to the patient's need that you could perhaps use the word love for* ... and he tried to do that not only with me, but with his other patients. He told me about his other cases; how it worked and how it didn't work ... then he went to Freud and he put this idea before him, and Freud was very annoyed. ... he told Ferenczi that he was adolescent or senile ... that he was sentimental and silly. He was very harsh. He came back just crushed, ... I saw how hurt he was.
>
> *(Eissler, 1952 p. 6)*

Severn also focused on Ferenczi's idea that, in order to maintain a non-erotic inter-action, personal analysis should be introduced for the analyst:

> The other point was the necessity for the analyst to have been thoroughly analyzed himself so that he didn't have any hidden pockets in his mind or emotions that might affect his attitude toward patients. ... *we also made notes on that with a view to possibly writing a book together about it.* He tried also pre-senting that idea to Freud. It didn't go down any better than the other.
>
> *(Eissler, 1952, pp. 6–7)*

Ferenczi in actuality, introduced the psychoanalytic focus on the role of the mother in child development and psychopathology (Roazen, 1975). In his work with trauma cases Ferenczi realized that early childhood experiences usually involved the mother (but not exclusively, like in Severn's case). As we now know, it is the early empathic response of the mother to the child that is crucial in the child's emotional development.

Non-interpretative measures

Ferenczi's relaxation therapy (Ferenczi, 1980i, 1988) was developed by him and Severn, to treat trauma. These cases were emotional disorders that were not addressed in the 1920s and 30s. These individuals needed more than interpretation or, in some instances, little or no interpretation. What they needed was responsiveness, empathy, and non-interpretative measures (Rachman, 1997a, 2003a; Rachman & Klett, 2015). Ferenczi described the boundaries of his non-interpretative empathic method:

> In some cases, I was even obliged to let patients stay in bed for days and weeks and relieve them of the effort of coming to my home [E.S.]. The sudden breaking off of the analysis at the end of the hour very often had the effect of a shock, and I would be forced to prolong the treatment until the reaction had spent itself ….
>
> My attempt to adhere to the principle that patients must be in a lying position during analysis would at times be thwarted by their uncontrollable impulse and get up and walk about the room or speak to me face to face … Difficulties in the real situation, often the unconscious machinations of the patient, would leave me with no alternative but to either break off the analysis or to depart from the general rule and carry it out without remuneration.
>
> *(Ferenczi, 1980i, p. 114)*

The kissing technique

Two of the most dramatic examples of non-interpretative measures that fueled Freud and the orthodox analytic community's view of Severn as evil, were the aforementioned kissing technique and the Madrid trip. Although the kissing technique involved Clara Thompson, not Severn, it cast a negative view upon Ferenczi's relaxation therapy and employment of non-interpretative measures with Severn. Ferenczi was clearly aware of the limitations of his relaxation therapy and didn't need Freud to denounce him for it. As previously discussed, Ferenczi began the discussion of his clinical interaction with analysands by describing Thompson's abuse of his empathic method on page 2 of the *Clinical Diary*, Ferenczi complained that Thompson was acting out her trauma disorder by bragging she could kiss her analyst. He was not describing it as an accepted method in his trauma analysis. Freud would have found this out, if he had discussed it with Ferenczi.

Judith Dupont, the editor of Ferenczi's *Clinical Diary* made it clear that Dm was Thompson (Ferenczi, 1988, p. 3, f3). Thompson described her experience with Ferenczi:

> A case … of a woman who had grown up in an intolerant small town community where childhood sexual activities … At the start of the analysis, it was apparent that she wished to make her body unattractive and avoided, to an extreme degree, … all physical contact. *A time came in the analysis where not*

only did it seem important to talk [about] whether her body was repulsive to the analyst, but to test it. To this end *she was encouraged to try a natural expression necessary for her to kiss the analyst not only once but many times* …

(*Thompson, 1964, pp. 67–69, italics added*)

Thompson's self-disclosure seems to indicate that she initiated the kissing technique in order to express her need for an *affirming, reparative parental figure* (Rachman, 1998) who could accept her as not being repulsive, either physically, emotionally, or sexually. Thompson was attempting to replace the trauma of paternal incest with empathic fathering. *Ferenczi encouraged her to express the deepest level of her incest trauma, but he did not tell her to do this by kissing him.* When Thompson decided to express herself with kissing, Ferenczi did not prevent her from using this form of expression. He *accepted* her need to express herself, affectionately perhaps, sexually in a safe, non-abusive environment (Rachman & Klett, 2015).

Freud accused Ferenczi of acting out his sexual needs with Thompson as he believed he had done, earlier in his clinical career, with Elma Palos. In actuality, the kissing of Ferenczi was Thompson's acting out her unresolved childhood trauma with her father. It was also a function of her rivalry with Severn. Thompson's acting out was equivalent to her shouting to the analytic community: "I mean more to Ferenczi than Severn because he allows me to kiss him!"

The irony of the criticism of the so-called kissing technique is that the interaction did not involve Severn. But Freud assumed that Ferenczi was using this same technique with Severn. Although, Severn helped develop the use of non-interpretative measures, according to my research, there is no indication that Severn kissed Ferenczi or Ferenczi kissed Severn (Rachman, 1993). If Ferenczi had developed this as a technique, why is there no report of the kissing technique with Severn in the *Clinical Diary* or in the Eissler/Severn Interview. What is more, Severn had developed an erotic transference to Ferenczi, yet, he (Ferenczi, 1988), or she (Severn, 1933), never reported any clinical activity of Ferenczi that can be considered erotic. It should be emphasized that Ferenczi's Confusion of Tongues theory of trauma (Rachman & Klett, 2015) clearly states that the analyst needs to take every precaution to create a *passion-free* clinical interaction. This is necessary so as to titrate, or carefully allow to unfold, the re-traumatization of the incest survivor. Ferenczi believed that the analyst must develop an attitude of self-scrutiny, through an ever-hovering attention to any countertransference reactions (De Forest, 1954), so that his/her sexuality does not intrude into the clinical interaction with an incest survivor (Rachman & Kleet, 2015). The Ferenczi/Severn adjustment to the analytic method has a mandate to guard against re-traumatization.

Ironically, Freud created a Confusion of Tongues experience between himself and Ferenczi by intruding his own concern about sexuality into Ferenczi's relationship with Thompson. As I have discussed elsewhere (Rachman, 2016b), Freud's own childhood trauma was relevant to his functioning. It is perfectly meaningful to argue that Ferenczi should have been aware of the unconscious erotic implications of Thompson kissing him, as well as his own potential countertransference reaction to her eroticizing their relationship. One could also raise the issue of why Ferenczi allowed the kissing by Thompson to continue once he heard about her acting out? He believed that the analytic material that emerged from the dramatic expression of the analysand's deepest unfilled needs and experiences in their most primitive form was therapeutic:

> we are helping him [her] to cope in general, hastening his release from analy-
> sis and the analyst, and we also hasten the transformation into memory of
> those tendencies towards repetition, hitherto resistant to change.
>
> *(Ferenczi, 1988, p. 3)*

Relaxation therapy and non-interpretative measures, Ferenczi and Severn believed, were necessary to reach the childhood trauma. The way to create this atmosphere in which these primitive feelings can emerge was to establish the empathic mode of clinical interaction.

Freud expressed his own middle-class morality in condemning Ferenczi's pioneering clinical work. Ferenczi thought Thompson was abusing his empathy. But wasn't Freud's technique of interpretation being abused by him in his aggressive interpretations in the case of Dora and the Wolf Man (see Chapter 8; Rachman & Mattick, 2012). Ferenczi was trying to inform Freud that psychoanalysis involves more than interpretation in the analysis of trauma. It also involved empathy. Ferenczi's clinical behavior with Thompson is open to investigation (Rachman, 2012c). But then, isn't Freud's behavior with his daughter, Anna, also open to investigation? Freud's analysis of his daughter Anna (Roazen, 1969) constitutes one of the greatest clinical transgressions in psychoanalytic history. But, no one, to my knowledge, has written a condemning letter about Freud's perpetration of "emotional abuse" in analyzing his daughter Anna.

In analyzing Anna, Freud broke his own rule of abstinence: *no erotic gratification* of a patient's needs. *Anna was charged with expressing her sexual feelings for her father to her father.* Then, her father was charged with analyzing these thoughts and feelings as if he was a scientific observer or analyst. The process of Anna expressing sexual feelings to her father was an emotionally laden interaction for her and her father. Freud had his own personal reaction in hearing Anna tell him she has a "beating fantasy" or sexual feelings about her father. Why does the issue of Freud's analysis of his daughter remain a taboo subject? (Rachman, 2003b).

The Madrid trip

In 1928, Severn accompanied Ferenczi and his wife Gisella on their vacation trip to Madrid, Spain. A record of this trip was captured in a photograph, which is part of The Elizabeth Severn Papers (Rachman, 2016d; see Chapter 18, Image 13). The photograph, in Severn's handwriting, has the notation, "Dr. & Mrs. Ferenczi, E.S. – Spain, 1928." The date indicates Severn was in analysis with Ferenczi for about three years when the photograph was taken. In 1928, Ferenczi published his paper on empathy, crediting Severn with a collaboration (Ferenczi, 1980h). We now have, for the first time, Severn's description of her emotional state during this period, which indicates that she was in a regressed state of dependence and dysfunction.

> In the summer, I was away from him a certain length of time. It was extremely difficult for me to live without the analysis. And I went on one trip with him and his wife to Spain because it was the lesser of the two evils for me. It was terrible. I didn't want to go, and I wasn't able really, to travel. I had to go to bed as soon as I arrived, and stay until he chose to move to the next place, then I got up and got on the train and went there and went to bed again. So that was rather a terrible experience ...
>
> *(Eissler, 1952, p. 12)*

Eissler asked Severn if Ferenczi saw her every day for a session, and she replied in the affirmative (Eissler, 1952, p. 12).

This important revelation by Severn indicates that Ferenczi agreed to allow Severn to accompany him and his wife on the Madrid trip when she made it clear she couldn't live without the analysis. Allowing her to accompany him and his wife on vacation, was considered an empathic response to Severn's traumatic childhood with her father. She needed a reparative father figure. In their trauma analysis, Severn quickly developed a positive father transference to Ferenczi. This transference also had unconscious erotic components. The positive transference was easily created as a result of Severn's need for a positive father figure, her desperate need for psychological help, and her previous negative analytic experiences. Ferenczi's warmth, kindness, and empathy synchronized with Severn's desperate need for emotional survival. The sexual undercurrent could be seen as an erotic transference enactment based on her childhood sexual trauma with her father (see Chapter 12). This issue was analyzed in the mutual analytic interaction they had (Rachman, 2012b).

But was Severn's accompaniment of Ferenczi on the Madrid trip an empathic measure or a non-therapeutic one, which encouraged dependence and regression? It is easy to understand how Freud would be upset with this clinical behavior by Ferenczi. Ferenczi allowing Severn to accompany him and his wife to Madrid was extramural contact, which is generally discouraged. This non-interpretative measure employed by Ferenczi, as we can see from Severn's own words, was probably instituted by Severn's urging. Such deviant clinical behavior by Ferenczi, urged by Severn, may have been one of the major ingredients that encouraged Freud to view Severn as evil. She was influencing Ferenczi not only to move away from traditional psychoanalysis but to move toward inappropriate clinical behavior, which encouraged acting out and the reinforcement of psychopathology. Severn, according to Freud's perception, asked outrageous things of Ferenczi to satisfy her unending emotional needs. Her response was based upon his unresolved needs (Rachman, 1997a). Freud felt that Severn was driven to destroy Ferenczi because she had no control of her own exaggerated needs, and Ferenczi was acting out his needs.

Although I do not agree with Freud's exaggerated, anxiety-ridden conclusions, he did have a meaningful point. Ferenczi, at times, seems to have been involved in confusing or acting-out clinical behavior. He was dedicated to cure this very difficult analysand. As Severn told Eissler, Ferenczi had lost a sense of himself as a clinician when he felt he would not be able to see Severn was going through her therapeutic regression. He did not fully understand the regressive process (as no one did at that time in analytic history).

I believe that Ferenczi's analysis with Severn should be viewed as a clinical experiment, a pioneering attempt to treat, analytically, a trauma disorder. Not Severn, Ferenczi, Balint, who was an observer of this analysis (Balint, 1992/1968), or anyone else in the analytic community had the experience or knowledge to fully understand this interaction. It took 35 years until Balint systematized the concept of therapeutic regression (Balint, 1992/1968), which was a significant contribution to understanding that the analyst's clinical behavior in treating trauma has to titrate and integrate the need for abstinence, empathy, and interpretation (see Chapter 22).

Ferenczi was attempting to integrate the use of interpretative and non-interpretative measures in the analysis of Severn. The Madrid trip can be seen as problematic. Allowing Severn to accompanying him on vacation encouraged dependence. But Severn in her interview with Eissler made it clear that she was in a seriously disturbed emotional state, on the edge of suicide. Ferenczi, it can be said, was extending the boundaries of empathy, perhaps to its outer limits. But, what about the use of two other therapeutic modalities that were available at that time, namely chemotherapy and residential treatment to treat Severn's serious psychopathology? Why wasn't medication used to help Severn reduce some of her symptomatology and stabilize her functioning. During the early part of the 1930s, psychoanalysis did not generally integrate medication into an analysis. The zeitgeist of the 1930s for treatment of emotional disorder was distinctly influenced by psychoanalysis, particularly derived from a Freudian perspective. Prior to the psycho–pharmacology revolution in the 1950s, there was great resistance to the use of medicine in psychoanalytic treatment of mental disorders. This was the case in spite of the use of agents such as amphetamine, opium, sedatives, and barbiturates in the treatment of psychiatric disorders. Although Freud, Ferenczi, and other pioneering psychoanalysts were originally trained as physicians, psychoanalysis developed as a psychological treatment freed from medical treatments. Ironically, Severn developed her form of clinical therapy with the integration of medical supplements, such as physical therapy, massage, exercise, etc. (see Chapter 11).

Ferenczi also wasn't dealing with an Oedipal problem, but most likely with severe borderline functioning. Severn may have needed chemotherapy. But would she have cooperated with a chemotherapy regime? It is doubtful Severn would have agreed to take medication. Her interest in Christian science was incompatible with taking medication or turning to a physician for dealing with one's emotional problems. Self-reliance was a key.

Georg Groddeck's sanatorium at Baden-Baden (Groddeck, 1977) was another treatment modality that Freud, Ferenczi, and their patients had used for rest and rehabilitation. Why didn't Ferenczi refer Severn to Groddeck's sanatorium when she was in serious emotional distress? He could have referred her to Groddeck while he was on vacation. She could have stayed for a brief period, until she gained her equilibrium. Since Groddeck was psychoanalytically oriented, there would be a consistent treatment orientation.

Countertransference analysis and self-disclosure: from opaque to transparent clinical intervention

As Fromm (1955) has described it:

> The central issue in Ferenczi's deviation from Freud is the relationship between analyst and patient. In Freud's view this relationship had to be absolutely neutral and impersonal. The analyst had to be like a mirror, showing himself as little as possible; his relationship to a patient had to be one of scientific detachment, devoid of any kind of emotional participation.
>
> *(Fromm, 1955, p. 1)*

Freud's own behavior did not match Freud's theory of clinical detachment. As Roazen (1975) has indicated, there were many instances where he deviated from his own dictum of clinical opaqueness. Ferenczi's deviations from Freudian technique were inspired by his mentor (Rachman, 1997a). Being a psychoanalyst inspires responding with human feeling and behavior no matter what the theory. There is no hiding from the emotional influence of a difficult analysand. What came together in the analysis of Severn was a combination of: working with difficult analysands, who needed empathy and non-interpretative measures to treat their developmental arrests; Ferenczi's identity as a healer (Rachman, 1997a, 2003a); his capacity to respond with clinical empathy; use of his own capacities for affection, warmth, and interpersonal engagement, and a willingness to extend himself in the direction of the analysand. It was Severn, according to Ferenczi's notation (Ferenczi, 1980h), who helped him first formulate the idea of clinical empathy and then the need of the analyst to be a partner in the co-creation of the analytic encounter (Ferenczi, 1988; see Chapter 16). As I have described, Severn needed to have a transparent analyst and a reparative parental figure (Rachman, 1998), who could be emotionally honest, non-traumatizing, and responsive, to help her work through her father-induced childhood incest and other emotional and physical traumas. As a Freudian-trained analyst who felt his mentor was looking over his shoulder at his ideas and clinical behavior, Ferenczi struggled with responding to Severn's need to have him analyze his negative countertransference.

7

TODSCHWEIGEN (DEATH BY SILENCE)

Removal of Elizabeth Severn's ideas and work from mainstream psychoanalysis

In the late 1980s Esther Menaker and I met on a weekly basis to discuss our dissident ideas about psychoanalysis. Colleagues had introduced us because they felt we both shared compatible dissident ideas about psychoanalysis. Esther had been one of the last analytic candidates at the Vienna Psychoanalytic Institute in the 1930s who had contact with the Freuds. She was analyzed by Anna Freud. Although she was trained as a Freudian analyst, when I met her she was no longer a Freudian. She told me about her journey from Freudian psychology to her admiration for Otto Rank to embracing Self Psychology (Menaker, 1982, 1989). We both were resentful of how Freud and his orthodox followers mistreated Ferenczi, Rank, and other dissidents. Our research, writings, and discussions were about the meaning we found in Ferenczi's and Rank's unrecognized contributions to psychoanalysis (Menaker, 1989; Rachman, 1997b). There was a pattern, we thought, in the way dissidents were silenced, as well as a psychodynamic explanation for this phenomenon. Esther offered the German phrase: "*Sie haben ihn Todschweigen*" or "They silenced him into death" (Menaker, 1989; Rachman, 1999). We translated the phrase as *Todschweigen: death by silence* (Rachman, 1999, p. 153). Esther told me about a dramatic example of a *Todschweigen* event she experienced as an analytic candidate at the Vienna Psychoanalytic Institute. In a seminar conducted by Helena Deutsch in 1933, the class was interrupted by a member of the Vienna Psychoanalytic Institute who came into the room to announce that Sándor Ferenczi had died. The reaction to this announcement was dramatic. Esther told me that a silence so deep and thick instantly settled over the seminar group, including Helena Deutsch its leader, that not one syllable was uttered. Esther received the non-verbal message from this dramatic silence: "Ferenczi is someone of whom we do not speak" (Rachman, 1997a). Helena Deutsch was conveying Freud, Jones, Abraham, Ettigon, and Rivere's silencing of Ferenczi as *a dissident and lost son of psychoanalysis*. When his death was announced in Deutsch's class, the mean-spirited attitude of punishing him for deviating and disobeying from Freud prevailed. An attitude of forgiveness and love for Ferenczi was missing at the Vienna Psychoanalytic Institute that fateful day in 1933. This unforgiving attitude; the need to punish the dissident, by use of *the silent treatment*; disowning a dissident son or daughter; and the removal of a dissident's works from study at traditional institutes and publication in approved journals, constitute the practice of *Todschweigen*.

Freud's Orthodox Jewish background

Ever since Freud's publication of his book *Moses and Monotheism* questions have been raised about the importance of Freud's Jewish background for his ideas and practices. The prevailing view in Freudian scholarship is that his father moved away from his Orthodox Jewish background and towards an assimilated reform Jewish belief system (Krüll, 1986; McGrath, 1991). In this shift to a liberal and secular Jewish belief system, an argument developed that Freud's Orthodox Jewish background had been unknowingly incorporated by him during his childhood years. Freud was exposed to traditional Jewish culture and values during his childhood through his interaction with his parents and the Jewish community in which he lived. Freud's parents were both from towns in Galicia where Orthodox Jewish religious and cultural practices were the standard of community life. His father, Jacob, came from a Chasidic background: his great-grandfather, Rabbi Ephraim Freud, and grandfather, Rabbi Shlomo Freud (after whom Freud was named) were learned Orthodox Jews. Freud's parental household was rich in Jewish culture and religion:

> His mother Amalie, spoke Galician Yiddish as her almost exclusive language, suggesting that this must have been Freud's own language until he began school. When we turn to examine psychoanalysis itself we discover that it shares a whole host of theoretical, technical and even sociological features with Judaism, particularly with Kabbalah and Chassidism.
>
> *(Drob, 1989, p. 2)*

The practice of *Todschweigen*, i.e. disowning a psychoanalytic dissident by suppressing and censoring his/her work because it represents the so-called repudiation of Freudism or traditional psychoanalytic thought or practice, may have its roots in Freud's traditional Orthodox Jewish background. I would like to raise the hypothesis that Freud's Jewish background, that is, his formal Jewish education and his Jewish family traditions (as well as his wife's) provided an awareness of the Orthodox tradition of disowning a child who seriously disobeys the father and the traditions of Judaism, such as by living a homosexual lifestyle or marrying a gentile. The Orthodox tradition in these two instances is to initiate *the tradition of Shiva*, the ritual of formal mourning for a deceased member of one's family (Lamm, 2000). The living dissident family member is declared symbolically deceased. Then the family sits Shiva, the traditional Jewish practice of mourning for the deceased individual. For seven days the family initiates a process of prayers, deprivation of comfort, and mourning. After the process is completed the disowned individual no longer exists for the family and the larger Jewish Community.

In the film, *Trembling Before G–d*, a 2002 award-winning documentary about Orthodox Jewish gay men and lesbian women, there is a particular touching and dramatic example of the playing out of a father disowning his son because he is homosexual (Dubrowski, 2002). Father and son do not have any personal contact; although, the son regularly calls his father, clearly pleading with him for some contact. In an emotionally wrenching scene, the son tries to make an appointment to visit his father, repeating the same kind of phone call he has regularly made for years. The father rejects his homosexual son, telling him he has no time to have him come over for a visit. Of course, what he does not say is that he has emotionally and interpersonally detached himself from his son. As an Orthodox Jew, he felt compelled to disown his son, although one sensed he still felt emotionally attached to him. The father's voice indicates an affection for his son, but the Orthodox prohibition on homosexuality is obeyed. There is a harshness, a mean-spirited, even abusive quality to this kind of parental behavior toward a child who disobeys parental and religious tradition.

The issue of parent-child obedience is a foundation of Orthodox Judaic law as handed down to the Jewish people by Moses. The fifth commandment states:

> Honor thy father and mother that thy days may belong in the land which the Lord gives.
>
> *(Exodus, 20:12)*

This commandment gives absolute power to the parents over their children. Abraham's willingness to sacrifice his son Isaac (Genesis: 22) to prove his faithfulness to God is a very powerful standard of obeying authority and not questioning the tenets of belief. Did exposure to Orthodox Jewish tradition of parent-child obedience have an influence on the young Freud that found its way into his own severe paternal behavior with his dissident children, such as Sándor Ferenczi and Elizabeth Severn, as well as Jung, Adler, and Rank?

Although I am suggesting that Freud originated the practice of *Todschweigen* in psychoanalysis and that this attitude toward dissidents may be related to his Orthodox Jewish background, I do not believe this practice of banishing, disowning, or silencing a dissident is exclusive to psychoanalysis or Judaism. I am trying to discern the specific process that forms *Todschweigen* within psychoanalysis. In actuality, I am suggesting that *Todschweigen* is not a product of Freud's psychopathology but of an orthodoxy in belief and thinking to which he was exposed and which he absorbed.

Pathology in family interaction produces something very akin to *Todschweigen*, what we may call, *giving a child the silent treatment*. Within a family, the silent treatment can involve a mother or father who reacts with prolonged silence to a child, demonstrating disapproval or anger. In one such clinical example a controlling, domineering, and emotionally volatile mother instilled a rigid sleeping routine for her daughter as a young child. Every night the child was placed in bed at 7pm in the evening. It did not matter what was actually happening in the home, to the child or parent; the child was placed in bed at the same time. All reactions, such as frustration, anger, or crying by the child, were met with silence by the mother. The more the child felt discomfort and struggled, the more silent and determined the mother became. Of course, these moments were an indication of a power-struggle dynamic. The situation became more and more of a crisis, cumulating in the mother deliberately employing the silent treatment to punish her daughter. This involved the mother discontinuing both verbal, emotional, and interpersonal interaction with her daughter. The child would submit and not fight the time to go to bed for fear of receiving the silent treatment. As an adult, the mother would use the same silent treatment to punish her daughter, sometimes for a day, several days, or a week at a time. During the longer periods of silence, the mother would wait until the father would come home from work and tell him to convey instructions to his daughter. The willingness to tolerate such a disturbed and damaging mother/daughter interaction is another powerful dynamic in that family. The mother's silence had a devastating effect on her child. She grew up as a highly anxious, emotionally volatile, angry individual who had serious problems with authority. The daughter as an adult had a severely disturbed relationship with her mother. She was emotionally abusive of her mother, acting out her childhood trauma of being mistreated through the use of the silent treatment. In an act of almost total denial, the mother was confused and had no idea why her daughter continually mistreated her.

Todschweigen of Sándor Ferenczi and Elizabeth Severn: silencing Ferenczi

Of Freud's disciples no one received a greater experience of *Todschweigen* than Sándor Ferenczi. Freud's favorite son went from being his collaborator, the psychoanalysis heir apparent, to being the target of Freud's dissatisfaction and anger (Rachman, 1997a, b). Jones, who became Ferenczi's rival for Freud's attention and affection, became Freud's collaborative in the *political assassination of Ferenczi*. There is no question about the suppression, censorship, and attempt to silence Ferenczi by Freud, Jones, and the orthodox community that surrounded them. I have been surprised at what can be considered an under-reaction by the traditional analytic community to the deliberate attempt at discrediting Ferenczi as a person and psychoanalyst. I have outlined the step-by-step process that non-traditional psychoanalysis employed to silence Ferenczi and remove his person and work from mainstream psychoanalysis (Rachman, 1997b). I would now consider the process to be emotionally abusive. Regrettably, The Budapest School of Psychoanalysis (Rachman, 2016) has been reluctant to criticize Freud's abusive behavior towards Ferenczi. Of course, this is understandable. Members of the Ferenczi community, already stigmatized by identifying with the dissident, walked a tightrope. Balint defended Ferenczi (Balint, 1969, 1992/1968), without directly criticizing Freud. There are some voices who have been more outspoken, (Aron & Starr, 2016; De Forest, 1954,

Fromm 1959; Masson, 1984; Mészaros, 1993; Rachman, 1997b; Roazen, 1975). Ferenczians did not want to revisit the original disturbing *Todschweigen* experience, where anyone who identified themselves with Ferenczi and The Budapest School, like Balint did, found themselves as the disowned sons and daughters, unable to be recognized as significant contributors to mainstream psychoanalysis (Balint, 1968).

Balint's attempt to counter the *Todschweigen* experience, however, was significant. He revised and extended Ferenczi's Confusion of Tongues ideas about trauma in an attempt to integrate them with Freud's Oedipal theory (Balint, 1992/1968; Rachman, 2003a). This attempt actually fulfilled Ferenczi's idea to have the Confusion of Tongues paradigm stand side-by-side with the Oedipal Theory (Ferenczi, 1980k). Ferenczi did not act out his anger toward Freud as Jones (1957) and Gay (1984) contended. He desperately wanted to remain Freud's faithful follower, as well as to develop his own identity as a psychoanalyst (Rachman, 1997a, b). As will be discussed in an upcoming section, psychoanalysis had not yet become more accepting of the creative dissident as a means to re-evaluate and contribute to the evolution of psychoanalysis (Rachman, 2007).

Silencing Elizabeth Severn

Todschweigen was so successful towards Severn that very few individuals in contemporary psychoanalysis have any idea that she existed or made a significant contribution. As I have been attempting to demonstrate in this volume, Severn could be viewed as a pioneering clinician before she went into analysis with Ferenczi (see Chapter 11). Several experiences shaped her development toward psychoanalysis: e.g. her personal analysis with Ferenczi; her consultation sessions with Freud; and her own study and clinical experience with psychoanalysis. It is from the vantage point of Severn as a student, practitioner, and innovator of psychotherapy and psychoanalysis, that her functioning can best be discussed.

Freud, I believe, felt that Severn was an intellectually and clinically gifted individual, or else he would not have labeled her "an evil genius" (Jones, 1957, p. 407). His need to create a *Todschweigen* experience about her within the psychoanalytic community is connected to her intelligence, her assertive (aggressive) personality, her emotional disturbance, and her influence on Ferenczi. I believe the Confusion of Tongues between Freud and Ferenczi was based upon his anxiety that Severn was taking Ferenczi away from him. He also assumed that Severn triggered the most disturbed aspects of Ferenczi's neurosis. In essence, Freud thought he needed to suppress Severn's influence on Ferenczi because she was a seriously disturbed individual who was not credible and should not have any influence on Ferenczi or the analytic community. There was no dialogue between Freud and Ferenczi about these concerns, although Ferenczi did originally inform Freud about the Severn analysis (Falzeder, Braband & Giampieri-Deutsch, 2000). Freud treated Ferenczi and Severn as if they were deviant children who were out of control and needed to be punished. Freud was angry at Ferenczi. Ferenczi needed Freud's approval and could not risk an open conflict. Severn became the scapegoat. In actuality, she was not leading Ferenczi away from psychoanalysis. Severn was in a training analysis, interested in becoming an analyst herself. She was trying to help cure herself with the analyst who she felt was the best equipped to help her recover from her severe trauma disorder, which analysts, such as, Otto Rank and Henry Stack Sullivan endorsed. Severn and Ferenczi were involved in a mutual analytic experience that was far-reaching, experimental, and pioneering. Freud did not suffer dissidents well.

Freud did not understand or accept the far-reaching clinical experiments in the psychoanalytic method that Ferenczi and Severn were developing. It is ironic that Feud was so rejecting of them, since he was such an important dissident himself. Freud began to think the worst of Ferenczi because of his departures from traditional analyses and because of his growing distance from Freud. The distance did not allow for any explanation of what he was doing. But, towards the end, when he tried to explain his Confusions of Tongues idea, Freud rejected him in the most dramatic way (Fromm, 1959).

Freud's analysis of his daughter, Anna: a *Todschweigen* experience

Freud's boundary violation in analyzing his daughter qualifies as a *Todschweigen* experience because *a silence was created* about it, which actually *became a taboo*. Neither Freud nor the traditional analytic community acknowledged that Freud analyzed his daughter. A prohibition has been institutionalized in the analytic community, creating the fiction that Freud had never analyzed Anna. Paul Roazen (1969) was the first scholar to put in print that this had happened. Roazen became a negative figure for the traditional analytic community for revealing this, as well as for his publication of a revisionist history of psychoanalysis (Roazen, 1975). To members of The Budapest School of Psychoanalysis, Roazen, on the other hand, became a hero because he had the courage to present Ferenczi and other pioneering dissidents as significant contributors to psychoanalysis. He helped lift the *Todschweigen* experience for dissidents. But, for traditional psychoanalysis he became an outsider, a critic, a Freud basher. He was labeled and disowned as someone whose work about Freud is not to be taken seriously or to be quoted in the traditional literature. Roazen then became a victim of *Todschweigen*. His history of psychoanalysis emerged from his interviewing Freud's students, colleagues, analysands, and friends. It was a significant departure from the hero-worshipping biography of Freud by Jones (1950–59). Jones' authorized history of psychoanalysis solidified the *Todschweigen* experience towards Ferenczi and Severn, while Roazen's work helped break the silence about these two figures and initiated the beginnings of the Ferenczi Renaissance.

Esther Menaker told me about her experience of Anna's analysis by her father. The acceptable rumor that floated around the Vienna Institute was that Princess Marie Bonaparte was Anna's analyst. In this rumor, a *Todschweigen* was created to silence the idea that Freud analyzed his daughter.

A traditional analyst's noble attempt to lift the *Todschweigen* on Freud analyzing Anna appeared in Elizabeth Young-Breuhl's biography of Anna Freud

(Young–Breuhl, 1988). Young-Breuhl may have been the first traditional analyst to openly discuss Anna Freud's analysis. She related the material that was available about the analysis as well as her speculations. From her discussion in her biography of Anna Freud, as well as a conversation I had with Young-Breuhl (Young–Breuhl, 1992), it was clear that she was attempting to create a dialogue about this controversial analysis that the traditional analytic community had avoided.

Contemporary experiences of *Todschweigen*

It is remarkable how viable Freud's, Jones', and other members' condemnation of Ferenczi has been on in the psychohistory of psychoanalysis. The original campaign to label Ferenczi as *mad* and *not a psychoanalyst*, or *emotionally disturbed*, continues in contemporary times. I have experienced three contemporary examples of *Todschweigen*. The first experience occurred at a weekend retreat conference at a prominent analytic center, in the 1990s. The weekend retreat was devoted to Ferenczi's ideas and work. On the Saturday morning a presentation about Ferenczi was given by a junior staff member. I had been scheduled to present, but, I was recovering from a serious automobile accident. I attended the conference as a respondent. The discussant of the Ferenczi paper was a senior analyst who identified herself as a Freudian. I was shocked by the discussant's remarks about Ferenczi, which were:

> I grew up in Europe as you know [the discussant grew up in Vienna, Germany]. There were many Hungarian people who were around in my childhood and later years. Ferenczi was Hungarian. I found these Hungarians to be sneaky people, who you cannot fully trust. They are romantic types who have ideas that are not intellectually sound.

I stopped listening after these initial statements, as I was filled with frustration and anger, so I do not have a remembrance of her other remarks. After the senior analyst concluded speaking, I eagerly awaited the audience responses to what I considered audaciously condemning remarks about Ferenczi. This senior Freudian analyst attacked Ferenczi's ancestry, as a person and as an analyst.

This attack on Ferenczi, as well as the others to be discussed, are a different example of *Todschweigen*. This form of *Todschweigen*, maintains a nefarious tradition in psychoanalysis, which began in pioneering times and was institutionalized by Jones (1957) when he began an open attack on Ferenczi as a person and clinician (Rachman, 1997a). The senior Freudian analyst openly attacked Ferenczi to politically assassinate him, as Jones had originally done, to continue to silence and discredit him. Criticizing Ferenczi's ideas is not at issue; however, these criticisms need to be intellectually sound and refer to verifiable behavior. I considered these remarks by the senior analyst as severely prejudicial and as having no place in a scientific meeting. To my surprise, five minutes into the discussion no one in the audience made any remarks about the senior analyst's attack on Ferenczi. I was about to initiate a confrontation with her when a colleague, to whom I had turned for some support, actively discouraged me. To the best of my recollection, this colleague said:

> Arnold, don't do it! No, no one is paying attention to what the senior analyst says anymore. We all know she has lost her marbles. If you confront her, everyone will feel you are attacking a helpless old person. They will turn away from you and Ferenczi.

My colleague and dear friend's reaction was meaningful, but I still struggled to keep my mouth shut. In the end, I decided to remain silent. I did not want to be remembered as the Ferenczi disciple who emotionally injured a beloved senior member of the Institute. But what was also shocking was that not one member of the analytic community to which I belonged made any remarks about this attempt to denounce Ferenczi. I left this conference making a silent pledge to myself:

> Arnold, *never* again *remain silent* when someone privately or publicly attacks Ferenczi!

There were other minor experiences of *Todschweigen* through the years, such as colleagues saying to me: "Isn't Ferenczi the one who let patients sit on his lap?; he was the one who had sex with his patients; didn't Freud break off from him because of his inappropriate clinical behavior." In these private encounters, I would present the research I had uncovered (Rachman, 1993; 1997a, b), which counteracted the false rumors and accusations that had become part of the dark undercurrent about Ferenczi. I was never convinced that my defense of Ferenczi ever changed any minds. Some of the people who believed these rumors went on to label me as a naïve, devotee of Ferenczi.

"Ferenczi/Severn analysis was regressive"

There were two additional experiences that shocked me and reminded me that the practice of *Todschweigen* was an important device, used by traditional psychoanalysis to continue *to silence unto death* Ferenczi and other dissidents, such as Severn. My second dramatic example of *Todschweigen* occurred in 2012. In discussing Ferenczi's analysis with Elizabeth Severn, a senior American psychoanalyst with a worldwide reputation did not hesitate to tell me:

> You know that Ferenczi's *analysis of Severn was regressive*. It cannot be considered a true analysis!

I disagreed with his condemnation of Ferenczi's work, saying that it was time to reassess this historic case. In addition, I added that the words he was using to denounce Ferenczi's work were the same as those used by Freud and Jones over 80 years ago. This Freudian scholar and psychoanalytic leader was perpetuating the *Todschweigen* experience first initiated by Freud, Jones, et al., in the early 1930s (Rachman, 1997b). As I have suggested, the Ferenczi/Severn analysis was necessarily controversial because he was pioneering the establishment of new diagnostic category, trauma disorder, and a new methodology to treat it, i.e. trauma analysis (Rachman, 2012a, 2014b). I was incredulous that a significant contemporary figure in psychoanalysis was deliberately perpetuating the *Todschweigen* experience with Ferenczi, so that his life and work would continue to be disowned by traditional psychoanalysis. I was angry at this influential individual for being so medieval in his thinking in the year 2012. It felt important to counteract the criticism of Ferenczi. I promised myself, once again, I would not be silent if someone denounced Ferenczi.

Professor Martin Bergman's denunciation of Ferenczi

In November of 2013, a dramatic example of a *Todschweigen* experience occurred at a narrative reading of the Freud/Ferenczi Correspondence. There were presenters, reading the parts of Freud, Ferenczi, Ferenczi's wife, and a narrator. Professor Martin Bergmann was an invited discussant. The event was well attended. After the narrative reading, Professor Bergmann was introduced as the distinguished invited guest to begin the discussion of the narrative presentation of the Freud/Ferenczi Correspondence. To the best of my recollection, Professor Bergmann said the following as his opening remarks:

> I found the narrative about The Freud/Ferenczi Correspondence very enjoyable, and the people being part of this narrative did a fine job. But, you didn't invite me here tonight just to say good things.
> What this correspondence shows is that *Freud was a psychoanalyst, Ferenczi was not a psychoanalyst. Ferenczi was not a psychoanalyst because he let patients kiss him!*
> *(Rachman, 2013)*

When Bergmann finished his denunciation of Ferenczi, I made sure I got the attention of the discussion leader and signaled I wanted to be the first person to speak after Bergmann's statements. I was determined to have a dialogue with Bergmann about his naked denunciation of Ferenczi. Here is what I said to Bergmann, which became a confrontation on my part:

> Professor Bergman, with all due respect, *I completely disagree* with your characterization of Sándor Ferenczi. I have researched this issue of the myth that Ferenczi had regular physical contact with his patients [see Rachman, 1993]. The only analysand with whom he had such contact was Clara Mabel Thompson. Thompson was the one who initiated kissing Ferenczi. He did not initiate the contact. [See Chapter 6]. What is more, Ferenczi did not have this contact with other analysands (Rachman, 1993). Thompson bragged to the analytic community that she could kiss "Papa Ferenczi anytime she wanted" [See Ferenczi,

1988]. Ferenczi allowed Thompson to kiss him in order to create a reparative therapeutic experience for her childhood trauma by her father.

(Rachman, 2013)

The remainder of our confrontation involved a stand-off. Bergmann would make statements that did not directly relate to or answer any of my comments. He would reiterate his condemnation about Ferenczi as an analyst and extol Freud as the role model for psychoanalysis. When I became frustrated with his lack of direct response to me, I asked him:

> Professor Bergmann, speaking of deviating from psychoanalytic standards, what do you think of Freud's analyzing his daughter, Anna, as an example of inappropriate analytic behavior?
>
> *(Rachman, 2013)*

Bergmann's response to my question was as follows:

> People always bring this issue up to discredit Freud.
>
> *(Rachman, 2013)*

With that response, I discontinued my attempt at a dialogue with Bergmann. My Yiddish grandmother's phrase for a sense of hopelessness came to me at that moment:

> *Es garnisht helfen.* It is useless!; nothing good will happen.

In the remainder of the discussion, there were two audience members who made comments relevant to the issue that I raised about Ferenczi's functioning. But, in an audience of over 100 individuals, not one analyst was able to voice any concern about Bergmann's denunciation of Ferenczi. After the meeting, I talked to a group of analysts about my confrontation with Bergmann. Several of them, who were silent during the discussion, congratulated me on standing up to him. In talking to another group of analysts, including one who was a contemporary Freudian, they agreed that it was appropriate to present a balanced approach to the Freud/Ferenczi controversy.

There were also criticisms of my exchanges with Bergmann. One analyst, in particular, thought my response to Bergmann was an indication that "I had a severe problem with anger." Fearing that I had offended Bergmann, I sent him a letter, inviting him to enter into a dialogue with me about Ferenczi. My letter was sent on November 15, 2013. I never received a response from Bergmann. He died in January 2014. I believe I was respectful to Bergmann. I found my voice to be able to help break the *Todschweigen* attempt by Bergmann to destroy Ferenczi as a significant contributor to psychoanalysis. Bergmann's accusations about Ferenczi can be seen as a direct line backwards to the *Kissing Letter* Freud send to Ferenczi. Bergmann in 2013 continued the tradition of *Todschweigen* started by Freud 83 years earlier in 1932, silencing and denouncing Ferenczi.

The silence of the psychoanalytic community

The dimensions of the *Todschweigen* psychodynamic I have discussed in the three previous examples were silence, anxiety, and confusion. This indicated to me that a Confusion of Tongues trauma had been provoked (Rachman & Klett, 2015). Ferenczi's student Balint (1968) reflected on both Ferenczi and his own experiences to revise and expand psychoanalysis. He concluded that Ferenczi's introduction of the Confusion of Tongues paradigm to provide a framework for understanding and treating trauma disorder, and his own expansion of this framework (Balint, 1992/1968), stimulated a *Todschweigen* dynamic in the analytic community (Rachman, 1997a, b, 1999). The confusion that ensued involved Freud and his followers believing that Ferenczi and then Balint were attempting to overturn traditional psychoanalytic theory and technique (Rachman, 1997b). *Ferenczi was not attempting to displace Freud, introduce his own version of psychoanalysis, or rebel against Freud* (Gay, 1984; Jones, 1957). They believed that Ferenczi was acting out his unconscious Oedipal conflict with Freud. Thompson (1964) indicated that Ferenczi should have broken with Freud and founded his own school of psychoanalysis, since he had evolved an alternative framework (Gedo, 1986). Freud had a need to have a uniformity in thinking and functioning, so he could protect his own discovery (Malcolm, 1981; Masson, 1984); a need to have adherents or company men protect his discovery (Fromm, 1959); and a need to protect his legacy of the Oedipal Complex (Masson, 1984). He couldn't accept an adherent, his favorite pupil, his adopted son, having his own ideas and methods. It is also possible that Freud was suffering from anxiety, confusion, and paranoia because he felt that Ferenczi was being aggressive toward him and feared he was being abandoned.

Ferenczi's Confusion of Tongues was exemplified by his anxiety, confusion, and desire to have Freud's approval for his deviations from Freudian psychology. Ferenczi could not understand that Freud was not able to affirm an adherent who was developing the first alternative to Freudian psychology (Gedo, 1986). It was Ferenczi's father transference to Freud, where he acted out his unresolved need for fatherly tenderness and affirmation, that emotionally blinded Ferenczi and caused him to seek to maintain a relationship with Freud, who expressed such severe criticism, rejection, anger, and, yes, emotional abuse towards him (Fromm 1959; Masson, 1984; Rachman, 1997a, b; Roazen, 1975). Furthermore, the Confusion of Tongues between them was exemplified by Freud wanting a loyal son/adherent in the tradition of Jewish Orthodoxy. Ferenczi did not comprehend that he was dealing with a Jewish Orthodox father figure. He projected his need for an unconditional loving father onto Freud. Ferenczi thought that Freud would allow him to develop his own identity and maintain the affirmation of the loving father (Erickson, 1950; Rachman, 1975). Ferenczi did not want to break away from Freud. He wanted his new ideas to be integrated into psychoanalysis so that it could evolve toward studying and treating trauma disorders (Rachman, 2007). But he was also emotionally hampered by his need to turn Freud into his original affirming father, which did not allow him to break away emotionally or interpersonally from Freud (Rachman, 1997a).

Emotional power of *Todschweigen*

The practice of *Todschweigen* in psychoanalysis has had a very powerful effect. As has been discussed, Ferenczi and Severn became virtual unknowns after Freud and his orthodox followers silenced them. After 1933, Ferenczi and Severn's work disappeared from psychoanalysis. Generations of analysts were prevented from studying their contributions (Rachman, 1997a, b). My own experience in analytic training took place from 1964 to the early 1970s at a psychoanalytic institute that saw itself as an eclectic psychodynamic training facility. Yet, in the seven years of the training program in which I was involved and which included individual, group, and child psychoanalysis, as well as mental health consultation training programs, *Ferenczi's name was never mentioned*. Furthermore, none of his ideas were taught in any class or mentioned in a supervisory session, and no analyst who was invited to lecture or give a special seminar mentioned Ferenczi. As I have mentioned, I discovered Ferenczi on my own. When I began to present my discovery about Ferenczi at my training institute, it was very well received by analytic candidates and some training analysts.

As much as Ferenczi was subjected to the *Todschweigen* experience, Severn's work was silenced and completely removed from psychoanalysis. In the psychoanalytic literature there have been only a handful of analysts who have written about Severn (Fortune, 1993, 1996; Haynal, 2010; Rachman, 2010a, b, 2014a, b, 2015b, c; Smith, 1998, 1999, 2001).

Silenced and banished from the analytic community: how *Todschweigen* endures Ferenczi's Confusion of Tongues paradigm (Ferenczi, 1980k, 1988) and its extensions (Balint, 1968; Rachman & Klett, 2015) identified the actual emotional trauma that occurs in parent/child interaction when a parent abuses a child. By analogy, *Todschweigen* can be seen as an emotionally abusive experience. Ferenczi suffered emotionally during the period when he analyzed Severn and developed his Confusion of Tongues paradigm. He removed himself from Freud because he felt he would be rejected for his clinical experiments with trauma analysis.

Another psychodynamic in the Confusion of Tongues trauma produced by the *Todschweigen* experience is the use of denial by the abuser. A dramatic example of this phenomenon is Freud's explanation to the analytic community for preventing the presentation and publication of the Confusion of Tongues paper. He said he was trying to protect Ferenczi from personal and professional disgrace (Rachman, 1997a, b). But in actuality what Freud was doing was silencing, disowning, and being abusive of Ferenczi. Freud's most dramatic disowning behavior occurred at their last meeting when he became angry, refused to shake hands goodbye, and turned his back on Ferenczi (Fromm, 1959). This abusive behavior was a reaction to Ferenczi asking Freud his opinion about his Confusion of Tongues paper before presenting it at the 12th International Psychoanalytic Conference in Wiesbaden. Ferenczi, once again, was asking Freud to affirm him in his dissidence, to be the loving father of his childhood. Ferenczi who felt rejected by Freud's silence after presenting his paper, held out his hand and Freud would not accept it in friendship. Ferenczi didn't realize that it was masochistic to continue to ask for Freud's approval. Ferenczi's Confusion of Tongues trauma with Freud did not allow him to give voice to any dissatisfaction or criticism of Freud and the analytic community for disowning him.

Being ostracized and disowned by one's family, group, or community is a dynamic that binds the victim to the abuser (Rachman & Klett, 2015). The individual's need for nurturance, love, and affirmation provides the *Todschweigen* experience with a dynamic of the individual clinging to the authority to prevent abandonment. One does not challenge the authority, even if the authority figure is abusive, because the individual does not want to risk abandonment. Losing one's connection to family and the community is like being cast into darkness and loneliness. Fear of being ostracized induces a profound sense of anxiety, annihilation, and a loss of self. I believe Ferenczi suffered in silence because he lost his voice and was afraid to lose the love of Freud, the father.

For *Todschweigen* to be effective, and it has been, it is necessary to understand the two-person dimension of this experience. As Ferenczi pointed out in the formulation of the Confusion of Tongues paradigm (Ferenczi, 1980k, 1988), the abused or traumatized individual loses his/her voice to speak about the trauma. With the working through of the trauma, the individual understands the authority figure is abusive because the individual finds their voice. Speaking about the trauma to the abuser, which is preferable (if possible), is most likely to be helpful. In this way, the individual breaks through the dissociation, confusion, repressed affect, suppression, and the silence of the trauma.

The *Todschweigen* experience that has silenced Ferenczi and Severn's work in psychoanalysis has been so effective because of the silence of the analytic community to the silencing of dissidents. During the original suppression of Ferenczi and Severn in the 1930s, there were little or no attempts to defend Ferenczi or Severn. Mészáros (2003) has raised the issue as to whether Balint, Ferenczi's heir apparent to The Budapest School of Psychoanalysis, did enough to defend his mentor when he was attacked by the analytic community. Severn had only Ferenczi to defend her. The three contemporary examples of *Todschweigen* discussed indicate that silencing the dissident still exists in the analytic community. Such silence has contributed to the power and endurance of the ostracism of dissidents. By not speaking out, silenced analysts contribute to the practice of *Todschweigen*. I must own up to my own contribution. At instances when I remained silent to the practice of *Todschweigen* in the cases of Ferenczi and Severn, I also became complicit in this practice.

In the second contemporary example of *Todschweigen*, I was able to find my voice when the analyst with a worldwide reputation clearly repudiated Ferenczi's analysis with Severn. At first, I did not repudiate his statements because I was afraid that this important analyst would get angry and retaliate against me. I placed myself in a position of a child who could be traumatized by a parental figure. But in a second conversation with him I was able to challenge his assertion that Ferenczi's clinical work with Severn was regressive. I also challenged his characterization of Ferenczi's analysis of Severn as regressive and using the same words used by Freud over 80 years ago as to criticize Ferenczi and Severn (Rachman, 1997b). What is more, I said it is time to review this analysis on the basis of new materials that may produce a new view of these two dissident analysts, and their positive contributions to psychoanalysis (Rachman, 2007a).

What became my most dramatic challenge to *Todschweigen* was the confrontation with Professor Martin Bergmann in November 2013. Although I had no idea that Bergmann would practice *Todschweigen* that day, I had promised myself I would find my voice to challenge any attempt *to denounce Ferenczi*. I did have some trepidation about challenging Bergmann; after all, he was 100 years old at that time. He was also a revered figure among the attendees of the event. Many people in the audience had been in his seminars. But I felt his audacious and mean-spirited attack on Ferenczi was an attempt to politically assassinate him in the same way Jones had done in his Freud biography. Once again, the audience was a co-conspirator in the *Todschweigen* experience, since no one challenged Bergmann. There were, however, analysts who agreed with me in private conversations.

I have been struck by the intensity and endurance of the practice of *Todschweigen* which, unfortunately, still exists. *Todschweigen* is just as present in contemporary psychoanalysis as it has ever been. The practice of *Todschweigen* needs to be understood and studied by the analytic community. We are still content to operate within different schools of psychoanalysis, with little interest in integrating dissident perspectives. Dissidence is the lifeline of any system of knowledge. The evolution of ideas and practices is fueled by those of us who respectfully challenge tradition rather than bow to it.

8

PSYCHOANALYSIS OF DIFFICULT CASES

Freud's case of the Wolf Man and Ferenczi's case of Elizabeth Severn

Freud confronts difficult cases

In order to fully understand Ferenczi's case of Elizabeth Severn, one needs to place their analysis in the context of the history of psychoanalysis. Ferenczi's case of Severn was an evolutionary development, connected to Freud's early clinical flexibility. The notion that there were difficult cases first emerged in Freud's original report of his iconic cases, such as the Rat Man (Freud, 1955a) and the Wolf Man (1955b). These cases presented particular difficulties in adhering to the basic rules of analytic interaction and presented interpersonal and emotional difficulties that arose between analyst and analysand. In the second decade of psychoanalysis, it became clear to Freud that there was a disparity between his theory of psychoanalysis, namely, the Oedipal theory of neurosis and attempts to treat clinically the so-called neurotic behavior (Freud, 1955c). At the Budapest Psychoanalytic Congress in 1918, Freud discussed his own difficulty in treating the obsessive/compulsive and phobia disorders. He made it clear that psychoanalysis needed to change to successfully treat these and other disorders:

> We shall then [have] the task of adapting our technique to the conditions ... we shall need to find the simplest and most natural expression for our theoretical doctrines. ... Often, perhaps, we may only be able to achieve anything by combining mental assistance with some material support ... application of our therapy will compel us *to alloy the pure gold of analysis freely with the cooper of direct suggestion* ....
>
> *(Freud, 1955c, pp. 167–168, italics added)*

Freud's history as a clinician incorporated non-interpretative measures from his early work with analysands:

In the 1890s, he went as far as to invite patients to meals with his family and, as late as 1909, he would have refreshments brought on for both himself and his patient.

(Coltrera & Rose, 1967, p. 36)

Feeding an analysand was also present in Freud's case of the Rat Man, Ernst Lanzer.

(Dr. Jerome Bergler, at a seminar called our attention to Freud's therapy notes on the Rat Man.) On one occasion his patient began his session by telling Freud that he was hungry, whereupon Freud gave him something to eat.

(Boyer and Giovacchini, 1967, p. 123)

Such non-interpretative behavior by Freud was very puzzling to the analytic community. According to Boyer and Giovacchini (1967), traditional analysts debated Freud's "non-analytic" clinical behavior, like the above-mentioned case, trying to understand it from his theoretical precepts of the Oedipal theory and the methodology of interpretation and the development of insight. In actuality, there was no means of reconciling the analysis of the Oedipal conflict with feeding an analysand. The Oedipal theory was incompatible with non-interpretative behavior. Freud, I believe, *strained* to fit his Oedipal theory into his clinical functioning, even though the case may have demonstrated the need for non-interpretative behavior. More traditional views of the treatment of the Rat Man have suggested that Freud's genius is evident in this case and the four other iconic cases (Anna O., Little Hans, Dora, and the Wolf Man). Mahoney (1986) said:

I would agree with Eissler that psychoanalysis empirically rests on the pillars of Freud's five case histories.

(Mahoney, 1986, p. 213)

Eissler elaborated:

[Freud's capacity] to perceive a complex phenomenon in its component parts, and as the product of an evolutionary process, does not seem to have been duplicated in anyone else as yet.

(Eissler, 1965, pp. 395–96)

The analysts concluded that:

For Freud not to feed a hungry man would have been out of character.

(Boyer and Giovacchini 1967, p. 323)

Freud's non-interpretative behavior, in this instance, was acceptable on humanistic grounds, not on theoretical ones.

I believe Freud's clinical behavior with the Rat Man, which was non–interpretative, was an indication that his clinical self was outpacing his theoretical self. He was willing to let the analytic method be open to change, but he maintained the Oedipal complex as the cornerstone of psychoanalysis, even though the clinical data did not fit the theory. For example, in the first pillar of Freud's iconic case histories, the case of Dora (Freud, 1955d), there is an issue of Freud's imposing the Oedipal theory on the adolescent girl, Dora (Ida Bauer), even though the clinical data indicates that sexual trauma had occurred and was a more relevant disorder to treat than an Oedipal complex (Rachman & Mattick, 2009, 2012).

Freud's designation of the Wolf Man as a difficult case

In his introduction to discussion of the case of the Wolf Man (Sergei Pankejeff) Freud spelled out that he considered Pankejeff a difficult case, but he also announced that it was only through the analysis of difficult cases that psychoanalysis can be changed:

> Something new can only be gained from analysis that presents *special difficulties*, and to the overcoming of these a great deal of time has to be devoted. Only in such cases do we succeed in descending into the deepest and most primitive strata of mental development and in gaining from these solutions for the problems of the later formulations and we feel afterwards that, strictly speaking, only an analysis which has penetrated so far deserves the name … *As regards these fertile difficulties the case I am about to discuss left nothing to be desired.*
>
> (Freud, 1955b, p. 20 – *Sigmund Freud's introduction to the Case of The Wolf Man, italics added*)

Freud Passed the mantle to Ferenczi

By the time Freud had established his method for analyzing neurotic conflicts by the use of free association, interpretation, and the development of insight as the standard procedure for conducting an analysis, both he and his heir apparent, Ferenczi, began to examine how an analysis should be conducted. In 1918, Freud and Ferenczi presented papers at the Budapest Analytic Congress on the formal introduction of deviations in analytic technique. This became the beginning of a new development in psychoanalysis: the examination of clinical psychoanalysis in order to creatively adjust to changing patient populations, clinical realities, and theoretical changes for the analytic encounter. At the same time, Freud realized that Ferenczi should lead the evolution in clinical psychoanalysis (Freud, 1955c), and in 1918 the center of psychoanalysis moved from Vienna to Budapest. At the Budapest Congress, Freud made two important statements about the evolution of psychoanalytic technique. First, he said that psychoanalysis must change in the willingness to go beyond interpretative behavior:

Developments in our therapy, therefore, will no doubt proceed along the lines; first and foremost, along the one which Ferenczi in his paper 'Technical Difficulties in an Analysis of Hysteria' (1919), has lately termed 'activity' on the part of the analyst.

(Freud, 1955c, pp. 161–162)

Freud's case of the Wolf Man, Sergei Pankejeff

In the time period in which Freud was analyzing the Wolf Man, Sergei Pankejeff, 1910–19, Ferenczi was involved in introducing the role of activity into clinical psychoanalysis (Ferenczi, 1980a–g). Ferenczi had already joined Freud by 1908, when Freud reported on his analysis of another one of his iconic cases, the Rat Man, Ernst Lanzer (Freud, 1955a). Both giants of psychoanalysis were initiating a re-evaluation of clinical psychoanalysis, during the same time period, influencing each other in a change of thinking and functioning. In reassessing the clinical functioning of the analyst, Freud led the way by his flexibility and responsiveness in introducing non-interpretative measures in the analysis of Ernst Lanzer and Sergei Pankejeff. In Freud's cases, as well as Ferenczi's early cases (Ferenczi, 1980 a–e), there were analysands who could not adhere to the general rule of psychoanalysis to free associate, integrate the analyst's interpretations, and develop insight into their emotional conflicts. Following the scientific method, Ferenczi, like Freud before him, changed his functioning to adapt to the reality of the clinical situation.

At the same time Ferenczi was influenced by Freud's cases, Freud was influenced by Ferenczi's cases of "Observations on larval forms of onanism" (Ferenczi, 1980c) and "Further development of the active therapy" (Ferenczi, 1980e), in which Ferenczi was creating active techniques to treat analysands who had difficulty free associating and adhering to the basic rules of psychoanalysis. Ferenczi paid tribute to Freud when he made it clear his teacher was the inspiration for his original clinical experiments (Ferenczi, 1980d). Freud acknowledged this credit (Freud, 1995b).

Sergei Pankejeff (the Wolf Man) as Freud's difficult analysand

Sergei Pankejeff (December 24, 1886 – May 7, 1979) was a Russian aristocrat from Odessa. Freud gave him the pseudonym of the Wolf Man to protect his identity, using a dramatic dream he had about wolves as the pseudonym. The dream of wolves will be discussed in detail in the section to come. Pankejeff was sent to Freud by his physician on the basis of three serious symptoms:

1. An inability to have bowel movements without an enema.
2. Debilitating depression.
3. The feeling there was a veil cutting him off from the world.

Before seeing Freud, Pankejeff suffered from depression in 1907 and went to Munich, saw many doctors, and stayed at many psychiatric hospitals between February 1910 and July 1914. He had a brief psychoanalysis with Freud in 1919. According to Freud, Pankejeff was not open to a full analysis until he set a termination date for the analysis, which was one year after the commencement of analysis. The setting of a date for termination was one of the non-interpretative measures Freud introduced in the analysis (Gardner, 1971).

Freud's analysis of Pankejeff centered on the interpretation of a dream of wolves, which he recalled in the analysis as an adult; the actual event occurred when he was five years old. The dream interpretation that Freud offered centered on Pankejeff witnessing a primal scene, i.e. his parents having sex from behind, doggy style. Later on in Freud's interpretation he changed his idea to Pankejeff having witnessed animals copulating, which was displaced to his parents. In order to discuss this difficult case the dream of wolves will be reproduced:

"IV: The Dream and the Primal Scene"

> I dreamt that it was night and that I was lying hung in my bed. My bed stood with its foot towards the window; in front of the window there was a row of old walnut trees. I knew it was winter when I had the dream, and night-time. Suddenly the window opened of its own accord, and I was terrified to see that some white wolves were sitting on the big walnut tree in front of the window. There were six or seven of them. The wolves were quite white and looked more than foxes or sheep-dogs, for they had big tails like foxes and they had their ears pricked like dogs when they paid attention to something. In great terror, evidently of being eaten up by the wolves, I screamed and woke up.
> *(Sergei Pankejeff's Dream of Wolves – Freud, S., 1918; From the history of an infantile neurosis – Reprinted in Gardner, 1971, pp. 173–74)*

Freud used Pankejeff's dream and his interpretations of it to establish his theory of psycho-sexual development. This case became a way to prove the validity of psychoanalysis by bringing together the main aspects of catharsis: the unconscious, sexuality, and dream analysis.

Reinterpreting Freud's interpretation

Basically, what Freud does in interpreting the dream of wolves as a primal scene memory for Pankejeff is locate the psychodynamics of this case in the analysand's unconscious Oedipal drama. Viewing the primal scenes produced an alteration in sexual development. Pankejeff's sexual life was splintered by it. As Freud asserted in his interpretations:

> His anxiety was a repudiation of the wish for sexual satisfaction from his father—the trend which had put the dream in his head. The form taken by

the anxiety, the fear of 'being eaten by the wolf', was only the ... transposition of the wish to be copulated with by his father, that is, to be given sexual satisfaction in the same way as his mother. His last sexual aim, the passive attitude towards his father, succumbed to repression, and fear of his father appeared in its place in the shape of the wolf phobia.

(Freud, 1914–15; Reprinted in Gardner, 1971, p. 188)

Freud used his analysis of the dream of wolves, Pankejeff's dream associations, early recollection, fantasies, and the transference relationship to demonstrate the efficacy of his fundamental theoretical assertions. As he had done earlier, as in the case of Dora (Freud, 1955d), there was an attempt to demonstrate that the Oedipus complex was the central psychodynamic:

> ... scenes from early infancy, such as are brought up by an exhaustive analysis (as, for instance in the present case), *are not reproductions of real occurrences*, to which it is possible to ascribe an influence over the course of the patient's later life and over the formation of the symptoms. *It considers them rather as products of the imagination*, which find their instigation in mature life, which *are intended to serve as some kind of symbolic representation* of real wishes and interests, and which owe their origin to a regressive tendency, to a turning away from the tasks of the present.
>
> *(Freud, 1955n, pp. 192–194, italics added)*

The analysis of Pankejeff also brought into focus Freud's idea that psychoanalysis was basically the study of imagination. The aim is to bring what is unconscious into consciousness. The material that emerges is like a fantasy; it can only be understood when it is brought to the surface and *analyzed*, which means interpreting the material.

Later on, these ideas became basic differences between Freud's orientation to a difficult case and Ferenczi's. At the point of the Pankejeff case, which Freud reported in 1919, Freud was still functioning in a clinically flexible way. Freud introduced four non-interpretative measures into psychoanalysis.

1. A cure was promised.
2. A termination date was set for the analysis.
3. The analysand was treated without a fee.
4. Freud collected money for Pankejeff's support (Rachman, 1997a).

These measures, Freud felt, were necessary in order to successfully analyze this difficult analysand. For example, Pankejeff had obsessive-compulsive personality characteristics, which he transferred onto the experience of the analysis. As Freud reported, the analysand made the analysis his existence. This *obsessive transference*, so to speak, did not allow what Freud called a *full analysis*. Setting a termination date for this analysis, was an attempt to use a non-interpretative measure to break the therapeutic impasse. The analysis with Freud did come to an end, but it continued with Ruth Mack Brunswick and members of the analytic community until Pankejeff's death in 1979 (Roazen, 1975).

When Ferenczi began to specialize in treating difficult cases, he learned that many of these cases had a history of childhood sexual abuse (Ferenczi, 1988; Rachman, 1997a). What is more, the Severn analysis (see chapters 12–17), helped Ferenczi understand the role of the actual trauma in the development of personality disorder. Severn helped Ferenczi to conceptualize and clinically respond to trauma, thus broadening psychoanalysis' boundaries beyond the Oedipal conflict. The evolutionary steps in this process were the development of the Confusion of Tongues paradigm (Ferenczi, 1980k), trauma analysis (Ferenczi, 1988), and the use of the non-interpretative measures (see Chapter 17). As we shall discuss in an upcoming section, Ferenczi realized that Severn did not suffer from an Oedipal disorder and therefore needed to be treated in a new way. He was willing to listen to Severn when she instructed him to listen to *what she needed* in order to be understood and helped. Was Pankejeff an Oedipal case? I believe this is open to question. In the section to follow I will raise the issue as to whether Pankejeff could be seen as an incest trauma case rather than an Oedipal one. And, if this hypothesis is correct, then the analysis of Pankejeff would have benefited from a Ferenczi/Severn-created trauma analysis.

An alternative interpretation of the case of Sergei Pankejeff, the Wolf Man

I would like to develop the hypothesis that Pankejeff was the victim, or in contemporary terms a survivor, of an incest trauma (Rachman & Klett, 2015). The idea of a personality disorder with an origin in the actual trauma of childhood seduction was not foreign to Freud; indeed, he originated the idea in founding psychoanalysis (Freud, 1954). Then Freud developed his analytic theory on the idea of the Oedipal drama, which moved actual seduction into the background and focused on the unconscious meaning of sexual experiences, which needed to be interpreted by the analyst. The primacy of the Oedipal conflict as the cornerstone of psychoanalysis, to which Freud became dedicated, produced a decided neglect of attention to actual trauma (Rachman, 2010b) and the analysis of the incest trauma (Rachman & Klett, 2015). In reinterpreting the Pankejeff sexual experience, reported by Freud, the alternative view of a Confusion of Tongues paradigm of childhood sexual experience will be used (Rachman & Klett, 2015).

As I read the extensive case interpretations of Sergei Pankejeff, I had several basic thoughts: Freud's formulations were an intellectual tour de force; as Freud did in the Dora case, he is using his considerable intellect to prove a lofty theoretical idea, but is ignoring some basic clinical issues; and Freud was *emotionally and intellectually blind* to the importance of the incest trauma. With all due respect to this revered case study of Freud, I would like to offer my thoughts on an alternative view, using my thinking and experience in the study and treatment of the incest trauma over the last 40 years. I have found Ferenczi's Confusion of Tongues concept invaluable in understanding the emotional, intellectual, and clinical experiences with incest survivors (Rachman & Klett, 2015). In this regard, I had a distinct emotional reaction to reading, and rereading, on several occasions, the dream of wolves. *I felt the dream of wolves was a dream of an incest survivor.*

Dreams of incest (Rachman, 2003a), I believe, contain elements of a re-enactment of childhood sexual abuse in the scenes depicted, objects represented, feelings expressed, and the symbolization used. Exploration of the dream material for indications of actual childhood seduction are added to the use of interpretative analysis. As this book demonstrates, the Ferenczi/Severn collaboration led psychoanalysis into the evolutionary phase of studying and treating trauma disorder originating in the incest trauma. This evolutionary step was not positively received by Freud. He did not receive the message, and through the practice of *Todschweigen* (see Chapter 7), he silenced the messengers. Ferenczi and Severn's work proposed the idea there are cases that are not of an Oedipal complex origin and, therefore, psychoanalysis needs to add a new methodology to treat them. We need to consider the data of the Pankejeff case from a fresh perspective to see if there is any data to substantiate a view of an incest trauma (Rachman & Klett, 2015).

First, I would like to refer to some compelling data from the analysand, Sergei Pankejeff, himself. In the 1970s, a German journalist, Karin Obholzer, read Muriel Gardner's book *The Wolf-Man by the Wolf-Man* in one night (Gardner, 1971). She became fascinated with the case and was determined to locate Pankejeff and interview him. She discovered him in Vienna and interviewed him from 1974 to 1976, which in itself, became a book, entitled *The Wolf Man Sixty Years Later* (Obholzer, 1982). What can we gain from Pankejeff's view of his own analysis by Freud and the reanalysis by Ruth Mack Brunswick? His assessment, in his own words, is comparable to Severn's view of her analysis with Ferenczi (Eissler, 1952; see Chapter 5). The data I will present seems to indicate that Pankejeff's incest trauma was not diagnosed, and, consequently, not analyzed.

Obholzer asked what Pankejeff thought about Freud's interpretation of his dream of wolves, and the primal scene interpretation? Pankejeff answered Obholzer with this response:

> *In my story, what was explained by dreams? Nothing as far as I can see. Freud traces everything back to the primal scene which he derived from the dream. But that scene does not occur in the dream. When he interpreted the white wolves as night shirts* or something like that, for example, linen sheets or clothes, that's *somehow far-fetched.* I think. That scene in the dream where the windows open and so on and the wolves are sitting there, and his interpretation, I don't know, those things are miles apart. *It's terribly far-fetched.*
>
> *(Interview between Sergei Pankejeff and Karin Obholzer in Obholzer, 1982, p. 35, italics added)*

In her interview, Obholzer asked Pankejeff, is it possible that there was another seducer besides Pankejeff's father, as the Oedipal interpretation suggested? Pankejeff's answer is very revealing and important:

> *Regarding my sister, there was this childhood seduction when she played with my member.* That's something very important when it happens in childhood. … when I was five … she played with my penis … We looked at a book with pictures of naked women … I felt like expressing something sexual and moved closer to my sister … Well, *this sister complex is really the thing that ruined my entire life.* For *those women who resemble my sister,* … *that was a prohibition* again, *that was incest again.*
>
> *(Interview between Sergei Pankejeff and Karin Obholzer, 1982, pp. 36–37, italics added)*

Pankejeff identified as incest his childhood sexual contact with his sister, which Freud reported as part of the case description. What is more, the analysand said he was traumatized by these experiences for his entire adult life. There is additional important data that Freud reported but ignored and did not interpret. Freud reported the following:

> … the patient suddenly called to mind the fact that, *when he was still very small,* … *his sister had seduced him into sexual practices. First came a recollection that in the lavatory, which the children used frequently to visit together, she had made the proposal: 'Let's show our bottoms,' and had proceeded from words to deeds* …
>
> *(Freud, 1918 in Gardner, 1971, p. 164, italics added)*

Freud, interestingly enough, reinforced the idea of the sister as an abuser:

> *But his seduction by his sister was certainly not a phantasy* … A cousin, who was more than ten years his elder told him … when she [sister] was a child of four or five [Sergei was then two or three years old], she had sat on his lap and opened his trousers to take hold of his penis.
>
> *(Freud, 1918 in Gardener, 1971, p. 165, italics added)*

In the study of the incest trauma, it is clear that young children who have been seduced can later become seducers (Rachman & Klett, 2015). So the question needs to be asked as to whether Pankejeff's sister was abused by a family member or servant, early in her life, because she became a sexual seducer. Furthermore, was this a family where actual sexual abuse was a part of the family interaction? Freud, in this case, as well as in the Dora case, (Rachman & Mattick, 2009), *did not discuss childhood seduction as an inherently pathological experience worthy of producing emotional disorder.* I am suggesting that sexual seduction of Pankejeff by his sister could account for his psychopathology. Oedipal interpretation was not relevant.

As a final argument for the significance of the incest trauma in the Pankejeff case, I would like to present an obscure reference to Pankejeff's seduction in Masson's book *The Assault on Truth* (Masson, 1984):

> Muriel Gardiner ... asked me to go through the unpublished material she had in her home concerning the Wolf-Man ... There I found some notes by Ruth Mack Brunswick for a paper she never published. *At Freud's request, she had re-analyzed the Wolf Man and was astonished to learn as a child he had been anally seduced by a member of his family – and that Freud did not know this.* She never told him. Why? Did Freud not know because he did not want to know? And did Ruth Mack Brunswick not tell him because she sensed this?
>
> *(Masson, 1984, p. xix, italics added)*

This piece of data has not been integrated into psychoanalysis. Is this because the person who reported this missing data was J.M. Masson, who was a victim of *Todschweigen* by the analytic community. The controversy over the Freud Archives (Malcolm, 1984), his criticisms of Freud (Masson, 1984), and his being fired from the Freud Archives as a researcher, have made Masson someone to silence and ignore. When I discovered the aforementioned quotation about Pankejeff's possible anal seduction, I discussed it with a well-respected analyst, who is an integral part of a traditional analytic institute and who responded with an immediate questioning of Masson's credibility:

> I would like other evidence besides Masson's assertions to consider this hypothesis.

Although additional evidence would be helpful, I would think, energy would be better spent trying to locate R.M. Brunswick's unpublished paper containing the revelation of Pankejeff's anal seduction. Whether this data was deliberately withheld is not known. But why is it that we still do not know whether Masson's assertions have any validity? I plan to contact J.M. Masson and the Freud Archives to see if Brunswick's paper can be located.

Freud asked Ruth Mack Brunswick to conduct a second formal analysis with Pankejeff in 1926 (Brunswick, 1928), when presumably she discovered the anal seduction data. This is what Pankejeff had to say about his analysis with Brunswick, who labeled him a paranoiac:

> Well, Mack interpreted my states by saying that not everything had been psychoanalytically interpreted by Freud. That's her explanation. But my explanation is different. *Because I know that I attributed very little importance to what she said to me ...*
>
> *(Obholzer, 1982, p. 55, italics added)*

Does Pankejeff's self-report on the analysis with Brunswick indicate that she continued the same theme of Freud's Oedipal analysis with Pankejeff and *did not want to correct Freud's analysis* with the idea of sexual seduction as an important psychodynamic in the analysis?

If we, for the moment, entertain Masson's report of Pankejeff's anal seduction described by Brunswick, we can add three pieces of data from Pankejeff's self-report of his analysis that are relevant. First, as has been reported, the analysand clearly stated that his sister was his seducer, being the aggressor in initiating sexual play with his penis. The sexual seduction was verified by a report of his cousin. Secondarily, his sister also initiated anal sexual play (bottoms) during their childhood. Thirdly, Pankejeff also reported that his sexual seduction by his sister had a dramatic effect on him, ruining his life. If a theory of sexual trauma is used to understand the case of Sergei Pankejeff, rather than an Oedipal theory, it allows for a new understanding of the case. *The Oedipal and primal scene interpretations of the dream of wolves are not a parsimonious interpretation of the data*: there is a simpler, more basic interpretation of the case material, which better fits the data. A new understanding of the psychodynamics to be considered is:

1. Pankejeff was sexually seduced by his older sister during his childhood. The sexual play involved his penis and anal areas.
2. There is a possibility that Pankejeff was seduced by his sister into sexual play on a regular basis, as he reported their using the toilet together as children.
3. If we add Masson's report of Brunswick's revelation of Pankejeff being anally seduced by a family member, we can hypothesize that his sister was the family member who anally seduced him.
4. The dream of the wolves can be seen not as a symbol of a primal scene, but as a dream of incest. The white wolves who were in the dream, sitting upright, can be viewed as a symbolization of the sister abuser as the sexual predator, whose repeated sexual intrusion made her *the dangerous predator animal* in Pankejeff's life.
5. Finally, Pankejeff's own self-report about his analyses with Freud and Brunswick indicated that their Oedipal interpretations of his illness did not lead to insights that produced any fundamental and lasting changes in intrapsychic or interpersonal functioning. It is possible that if incest trauma had been analyzed, it may have produced more meaningful results.

Freud introduced non-interpretative measures for difficult cases

Freud, it should be understood, initiated the reassessment of the functioning of the analyst in difficult cases, using the iconic case of the Wolf Man as the prototype. To counteract the difficulties in the Pankejeff case, as discussed, four non-interpretative measures were introduced (Roazen, 1975). Was Freud so certain that he understood the psychodynamics of the case—because he felt he had discovered the Oedipal idea of the structure of an infantile neurosis in terms of the dream of wolves, Pankejeff's early recollections and fantasies, and in the transference relationship—that he could ensure the anxiety-ridden, depressed analysand that he could cure him? Pankejeff was chronically depressed, and psychiatric treatment before the analysis with Freud was unsuccessful. These factors combined to create hope and motivation for the analysis to succeed. Unfortunately, Freud's valiant attempt to motivate Pankejeff to fully engage in the analysis did not succeed.

Freud introduced a second non-interpretative measure, setting a unilateral termination date of one year to end the analysis. Pankejeff's obsessive-compulsive personality helped turn the analysis into a severe obsessive-compulsive experience. He turned the analysis into his life. Pankejeff's analysis seemed interminable, although Freud's idea of setting a termination date seemed like a meaningful idea to limit the analysand's psychopathological tendency to intellectualize rather than emotionally respond. But, I would venture the hypothesis that another significant factor was that Freud, Brunswick, and the other analysts who followed, conducted a traditional interpretative Oedipal analysis. Uncovering the incest trauma could have led to analyzing the childhood seduction, which Pankejeff reported ruined his life.

The third and fourth non-interpretative measures related to financial matters. Pankejeff not only lost his fortune, but then had serious financial difficulty thereafter. Freud not only treated him without a fee, but helped raise money for his support. It seems an indication of Freud's humanism, generosity, and dedication to an analysand. Apparently, Pankejeff was not the only analysand who Freud treated without a fee:

> Freud treated without payment, Heinz Hartmann, Kate Levy, Eva Rosenfeld … and doubtless others.
>
> *(Roazen, 1975, footnote, p. 126)*

Freud's behavior had an influence on others, such as Ruth Mack Brunswick, who also treated Pankejeff without a fee. The change in clinical behavior in treating an analysand without a fee and contributing to the individual's welfare suggests that Freud was introducing a kind of an empathic role for the analysand (but, he did not label it as such).

Learning from the case of Sergei Pankejeff

The fascinating case of Sergei Pankejeff provides a rich treasury of data about how the founder of psychoanalysis struggled to deal with a difficult individual who could not be analyzed in the traditional way. Freud attempted his Oedipal analysis, and when his success was limited, he introduced modifications in his clinical behavior. Freud's difficult case raised many issues. Freud's development of the Oedipal conflict theory of neurosis was so paramount for him that I believe it *intellectually blinded* him to being attuned to the incidence of the incest trauma in some of his most iconic cases. In the past, Paul Mattick and I (Rachman & Mattick, 2009, 2012) have introduced the incest trauma theme in the case of Dora (Ida Bauer). We believe Freud was intellectually blinded to the data he reported about sexual seduction in Bauer's experiences with the family friend Harr K., because he was determined to prove his analysand suffered from an Oedipal conflict with her father. Similarly, in Pankejeff's case Freud continued to be intellectually blinded to the incest trauma. If the incest trauma had been identified then, the analysis of it would have helped establish the incest trauma as a significant part of psychoanalysis. Besides the intellectual factor of the Oedipal theory, there was a personal factor in Freud's personality that blinded him to the incest trauma (Rachman, 2016b).

Another issue in this case was the application of theory to clinical practice. In the analysis of Pankejeff there was a marked determination to prove that the Oedipal conflict framework was the *cornerstone of psychoanalysis*. The Oedipal theory became more important than the actual clinical experience. It is understandable that Freud wanted to prove his theoretical framework and initiate a new perspective for understanding human behavior. However, there seems to have been a disconnect between developing a theory and modifying it based on the findings of the clinical data. As has been described, Pankejeff's clinical data didn't fit the theory. Freud, I believed, fit the clinical data into the theory. We need to heed Kohut's admonition: *We need to wear our theories lightly*. Freud neglected his clinical data in favor of his theory. The Oedipal theory became more important than the reality of the clinical experience. The need for conformity was so intensely established among Freud's followers that they never questioned the interpretation of the Ida Bauer or Sergei Pankejeff cases. Of course, we also know that when a follower presented an alternative theory or clinical method, they risked being silenced by the *Todschweigen* experience. Freud changed his clinical functioning but would not entertain a change in theory.

One can see how disturbing the Severn/Ferenczi alliance was for Freud, in the light of his single-minded theory, authority-oriented domination of psychoanalysis. Freud did try to change his clinical behavior in the difficult case of Pankejeff. His new methodology was based upon a one-person experience. Freud decided to introduce the changes. The changes were not co-created. The introduction of non-interpretative measures in the Ferenczi/Severn analysis was based on a two-person experience. Ferenczi introduced a perspective where he attuned to, inquired about, and responded to Severn's subjective experience. In so doing, the difficulties in the therapeutic relationship were explored by both analyst and analysand. This exploration led to a co-created clinical experience, rather than the analyst imposing a change on the analysand, however well-meaning this intervention might be. A democratic attitude emerged in the psychoanalytic situation. Ferenczi learned to empathize with Severn's complaints, rather than interpret them as resistance. He and Severn pioneered the retrieval of childhood sexual experiences which lead to a new perspective, the Confusion of Tongues, and a new methodology, trauma analysis (see chapters 12–17). These developments separated Ferenczi and Severn from Freud. The idea of allowing the analysand a voice in the theory and practice of psychoanalysis alarmed Freud. He wanted psychoanalysis to remain an analyst-dominated enterprise. He was appalled that Ferenczi could let Severn be so influential in their analysis. Freud did not welcome the Ferenczi/Severn development of a two-person experience. As Fromm (1959) has suggested, Freud needed to be the authority. He could not be both a teacher and student. Jung was so angry and disillusioned by this, when Freud would not let Jung analyze a dream of his on their Atlantic crossing to the Clark Conference in 1909, that it was the beginning of their eventual termination of their relationship (Rachman, 1997a).

A fundamental issue of the analysis of difficult cases, such as Serge Pankejeff and Elizabeth Severn, is the analyst's capacity to change. This change means, as Ferenczi reported, to be able to admit that the analyst can make mistakes and change his/her functioning (Ferenczi, 1980h). Pankejeff, as discussed, presented three fundamental symptoms at the beginning of his analysis: (1) debilitating depression; (2) inability to have a bowel movement without an enema; (3) the feeling that a veil cut him off from the world. In 40 odd years of working with cases of incest trauma (Rachman & Klett, 2015), I have recognized these three symptoms with some regularity in survivors of the incest trauma. In the Case of W. (Rachman & Klett, 2015, pp. 189–230) the analysand showed these three same symptoms (as well as others), the origins of which were in the experience of severe childhood sexual trauma by his mother and father. These symptoms were treated by a trauma analysis, not an Oedipal–Interpretative analysis. In fact, W., had a *previous treatment with a traditional perspective that did not identify or treat* the incest trauma.

Returning to Pankejeff's case, did his three basis symptoms, which brought him into treatment, change in any significant way during the course of his analysis with Freud, Brunswick, and the other analysts? In his own words Pankejeff indicated that these analyses were not relevant. What is more, he indicated that he and the analysts who treated him were not emotionally connected. In his one-person experience, the analysand felt the therapeutic focus was irrelevant and not helpful, and the analyst was unaware of the analysand's dissatisfaction.

Ferenczi as "the analyst of difficult cases"; from activity to mutual analysis

Freud's choice of Ferenczi to lead the evolution of clinical psychoanalysis was based upon personal and professional considerations (Rachman, 1997a). Ferenczi became Freud's favorite follower (Roazen, 1975) as soon as they met (Rachman, 1997a). Their personal relationship developed over a 25-year period (1908–1933), and, even though there were difficulties (Ferenczi, 1988; Grosskurth, 1991; Masson, 1984; Rachman, 1997 a, b; Roazen, 1975), there was mutual affection and respect to the end (Freud, 1933). What Freud first saw in Ferenczi as a friend and clinician, Severn later saw as an analyst who could also be a friend. In 1929, 21 years into their relationship, Freud was concerned about Ferenczi distancing himself from psychoanalysis as he concentrated on the development of his own, alternative frame of reference. However, Freud was interested in maintaining their relationship:

> For you have outwardly distanced yourself from me in the last few years. Inwardly, I hope, not so far that a step toward the creation of a new

oppositional analysis might be expected from you, my paladin and secret Grand Vizier.

(Falzeder, Brabant & Giampieri-Deutsch, 2000, pp. 173–174 –
Letter from Freud to Ferenczi, December 13, 1929)

The qualities Ferenczi possessed, which made him a master clinician, were what attracted both Freud and Severn to him. Ferenczi had a warm, outgoing personality, which helped establish a positive relationship with family, friends, colleagues, and analysands. A dramatic example of his personal attractiveness was illustrated by a social incident in a nightclub (Rachman, 1997a). Ferenczi and his colleagues went to celebrate at a nightclub after one of the famous Wednesday evening meetings of the Viennese Society. The African-American singer Josephine Baker was the performer. During her performance she went over to Ferenczi and rubbed some of her hair pomade on his bald spot. Everyone had a good laugh. Baker felt she could approach Ferenczi and have physical contact with him. No one in the group of analysts, including Ferenczi, took offense or felt Baker had violated personal boundaries. Apparently, Ferenczi was approachable. Another incident also demonstrated Ferenczi's accessibility and personal warmth: at a meeting of a group of analysts Ferenczi greeted everyone, including the dour Ernest Jones, with a kiss on the cheeks (Rachman, 1997a). This kind of a personal availability, emotional warmth, and willingness to be interpersonally engaged made Ferenczi attractive to analysands like Severn.

Ferenczi saw himself as a healer, someone who was dedicated to helping analysands solve their emotional problems. He had a dedication to healing; he would take difficult cases and continue to see them, as long as they were willing to see him. Ferenczi seemed to have infinite patience and motivation to cure, which pushed him to make changes in his own functioning, moving beyond the traditional concept of resistance. In this two-person psychology *the analyst does not give up on the analysand's capacity to change.* Change is imbedded in the interpersonal analytic encounter. *Ferenczi, therefore, was willing to examine his own functioning, as well as the analysand's functioning.* In his analysis with Severn one can say that Ferenczi pushed his own functioning to the limit. He seemed to believe he could respond therapeutically to the many needs and difficulties in the relationship by examining and extending his own functioning. Ferenczi first attempted to respond to Severn's needs by traditional means. But Severn had tried traditional therapy and psychoanalysis with no success. She realized that her emotional difficulties were not Oedipal issues but, as previously discussed, beyond neurotic conflicts. As we shall see (Chapter 12; Eissler, 1952) Ferenczi could not satisfy all of Severn's needs.

Ferenczi's designation as the analyst of difficult cases was formalized by Freud after Ferenczi sent him a copy of his 1928 groundbreaking paper "The elasticity of Psychoanalytic Technique" (Ferenczi, 1980h):

Your accompanying production [Elasticity Paper] displays that judicious maturity you have acquired of late years, in respect of which no one approaches you … There is no doubt that you have much more to say on similar lines, and it would be very beneficial to have it.

(Jones, 1952, p. 241)

Freud was endorsing Ferenczi's introduction of clinical empathy into psychoanalysis, which signified that the next evolutionary step in psychoanalysis would be the analyst's role as an understanding, responsive partner. Freud, by the third decade of psychoanalysis, was willing to examine clinical psychoanalysis and allow Ferenczi to give direction to the changes in analytic method.

> … the 'Recommendations on Technique' I wrote long ago were essentially of a negative nature … the most important thing was to emphasize what one should not do, and to point out the temptations in directions contrary to analysis. Almost everything positive that one should do I have left to 'tact,' … The result was that the docile analysts did not perceive the elasticity of the rules I had laid down and submitted to them as if they were taboos. Some time all that *must be revised* without, it is true, doing away with the obligations I had mentioned.
>
> *(Jones, 1953, p. 241)*

Freud was willing to endorse Ferenczi's introduction of clinical empathy as the necessary correction for treating disorders beyond neurosis. Ferenczi made it his mission to empathize with difficult analysands. He searched for understanding of the difficulties in the psychoanalytic situation. The search for understanding replaced *blaming the analysand* for being resistant. The analysand was no longer seen as disobeying the basic rules of psychoanalysis, *unable to be a good candidate for psychoanalysis*. Ferenczi changed the trajectory of clinical functioning from *blaming the patient to understanding the patient*. The capacity for an analyst to maintain an empathic way of being with a difficult analysand was put to the test with Severn's analysis. Her *childhood* trauma led to such damage that Ferenczi needed to rebuild a healing parent/child relationship before Severn could integrate a therapeutic relationship with an analyst.

The very difficult case of Elizabeth Severn: the outer boundaries of clinical behavior

It can be said that Ferenczi, the analyst of difficult cases, ended his clinical career with the analysis of his most difficult case. One wonders if Ferenczi knew the difficulties he was facing with Severn when he agreed to begin their analysis. Severn had some idea of how difficult she was from her previous unsuccessful attempts at treatment, as well as the deep-seated depression and suicidal thoughts she had. Ferenczi seemed to be aware of her emotional difficulties, as he helped Severn become aware that her emotional difficulties were imbedded in her childhood traumas (Ferenczi, 1988).

Ferenczi's philosophy of clinical psychoanalysis was very different from Freud's (Rachman, 1997a). Even though they shared their initial clinical origins in working in a flexible and responsive way with difficult cases, Ferenczi always saw himself as a "healer/partner" in the therapeutic encounter. Freud's identity was a theoretician and system builder.

From this very early clinical case to the introduction of activity in difficult cases (Ferenczi, 1980a–g), to the introduction of clinical empathy (Ferenczi, 1980h) to the development of relaxation therapy (Ferenczi, 1980h–k), to mutual analysis (Ferenczi, 1988) and the analysis of Elizabeth Severn (Eissler, 1952; Ferenczi, 1988, Severn, 1933), Ferenczi moved closer and closer to a shared responsibility in the therapeutic encounter, where the analyst's attitude is geared toward understanding the analysand from his/her subjective experience. The traditional analytic community and some of Ferenczi's own analysands, like Clara Thompson, reacted negatively to the technical measures Ferenczi introduced in the analysis of Severn. It is ironic that Thompson was critical of Ferenczi's clinical behavior, since she was one of the analysands who violated the boundaries of the empathic method developed in the Ferenczi/Severn trauma analysis (see Chapter 6).

Elasticizing the boundaries of the analytic encounter was one of Ferenczi's contributions to the evolution of clinical psychoanalysis (Rachman, 1998, 2007). In the analysis of Severn the boundaries of clinical behavior were expanded in the most flexible and responsive way. The use of non-interpretative measures was a central focus in the analysis of Severn. This was so because of four factors: 1. Ferenczi believed in a flexible and responsive analytic encounter (Rachman, 1997a, 2003a); 2. Severn also had a flexible and responsive idea about clinical therapeutics (Severn, 1913, 1920, 1933); 3. Severn demanded new forms of flexibility and responsiveness, and Ferenczi experimented with providing them. This resulted in the development of new forms of non-interpretative measures (see Chapters 11–15); 4. Ferenczi and Severn were an emotional, intellectual, and interpersonal match. This compatibility allowed a permeability of boundaries between this therapeutic dyad.

Freud's case of Sergei Pankejeff (the Wolf Man) and Ferenczi's case of Elizabeth Severn (R.N.) have common denominators. Each clinician believed these cases were important in defining their theory and clinical practices. Freud moved from considering sexual seduction to fully embracing the Oedipal theory of neurosis. Ferenczi courageously attempted to expand psychoanalysis to consider the Confusion of Tongues theory of trauma disorder. Unfortunately, Freud thought Ferenczi was regressing, returning psychoanalytic theory and practice to its repudiated origins. In actuality *Ferenczi was not regressing but progressing*. He realized that the so-called difficult cases of Freud, and the other orthodox analysts who were referred to him, constituted a new group of non-Oedipal, trauma-induced disorders. Trauma disorders needed a new set of ideas and methodology, which Ferenczi and Severn helped to develop.

9

ELIZABETH SEVERN AS A PERSON

Severn's life and family background

Elizabeth Severn was born Leota Loretta Brown on November 17, 1879 in Milwaukee, Wisconsin, and died in New York City in February 13, 1959 at 80 years old. Severn's life and family background were chronicled in her daughter' Margaret's autobiography, *Spotlight: Letters to my Mother* (M. Severn, 1989). This material consists of about 3,000 typed pages, which Margaret Severn prepared, working with a typist, when, in retirement, she moved to Vancouver, B.C., Canada. According to Peter Lipskis, Margaret's personal friend, she wrote this autobiography at his suggestion after she attempted suicide in April 1983. It contains a chronological account of her life from childhood, when she lived with her grandparents, through her reunion with her mother after a traumatic separation, and on to her dance career as an adolescent and then as an innovative modern dancer into her adult life. This autobiography consists of her reminiscences and a select number of letters Margaret wrote to her mother throughout her adolescence and adult years when she traveled on the road in the United States and Europe performing as a dancer. The manuscript in its original form is housed in its entirety at the New York Public Library for the Performing Arts, Dorothy and Lewis B. Cullman Center, New York City (Severn, M., 1988). Margaret finished the manuscript in 1989 and sent it to 100 publishing houses, but no one was interested in its publication. It remains unpublished to this day (Lipskis, 2010). Sections of *Spotlight* were published in the journal *Dance Chronicle*.

Elizabeth Severn's mother

It is remarkable that very little is mentioned about Elizabeth Severn's mother, who was referred to as "Amma." No mention is made to her mother in Ferenczi's *Clinical*

Diary (Ferenczi, 1988), which chronicles her analysis with Ferenczi. Reference to parental relationships was exclusively with the father, Charles Kenneth Heywood. The father was identified by Severn and Ferenczi as the primary traumatogenic agent in Severn's development of psychopathology (Rachman, 2014b, 2015a). Severn also does not mention her mother in her own clinical writing or when she was interviewed by Kurt Eissler in 1952. Her daughter Margaret recalled that her maternal grandmother, "Amma" Brown, was "rather dull" (Lipskis, 2015a). Since there is such a sparsity of data about Severn's mother, we can extrapolate about the mother from the transference relationship Severn developed with Ferenczi. Severn's adult psychopathology was attributed to the horrific traumas inflicted upon her in childhood by her psychopathic father. There was no discussion of the mother in Severn's disorder or personality development. It is very likely that Severn's mother experienced great anxiety being married to a man Ferenczi described as psychopath and criminal (Ferenczi, 1988). Peter Lipskis believed he had committed criminal acts (Lipskis, 2015a).

The mother also was a bystander to the abuse her daughter suffered at the hands of her husband. These circumstances indicate mother and daughter suffered great anxiety, perhaps debilitating anxiety and terror, with the father during Severn's childhood years (Youcha, 2014). If Severn's mother was dull in spirit and/or intellect, she was likely incapable of actively removing herself from her husband's pathological influence on her daughter or on her own disturbing experiences. Severn's mother staying with this disturbed man is reminiscent of battered women who stay with husbands who regularly abuse them. It is also similar to the mothers who became *bystanders* in their children's sexual abuse by their husbands, which seems to have been the situation in Severn's childhood experience (Rachman & Klett, 2015).

Elizabeth Severn's father

The data we can turn to in gathering information about the father's behavior and relationship to his daughter is found in Ferenczi's *Clinical Diary* (Ferenczi, 1988). In actuality, this data may be the deepest level of material that is available because it emerged during Ferenczi's analysis of Severn's childhood traumas. In this analysis, Severn and Ferenczi retrieved the memories of her being abused emotionally, physically, and sexually by her father from about one and a half to ten years old. According to this retrieved data, the father was considered a "criminal," a psychopath. The childhood trauma data in the *Clinical Diary* indicates he tried to poison her; he sexually abused her; he threw her out the house; and he cursed her and damned her.

Peter Lipskis, my Severn informant, also believes that Charles Heywood was a shady, criminal type who was involved in anti-social behavior. The father may have been involved in the use of cocaine, alcohol, and prostitution. Margaret Severn, according to Lipskis, did not speak of her father in a respectful way. What is more, she recounted a very disturbed experience between her mother and father. She remembered he brought her mother, Elizabeth, to a house and in the basement showed her a corpse. There was some remembrance that Elizabeth was a teenager at this time and she described what she saw (Lipskis, 2015a). Consequently, both Ferenczi and Severn believed the father was a significant traumatogenic factor in the development of her emotional disorder.

Elizabeth Severn's marriage

Severn and her husband Charles Heywood came to the Chicago area from Southern Illinois with the promise of a job for her husband as an accountant. When the job didn't work out, they returned to Illinois with their daughter, Margaret. According to the daughter, her parents began their relationship as a positive experience:

> When my parents were first married, I believe they were very romantically in love, but by the time I was four they had decided to separate.
>
> *(M. Severn, 1989, p. 2)*

Severn changed her name

While Severn was married to Heywood, her married name was Leota Heywood. After the divorce from Heywood, Severn decided to change her name. Severn and Margaret had moved from the Midwest and were living in San Antonio, Texas, where they went to form a new life.

> There is a letter fragment, probably among Margaret's artwork, etc., acquired by Uno Langmann [Gallery owner, Vancouver, B.C., Canada], in which Elizabeth Severn wrote that her divorce and name change had been finalized.
>
> *(Lipskis, 2015b)*

In her autobiography, Margaret did not indicate why her mother chose her new name to be Elizabeth Severn (Lipskis, 2015b). Apparently, the last name Severn was taken from the River Severn in the United Kingdom. It is the United Kingdom's longest river, about 220 miles long, flowing from its source in Wales through England and emptying into the Bristol Channel and then on into the Celtic Sea. The river is named for Sabrina, the Roman name for Hafren, the Welsh goddess of the river (Ross, 1967). Severn was a believer in myth and apparently was fond of the mountainous areas through which the River Severn flows. The most important part of the name change was symbolic. It was Elizabeth Severn giving herself a new life, making herself into a healer, metaphysician, lecturer, and author. It was a symbol of a metamorphosis: she was leaving her emotional disturbance, hospitalization, and failed marriage behind and identifying with the enduring power of a river that gave birth to myth, industry, and beauty.

Severn's hospitalization for emotional illness and her separation from her daughter

Elizabeth Severn's forced separation from her daughter Margaret was described as follows:

> My father whisked me away to the home of his parents in Wayne, Michigan. I did not see my mother for two years. I never saw my father again.
>
> *(M. Severn, 1989, p. 3)*

Apparently, the father brought his daughter to live with her paternal grandparents, when her mother, Elizabeth Severn, was hospitalized for emotional illness sometime in the early 1920s, during the early days of her marriage. The separation lasted for two years. On the one hand, Margaret's stay with her grandparents would turn out to provide a safe place to live with close family while she was separated from her mother, but on the other hand, it turned out not to be an emotionally or physically safe situation. Her grandfather became a predator, sexually abusing her and imprinting her life with emotional problems. (See the next section for a full discussion).

Elizabeth Severn returned

After the two-year absence from her daughter, Severn made a dramatic return into Margaret's life:

> One day ... I heard the most beautiful sound I have ever heard in my whole life. It was the voice of my mother ... she was so thin and pale that she looked more like an apparition than a living person ... the next moment I was enveloped in her embrace.
>
> *(M. Severn, 1989, p. 10)*

The way Margaret described her mother's return indicated that Elizabeth thought her daughter was kidnapped, and taken away from her. Severn seemed to return in a sequitis way to her daughter since the scene described takes place outdoors, away from her daughter's grandparents. The father had taken Margaret away from her, as if she were kidnapped. In a way, Severn seems to have re-kidnapped her daughter, when she said to her daughter:

> 'Come quickly' ... my mother cried but ... '*I am her mother.* Tell them they will never get her away from me again!'
>
> *(M. Severn, 1989, p. 10, italics added)*

The Severns quickly boarded the train for San Antonio, Texas, to begin a new life. After this, they were only separated by their careers, Elizabeth practicing her clinical work in various cities and Margaret touring in the United States and Europe as a modern dancer.

Elizabeth's personal relationships: Leon Dabo

Elizabeth Severn's 1921 unpublished novel *Crystals* (Rachman, 2016d) is about an independent woman's romantic involvement and disillusionment with an artist. It is presumably based upon her relationship with Leon Dabo.

> Margaret's apartment had a half-dozen framed Dabo oil-paintings, at least one dated 1916. The largest canvas was a tree in a green 'mystical' landscape: the others were vase flowers similar to some presently at the Sullivan Goss Gallery in Santa Barbara, California.
>
> *(Lipskis, 2015c)*

They were bought by Uno Langmann, Fine Arts Gallery in Vancouver, following an informal 2003 appraisal by Christie's in New York.

Leon Dabo was a painter considered part of the Tonalism movement. He studied in Paris with de Chavannes at the Ecole de Beaux-Arts and the Academy of Fine Arts Munich. James Abbot McNeill Whistler had a profound influence on Dabo's style. His paintings became known for their feeling of spaciousness, with large areas of the canvas that had little but land, sea, or clouds (Narody, 1969). Lipskis provided more information on Dabo:

> Relevant to his involvement with Elizabeth Severn, Dabo was a debonair gentleman fond of expensive liqueurs and chronically short of cash who could paint like a stream ... He hobnobbed with celebrities like Marc Chagall and George Bernard Shaw. At the 1913 Armory show in New York, Theodore Roosevelt admired Dabo's scene of a Canadian snowfall. Helen Hayes Whitney wrote a poem about the canvas's ..."
>
> *(Lipskis, 2015c)*

Mara Lysova: an "adopted family member" of the Severns

Mara Lysova was an individual still living at the time of this writing, who had direct contact with both Elizabeth Severn and her daughter Margaret. Mara was a German-Jewish girl who emigrated to the United States from Berlin, Germany, with her parents. She was enrolled at Julia Richmond High School in New York City. Mara danced at a Christmas pageant at the school while Margaret Severn was in the audience. Margaret came back stage to meet the young dancer. Mara was 15 years old at that first meeting. They spoke in French and German. A relationship quickly began:

> Margaret saw that I was very sad. I became a family member. She realized I needed a friend.
>
> *(Lysova, 2007a)*

Significant events grew out of their meeting. First Margaret realized that Mara needed a friend. The Severns opened their hearts and household to Mara. She became a member of the Severn household. Margaret became her mentor.

> Margaret took my mother's place. My mother was very unhappy with me [my parents] were strict, cultured. Very critical of other Jews. They didn't have room [in their life for a child]. They were so in love with each other.
>
> *(Lysova, 2007)*

Mara felt that Margaret Severn opened up her heart to her, believed her story about parental deprivation and rejection, and wanted to help her. Margaret not only showed empathy for a young girl in distress, but wanted to actively do something to help the situation. Margaret did not marry and had no children. Mara may have become her adopted daughter. What is more, Margaret may have had some of the same therapeutic presence and desire to help as her mother, Elizabeth.

Peter Lipskis put me in contact with Mara Lysova, who was still living in California. In 2007, I interviewed her on several occasions by telephone. Margaret developed not only a friendship but a therapeutic relationship with Mara. She maintained contact with her to help Mara with her anxiety. She characterized Margaret as brilliant and spiritual: "I would read these letters and feel better" (Lysova, 2007). When I asked Mara Lysova if she had kept the letter exchange, she expressed regret that she had not thought of keeping them.

The second event that grew out of Mara's contact with Margaret Severn was the interpersonal relationship that occurred between them and her mother, Elizabeth. Mara was invited to help with Elizabeth Severn's weekend get-togethers. Elizabeth Severn would have people over for coffee and cookies on a Saturday or Sunday afternoon. Mara would help serve the refreshments. However, Margaret didn't sit at the table during this experience.

> I think Margaret said they were clients. Maybe she had group sessions.
>
> *(Lysova, 2007)*

Mara had distinct ideas about the relationship that she observed between Elizabeth and Margaret Severn. She described Elizabeth Severn as a stocky but not fat woman. E. Severn had a majestic air about her: "Someone said, she was a self–assigned psychiatrist … she was known as Dr. Severn" (Lysova, 2007). Lysova's description matches Ferenczi's observations of Severn as noted in his *Clinical Diary* (Ferenczi, 1988). Mara described the relationship between Elizabeth Severn and her daughter, Margaret, as "such a tight relationship, I was stunned…. [Margaret] would never leave her, she could never live without her" (Lysova, 2007).

Mary Wilshire

Mary Wilshire was a Jungian therapist. Wilshire was a wealthy Californian. Wilshire Boulevard in Los Angeles, California, was named after her forbearers. Peter Lipskis believed she may have been an analysand of Elizabeth Severn. Margaret Severn was fond of her:

> She is wonderful – I never heard of anybody working as hard as she does.
>
> *(Rachman, 2016d – Letter from Margaret to*
> *Elizabeth Severn, January 30, 1924 on the train to Denver)*

But Margaret had her criticisms of Wilshire as an analyst:

> I wonder how thorough an analysis she gives that she has discovered certain governing principles of the human psyche which explain every phenomenon of the human mind.
>
> *(Rachman, 2016d – Letter from Margaret to Elizabeth Severn,*
> *January 30, 1924 on the train to Denver)*

Perhaps, the most interesting comments about Wilshire are Margaret's comparing Wilshire's functioning to her mother's:

> I don't know – there is something about most teachers or healers, *which you have not got,* that always annoys one. They are so used, I guess, to securing the perfect confidence and trust of the patient, but they think they have to speak with the assurance of God himself, and that always arouses an antagonism in my spiffy little nature. I listen to them with a skepticism which is quite unwarranted ...
>
> *(Rachman, 2016d – Letter from Margaret to Elizabeth Severn,*
> *January 30, 1924 on the train to Denver)*

Margaret, in this letter was expressing a series of complex ideas, not only about her mother's friend, Mary Wilshire, but in a projective way, about her own mother. Wilshire and Elizabeth Severn share similar qualities. They are both teachers or healers; they are self-assured individuals; they are people about which she has mixed emotions. As we shall see in the sections to follow, Elizabeth and Margaret have had a profoundly complicated relationship.

Margaret Severn: A devoted daughter and pioneer of modern dance: separation from mother

Elizabeth Severn's daughter became a person of prominence in her own right. Margaret, as reported, had a very difficult beginning to her life, which she chronicled in her autobiography, *Spotlight* (M. Severn, 1989), but which she was able to overcome. Margaret seemed to have the resilience that her mother demonstrated (see Chapter 23). She described negative feelings toward her father:

> I had a strong feeling of dislike for my father ... he never kept his word ... he insisted on my eating some soft-boiled eggs (... I found nauseating). I truly hated him.
>
> *(M. Severn, 1989, p. 2)*

Her trauma was not of only the father's negative behavior toward her, but how he initiated a separation between Margaret and her mother Elizabeth. She described it in a dramatic fashion:

> I was four years old when they decided to separate and a family meeting was called to Chicago to determine whose care I should remain … Uncle Harry, Aunt Rose, and my father, all arguing violently with my mother … years later in a nightmare I relived this situation, but with a difference: in the dream I had a huge sword, and … cheerfully sliced up my father.
>
> *(M. Severn, 1989, p. 2)*

Margaret described the forced separation from her mother as one of the significant traumas of her childhood:

> Finally, Uncle Harry … said, 'Let's go for a little walk … I was being taken away from my mother … we went back to the house but my mother was no longer there … my father … whisked me away to the home of his parents in Wayne, Michigan. I did not see my mother for two years. I never saw my father again.
>
> *(M. Severn, 1989, p. 3)*

Margaret during the period of four to six years old was separated from her mother. Her mother apparently was being treated for emotional disorder. Her mother returned when she was six years old. They were not separated again, except when they travelled for their careers. Margaret never saw her father again after the separation at four years old.

Margaret Severn's childhood sexual abuse

In a family tragedy, Margaret's stay with her paternal grandparents produced a period of sexual abuse by her grandfather. Elizabeth Severn was sexually abused by her father (see Chapter 12). Mother and daughter shared the same trauma. Margaret discussed her childhood sexual abuse by her grandfather and how it established a perverse bond of affection with him. On the one hand, she and her grandfather became inseparable, affectionately attached. On the other hand, she described him as a raving maniac, a tyrant:

> He was a man of violent temper and was feared by most of those who knew him, but not by me.
>
> *(M. Severn, 1989, p. 3)*

Margaret described her grandfather and her as inseparable:

> I was the apple of his eye and he was my devoted slave though actually in a larger sense, a tyrant. He kept me with him constantly, dragging my sled behind him as he trudged through the snow on his round of chores.
>
> *(M. Severn, 1989, p. 3)*

The complexity of the relationship erupted into abuse:

> from my grandfather I had learned the passion of man-strange, overpowering, both beautiful and terrifying emotions much too shattering for the psyche of a young child and therefore a threat to the very core of her existence.
>
> *(M. Severn, 1989, p. 7)*

Margaret's description of her childhood sexual abuse and its ramification on her personality development was the trauma experience originally described by Ferenczi in his pioneering paper "The Confusion of Tongues" (Ferenczi, 1980k) in regard to Margaret's mother's sexual abuse. There is a striking parallel between Margaret's abusive experience and her mother's (see chapters 10 and 12).

Here is what Margaret Severn said in this regard:

> the pent up passion of my grandfather vented itself on this body of his small granddaughter. I became the object and the satisfaction of his desire, the very center of his life.
>
> *(M. Severn, 1989, p. 8)*

Relationship between Elizabeth and Margaret Severn

The relationship between Elizabeth and her daughter Margaret was complicated by Elizabeth Severn's emotional disturbance and her dedication to a career as a clinical therapist. However, the relationship was not only determined by her mother's behavior. Margaret's desire to be and dedication to becoming a dancer also determined the trajectory of their lives. Mother and daughter had a very close emotional relationship, which was very unusual in its structure. After returning to her daughter from her hospital stay when Margaret was six years old, Elizabeth did not become a conventional mother. However, Elizabeth was conventional in her desire to have a close emotionally meaningful relationship with her daughter. She also had the capacity to form an affectionate attachment with Margaret, which was indicated in a letter Margaret sent to her mother:

> Reflecting on why I was glad you were coming to live with me, I was thinking you're the most INTELLIGENT person I ever met, and what an honor and an instruction to live with such a bright person. I ought to become bright myself from association. And you're not only intelligent, you're nice too.
>
> Your friend for infinity,
>
> *Margaret (Letter from Margaret to Elizabeth Severn*
> *February 15, 1993, Paris; Rachman, 2016d)*

Although Elizabeth and Margaret Severn maintained such an emotionally close and loving relationship, they were physically separated on many occasions because of their professions. They did not maintain a joint living situation during Margaret's teenage and young adult years. The mother was a therapist throughout her daughter's life, establishing herself in various cities where she developed a clinical practice. These locations included San Antonio, Texas, New York City, Budapest, and London. Elizabeth Severn was free to make such decisions because her daughter chose a profession, professional dancing, in which changing locations was an integral component. Margaret Severn felt she was destined to be a dancer, which she described in dramatic fashion:

> There was one thrilling night ... huge clouds gathered in the sky; in my heart I felt they had come for me and I was glad ... the storm raged in fury ... filled with wild exultant joy, I rushed ... into the night, and I danced there joyously under the flares of lightening with crashes of thunder for music. I felt a great ecstasy but no fear ... the wind and the rain loved me and I loved them.
>
> *(M. Severn, 1989, p. 6)*

Margaret seemed to have made her decision to become a dancer that night in her childhood:

> What the forces of nature were telling me that night was really true. I have always felt at one with them, almost closer to fire and earth, water and air, than to my fellow human beings ... the tumultuous emotions connected with the visual effects were even more important, giving meaning, background and color to the actual steps of a dance that I created some twenty years later.
>
> *(M. Severn, 1989, pp. 6–7)*

Margaret was encouraged to follow her love for dance by her mother. She began her dance career as a teenager of 15 years old, traveling away from home. Elizabeth was able to emotionally support her daughter, not only to travel but to live on her own on the road. The mother/daughter relationship was maintained at a loving, supportive level by therapeutic letter writing that the two maintained over the period that Margaret pursued her dance career, over her teenage years through her adult years. In her letters to her mother as a teenager, Margaret did report there were moments when she felt unsafe, but these moments did not discourage her from being on her own nor did she tell her mother she wanted to return home. Elizabeth Severn never suggested Margaret give up dancing. Whatever concerns Elizabeth Severn had for her daughter's safety and difficulties, she did not let them interfere with her daughter's functioning.

If one examines the correspondence between Margaret and Elizabeth Severn (E. Severn, 2013; M. Severn, 1989), it is clear that they maintained an intimate and loving relationship while at a distance via letter writing. At times, the letter writing was conducted on a daily basis. Margaret told her mother every detail of her daily life as well as her psychological condition as she danced her way across the United States and Europe. It was as if she carried her mother with her every day they were apart.

A typical version of this therapeutic correspondence is illustrated in the letter Margaret sent to her mother when she was 22 years old and appearing as a dancer in Memphis, Tennessee:

> Dearest,
>
> Well, me nerves is going! I got worried and upset over the act last night and had that bad pain in my side again … when the act goes well I feel well but if it doesn't, you know, it just makes me feel sick. This hotel still has its 75¢ lunch and $1.25 dinner – the food is really excellent but the room, $4.00, is very good … in addition to the general strain of things, resulted in my having a neat little fit of hysteria after the matinee. Oh ya – I was mad! And then there was no letter from you – I nearly sent you a very abrupt telegram today but decided to save the money. Instead, I hired a car and driver for over an hour … I never saw a more extraordinary sunset than has just now taken place – heavy cloud banks of vermillion and gold stretched far across a sky of emerald green, vivid blue and deep indigo. (Red leaves, blue leaves, green leaves and other leaves).
>
> Very sincerely yours,
> Other Leaves
>
> *(Rachman, 2016d – Letter to Elizabeth Severn,*
> *September 20, 1923 – Memphis, Tennessee)*

This letter indicated the practical, emotional, and creative ebb and flow that was exchanged between daughter and mother. Margaret tells her mother about her work issues, shares her emotional reactions to how she coped with her difficulties and adds her creative vision of her environment. Margaret maintained an intimacy with her mother, not hesitating to tell her every detail of her daily life as well as expressing her emotional reactions. The letter writing sustained the emotional viability of their relationship, not only because Elizabeth was an expert in maintaining therapeutic contact at a distance, but also because she believed she had telepathic powers (Severn, 1913, 1920). She believed she could send and receive messages, vibrations, emotional content, which could have healing powers (see Chapter 11).

Another special interaction that Margaret and Elizabeth shared was an appreciation of the arts, e.g. dance, painting, and poetry. Margaret ended her letter in 1923 from Memphis waxing poetically about the physical environment in which she was living. She even went on to sign off her letter referring to herself as "Other Leaves." She always had an affectionate opening and closing salutation to her mother.

Elizabeth Severn's analysis of her daughter Margaret

Elizabeth entered into an analytic relationship with her daughter as early as 1916, when Margaret was 15 and living apart as a dancer for the first time. In a letter during this period Margaret asked her mother for help with her emotional troubles, not as a mother, but as a clinician.

> Darling mother. Maybe you won't get this letter before you leave, but I have to write it … I wish you'd hurry and come back and help me out of my troubles. You've been away a long time. I have many dreams.
>
> *(Rachman, 2016d – Letter from Margaret to Elizabeth Severn – April 15, 1916)*

The mother as analyst as depicted in a remarkable drawing Margaret produced in 1927, when she was in her twenties (see Image 3). Margaret, who was a gifted illustrator, depicted herself in a full-page drawing as an enraged person. Her eyes are piercing, her nostrils flared, with her mouth baring her teeth. There are two notations that accompany the drawing. On the right side of the drawing is the title of the

IMAGE 3 Drawing by Margaret Severn: "Correct attitude of psychoanalyzed daughter toward telepathic mother," 1927

drawing, "Portrait of correct attitude of psychoanalyzed daughter toward telepathic mother." On the left side of the drawing is the commentary: "But, if you perfect your system twill save a lot of money and cables." The drawing clearly communicates an enraged daughter toward her mother. Margaret's notation indicated that her mother's analysis of her was the basis of the rage. Margaret is suggesting that she is expressing her anger toward her mother as an analysand is supposed to do, being true to her feelings. Her mother was apparently analyzing her at a distance. The mother and daughter were in two different cities. As was Elizabeth's method, she believed in an esoteric means of communication, such as telepathy. Elizabeth is sending telepathic messages to her daughter to help her with emotional issues, but this mode of communication doesn't seem adequate. Margaret is asking her mother to be of greater help to her. The period of 1927, which the drawing depicted, was a difficult period for Elizabeth Severn. She was two years into her psychoanalysis with Ferenczi, where she was struggling with feeling that her analyst was having negative feelings toward her, to which he would not admit (see Chapter 12). This struggle drained Elizabeth's emotional energy, which may have made her less available to confront her daughter's anger or any other of Margaret's series of emotional issues. Margaret relied on her mother for a psychological understanding in the letters exchanged between them. Margaret did not seem to turn to any friends to share her troubles. Although her mother may have initiated the analysis, she may not have been fully available to her daughter, in the way she had been before entering analysis with Ferenczi.

Margaret seems to have recovered from her angry outburst with her mother. In a letter five years later in 1932, Margaret wrote:

> How did you get the idea that the attack by a man in the dream showed that I was horrified and terrified? I am very nervous today. I see how all these violent emotions of the past have had their chief outlet through my work and that is what's put the terrific nervous pressure into it which has excited the audiences and at the same wrecked me. If I don't control the nervousness, I feel like I used to describe feeling in Epsom, a bag of firecrackers ready to explode.
>
> (Rachman, 2016d – M. Severn, 1933, Letter from Margaret to Elizabeth Severn, December 1, 1933, Paris)

It is clear from this letter that Margaret had developed an intense personality, where she needs to negotiate anger. She was able to integrate her anger into her dancing. Like her mother, she had maintained a capacity to maintain a portion of her personality for positive functioning. They both referred to their Orpha functioning, which is the positive part of the personality (see chapters 10 and 23). The therapeutic relationship between Elizabeth and Margaret was also a basic factor in maintaining a sense of equilibrium in Margaret's personality functioning.

Almost a year later, Margaret was sharing with her mother her positive emotional state:

> … Now that I am in good spirits, but it was hard to break off the analysis just as we commenced to get somewhere and my sense of making the change

of bridging the great chasm between grandpa and you, filled with so much dread and worry yesterday, plus my confusion on the homosexual matter, that I just didn't know whether I was sitting on my tail or my ears!

(Rachman, 2016d – Letter from Margaret to
Elizabeth Severn, January 19, 1933)

This communication between daughter and mother reveals the deep level of sharing in the analysis, with Margaret discussing such topics as child abuse and homosexuality. This disclosure revealed the inherent difficulty in analyzing your own child. This is what I observed in my discussion of Freud's analysis of his daughter, Anna (Rachman, 2003b). In this instance, we have the daughter, Margaret, discussing with her mother, Elizabeth, her homosexual feelings, which may involve feelings about her mother. This is the limitation that makes analyzing your child non-therapeutic. The zone of transference and countertransference is hopelessly contaminated. A child, no matter how intelligent, self-aware, or self-disclosing is not really emotionally free to disclose and examine their feelings about their parent to their parent. The same limitation is true of the parent. Perhaps, we should reconsider the drawing, under consideration, by suggesting that Margaret's anger was also generated by the factor of her mother's analysis of her. Even if Elizabeth could provide the necessary time, energy, emotional connection, or insight to satisfy her daughter's needs, the analysis was limited by her analyst being her mother.

In a letter to her mother, Margaret indicates the difficulty the analysis with her mother presented.

I suppose the state of my analysis is the chief cause of my troubles, but it makes me think that it is dangerous to attempt analysis when I must be in a condition to work. I am an absolute wreck, I have had bad dreams but I haven't the strength to write them out, in fact, I guess I will have to stop now. More anon.

(Rachman, 2016d – Severn, 1933 – Letter from Margaret to
Elizabeth Severn, January 21, 1933, Paris)

The mother/daughter analysis apparently continued during the period when they lived together in New York City in the 1940s and 1950s. Peter Lipskis elaborated on this:

My recollection is that Margaret had daily psychoanalysis with her mother when they lived together in New York (during World War II). Before that Margaret often wrote about her dreams, sometimes trying to analyze them. The net result was the 'forgotten memory' of being sexually abused by her grandfather.

(Lipskis, 2016a)

We can now also add to the understanding of the drawing a projection of Margaret's feeling of intrusion by her mother into her psychological space. The drawing is symbolic of an object that opens its eyes wide, flares its nostrils, and bares its teeth to protect itself from harm by an intruder.

Fifty-five years after the 1927 drawing, Margaret exposed her capacity for anger to one of her best friends, a former dance student and colleague. When she was in her eighties, she lacerated her friend for incorrectly addressing her letter:

> Excuse my French, but you really are an idiot!!! You *still* do not complete the address when writing to me. You now put 'Canada' but omit the B.C., which is the same as if I addressed you at 'Oxnard, U.S.A.' B.C. signifies 'Provence of British Columbia! There are eleven provinces in Canada and they all hate the United States ... well, anyhow ...
>
> *(Rachman, 2016d – Letter to Marian,*
> *Vancouver, B.C., June 18, 1982)*

Toward the end of this letter, however, Margaret goes on to engage her friend in a friendly discussion of her present life. What is more, she expresses affection to her, the same person she had previously severely criticized. Margaret apparently was an emotionally volatile individual who felt free to directly express her anger.

Margaret's personal presence

Fortune (2015) has recently verified Margaret's volatility. He described her as follows:

> Margaret was a 'grand dame' and visiting her was like receiving an audience with royalty. She had a strong presence; she could be warm and charming, or she could quickly turn volatile if she did not like what you were saying, or what you said was too inconsequential, such as an innocent comment on the weather.
>
> *(Fortune, 2015, p. 23)*

This personal description of Margaret may give us insight into her mother as well. Elizabeth Severn was described by Ferenczi in a similar fashion (Ferenczi, 1988, see Chapter 12). Mother and daughter were strong formidable personalities, who freely expressed their thoughts and feelings, which influenced their relationships. Certainly, Elizabeth Severn's relationship with Ferenczi was characterized by difficult interchanges, as she voiced her needs, at times, in angry demands. Fortune's description of Margaret's presence as she lived in retirement in Canada evoked her mother's presence:

> Being in Margaret's presence in her apartment furnished with numerous possessions that had also been her mother's – including many from when Elizabeth had lived in Budapest – [which include her analytic couch], transported me back to another time and place.
>
> *(Fortune, 2105, p. 24)*

Margaret was a physical presence as an adult. This is clearly demonstrated in a well-known portrait of her. The portrait, which was cited on page 162 of Jeffrey Moussaieff Masson's book on Freud (Masson, 1984), clearly depicts Margaret's physical attractiveness at the height of her dancing career in 1926. It was painted in

Portrait of Mrs. Elizabeth Severn
by Olga Dormandi, ca. 1926

IMAGE 4 Oil painting of Margaret Severn by Olga Kovàcs, 1926

Budapest by Olga Széhey–Kovàcs (Olga Dormandi), Judith Dupont's mother (see Image 4). Margaret was painted as a beautiful, sensual woman. Margaret told her friend, Peter Lipskis, she remembered posing for the artist Olga Kovàcs in Budapest in 1926, who had a paint brush in one hand and held an infant (Judith Dupont) with the other (Lipskis, 2015b). The photograph of this painting in Masson's book initiated a controversy. In a series of letters exchanged between Margaret and Masson; which are part of The Elizabeth Severn Papers (Rachman, 2016d), Margaret raised an error about the portrait. In a two-page handwritten letter after Masson's book was published, Margaret wrote an angry letter to Masson that the portrait was misidentified as being Elizabeth Severn:

> I am very disturbed at this ridiculous error and am anxious to know if something can be done about it and what kind of correction can be made.
>
> *(Rachman, 2016d – Letter from Margaret Severn to*
> *J. M. Masson, May 1, 1986)*

In actuality, the portrait was of Margaret.

Margaret also sent a letter to an associate editor of Farrar Straus and Giroux, Masson's publisher, inquiring whether the *misidentification of* her as Elizabeth Severn will be corrected, making the following statement:

The caption [of the painting] referred to the 'dancing' of Elizabeth Severn when as actually I am the dancer and she a psychotherapist, never danced a step in her life. The mistake was really horrendous and I would like to know if any corrections of it have been effected?

(Rachman, 2016d – M. Severn, Letter to Barbara Williams,
Vancouver, B.C. [not dated])

Masson's publisher responded to Margaret's criticism by saying he would change the photograph of her to one of her mother, printed in London in 1912 by Ethel Wright, in any second edition of the book. What is more, Masson responded to Margaret's concerns about the misidentification of the photograph apologizing for the error, which he said originated with Judith Dupont:

it was Dr. Dupont who told me. I assume she would know, since it was her mother, Olga Széhey–Kovàcs (Olga Dormandi) who drew your portrait. Clearly Dr. Dupont did not realize it was of you, not of your mother.

(Masson, 1986 – Letter to Margaret Severn
from J. Masson, May 27, 1986)

Masson's assumption was verified in a letter written in French, which indicated that Dupont sent a picture to Masson she thought was Elizabeth Severn (Dupont, 1982). In the collage on the cover of my book, *Sándor Ferenczi: The Psychotherapist of Tenderness and Passion* (Rachman, 1997a), I corrected the error by placing Elizabeth Severn in the picture instead of Margaret (see Image 5).

IMAGE 5 Collage cover by Arnold William Rachman, "Analysis of Elizabeth Severn by Sándor Ferenczi," from his book, *Sándor Ferenczi: The Psychotherapist of Tenderness and Passion*

Margaret's dance career: a pioneering modern dancer

Severn's greatest fame as a dancer was connected with her combining modern dance with the use of face masks made by W.F. Benda, first at Carnegie Hall, then in the 1920 Greenwich Village Follies directed by John Murray Anderson (Lipskis, 1993). At the pinnacle of her career she was part of the dance world elite, rubbing shoulders with the likes of Michel Fokine, Martha Graham, and Agnes De Mille (Scott, 1995). Her career began at age 15 in a Metropolitan Opera production and with Denishawn in California. She was in the 1920 production of the Greenwich Village Follies directed by John Murray Anderson. She was photographed by Arnold Genthe and Nicholas Murray, and appeared in the pages of *Vanity Fair*, *Vogue*, and *Cosmopolitan* magazines. Thereafter, Margaret made her own expressive masks, and from 1922 to 1928 she performed mostly in vaudeville theatres throughout North America in a variety of acts, one of which included Spanish dancers from the famous Canosino family. In 1929 she opened the Margaret Severn School of Dance on Madison Avenue in New York City. In 1931 she took part in a debate on modernism, siding with Ruth St. Denis and Michel Fokine against Martha Graham, Agnes De Mille, and John Martin of *The New York Times*.

Margaret Severn settled in Paris in 1932 and joined the Company of Bronislava Nijinska a production with Fernando Chilispin. In 1934 she danced in the company of Ida Rubenstein, working with Fokine, Kurt Joos, Kurt Weil, and Stravinsky. From 1935 to 1938, she became a principal dancer in the Ballets Russes de Paris, which toured in Europe. In the United Kingdom, John Masefield, the Poet Laureate, dedicated a poem to her.

Margaret returned to New York in 1939, where she continued to give concerts and teach. Margaret and Elizabeth Severn lived in New York City until Elizabeth's death in 1959. Margaret continued living in New York City until 1971, after which she retired to Vancouver, B.C., Canada. Her personal friend and companion, the filmmaker Peter Lipskis, produced two documentaries about Margaret: the award-winning *Dance Masks* (Lipskis, 1980) and *Portrait of an Artist as a Young Woman* (Lipskis, 1992).

Margaret's remarkable psychological accomplishment was that she enjoyed a pioneering career in modern dance without the regular physical presence of her mother. She did not have a father presence, since her father was divorced from her mother and his psychopathology could not, in any event provide her with emotional support and affirmation. It was the voluminous correspondence between Elizabeth and Margaret Severn that could be seen as a form of therapeutic interaction. In fact, in her earlier clinical work (see Chapter 11) Elizabeth Severn used distant contact, letter writing, telephone, and telepathy as ways of staying in contact with patients when personal contact was not possible. Elizabeth Severn reported that this type of distant contact had positive value for maintaining the relationship and conveying emotional information (Severn, 1913, 1920).

Severn's use of letter writing for clinical purposes was another indication of her pioneering clinical ideas (see Chapter 11), which we can consider she used as a mechanism to maintain her relationship with her daughter although they were at a distance for a significant period of their lives. The use of writing as a therapeutic means and a clinical method for treating trauma and other disorders exists in contemporary psychotherapy (Batten, 2002; Bjoroy, Madigan and Nylund, 2015; Pennebaker, Kiecolt-Glaser, Glaser, 1988; Smyth & Helen, 2003; Stanton & Danoff-Bury, 2002). Focused expressive writing is clearly connected to The Budapest School of Psychoanalysis (Rachman, 2016a), where emotional expression is a meaningful alternative mode to the intellectual-oriented interpretative mode of responding.

Psychoanalytic detectives

Fortune (2015) has recently discussed the issue of the researchers who pursued Margaret Severn to collect information about her mother's relationship with Ferenczi. Fortune interviewed Margaret on a regular basis as he became one of the psychoanalytic detectives he discussed in his recent article. He described Jeffrey M. Masson and Kurt Eissler as the original psychoanalytic detectives. These researchers had a vested interest in collecting information about Elizabeth Severn as Ferenczi's most well-known and controversial analysand.

Margaret Severn and Jeffrey M. Masson

Fortune described how the psychoanalytic detectives pursued Margaret Severn in order to investigate her mother. First, he described Masson's pursuit of Margaret, as he became interested in interviewing her:

> like a psychoanalytic bird-dog … she confided in me that she was, 'having none of that,' as she clearly had a negative view of Masson's work.
>
> *(Fortune, 2015, p. 24)*

At first glance, Margaret's negativity towards Masson does not seem reasonable. He was the analytic scholar who first identified Ferenczi's case of R.N. as Elizabeth Severn; this helped return Severn to a significant place in psychoanalysis at a time when Ferenczi's *Clinical Diary* was being published for the first time. In my contact with Masson he expressed positive thoughts about Elizabeth Severn and encouraged me to continue writing about her. He considered her, as well as Ferenczi, as important, unappreciated figures of psychoanalysis. A possible explanation for Margaret's anger toward Masson may involve, at least, two factors. Fortune may have identified an important factor in the behavior of the psychoanalytic detectives toward Margaret. According to Peter Lipskis (2015b), Margaret felt harassed by the analytic researchers who were interested in interviewing her about her mother's contact with Ferenczi. She felt her mother had a negative reputation in psychoanalysis. Margaret was defensive, believing that the psychoanalytic detectives were basically interested in uncovering that something untoward happened between Ferenczi and Severn. Margaret seemed very angry over the identification of her picture as her mother, possibly because she felt she wanted to be recognized as an important figure in dance and separate from her mother.

Margaret Severn and Kurt Eissler

Fortune (2015) also gives us a glimpse into Kurt Eissler's behavior with Margaret as one of the prime psychoanalytic detectives. Apparently, Eissler had instituted a campaign to enlist Margaret in helping him to refute Masson's assertion that Freud ignored the importance of child abuse. As described in Chapter 5, Eissler and Masson had a falling out over Masson's criticism of Freud, which was made public. Eissler fired Masson from the Freud Archives. What we can now add to this drama is Fortune's commentary about Eissler's attempt to develop a relationship with Margaret Severn. This is how Fortune described it:

> Eissler doggedly tried to marshal evidence to rebut Masson's damning critique of Freud. Through Margaret Severn he was hoping to get inside information to shed light on the Elizabeth Severn case – ... was Elizabeth Severn actually sexually abused, or was it Oedipal phantasy?
>
> *(Fortune, 2015, p. 25)*

According to Fortune, Eissler launched a campaign to get Margaret to agree to be interviewed. Margaret was so aggressively pursued by Eissler that it rose to a level of emotional harassment:

> Eissler wooed Margaret. Along with regular phone calls to her from New York, he sent cards, flowers and chocolates to enlist her trust.
>
> *(Fortune, 2015, p. 25)*

A final attempt at seduction was Eissler's invitation to Margaret to come to New York and enter analysis with him. How could Eissler have justified analyzing Margaret in order to uncover information about her mother's analysis? Eissler must have been so upset by Masson's criticism of Freud and the dissolution of their once close relationship that he became consumed with proving Masson wrong and defending Freud.

Margaret Severn and Christopher Fortune

Unfortunately, we do not have the letters Elizabeth Severn sent to her daughter. There are two explanations for the missing letters of Elizabeth Severn. The first version emerged from Christopher Fortune's article which introduced Elizabeth Severn to the analytic community. He offered the following explanation:

> For over 30 years Elizabeth and Margaret Severn maintained an intimate, almost daily correspondence. In 1986, Margaret *honoring Elizabeth's last request burned her mother's letters.*
>
> (Fortune, 1993, p. 105, f5, italics added)

Peter Lipskis, Margaret's personal friend and biographer during the period she lived in Vancouver, British Columbia, has told me another version of the destruction of the Elizabeth Severn letters. When I asked him to discuss Elizabeth Severn's missing letters, he immediately volunteered a different explanation from the one Fortune had written. Lipskis (Lipskis, 2016b) said Margaret destroyed her mother's letters to her in a moment of frustration and anger. According to Lipskis, who claimed he was an eyewitness to this event, Margaret had an accumulation of negative feeling from the psychoanalytic detectives who had interviewed her about her mother. Peter had said to me that Margaret, who was very proud of her mother's career and relations with Ferenczi, was very angry that the researchers were questioning her mother's relationship with Ferenczi. They were insinuating that there were boundary violations between Severn and Ferenczi. Margaret, according to Peter, was indignant and angry that these researchers insinuated her mother had been immoral or unethical in her relationship with Ferenczi. One day Margaret became enraged with the questions and insinuations and decided to destroy her mother's letters, so that there would be no material that could be misinterpreted to prove these false accusations. What would remain would be Margaret's account of the Severn/Ferenczi relationship, which contains no account of inappropriate behavior. If one inspects Elizabeth Severn's materials about the Ferenczi relationship (Eissler; 1952, Severn, 1933) and Ferenczi's (1928–1933, 1988) as well as the reports of outside sources (Haynal, 2013; Rachman, 1993), there is no evidence of any sexual contact between Ferenczi and Severn.

Margaret's protective attitude towards her mother's career as a clinician and psychoanalyst was also evident in her protecting her mother's papers and artifacts for prosperity. She made a concerted effort to maintain and store her mother's papers after her death in 1959. After Margaret's death in 1997, The Elizabeth Severn Papers were bequeathed to Peter Lipskis. Not only was he dedicated to fulfilling Margaret's wishes to maintain her mother's legacy, but he was also committed to contributing to the creation of an awareness of Margaret Severn's legacy as a pioneer of modern dance.

10

SEVERN FINDS FERENCZI

From psychiatric patient to analysand to analytic partner

Psychiatric diagnosis

Ferenczi's diagnosis of Severn's psychiatric condition is clearly stated in his *Clinical Diary* (Ferenczi, 1988, p. 8) where, in his January 12, 1932 entry, he said: "Case of Schizophrenia Progression (R.N.)." In the 1930s, when the *Clinical Diary* was written, the prevailing idea was that schizophrenia was a progressive disease. It was thought that over time a patient with schizophrenia will show behavior and brain deterioration. This issue is still being debated. Recently in a research symposium the results indicated that schizophrenia does not have a negative trajectory in either brain functioning and symptomology. Kahn (2013) expressed the conclusion that perhaps a subgroup of people who are diagnosed as schizophrenic show decreasing brain volume and do worse symptomatically, but it is not so for the group as a whole.

Ferenczi's diagnosis of schizophrenia in Severn's case seemed to be based upon the severe childhood traumas inflicted upon her by her father and the disturbing symptomology she developed. Severn's diagnosis can be re-evaluated from a contemporary perspective. In my discussions with colleagues two different diagnoses based upon contemporary standards were offered about Severn's psychopathology. Finnegan (2013), who is an analyst who specializes in treating Multiple Personality Disorders (MPD), believes that Severn suffered from MPD. He thoroughly compared Ferenczi's notations about Severn in the *Clinical Diary* with clinical notes he had gathered in some of his clinical cases and found meaningful parallels to MPD. Kellerman (2009), who is a psychoanalyst and diagnostician, believed Severn's psychopathology and functioning indicated borderline personality disorder (Kellerman, 2014). My own predilection is to agree with Kellerman. Severn had severe symptomology, as we shall see when her traumatology is outlined. Although Severn suffered from severe symptoms, she was very functional as a professional from about

1907 to 1925 before she saw Ferenczi. She also had a very active intellect and became a self-taught, successful therapist (see Chapter 7). Severn also enjoyed an emotional and meaningful relationship with her daughter, Margaret, as well as with friends and and clients (see Chapter 9). There was no indication that Severn's symptoms or disorder progressed in severity, either in the period before she entered analysis with Ferenczi or in her recovery period (see Chapter 20). There was, however, a period of increased severity during the therapeutic crises of mutual analysis (see Chapter 16), when her childhood traumas were being retrieved.

Severn's previous analyses

Severn openly reported her psychiatric history in the interview Eissler conducted with her 19 years after ending her analysis with Ferenczi (Eissler, 1952). Early in the interview she said the following:

> I had attempted analysis with at least three men ..., two of them had been students of Freud.
>
> *(Eissler, 1952, p. 3)*

She went on to tell Eissler about the three therapeutic experiences she had had. She saw Drs. Ash, Jellife, and Rank. First, she mentioned a Dr. Ash "... who was analyzed by Freud" (Eissler, 1952, p. 3); Severn liked him, but she thought his analysis of her was limited because Ash had complained about his own analysis with Freud. As Severn noted, Ash actually stopped his analysis with Freud because it was not producing change. Ash said Freud didn't understand his homosexuality (Eissler, 1952, p. 11). This dramatic self-disclosure by Ash to Severn can be understood as an example of her capacity to create transparency in an analytic encounter. After Ash, she saw Jellife. She described him as intellectually capable, but "a very sadistic man!" (Eissler, 1952, p. 4). She had heard very positive things about him, but was very disappointed in the analysis. Her third contact with analysis was with Otto Rank. Apparently, as Rank moved his practice to America, he further developed his birth trauma theory (Rank, 1994) into a clinical paradigm (Rank, 1978). Severn described her analysis with Rank as a "three-month course" with an education focus on Rankian theory (Eissler, 1952, p. 4). She described the experience with Rank as follows:

> if you could recall the feelings of being born, every subsequent difficulty in your life would be eliminated. An extraordinary theory don't you think? [Eissler answered "yes"]
>
> Rank was one of those analysts ... Freud's pupils, "who decided they knew as much as Papa did, if not a little more, ... I found him completely wrapped up in the one idea of the birth trauma, and incapable of thinking of anything else.
>
> *(Eissler, 1952, p. 4)*

Severn said that the therapy with Rank, "… didn't help me any" (Eissler, 1952, p. 5). Severn's observations about Rank closely paralleled Freud's and Ferenczi's evaluations.

Severn chose Ferenczi over Freud

Severn's dissatisfaction with Rank led her to seek out a new analyst. Rank recommended Ferenczi. Severn made a meaningful choice of whom to see for her final therapeutic experience. Although she was not impressed with Rank, he had a significant reputation when he arrived in the United States from Europe in the 1920s and she saw him. One could argue she could have sought out analysis with Freud, after all she considered herself a student of psychoanalysis by that time. She was perfectly aware of Freud's reputation as being considered the world's foremost psychoanalyst, being its founder. She did consult Freud, for the first time during the early months of her first year of analysis with Ferenczi. Severn told Eissler she chose Ferenczi over Freud for analysis:

> and I had chosen him [Ferenczi] because I thought he was more of a physician than Freud was. In other words, that he was more interested in the patient; I believed that Freud was primarily interested in the science … I had no reason to change that opinion in later years.
>
> *(Eissler, 1952, p. 2)*

Severn believed that there was a fundamental difference between Freud and Ferenczi as people. Furthermore, she said she never regretted that she had chosen Ferenczi as her analyst. The further on they went into the analysis, the more they co-created the analysis and became therapeutic partners. Severn never thought about prematurely terminating with Ferenczi, saying:

> I believe [he] was doing his level best all the way.
>
> *(Eissler, 1952, p. 3)*

The search for therapeutic help and Severn's reaction to her three analyses is very illuminating. She was determined to get better, to never give up, to find an analyst who could meaningfully treat her. It should be emphasized that by 1924, when she saw Rank, Severn considered herself a student of psychoanalysis. She had moved on from esoteric healing, Christian science and applied psychology to psychoanalysis. Severn had negative feelings about Freudian analysis from her experiences with Drs. Ash, Jellife, and Rank, as well as with Freud. Her personal reaction to Freud was that he appeared intellectualized, reserved, and rigid.

Eissler asked Severn why she first went to see Freud. Her reply was:

> Well, of course I had made a choice for myself of Ferenczi rather than Freud, without having seen Freud. I had made that choice on the basis of mostly knowledge from people who had known either one/or the other of them.
>
> *(Eissler, 1952, p. 11)*

Severn believed it was preordained that Ferenczi should be her analyst. She believed that there was a mystical connection between herself and Ferenczi. Ferenczi described Severn's idea of a match between them in the following way:

> in the case of R.N. (Severn) like someone in love, the patient tries to extend her interest in my person for her back into the past. With the help of an intermediary, a Hungarian who at that time inhabited that distant land (she had only recently learned that he used to live there), the patient believes she discovered precisely me, through mystical thought-transference (N.B. thirty-one years ago), as the only person who would be able to help patients in great distress.
>
> *(Ferenczi, 1988, p. 43)*

Ferenczi also reported that another of his analysands (S.I.) also told him that, although she had never heard of him before they began their analysis, she felt: "that I alone could save her. All other attempts at analysis had indeed failed, but she came to me with symptoms of intense transference" (Ferenczi, 1988, p. 43). In my 40 years working with severe trauma disordered individuals, I have found similar incidents of an analysand believing in the "chosen analyst." A woman who was severely sexually abused as a young child by two family members, and was interested in mythology, mysticism, and psychoanalysis, expressed what Ferenczi called intense transference. She told me she had a vision that Ferenczi was very happy that she was seeing me for analysis. Additionally, she told me she had "read my aura," as well as Ferenczi's, and they were compatible. She said we both had very positive auras. I asked this analysand to help me understand the methodology behind reading one's aura, since I was completely ignorant of this practice. She brought me in a book about reading auras (Butler, 1998). According to this field of paranormal studies, everyone has an aura, which is an invisible field of energy believed to radiate for each person (Lindgren, 2000). Traditionally, the aura is a designation of an individual's power or spirituality. It is also considered as a map of the thoughts and feelings surrounding a person (Brennan, 1988). This incest survivor said she was interested in reading my aura because she wanted to be sure I was a "healing person." After reading my aura, she concluded that, like Ferenczi, "I had a very positive, healing aura."

Difficult analysand and analyst of difficult cases

The description of Severn's psychological problems, her unsuccessful attempts at therapeutic help, the desperate emotional state in which she lived, combined to create great difficulties for her. Issues in Severn's personality functioning, such as aggressiveness, which Ferenczi saw as a negative, added to the difficulties (Ferenczi, 1988). Did these characteristics contribute to her unsuccessful attempts at analysis with Ash, Jellife, and Rank? Did they experience her as a person who couldn't be analyzed, because she would not let them analyze her. Or was it that these parochial, patrocentric analysts of the pioneering period were not accustomed to a woman who knew what she needed, how to get it, and even what kind of therapeutic partner she needed to help her meet her needs. One must remember, this kind of self-assured, independent thinking from an analytically-informed, dramatically expressive active analysand, such as Severn, was not typical among analysands of the 1920s and 1930s. Freud's clinical cases, as he described them, were sick people who needed the wisdom and authority of a physician/analyst. Severn was very astute in choosing Ferenczi over Freud. Her intuitive capacities helped her to understand that Freud's approach to clinical interaction was intellectual, sparse, and emotionally distant. She observed this from the behavior of analysts whom she saw; Ash and Jellife were analyzed or trained by Freud. Severn knew what kind of analyst she needed. Rank, for all his shortcomings, helped her change her life by referring her to Ferenczi.

Severn's analytic task

One of the contributions that the Eissler interview makes to our understanding of Severn is a description of her emotional disturbances in her own words. This helps us better understand her emotional disorder as well as to re-evaluate the negative comments made about her by Freud and his orthodox followers. This is how Severn stated her basic emotional issue:

> I was in a desperate state because I didn't feel that I would live unless I got rid of this thing that was troubling my unconscious … the feeling that I couldn't live, that I would have to kill myself, was overwhelming at times. And if I couldn't get rid of it, I certainly didn't want to live.
>
> *(Eissler, 1952, p. 5)*

Severn's emotional declaration of potential destruction pointed her analysis toward the fear of killing herself (Eissler, 1952, p. 5). As we shall see, the therapeutic relationship between Severn and Ferenczi became the vehicle for unravelling the drive towards self-destruction. Their relationship, which was both therapeutic and chaotic, encompassed the trauma and the cure. Severn knew what her analytic task was:

> a very serious amnesia in my life in my childhood – a complete amnesia – of which I had no knowledge whatsoever … I had, particularly a desire for suicide.
>
> *(Eissler, 1952, p. 1)*

The analyst of difficult cases

In 1925, Severn, it can be said, made the most significant emotional decision of her life. She decided to trust her emotional recovery from her severe disorder to

Ferenczi. By this time Ferenczi was known as *the analyst of difficult cases* (Rachman, 1997a, 2003a; Rachman & Klett, 2015). Everyone in the analytic world was aware of Ferenczi's analytic powers with cases in which other analysts had been unsuccessful, or with difficult cases that analysts did not want to treat. At the time of the Ferenczi/Severn analysis, Henry Stack Sullivan referred Clara Thompson to Ferenczi. Thompson was dissatisfied with her first analyst and turned to Sullivan for a referral (Rachman, 1997a, 2003a). Sullivan didn't hesitate to recommend Ferenczi, who he thought was the best analyst among Freud's followers. Perhaps Sullivan knew about Thompson's childhood trauma when he referred her to Ferenczi. The analysis seemed to be very helpful for her. Ferenczi discussed it under the case of Dm in his *Clinical Diary* (Ferenczi, 1988). As has been discussed, Thompson was an incest survivor. Thompson was a difficult case, not only because of her trauma background but because she was seductive in the transference with Ferenczi and she was also jealous of Ferenczi's intense attention to Severn.

Compatibility between Severn and Ferenczi

There was an intellectual, emotional, and interpersonal match between Severn and Ferenczi. Intellectually, Severn was exceptional. She had no extensive formal education, yet, she was a self-motivated student of mysticism, psychology, philosophy, psychotherapy, human behavior, and psychoanalysis (Rachman, 2016a). As will be outlined in Chapter 11, Severn used her intellect to evaluate, experiment with, and develop a variety of methodologies, some parallel to Ferenczi's technical innovations. Severn conducted sessions that varied from minutes to hours, saw people in her office, made house calls, and conducted weekly to daily sessions (see Chapter 11). Ferenczi was considered a *clinical genius* because of his capacity to be flexible, responsive, and innovative with difficult analysands, within the analytic framework. In fact, it was Ferenczi who taught psychoanalysis to expand beyond interpretation and the development of insight (Rachman, 1997a, 2003a). In parallel careers, which began roughly at the same era, in the early 1900s, Ferenczi and Severn developed their clinical functioning in similar ways.

Severn showed a capacity to interact and maintain a peer relationship with not only Ferenczi but with Freud and Eissler. As we saw in Chapter 5, Severn interacted with Eissler, the founder and secretary of The Freud Archives, as if he was her peer. At no point did she seem deferential to him. She interacted as his intellectual and professional equal. To his credit, Eissler treated Severn in a gracious and thoughtful manner, as she was genuinely his equal (Eissler, 1952).

Another example of Severn's intellectual and interpersonal capacities is illustrated in her consultation sessions with Freud. Severn consulted with Freud three times: twice while in analysis with Ferenczi (in the winter of 1925 and during the analysis of 1925–33) and once in 1938, five years after the termination of the analysis with Ferenczi. The first consultation was arranged by Ferenczi because Severn wanted to see The Master. Perhaps, Severn also wanted to see if Freud had something to offer her. In the second consultation session Severn discussed with Freud her notion that the early analysts had defects in their training. She felt their personal analysis was conducted in an intellectual manner and their transferences had not been fully worked through. Telling this to Freud can be seen as an example of the Yiddish concept of "Chutzpah," unmitigated gall. Severn could be seen as audacious, bold, courageous, and, maybe, insolent. Freud, according to Severn's recall did not take these criticisms of psychoanalysis as an insult (Eissler, 1952). These kinds of audacious interactions with Freud may have contributed nevertheless to Freud's negative evaluation of her. She pointed out a shortcoming of Freudian psychoanalysis that matched what Ferenczi and Rank (1925) put forth in their critique that recommended the field expand toward a more emotional and expressive way of functioning.

Severn and Ferenczi had compatible personalities. They were both outgoing and friendly, and they both expressed compassion, concern, and warmth. One could say that Severn was more assertive than Ferenczi. Perhaps some, such as Freud, Jones, Thompson, and others, would say Severn overpowered Ferenczi. I do not think this is accurate. If we take Ferenczi's struggle to join Severn in a mutual analysis (see Chapter 16), one can see the emotional struggle with which he grappled over a year's period to become a partner in the analysis. He wasn't overpowered by her to participate. Ferenczi needed to work through his intellectual and emotional anxieties in order to become a partner with Severn. He realized it was a necessary clinical departure to attempt to solve an intractable situation. The difficulties in their relationship will be more fully examined in the chapters to follow.

Clinically, the compatibility between Severn and Ferenczi was fundamental. Both identified themselves as healers (Ferenczi, 1988; Severn, 1933). They both became interested in understanding and treating trauma disorders. Severn's interest in the healing of trauma disorders arose out of her attempt to understand and cure herself; Ferenczi's interest in working with difficult cases, which included incest and trauma disorders, arose from his childhood experience of maternal deprivation (Grubrich-Simitus, 1986) and his own childhood sexual abuse (Chapter 12). Their compatibility also existed in their active, empathic and flexible clinical attitude, which allowed both to introduce a variety of innovative techniques in their own clinical practices (Ferenczi, 1988; Severn, 1920).

There was a theoretical compatibility, which was clearly a belief in psychoanalysis, albeit a modified version of Freudian psychology. Of course, Ferenczi was an avid student of Freud who extended the boundaries of psychoanalysis in the development of the study and treatment of trauma (Rachman & Klett, 2015). Severn, although she began her clinical career using mysticism, belief in the paranormal, Christian science and applied psychology, (see Chapter 11) eventually became a believer in psychoanalysis:

> I can see Freud's point of view that he had worked everything out so carefully and that he had spent his life doing it and was satisfied apparently that he had gone as far as could be, and that most of the contributions his other pupils had made were really not much of an improvement on what he had done.
>
> *(Eissler, 1952, p. 7)*

Severn also shared a perspective with Ferenczi: "… we begun some mutual research work and he discussed all the technical points with me" (Eissler, 1952, p. 2).

11

SEVERN AS A CLINICIAN

In the early part of the twentieth century, Severn became a self-educated and self-taught therapist. Psychoanalysis has acknowledged the achievements and pioneering contributions of women who helped shape the field. Anna O./Bertha Pappenheim is acknowledged as one of the founders of psychoanalysis by Freud (Breuer & Freud, 1895). Freud credits Bertha Pappenheim with developing the *talking cure*, when she convinced Josef Breuer to let her verbalize her emotional issues in a non-hypnotic state. In this volume, Elizabeth Severn is considered one of the founders of the Ferenzian alternative to Freudian therapy.

The Elizabeth Severn Papers (Rachman, 2016d) now provide us with significant material that can shed light on Severn's career as a clinician from 1908 to 1959. These materials draw a picture of Severn as a significant clinician in her own right before, during, and after her analysis with Ferenczi. As mentioned, she was a student of many disciplines, such as mysticism and psychology.

In her own personal treatment, she had chosen to see a number of Freudian-trained psychoanalysts (Eissler, 1952). At the onset of her analysis with Ferenczi in 1925, Severn saw herself as a polished clinician, who had been practicing psychotherapy for about 25 years and had a contribution to make to her own psychoanalysis. We must reassess the view of Severn as only a disturbed patient who created clinical, professional, and personal turmoil for Ferenczi. She was a functioning, successful clinician and thinker. Severn's professional career can be divided into four phases:

1. A massage therapist, 1900–1907
2. Metaphysician, 1908–1910
3. Therapist and practicing psychotherapist, 1911–1924
4. Practicing psychoanalyst, 1933–1959

Pre-clinical experience: encyclopedia salesperson

Severn's career as a self-taught clinician began when she was a door-to-door encyclopedia salesperson (Fortune, 1993) and eventually developed into becoming a psychoanalyst. Severn, after she separated from her husband, Charles Heywood, shortly after reuniting with her daughter, needed to find a way to earn a living. This was just after the turn of the twentieth century, when women began to have careers. She had suffered from severe childhood trauma, which was uncovered in her analysis with Ferenczi (Ferenczi, 1988; Rachman, 2010a, 2012b, 2014b, d, 2015a, b). During this earlier period of her life, however, Severn was not aware that her horrific childhood traumas were at the center of her ongoing emotional disturbances, such as severe depression and crippling headaches. On the other hand, Severn had a functional part of her personality, which she developed as a child, which was characterized by a talented, very intelligent, creative, motivated, assertive, and likeable individual (Ferenczi, 1988; see Chapter 23). Although Severn's personality was fragmented due to the severe childhood traumas, she was able, under most circumstances, to allow the functional, positive part of her personality to be available to her. It was this functional part of Severn's personality that allowed her to perform the difficult task of going door-to-door, in the Midwest of the United States and selling encyclopedias. This positive function was labeled as her Orpha-function (see Chapter 23). Severn, also had a grandiose, arrogant, confident part of her personality, which allowed her to believe in herself. Severn was successful in two important ways as an encyclopedia salesperson. She was able to earn a living, which, of course, was essential. But, there was an additional unforeseen benefit. She became aware that the individuals, to whom she called upon to sell her wares, turned to her in a personal way, sharing themselves with her. Through this experience, Severn began to become interested in working with people in a therapeutic way.

Massage therapist: 1900–1907

A second step in Severn's path toward becoming a therapist was the unexpected opportunity she capitalized upon in the woman's salon she frequented. She overheard that some of the women who seemed to have emotional issues were looking for someone who could provide body massages to help them relax and reduce their tensions. She felt she could offer this service and volunteered to become a kind of *massage therapist* at the salon. The massage service was so successful that Severn decided to open her own service. Consequently, her first type of clinical practice was as a massage therapist for women with nervous conditions (M. Severn, 1989). Her daughter, Margaret, described the origin of this second state in her clinical career:

> My mother ... had her hair washed in a shampoo parlor ... on a certain day she found a considerable commotion in progress. It seems that one of their principle clients was very angry because she had an appointment for a massage, but the masseuse had failed to show up. My mother quickly intervened

and said 'I can give the massage' … a few minutes after the treatment had started, the client began to sigh peacefully, felt extremely well, and was so pleased with the massage that she made an appointment for the next day and brought friends with her.

(M. Severn, 1989)

At this point, Severn realized she had a talent for working therapeutically with people who had emotional problems. She was able to draw upon several positive qualities of her personality to accomplish this type of career. She brought her like-ability, assertiveness, confidence, intuitive understanding of human behavior, a sense of empathy, and a willingness to be responsive and meet the needs of others. She was also attuned to her own inner needs and what was therapeutic for her. This capacity was further developed in her analyses with Ferenczi. Severn knew what she needed in her interaction with Ferenczi to heal.

Severn's daughter, Margaret, was able to describe her mother's special personal qualities that enabled her to become a clinician:

She had a very charismatic personality and was an excellent speaker so that there was no difficulty in attracting patients or in keeping them, because she was always able to help and heal them. People found her to be an inspiration and feel better just for coming into her presence. She accepted only a limited number at a time as she preferred to concentrate with great intensity on the particular problems of each individual.

(M. Severn, 1989)

The concept of a *therapeutic presence*, which her daughter credits to Elizabeth Severn, is an important dimension of a clinician, which is rarely discussed. There have been psychoanalysts who seem to possess this quality, e.g. Balint, Freud, Ferenczi, Freida Fromm-Reichman, Kohut, and Winnicott. In my own experience, I have been fortunate to have felt the therapeutic presence of Betty Feldman, Ben Fielding, Erika Fromm, Eugene Gendlin, Asya Kadis, Joseph Lichtenberg, Esther Menaker, Carl Rogers, and Harold Searles. The idea of a therapeutic presence is not having charisma, but an ability to engage another person in a healing relationship. Severn's capacity to engage people was not built on manipulation, control, and emotional attraction. Her therapeutic presence was the capacity to be fully in the moment with the person, so that she could give herself fully. She knew how to give to another by attuning to the inner needs of others. As we shall see, Ferenczi was able to accept and integrate her therapeutic presence as an integral part of their analysis. He accepted her both as a person and therapist.

Clinical metaphysician: 1908–1911

The first two career stages, salesperson and massage therapist, led to the opening of a clinical practice. Severn was one of those rare individuals who was able to educate herself in a career that combined intellectual, emotional, interpersonal, and creative capacities at a time when there were no formal training programs for psychotherapy and/or psychoanalysis. She began her clinical practice in or about 1908, when Freud was about to report his case of the Rat Man/Ernst Lanzer (1878 – 1914). It is interesting to note that Freud's clinical behavior at this time, which involved providing food for the analysand, was considered unconventional (Mahoney, 1986). The traditional analytic community, which later examined Freud's behavior, found it to be an expression of Freud's humanism, not a sign of a personal or professional defect. Ferenczi and Severn never enjoyed such a positive evaluation of using a non-interpretative measure. The year Severn began her clinical practice in 1908, Ferenczi was just meeting Freud for the first time (Rachman, 1997a). To announce her first clinical practice, Severn sent out the following statement:

> Mrs. Elizabeth Severn desires to announce … the opening of her office [in] San Antonio, Texas … [she] very effectively puts into practice the principle that Health, Happiness and Success on every plane may be ours. In her exhaustive study of mind, Mrs. Severn has become a deep student of the occult, yet she maintains the scientific attitude that aims always to make practice the truth promulgated.
>
> *(Rachman, 2016d; see Image 6)*

At this point, Severn identified herself as a metaphysician, that is a student of the science of mental phenomena and the laws of the mind employed as synonymous with psychology (Zalta, 2012).

By the time Severn initiated her clinical practice in 1908, what were Freud and Ferenczi doing? Freud had established psychoanalysis as the new study and treatment of psychological disorders, written *The Interpretation of Dreams*, and discussed his iconic cases: e.g. with Josef Breuer, The Case of Anna O./Bertha Pappenheim, Little Hans/Herbert Graf, Dora/Ida Bauer, and the Rat Man/Ernst Lanzer. All were published by 1909. What is more, in 1909, Freud, with the help of Jung and Ferenczi, helped introduce psychoanalysis into the United States at Clark University, in Wooster, Massachusetts. In February 1908, Ferenczi met Freud for the first time. By 1909, Ferenczi collaborated with Freud on *The New Introductory Lectures* at Clark University (Freud, 1990). As Freud and Ferenczi introduced psychoanalysis, Severn began her own version of therapy.

Dr. Elizabeth Severn, psychotherapist: 1911–1915

In the years of clinical practice from 1911–1915, Severn referred to herself as "Dr. Elizabeth Severn, Psychotherapist." There is no indication in The Elizabeth Severn Papers (Rachman, 2016d) that Severn had gone through an academic study program to receive a doctorate. It is likely that her self-confidence and, perhaps, a sense of arrogance, fueled her belief she was learned enough to call herself a doctor. Perhaps, she felt she had earned the title of doctor because she was a self-taught

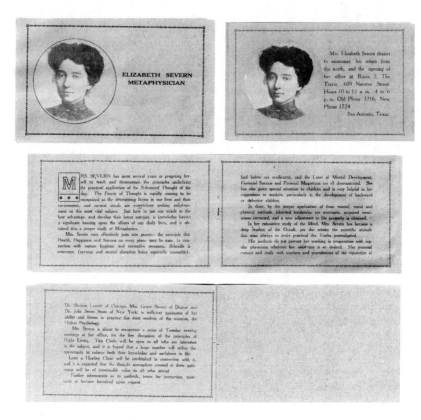

IMAGE 6 Elizabeth Severn's announcement of the opening of her first office as a clinician in San Antonio, Texas in 1908

accomplished clinician and teacher. There were two instances where psychoanalysts referred to Severn as a doctor. In the photograph of Ferenczi, in the Foreword, p. ii, he referred to her as "Dr. Elizabeth Severn" (Rachman, 2016d). Severn distributed notices of her different clinical practices and lectures, located in various cities.

In the Eissler/Severn Interview (see Chapter 5), the typed manuscript of the interview noted that Eissler addressed her as Dr. Severn (Eissler, 1952). Severn was a student of psychology and therapeutic experiences. She was influenced by the founder of Christian science, Mary Baker Eddy, and Emile Coué, a French psychologist who introduced a clinical method of self-improvement (Dupont, 1988 f2, 3, pp. 33–34). Eddy's ideas about Christian science first became popular in the United States in the nineteenth century (Gardner, 1993). Christian science emphasized a form of self-healing, free from drugs, medicine, and physicians. The healing for illness came from the individual and a belief in his/her own mental capacities for cure. This perspective located healing in the believing individual not in an outside force. Eddy believed that illness was a result of an individual's belief system. She described this idea in this following way:

Your aid to reach this goal (of healers) is *spiritualization* ... let my thoughts and aims be high, unselfish, charitable, meek, *spiritually-minded*. With this attitude of thought your mind is losing materiality and gaining spirituality and that is the state of mind that heals the sick.

(Gotteschalk 2006, p. 354 – Letter from Mary Baker Eddy to James A. Neal, January 29, 1898)

Mary Baker Eddy's philosophy of healing, which focused on self-reliance, belief in a higher spirit, avoiding medical treatment, and curing by psychological means, was compatible with Severn's own sense of spirituality, self-reliance, and self-determination, providing the untrained Severn with a theory of healing that could be integrated with her assertive and independent personality. This theory became a part of the intellectual framework for her clinical practice. Severn's integration of Eddy's philosophy predates the development of contemporary orientations that incorporate biofeedback, psychoneuroimmunology, positive psychology, and mindfulness. These perspectives emphasize the idea that mind can heal the body (see Image 7).

Severn's psychotherapy cases: 1913–1920

Severn published three books about her clinical theory and practice. Her first book, *Psychotherapy: Its Doctrine and Practice*, published in 1913 (Severn, 1913), outlined her extensive practice as a psychotherapist. She presented 49 clinical cases, mostly referred by physicians. The patients were difficult cases who did not respond to the traditional medical cures. In retrospect these cases were referred to Severn because they needed something other than medicinal treatment. Severn had a reputation for working with difficult cases, being psychologically minded, and employing innovative techniques. She became known for being successful in these physician-referred cases. Severn actually preceded Ferenczi as being the *expert in difficult psychological cases* (see Images 8, 9, 10, and 11).

Severn developed what she termed *severe measures*, which were techniques beyond the usual measures (Severn, 1913, p. 155). In the clinical practice of psychotherapy, her innovative interaction was characterized by the following:

1. Giving of direct suggestions
2. Compassion, concern, empathy
3. Auto-suggestion, commands, prohibitions
4. The affirmation of the patient's positive attributes or functioning
5. Sending *unconscious healing vibrations* from the therapist to the patient
6. Making of house calls
7. Use of physical touch to soothe patients
8. Promising a cure
9. Application of magnetic energy
10. Aspects of the talking cure, e.g. direct interpretations, compassion, conveying of hope, imparting knowledge, catharsis, and psychodynamic formulations

IMAGE 7 Announcement of Dr. Elizabeth Severn's course on Thought-Force in Washington D.C. in the winter of 1912

11. Use of adjunctive medical treatments, e.g. ice packs, use of bandages, prescribed rest, advice on food consumption
12. *Absent* therapy, e.g. telephone therapy, sending vibrations, writing letters
13. Extramural contact with patients, e.g. therapeutic interactions outside the consultation room, maintaining ongoing contact with a patient
14. Music therapy
15. Analyst self-disclosure
16. Self-treatment/self-analysis.

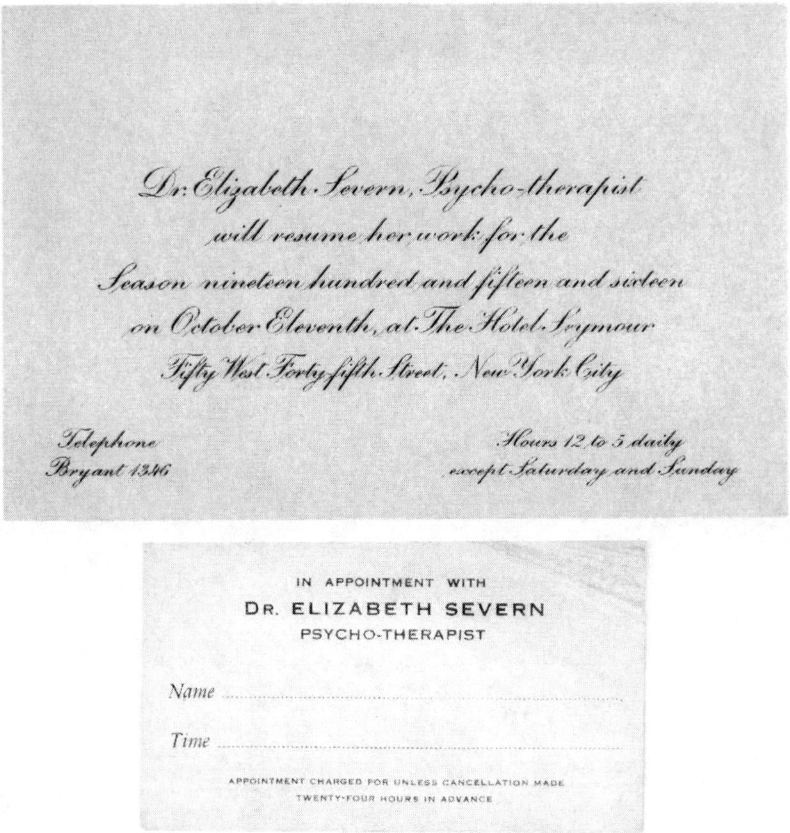

Dr. Elizabeth Severn, Psycho-therapist
will resume her work for the
Season nineteen hundred and fifteen and sixteen
on October Eleventh, at The Hotel Seymour
Fifty West Forty-fifth Street, New York City

Telephone
Bryant 1346

Hours 12 to 5 daily
except Saturday and Sunday

IN APPOINTMENT WITH
DR. ELIZABETH SEVERN
PSYCHO-THERAPIST

Name ....

Time ....

APPOINTMENT CHARGED FOR UNLESS CANCELLATION MADE
TWENTY-FOUR HOURS IN ADVANCE

IMAGE 8 Dr. Elizabeth Severn's announcement of her office at the Hotel Seymour in New York City and Dr. Elizabeth Severn's appointment card

Severn's claims about her eclectic therapeutic techniques ranged from modest successes to extravagant claims of cures. She also cited a few cases where there were no successes because, she said, the individuals were not "amenable to suggestion or motivated to make changes" (Severn, 1914, p. 159).

There were a wide variety of therapeutic interactions in the 49 cases, which indicate Severn's creativity, flexibility, responsiveness, and wide-ranging capacity as a clinician. The employment of *direct suggestion* was an important dimension of Severn's approach during her period of being a psychotherapist. Suggestion, which has been a controversial issue in psychoanalysis (Raso, 2005) since its inception, was employed by Severn as a primitive form of interpretation. Severn was convinced she understood the psychological aspects to human behavior and was willing to directly offer suggestions to her patients. The case of Miss G. illustrates Severn's use of suggestion:

Miss G. was a talented business woman who was self-referred after hearing Severn giving a lecture about her clinical practice. She was: "broken down from overwork" and lacked vitality, ambition, and interest in life. Although she described

IMAGE 9 Dr. Elizabeth Severn in her office at the Hotel Seymour in New York City in 1924

neurotic symptoms, Severn felt: "No deep psycho-analysis was required in the case." Apparently, Severn, at this time, was aware of psychoanalysis in her initial clinical practice. Severn described that:

> the patient responded quickly to the suggestions made resulting … in better, … appetite and more strength … A few subsequent treatments were necessary a few months later … after which she remained perfectly well.
>
> *(Severn, 1913, p. 172)*

Severn's suggestions can be characterized as *direct interpretations*. One can paraphrase Severn's use of direct suggestion in this case in the following way:

> You are suffering from a psychological disorder. You are so overworked that you are physically and psychologically exhausted. I will recommend a regime for you that will help you recover.

Apparently, Miss G. regained her appetite and her physical and emotional strength with a few direct suggestions. Severn was actively engaging Miss G. in her own cure.

A more complicated case study involved a man who had complications after three operations on his knees. Severn described the issues in this case as follows:

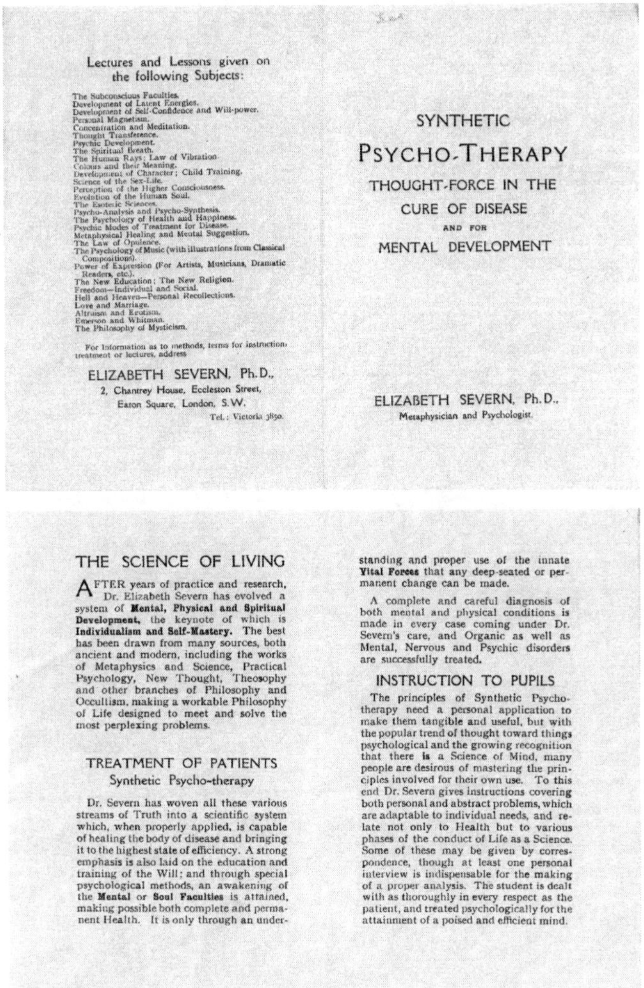

Lectures and Lessons given on the following Subjects:

The Subconscious Faculties.
Development of Latent Energies.
Development of Self-Confidence and Will-power.
Personal Magnetism.
Concentration and Meditation.
Thought Transference.
Psychic Development.
The Spiritual Breath.
The Human Rays; Law of Vibration.
Colours and their Meaning.
Development of Character; Child Training.
Science of the Sex-Life.
Perception of the Higher Consciousness.
Evolution of the Human Soul.
The Esoteric Sciences.
Psycho-Analysis and Psycho-Synthesis.
The Psychology of Health and Happiness.
Psychic Modes of Treatment for Disease.
Metaphysical Healing and Mental Suggestion.
The Law of Opulence.
The Psychology of Music (with illustrations from Classical Compositions).
Power of Expression (For Artists, Musicians, Dramatic Readers, etc.).
The New Education; The New Religion.
Freedom—Individual and Social.
Hell and Heaven—Personal Recollections.
Love and Marriage.
Altruism and Erotism.
Emerson and Whitman.
The Philosophy of Mysticism.

For Information as to methods, terms for instruction, treatment or lectures, address

ELIZABETH SEVERN, Ph.D.,
2, Chantrey House, Eccleston Street,
Eaton Square, London, S.W.
Tel.: Victoria 3850.

SYNTHETIC
PSYCHO-THERAPY
THOUGHT-FORCE IN THE CURE OF DISEASE AND FOR MENTAL DEVELOPMENT

ELIZABETH SEVERN, Ph.D.,
Metaphysician and Psychologist.

THE SCIENCE OF LIVING

AFTER years of practice and research, Dr. Elizabeth Severn has evolved a system of **Mental, Physical and Spiritual Development**, the keynote of which is **Individualism and Self-Mastery.** The best has been drawn from many sources, both ancient and modern, including the works of Metaphysics and Science, Practical Psychology, New Thought, Theosophy and other branches of Philosophy and Occultism, making a workable Philosophy of Life designed to meet and solve the most perplexing problems.

TREATMENT OF PATIENTS
Synthetic Psycho-therapy

Dr. Severn has woven all these various streams of Truth into a scientific system which, when properly applied, is capable of healing the body of disease and bringing it to the highest state of efficiency. A strong emphasis is also laid on the education and training of the Will; and through special psychological methods, an awakening of the **Mental** or **Soul Faculties** is attained, making possible both complete and permanent Health. It is only through an understanding and proper use of the innate **Vital Forces** that any deep-seated or permanent change can be made.

A complete and careful diagnosis of both mental and physical conditions is made in every case coming under Dr. Severn's care, and Organic as well as Mental, Nervous and Psychic disorders are successfully treated.

INSTRUCTION TO PUPILS

The principles of Synthetic Psycho-therapy need a personal application to make them tangible and useful, but with the popular trend of thought toward things psychological and the growing recognition that there **is** a Science of Mind, many people are desirous of mastering the principles involved for their own use. To this end Dr. Severn gives instructions covering both personal and abstract problems, which are adaptable to individual needs, and relate not only to Health but to various phases of the conduct of Life as a Science. Some of these may be given by correspondence, though at least one personal interview is indispensable for the making of a proper analysis. The student is dealt with as thoroughly in every respect as the patient, and treated psychologically for the attainment of a poised and efficient mind.

IMAGE 10 Announcement of Elizabeth Severn, Ph.D., psychologist

> his legs remained stiff and immovable ... not a true *paralysis*, ... after a careful examination, I was convinced that a cure could be effected, and was so sure that I promised him that he might walk again within a month.
>
> *(Severn, 1913, p. 174)*

We can see from this case that Severn paralleled Freud's use of non-interpretative measures in promising a cure for the Wolf Man, in approximately the same period (see Chapter 8). Severn saw him for three sessions a week. She was sure that although this began as a medical issue of paralysis, there were: "distinct psychic elements in this case," which needed careful handling and readjustment in developing the necessary will-power to make him attempt any use of himself ... (Severn, 1913, pp.

IMAGE 11 Announcement of Elizabeth Severn, Ph.D., lecture series, Omaha, Nebraska

174–175). Severn's treatment in this case involved a combination of four methods: magnetic treatment, massage, direct suggestion, and behavior therapy.

Magnetic treatment was one of the earliest methods of treatment Severn used at a time when she described herself as a metaphysician. It was popular at the beginning of the twentieth century, but is now seen as a pseudoscientific alternative medicine (Park, 2000). The idea that the application of magnetic energy in the form of bracelets, body garments, etc. is still with us, in the television and print commercials by athletes who promise increased performance by their use. Severn applied magnetic treatment to the patient's knees. In addition, she applied massage to this same area to produce increased circulation. The next form of treatment was her special form of direct suggestions to change behavior. In this instance, direct suggestion took the form of commands, because Severn had decided that the patient needed a very active approach to counteract becoming non-mobile after his operation, which was considered medically successful. Severn's method in this instance may have been an overly aggressive use of the role of suggestion and activity, but she may have anticipated the idea of *learned helplessness* (Peterson, Maier & Segilinow, 1995). This idea is that in adverse situations individuals can feel helpless and give up trying. In Severn's case, the individual may have given up after three operations on his knees did not produce positive results. Severn's method of direct suggestion and behavior therapy was described in the following way:

> I encouraged and even forced him to move about the room on crutches … when this fear-thought was finally removed, he became more facile … [then] … he walked alone down two flights of stairs to the street … the following week he came to my office in a motor car … two weeks later even these [crutches] were discarded … the last I heard, he was getting about very comfortably.
>
> *(Severn, 1913, pp. 175–176)*

The use of direct suggestion and behavior therapy in Severn's quote, was modulated from an aggressive stance to a graduated, less intrusive one, as the patient responded to Severn's suggestions. Severn had the capacity to show flexibility and responsiveness mixed with empathy when applying her direct form of psychotherapy. This is something Ferenczi also understood when he realized that his introduction of the active role of the analyst needed to be calibrated (1980f).

Severn was *intuitively informed* in her use of massage, which in contemporary times was demonstrated in research of healing through touch (Krieger, 1993; Rosa, Rosa, Sarner & Barrett, 1998). Later on in the twentieth century, after Severn had been practicing for several years, another influence became popular in American psychology; this influence was called applied psychology by its founder Emile Coué (Abraham, 1926; Brooks, 2015; Coué, 2006). He developed the idea of auto-suggestion (self-hypnosis). Coué's experience with people paralleled Severn's experience as an encyclopedia salesperson. While a practicing pharmacist, Coué noticed that medial remedies given to patients with positive autosuggestions and positive encouragements provided them with the motivation to feel better. The autosuggestions combined with the medicines worked better than giving the patients only the remedies. Coué believed that each person had the solution to his/her own problems. He is reported to have said, *you have in yourself the instrument of cure.* His Law of Concentrated Attention stated that when one is concentrated on an idea and repeats it, over and over again, you spontaneously tend to believe it. This notion produced Coué's most famous saying: *Everyday, in every way, I am getting better and better.* Applied psychology provided Severn with a more modern, positive, self-reliant, assertive, and active philosophy of psychological cure she would integrate, as she began to move away from mysticism and toward a psychological framework.

Coué's ideas have relevance for contemporary thinking, like the placebo effect in medicine, in that, a patient believes in the medication as a cure, even if it contains no medicinal properties. Positive thinking was a precursor to transcendental meditation. When a Hindu Yogi was studied at Menniger's Clinic in the mid-twentieth century, it was shown that meditation can alter the heartbeat (Boerstler & Kornfeld, 1995).

Self-treatment/self-analysis

Severn applied her own brand of healing developed to treat patients to also treat herself. In the period prior to entering analysis with Ferenczi, Severn used self-treatment and self-analysis to deal with her own personal difficulties. In this way, she shared a function with Freud, who analyzed himself. Severn, however, when it was necessary, turned to others for psychiatric treatment or psychoanalysis. Freud was not only unable to turn to others for analysis, but refused the offer of help by friends, such as Jung and Ferenczi. Severn described two examples of self-treatment:

> The first was a spraining of the ankles due to a hard fall … the ankle was so badly swollen I could not tell whether it was sprained or broken, but concluded to treat it as though it were only a sprain. I wrapped it up in iced bandages and then lay down to concentrate. … on waking … the swelling and discoloration were almost gone, so I knew my surmise had been correct and no breakage had occurred. … I got up and began to exercise them gently … then more vigorously … and had no further trouble.
>
> *(Severn, 1913, pp. 176–177)*

A second example of self-treatment involved being thrown from a horse:

> [I had] severe blows at the base of the brain and the end of the spine, rendering me unconscious for a few moments … I was numb all over and considerably dazed … my lower limbs were paralyzed … no longer possible to speak. I felt a momentary fear at the apparent gravity of my condition … but my mind was perfectly clear, so that I was able to give myself the necessary treatment to restore the lost equilibrium.
>
> *(Severn, 1913, p. 177)*

She enlisted friends to read to her during the night because she could not sleep; they also applied massage. In the morning, her internal stress had passed. By the afternoon, she was up and dressed. In the evening of the next day, she went to the theatre. She showed no signs of further disturbance, she said. Severn anticipated a contemporary example of a brain pathologist training herself to recover from a stroke (Taylor, 2006). In these two examples of self-treatment she described, Severn's desire to apply her psychological treatment to physical injury seems problematic and may push self-reliance to an extreme. In the case of an ankle injury, she relies on her own assessment that she did not have any broken bones. In the second example, she seems unconcerned that she may have had a brain concussion. In both instances, she did not consult a physician, which seems like an irrational thing to do under the circumstances of physical injury. In self-treatment, in these instances, is she illustrating a form of self-reliance that distorts her capacity to seek out physical treatment. Severn was influenced by Christian science, which believed in non-medical treatment and self-reliance, I think, to a fault.

In the period prior to 1920, she described the self-treatment of a severe eating disorder. She disclosed the following:

> I had for years been unable to eat anything with comfort, and had been obliged to eliminate one food after another, [left with a] abstemious (austere) diet.
>
> *(Severn, 1913, pp. 51)*

She described a self-treatment, which she called "experimenting with my own sub consciousness" (Severn, 1913, p. 52). She decided to confront her serious dislike of pancakes. First, she set up a regime to deliberately eat pancakes for breakfast, which was not successful. Then Severn described her special efforts to change her neurotic behavior.

> I redoubled my efforts, and on the third day ate pancakes again, this time in peace and comfort … from that day to this, I have been free to eat what I chose at any time and whatever nature in perfect peace.
>
> *(Severn, 1913, pp. 52–53)*

Severn, without the benefit of a second party, was able to change her behavior. She does not ascribe the change to a process of insight or understanding. Rather, it was a kind of drastic behavior modification applied to her own functioning. If we examine Severn's statement "I redoubled my efforts …" (Severn, 1913, pp. 52–53), we see we have a similar kind of clinical interaction initiated during the Ferenczi/Severn analysis. In Ferenczi's report on their analysis, in his *Clinical Diary* (Ferenczi, 1988) we hear Severn's clinical functioning echoing in Ferenczi's statement about working with Severn:

> When the case did not show any progress *I redoubled my efforts*; in fact I made up my mind not to be frightened off by any difficulty, … with the help of such *extreme exertions*.

In this description of Ferenczi's clinical work with Severn, we can see the echoes of Severn's self-treatment, e.g. therapist's activity; therapist's self-disclosure; use of non-interpretative measure, and intensifying the contact.

Development of a psychological perspective as a psychotherapist

The next phase in Severn's clinical development occurred in the period of 1920 to 1925, prior to entering analysis with Ferenczi. In this period, Severn moved towards an understanding of psychology and psychoanalysis. Her developing views and methods during this third phase of her clinical career were outlined in her second book, *The Psychology of Behavior* (Severn, 1920). Severn gave a copy of this book to Ferenczi with a very sweet and poetic inscription in her own handwriting (see Foreword, p. iii).

Severn moved away from calling herself a metaphysician to using the term psychotherapist (Severn, 1920, p. 3). At this time she believed that "Modern Psychology is going to contribute to human understanding" (Severn, 1920, p. 2). In an announcement of the opening of an office for clinical practice in New York City in 1915, she listed herself as "Dr. Elizabeth Severn, Psycho–Therapist." In a lecture given in London during the same period on the topic of "Psycho–Therapy," she listed herself as "Elizabeth Severn PhD" (Rachman, 2016d). Moving away from the mystical, she believed that the task of psychotherapy was:

> to analyze and learn to handle the various and complex elements of the human mind ... [Furthermore] we now have well organized methods of psychological experiment based on careful introduction and observation ... that man is able to study his own mind ... from researches in the field of Abnormal Psychology.
>
> *(Severn, 1920, pp. 9–10)*

Development of a psychoanalytic perspective

Severn was beginning to use a psychodynamic view of treatment in her psycho-therapy period, as illustrated in the following quotation:

> A patient was confined to bed. [patient needed] mental treatment, where the ... subconscious ... is thoroughly with the healer ... so that in within an hour she got up ... entirely healed.
>
> *(Severn, 1913, p. 188)*

As Severn moved toward a psychoanalytic perspective, she took the next step and became a student of psychoanalysis through reading the work of James Jackson Putnam (1846-1918), who helped bring Freud to America for the Clark University Lectures in 1909 (Putnam, 1915). Severn clearly stated her growing intellectual interest in psychoanalysis in the following quotation:

> Taking its origin in pathological studies made by Dr. Breuer of Vienna, in 1881, and later by his brilliant successor, Dr. Freud today presents us with a

large mass of scientific observations and theories concerning human emotions and experiences [this] had a practically simultaneous birth with the more thoroughly established and invaluable works of the great psychologists, Lange [Carl George Lange, 1834-1900 (Schcoldann, J., 2011); Lange's idea was that all emotions are developed from, and can be reduced to, psychological reactions to stimulus.] William James, (1842–1910); published a similar work in 1885. This theory became known as the James – Lange theory of emotion.

(Severn, 1920)

Severn's belief in psychoanalysis becomes evident in the following statement:

All 'feelings' have in fact, their origin in the unconscious life and form the most vital part of the mental organism … all feeling as an unconscious form of thought.

(Severn, 1920, p. 25)

For the best results the work of a Psychoanalyst is indispensable. He acts as an agent or substitute upon which the patient can transfer the unconscious psychic forces.

(Severn, 1920, p. 43)

In her interview with Eissler, she described herself as a clinician who had evolved toward psychoanalysis:

psychotherapist thirty-five years ago, gradually worked my way up into psychoanalysis.

(Eissler, 1952, p. 1)

Severn was a thoughtful student of psychoanalysis, but definitely not an orthodox follower. She criticized Freudian psychology when she said:

[The] Freudian method … places too much emphasis upon the analytical process with a corresponding weakness on the constructive side.

(Severn, 1920, p. 257)

Later on in her analytic studies, when she consulted with Freud during her analysis with Ferenczi, she felt Freud was intellectually gifted, but was emotionally constricted (Eissler, 1952).

An analysand of Severn

At a symposium, focused on Elizabeth Severn as a significant figure in psychoanalysis and sponsored by The Sándor Ferenczi Center at the New School for Social Research, on September 20, 2015, in New York City, an analysand of Elizabeth Severn presented his experience of being in analysis with Severn. Jim Righter who is now in his eighties, was a 15-year-old when he was referred to Severn by his grandmother, who was a personal friend of Severn. Righter saw Severn in her New York City office at East 87th Street, Manhattan, where she had an apartment that also served as her office (see Chapter 20). Living there since the 1940s, Severn's apartment/office was an arrangement for her clinical practice that Freud had pioneered and generations of psychoanalysts both in Europe and the United States had adopted.

Righter, in his presentation, described Severn in their sessions as an old lady. Severn was 70 years old when Richter saw her in 1949. He was referred by his grandmother, as an unmotivated student who was more interested in social activities than his studies. His description of their clinical interaction in 1949 is consistent with a responsive, flexible, active analytic approach already described in Severn's stages of clinical development. Righter said Severn acted like a Freudian, who didn't say much. Apparently, she had first tried the traditional approach of free association with her adolescent analysand, but it was not helpful. Then Severn introduced the projective technique of drawing with a series of colored crayons. She asked Righter to draw whatever came to mind, with the crayons and drawing paper she provided in the sessions. He drew a series of emotionally expressive abstractions, which were an indication of the personal material that could not be expressed through the free associative method. These drawings were explored analytically after they were completed, searching for the psychological issues beneath his seemingly unresponsive exterior.

Righter was animated, enthusiastic, and positive about his therapeutic work with Severn. He gave the impression that the switch from the free association to the projective drawing method was helpful to him in becoming more engaged in the therapeutic process and expressing his underlying feelings. Righter described Severn as a positive, helpful, kind analyst (Righter, 2015).

Testimonials to Severn

Severn saved letters from her patients praising her clinical skill and her writings. Her books appear to have made a positive impression on the public. A group of these testimonials will illustrate Severn's intellectual, theoretical, and communication ability to reach people. Here is a group of letters by one such person:

October 21, 1918

Dear Doctor Severn:

I have read your book with a thrill and gratitude ... – – I did not think any woman of the day contains such a mind as your invincible philosophy ... You have changed my mental bearing and enriched me more than I can tell ...

December 3, 1918

How much independent thinking you have done, and how little you have depended on this ...you prove your science by the clarity and penetration and poise of your own finely attuned and delicate adjusted intellect.

December 11, 1918

I have re-read Psychotherapy [Severn, 1913], with added profit and admiration … you have stated profound truth in a clear and facile style … I was beating my head against stupidity. Now I see the root of all is in the minds of myself and others. The little I have achieved in life is largely due to the fact that I unconsciously followed your teaching.

Sincerely yours,

Edward Shaughnessy

(Shaughnessy, 1918 – Letters to Elizabeth Severn, October 21,
December 3 and 11, 1918. In Rachman, 2016d)

The patient Edward Shaughnessy was able to deal with his neurotic behavior by reading and re-reading Severn's first book, published in 1913, entitled *Psychotherapy: Its Doctrine and Practice*. This book outlined her extensive eclectic clinical practice from 1908 until 1913. According to the letters cited, five years after the publication of the book, an individual was able to use the material in the book as a therapeutic aid. This individual wrote a series of other letters to Severn, indicating that he had developed a very *positive transference* to Severn *at a distance*. This phenomenon, *transference at a distance*, occurs in human behavior, which can explain the phenomenon of how self-help books can become bestsellers. The authors of such books present an understanding of human behavior in a language to which lay people can relate. Individuals are also interested in receiving help with their emotional problems. Severn seems to have had this interest and capacity. One could suggest that she produced an early self-help book, before this genre became an integral part of the twentieth century.

This capacity to attract patients through her writing continued into her latter clinical days. In 1946, an individual who read her 1933 book, *Discovery of the Self* (see Image 12), wrote her a letter that indicates her popularity and capacity to project a *therapeutic presence* in person as well as in writing. The letter said:

I have recently read your book, 'Discovery of the Self' and I really believe you can help me, so I should be glad to know whether you could arrange a consultation…

(McGrum, 1946 – Letter to Elizabeth Severn, Birmingham,
England, May 25, 1946. In Rachman, 2016d)

There are also other testimonials to Severn's capacity as a therapeutic agent, which span a 35-year period of her clinical functioning. In a long, complicated letter, an individual in 1920 outlines her struggle to integrate and maintain the therapeutic help Severn had provided:

Dear Doctor Severn,

… My health is splendid … I am no longer hysterical, I can manage to love myself … I feel tearful very often but haven't indulged in a cry more than

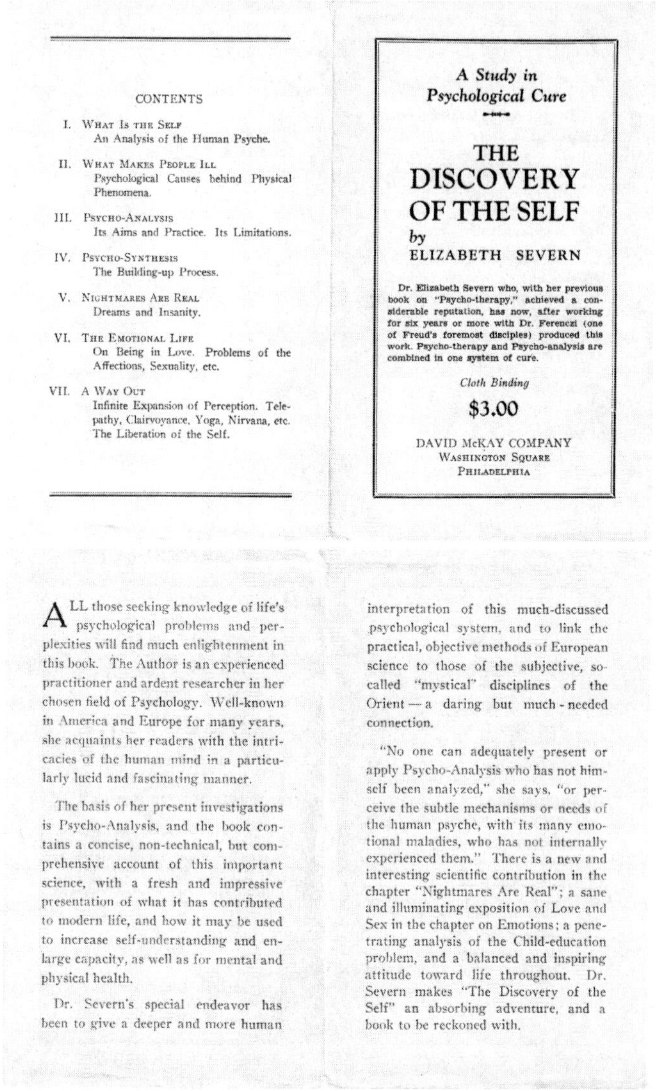

CONTENTS

I.   WHAT IS THE SELF
     An Analysis of the Human Psyche.

II. WHAT MAKES PEOPLE ILL
     Psychological Causes behind Physical
     Phenomena.

III. PSYCHO-ANALYSIS
     Its Aims and Practice. Its Limitations.

IV. PSYCHO-SYNTHESIS
     The Building-up Process.

V.   NIGHTMARES ARE REAL
     Dreams and Insanity.

VI. THE EMOTIONAL LIFE
     On Being in Love. Problems of the
     Affections, Sexuality, etc.

VII. A WAY OUT
     Infinite Expansion of Perception. Tele-
     pathy, Clairvoyance, Yoga, Nirvana, etc.
     The Liberation of the Self.

*A Study in
Psychological Cure*

THE
DISCOVERY
OF THE SELF
by
ELIZABETH SEVERN

Dr. Elizabeth Severn who, with her previous
book on "Psycho-therapy," achieved a considerable reputation, has now, after working
for six years or more with Dr. Ferenczi (one
of Freud's foremost disciples) produced this
work. Psycho-therapy and Psycho-analysis are
combined in one system of cure.

Cloth Binding

$3.00

DAVID McKAY COMPANY
WASHINGTON SQUARE
PHILADELPHIA

ALL those seeking knowledge of life's psychological problems and per-plexities will find much enlightenment in this book. The Author is an experienced practitioner and ardent researcher in her chosen field of Psychology. Well-known in America and Europe for many years, she acquaints her readers with the intri-cacies of the human mind in a particu-larly lucid and fascinating manner.

The basis of her present investigations is Psycho-Analysis, and the book con-tains a concise, non-technical, but com-prehensive account of this important science, with a fresh and impressive presentation of what it has contributed to modern life, and how it may be used to increase self-understanding and en-large capacity, as well as for mental and physical health.

Dr. Severn's special endeavor has been to give a deeper and more human interpretation of this much-discussed psychological system, and to link the practical, objective methods of European science to those of the subjective, so-called "mystical" disciplines of the Orient — a daring but much-needed connection.

"No one can adequately present or apply Psycho-Analysis who has not him-self been analyzed," she says, "or per-ceive the subtle mechanisms or needs of the human psyche, with its many emo-tional maladies, who has not internally experienced them." There is a new and interesting scientific contribution in the chapter "Nightmares Are Real"; a sane and illuminating exposition of Love and Sex in the chapter on Emotions; a pene-trating analysis of the Child-education problem, and a balanced and inspiring attitude toward life throughout. Dr. Severn makes "The Discovery of the Self" an absorbing adventure, and a book to be reckoned with.

IMAGE 12   Brochure announcing the publication of Elizabeth Severn's 1933 book, *The Discovery of the Self*

half a dozen times in the last few years. Pretty good, I think, considering at one time I had no control over myself at all. When I get depressed, I give myself a good scolding and point out to myself all my blessing … when I am out on a clear night and look at the stars, I feel soothed and comforted … I do hope I can see you for I feel sure you would say to me how well you look, you never looked so well before … have a little talk and to reas-sure you that I think you have made a complete success of my case for your work still has its effects on me … I can stand to one side and see myself from all angles … .

> I am
> Always yours faithfully
> Mathilde

(Letter from Mathilde Rochon to Elizabeth Severn, November 29, 1920, Washington, D.C. In. Rachman, 2016d)

This letter seems to indicate a positive change in the functioning in an individual, with multiple emotional issues, over years as a result of her therapy with Severn.

A fragment of another letter from Severn, when she was in her 70s and practicing psychoanalysis, indicates a very grateful former patient:

> On the whole, I feel very much more content and I think this is as it should be – My thanks go out to you every day and I'm constantly grateful for the remarkable education you have given me.
>
> With love to you and Margaret
> Phebe Cates

(Letter from Pheobe Cates, 1955 letter to Elizabeth Severn, January 12, 1955, Paris. In Rachman, 2016d)

12

THE DEVELOPMENT OF
TRAUMA ANALYSIS

The development of trauma analysis (Rachman, 2012b, 2014a, b, 2015a), which was co-created by Severn and Ferenczi, was through clinical interactions that focused on treating trauma disorder, and expanded analytic theory and clinical practice beyond the Oedipal complex and the analysis of neurotic conflict. Severn described this new kind of clinical experience, calling upon her own contributions with Ferenczi:

> [Re-living the trauma] … is an important measure which was worked out between Ferenczi and myself in the course of my own long analysis with him – a development which enabled the patient to re-live as though it were now, the traumatic past, aided by the dramatic participation of the analyst.
>
> *(Severn, 1933, pp. 93–94)*

As has been discussed, Severn's emotional problems were not of an Oedipal nature. Freud had many opportunities to introduce an alternative to the Oedipal analysis of emotional disorder in his clinical thinking about the cases of Dora/Ida Bauer and the Wolf Man/Sergei Pankejeff (see Chapter 8). However, he believed in a unitary conceptualization of emotional disorder, which was a theory of memories and its treatment. It can be questioned whether Freud's original cases were examples of Oedipal disorders. These cases can also be seen as instances of trauma disorder due to childhood sexual abuse, which produced borderline personality disorder. Did Freud develop the Oedipal theory for neurosis because he had different kinds of analysands than Ferenczi? Or were there differences in their clinical attitude and responsiveness. Ferenczi's open, emotionally active, and dramatic interaction was in contrast to Freud's intellectual and austere interaction. Freud's analysands did not seem to challenge the analyst, ask for certain kind of responses, or be critical of the analyst's functioning. It is clear from interviews with the Wolf Man/Sergei Pankejeff years after his analyses with Freud and Brunswick (see Chapter 8) that Pankejeff was critical of the analyses and the analysts, but never voiced these negative views directly to Freud or Brunswick. Ferenczi, however, created a clinical atmosphere where an analysand could express his/her negative or positive feelings, as well as ask for a particular kind of response from the analyst.

In analyzing Severn, Ferenczi was presented with an individual who suffered from emotional issues beyond a neurotic disorder, more in the range of a borderline condition. In addition, as was revealed in her analysis with Ferenczi, the origin of her borderline disorder was severe childhood traumas, which were never uncovered in Severn's three previous attempts at psychoanalysis. Ferenczi was familiar with the analysis of difficult cases like Severn, whose psychopathology and personality disorder presented unusual circumstances for the analytic process and the analyst. In fact, Severn was beyond being an example of a difficult case, because she had her own unique personality characteristics that added to the challenge of her analyses. She was intellectually, emotionally, and interpersonally assertive; had three failed analyses before seeing Ferenczi; was desperate to solve her severe depression and suicidal feelings; was determined to contribute to her analysis (see Chapters 9 and 10); and was an experienced and innovative clinician, in her own right, before she joined Ferenczi (Severn, 1913, 1920; see Chapter 11).

Reconstructing the Ferenczi/Severn analysis

The description of the stages of the trauma analysis that developed between Ferenczi and Severn was reconstructed from Ferenczi's report of this clinical interaction contained in the *Clinical Diary* (Ferenczi, 1988), which he wrote in 1932. At the time of writing, he was struggling with the analysis ending as well as with his own vulnerability, as he was in the terminal stages of pernicious anemia (Rachman, 1997a). Ferenczi was in a period of denial, which did not allow him to confront either issue (see Chapter 18). The *Clinical Diary* was not published in his lifetime or in Freud's, or in his student and successor Michal Balint's lifetime, because the description of Ferenczi's clinical work was considered so far out of the mainstream of traditional psychoanalysis that it would further damage Ferenczi's reputation (Balint, 1969a, pp. 219–220). Ferenczi knew his descriptions of theoretical deviations and clinical innovations would further alienate him from Freud. What is more, Freud would not accept the analysis of a trauma disorder as Ferenczi described it in the *Clinical Diary*. Freud only wanted to maintain the Oedipal complex as the cornerstone of psychoanalysis (Rachman, 2012a). Freud's concern was Ferenczi's inspiration. Severn was suffering from a trauma disorder rather than an Oedipal conflict, and she helped Ferenczi to understand that her childhood traumas were the source of her psychopathology. I have discerned five stages in the Ferenczi/Severn analysis.

Stage one: early feelings of antipathy

Ferenczi harbored negative feelings toward Severn in the early period of their analysis, which he described as antipathy in the *Clinical Diary*. These negative feelings as Ferenczi described them were:

1. [Severn had] excessive independence and self-assurance.
2. Immensely strong-willed reflected by a marble-like rigidity of her facial features.
3. "Altogether a somewhat sovereign [look] of a queen, or even the royal imperiousness of a king – all these characteristics that one cannot call feminine" (Ferenczi, 1988, pp. 96–97).

As we shall see as we continue on with the description of the analysis, Ferenczi struggled with the awareness of confronting this negative countertransference reaction to Severn:

> Instead of making myself aware of these impressions I appear to proceed on the principle that as the doctor I must be in a positive or superior position in every case. Overcoming my obvious apprehensions when faced with such a woman, I appear to have assumed, perhaps unconsciously, the attitude of superiority of my intrepid masculinity, which the patient took to be genuine, whereas this was a conscious professional pose, partly adapted as a defensive measure against anxiety,
>
> *(Ferenczi, 1988, p. 97)*

In Stage Five, the analysis of the countertransference will be outlined. Until this analysis was fully implemented, the Ferenczi/Severn analysis could not reach the working-through stage in Severn's clinical experience. Unfortunately, because of Ferenczi's death, the analysis was never able to proceed toward the working-through stage (see Chapter 22).

Stage two: unfolding the transference

The analysis was an intense emotional, interpersonal, and intellectual struggle as Severn acted out her emotional issues as well as expressed her need to participate in her analysis. Ferenczi's clinical attitude of openness, emotionality, and empathy allowed Severn to fully express both her transference reactions and assertiveness. He described how Severn suffered for weeks from lack of sleep and breathing difficulties. She was enraged with Ferenczi and the analysis. She was angry and dissatisfied because the analysis returned her to her childhood traumas or shocks (see Chapter 10). Severn began the analysis feeling that she was functioning under a black cloud. She knew there was something buried underneath her emotional struggle (Eissler, 1952). The joint enterprise of Severn's dedication to being healed of her severe emotional wounds and Ferenczi's openness in providing a holding environment for her traumas helped unfold the recall of the memories connected with the emotional, physical, and sexual abuse by Severn's father (see Chapter 10). The analysis of this childhood trauma opened up old wounds for Severn as she expressed her hurt by:

> Swearing and screaming during the entire session, accusation, insults, etc., she insists I should admit my helplessness, finally she even has the idea that I should repeat the trauma if it will only help.
>
> *(Ferenczi, 1988, p. 156)*

As Ferenczi struggled to understand and analyze Severn, she did not let up in her complaints about his functioning:

> [Severn has] … complaints about the absence of the degree of interest and sympathy, even love, that alone give her confidence in my ability to glue her lacerated soul into a whole.
>
> *(Ferenczi, 1988, p. 155)*

Ferenczi felt assaulted by Severn's outbursts and assaults on his personal and clinical functioning. It triggered hurt, self-doubt, and confusion in Ferenczi: in fact, this dynamic of Severn fully expressing her dissatisfactions with her analyst's functioning was a very important expression in the transference relationship of her childhood traumas with her father. As the analysis helped unfold the retrieval of her father's horrific abuse of her as a child, and as she emotionally relived the pain of that abuse, she yearned for Ferenczi to become her idealized positive father figure. Ferenczi was caught in an emotional dilemma, empathically responding to her need for a reparative father figure (Rachman, 1998) and feeling self-critical when he did not seem to satisfy Severn. Her needs, demands, and expression of dissatisfaction was a great challenge for Ferenczi, but he was willing to accept it. Of the pioneers of psychoanalysis in the Freud/Ferenczi era what other of this group would have met the challenge of analyzing Severn? Ferenczi's dilemma of feeling inadequate in his capacity to satisfy Severn's need for a totally reparative therapeutic experience highlighted the issue of a countertransference reaction, an analytic dynamic neglected in the era in which the Severn analysis was conducted. One of the significant contributions this clinical interaction made to the evolution of psychoanalysis was embracing countertransference analysis as a necessary psychodynamic in the psychoanalytic encounter and relationship.

Stage three: analysis of the analyst, countertransference analysis

Severn can be credited with a new perspective for the function of countertransference in the psychoanalytic encounter. As has been discussed, the introduction of the countertransference reaction by Freud was seen as a negative event in the analysis. The implication was that the analyst had made a mistake and needed to correct it, as soon as possible, so that the analysis could proceed. Countertransference reactions should be a secret of psychoanalysis, as Freud conveyed to Jung (McGuire, 1974). This negative connotation toward countertransference was translated into an interesting compromise for analytic candidates in their training. In my training days of the 1960s, it was implied that candidates for graduation should include, in the case study, or control case, a brief paragraph about the analyst's countertransference issue. I emphasize the concept of issue, *not issues*. The standard that emerged from this view of countertransference was limited. The candidate should demonstrate that he/she knew the meaning that countertransference should play a minor role. A candidate should not focus on the importance that countertransference played in your clinical work and control case, or elaborate on a variety of ways countertransference played a role in the control analysis. Any exaggerated write-up of countertransference would demonstrate to the evaluation committee that the candidate was emotionally unstable and unfit to be an analyst. When, as a candidate, I examined previous case studies to gain an understanding of an acceptable case study write-up, all such case studies contained only a one-paragraph statement of countertransference.

The Severn/Ferenczi analysis was a deviation from this limited view of countertransference. In actuality, it turned the countertransference reaction, as it was first conceived, into the *analysis of the analyst*. It is clear that Ferenczi was remiss in not initiating the analysis of his negative countertransference reaction towards Severn. He paid his greatest emphasis in the clinical interaction in diagnosing retrieving and analyzing Severn's childhood trauma. This constituted a major effort, since it was likely that a trauma analysis was never previously accomplished. Was he so concentrated on understanding Severn's trauma and searching for therapeutic ways to respond, *which, as yet, had not been devised*, that he lost touch with his own subjective experiences? Ferenczi's negative feelings toward Severn may have interfered with a capacity to examine his own subjectivity. For example, my colleague Paul Mattick and I have suggested that in a re-evaluation of the Dora case/Ida Bauer (Rachman & Mattick, 2009, 2012), we felt that Freud was overwhelmed by a countertransference reaction to Bauer's need for empathy. We argued that Ida Bauer revealed her sexual abuse by Herr K. and maternal deprivation experiences to Freud, which he did not include in the analysis. Bauer, who suffered from some serious psychological symptoms that could be linked to her actual traumas, needed to experience empathic understanding rather than Oedipal interpretations. Was Freud emotionally blind to the sexual trauma. Reflecting on Bauer's premature termination of the analysis, Freud wondered if he should have considered giving her the empathy for which she asked.

There were two other very important impediments to Ferenczi's neglect of his countertransference reaction. The two difficulties that evaded Ferenczi's consciousness during the Severn analysis were his growing alienation from Freud and his deteriorating physical health. During the years from 1930 to 1933, when Ferenczi was struggling in the analysis with Severn, he withdrew from Freud because he knew his work with Severn and other trauma survivors would lead to severe criticism and rejection (Rachman, 1997b) once Ferenczi began to devote himself to only treating trauma disorders and introduced non-interpretative methods to treat these cases (Rachman, Kennedy & Yard, 2005, 2009). Freud felt he was acting out against him and rejecting psychoanalysis (Gay, 1984; Rachman, 1997a, b). Having to cut himself off from the most important person in his professional and personal life was extremely painful for Ferenczi. He did this not out of anger, rivalry, or competition, but to protect himself from rejection and even from professional and personal annihilation. If one examines Fromm's report of the last meeting between Ferenczi and Freud over the presentation of his controversial paper "The Confusion of Tongues" (Ferenczi, 1980k), we can feel the hurt, agony, and pain Ferenczi suffered when Freud rejected him in such a mean-spirited way (Fromm, 1959). Freud's naked rejection in that moment in August of 1933 verified that Ferenczi was astute in protecting himself from emotional harm. But such moments and the ones which preceded them, e.g. the campaign to convince Ferenczi not to present his Confusion of Tongues paper at the Wiesbaden Congress (Rachman, 1997a, b) so flooded Ferenczi's psychic functioning that he became preoccupied with feeling rejected by Freud. He performed the analysis with Severn under the emotional strain of feeling Freud and the orthodox community believed he was not performing psychoanalysis and should be suppressed in doing his brand of therapy (Eissler, 1952). Ferenczi's difficulty in examining his countertransference may be related to his preoccupation with Freud's rejection that he could not tolerate opening himself open to self-criticism. In the Severn analysis, Ferenczi turned to Severn and his Hungarian colleagues for empathy and affirmation.

Finally, Ferenczi's clinical functioning in the analysis of Severn was also influenced by his ailing health. During the period of struggling with understanding and responding to Severn's needs in 1930–33, Ferenczi was entering the terminal phase of his physical and emotional struggle with pernicious anemia (Rachman, 1997a), which took his life on May 22, 1933. It is meaningful to speculate that Ferenczi's emotional functioning was clouded with his anxiety about the condition of his health. What is more, he did not confront his illness or share his vulnerability with Severn (Eissler, 1952). It is likely Ferenczi's reluctance to face his impending demise was relevant to his not examining his countertransference. He didn't want to match his physical vulnerability with emotional vulnerability. Redoubling his efforts to cure Severn of her traumas was in his eyes a way to maintain his emotional strength.

Stage four: mutual analysis

The experience of mutual analysis was a struggle for both Ferenczi and Severn, since it signaled such a remarkable departure from psychoanalytic thinking and behavior. Mutual analysis was Severn's idea. She realized that Ferenczi could not identify and analyze his negative countertransference reaction, which was interfering with an empathic response to her, thereby creating an impasse in the therapeutic relationship. Her familiarity with the psychoanalytic process from her previous analysis as well as her own theoretical studies informed her of this as an issue. What is more, Ferenczi seemed to be functioning in this analysis without any awareness that his own subjectivity was a causal factor in the impasse between them. It was necessary, in this instance, for the analysand to take the lead in identifying the psychodynamic in the analytic difficulty. As Dupont (1988) has pointed out, the analytic process has a shadowy area that needs to become known to the analyst. The analyst needs to be open to learning from the patient (Casement, 1985). This is what Ferenczi faced in responding to Severn's suggestions that he allow her to analyze him so that his countertransference reaction could become part of the analytic process. His struggle to accept this suggestion became a blueprint for a two-person psychology for psychoanalysis (Aron, 1990).

As Ferenczi stated in his *Clinical Diary* (Ferenczi, 1988), the mutual process was: "a transformation of mutual analysis into simply being analyzed" (Ferenczi, 1988, p. 71). This process was anything but simple. Severn and Ferenczi spent over a year negotiating the practical details of taking turns being analyst and analysand:

> ... who should begin, each offered to let the other go first; (the total period of two hours was strictly adhered to); I thereby had to return, somewhat shame-facedly, to the analysand's earlier suggestion that I let myself be analyzed completely *first* before proceeding with analysis. Not without a certain feeling of depression and shame.
>
> *(Ferenczi, 1988, pp. 71–72)*

As Ferenczi alluded to in the discussions of the particular arrangements for mutual analysis, he suffered intense emotional difficulties in negotiating his surrender to Severn. This struggle in 1932 involved intense feelings of shame, humiliation:

> It had already cost me considerable effort to acknowledge the fact of our being equals in mutual analysis, and now the plan for a one-sided analysis of me by the analysand meant further degradation, or humiliation.
>
> *(Ferenczi, 1988, p. 72)*

One of the most difficult issues for Ferenczi to accept was clearly stated by him:

> I had to demote myself to the position of a child (Ich musste zum Kinde degradieren) and recognize the analysand as the authority keeping watch over me.
>
> *(Ferenczi, 1988, p. 72)*

No sooner had Ferenczi decided to surrender and allow himself to become Severn's equal than he developed a severe headache. Ferenczi did not allow his psychosomatic reaction to prevent him from going through with the mutual analysis. In fact, he revealed the depths of his anxiety.

The actual fear of being analyzed is the fear of being dependent.

(Ferenczi, 1988, p. 73)

In order to conquer the anxiety of losing his sense of authority, status, and control as an analyst Ferenczi needed to feel he could surrender to an analysand in whom he felt confidence:

So long as I do not have the full confidence ... I cannot surrender myself into his [her] power.

(Ferenczi, 1988, p. 73)

Ferenczi knew that the countertransference analysis was necessary even though he did not initiate it:

analyzing the analyst so that all potentially dangerous impulses, or at least all neurotic impediments to comprehension (which could lead to error) are allowed to become clearly manifest in the analysis ... that the other's understanding is free from complexes.

(Ferenczi, 1988, p. 73)

Stage five: the retrieval and analysis of Ferenczi's childhood sexual trauma

The Severn/Ferenczi mutual analysis produced a remarkable discovery. In helping Ferenczi analyze his countertransference reaction to her, she helped him to fully uncover the origin of his negative feelings toward her. Ferenczi was aware of the limitations in his own analysis with Freud, which he felt did not analyze his negative transference. In a letter dated January 20, 1930, Freud defended himself by replying that the issue of negative transferences was not known well enough and that there was not sufficient time in their short analysis (initially, three weeks in duration) (Falzeder, Brabant & Giampieri-Deutsch, 2000). If the analysand is aware of negative countertransference in the therapeutic relationship, isn't it the analyst's responsibility to also respond? Not responding to negative transference creates an illusion and invalidates the analysand's experience. Empathy is also missing in not responding. Freud's reaction to Ferenczi's criticism of his functioning as an analyst is contrasted with Severn's criticism of Ferenczi. In the example we are discussing, Severn's insistence that Ferenczi needed to examine his own functioning because it was causing the therapeutic impasse, was met by Ferenczi, eventually, as he struggled to understand it and, eventually, was able to respond to it in an empathic way. Once he decided to surrender to Severn, feeling he could trust her with his own emotional life, Ferenczi joined her in fully analyzing his childhood trauma.

When Severn took turns being Ferenczi's analyst, he began to develop insight into his negative feelings to Severn. From February 24, 1932 to May 5, 1932, Ferenczi's and Severn's clinical interaction produced a series of insights for Ferenczi, chronicled in his *Clinical Diary* and outlined in the following sequence (Rachman, 2010a, 2012b, 2014a, b, 2015a):

1. "[In] RN [Severn] I find my mother again, namely the real one, who was hard and energetic and of whom *I am afraid. RN knows this*" (Ferenczi, 1988, p. 45 – Clinical Entry, February 24, 1932, italics added).

As he began to develop insights into his countertransference reaction, Ferenczi went deeper into the countertransference analysis and a remarkable event occurred:

2. "I submerged myself deeply in the reproduction of the infantile experience; the most evocative image was the vague appearance of female figures, probably servant girls from earliest childhood" (Ferenczi, 1988, pp. 60–61 – Clinical Entry, March 17, 1932).

Ferenczi was going to analyze his countertransference reaction to rock bottom. The recovery of childhood memories began the process of analyzing the origins of Ferenczi's negative feelings toward women. What emerged was a *recovered memory of child abuse*:

3. [a] mad fantasy of being pressed into this wound in the corpse.
4. "a house maid probably allowed me to play with her breasts but then pressed my head between her legs … I became frightened and felt I was suffocating" (Ferenczi, 1988, p. 61 – Clinical Entry, March 17, 1932).

As the countertransference encounter between Ferenczi and Severn continued, he was helped to developed insight into his negative reaction toward women:

5. "This is the source of my hatred of females. I want to dissect them for it, that is, to kill them" (Ferenczi, 1988, p. 61 – Clinical Entry, March 17, 1932).

This led to the insight about the emotional connection between his mother and Severn:

6. "The patient's demands to be loved corresponded to the analogous demands on me by my mother. I did hate the patient, in spite of all the friendliness I displayed" (Ferenczi, 1988, p. 99 – Clinical Entry, May 5, 1932).

Ferenczi also developed the awareness that Severn's negative reaction to him and their impasse was a transferential enactment of the original trauma that she suffered in her childhood with her father.

7. "… This was what she was aware of to which she reacted with the same inaccessibility that had finally forced her criminal father to renounce her" (Ferenczi, 1988, p. 99 – Clinical Entry, May 5, 1932).

In a four-month period, Ferenczi and Severn analyzed Ferenczi's countertransference reaction of negative feeling towards women and retrieved his childhood sexual abuse. Ferenczi reported that the mutual analytic encounter produced a diminution in the previously intractable erotic transference so that a more traditional analytic interaction could be reinstated. However, Ferenczi recommended that mutual analysis should only be used as a last resort. Ferenczi realized that there were limitations to encouraging analyst vulnerability and there were times that the analyst needed to assert his/her authority to help the analysand. Becoming attuned to the subjectivity of the analysand did not mean relinquishing the mandate of the analyst to give direction and meaning to the analysis (Rachman, 2012b). Ferenczi credited Severn with a significant contribution to overcoming their therapeutic impasse. In essence, the most helpful clinical behavior was Severn's attunement to Ferenczi's subjectivity (Rachman, 2010a). Finally, Ferenczi self-disclosed his appreciation to Severn:

8. "... [Severn said] her analysis would never make any progress until I allowed her to analyze those hidden feelings in me. I had resisted for approximately a year but then I decided to make this sacrifice" (Ferenczi, 1988, p. 99 – Entry, May 5, 1932).

Stage six: changes in the analysand and the analyst

After much analytic work, Ferenczi reported a change in Severn's attitude toward him:

> [W]ith particular gentleness; the analysis even enables her to transform her own hardness into friendly softness.
>
> *(Ferenczi, 1988, pp. 43–44)*

Severn's positive reaction to Ferenczi was not transitory. Ferenczi reported a new way of relating by Severn:

> I was received with a radiant face and a conciliatory gesture: numerous apologies for having provoked and infuriated me through lack of self-control.
>
> *(Ferenczi, 1988, p. 48)*

Ferenczi was able to use the newly developed atmosphere to explore and decipher levels of the Severn's trauma to move the analysis toward individuation, separation, and termination:

> As the final act, following deep catharsis, I imagine a period of reconciliation and finally separation ... with the feeling of being delivered from traumatic fixation ... from emotions of a compulsive nature with regard to love and hate. The traumatically oriented character ceases to exist, and the other, natural aspects of the personality are able to unfold.
>
> *(Ferenczi, 1988, pp. 49–50)*

Ferenczi reported an essential change in Severn as a result of his self-disclosures:

> Once I had openly admitted the limitation of my capacity, she even began to reduce her demands on me.
>
> *(Ferenczi, 1988, p. 99)*

Ferenczi believed the changes in Severn's functioning would continue:

> [T]hen the former disintegration and consequently the tending to project (insanity) will in fact be mutually reversed.
>
> *(Ferenczi, 1988, p. 159)*

13

ANALYZING THE FERENCZI/ SEVERN ANALYSIS

One of the most comprehensive, thoughtful, and critical evaluations of the Ferenczi/Severn relationship has been made by Maroda (1998). This criticism is based upon the evaluation of the analysis as a malignant regression caused by Ferenczi's indulgences of Severn's demands for all of her unresolved developmental needs to be met. Ferenczi, Maroda also believed, did not honestly share his countertransference feelings with Severn, which also impeded the therapeutic relationship. These criticisms actually focused on the last years of the analysis when the controversial method of mutual analysis was one of the therapeutic focuses, and Severn was in an emotional turmoil. Ferenczi was also struggling with intense physical and emotional problems. The prior seven years of the analysis were not part of Maroda's evaluation.

Maroda (1998) implied that the Ferenczi/Severn analysis could be used as a blueprint for a failed analysis. She also admits there are special considerations in a very difficult case like Severn:

1. "knowing how to establish and regulate therapeutic levels of regression ... *remains a significant challenge*";
2. "managing *countertransference when ... persons have a traumatic history can be likened to lion-taming for its level of difficulty*";
3. "a certain degree of reliving of the original trauma – this time with a different outcome";
4. "*a certain* degree *of gratification is necessary for some patients*";
5. "some physical contact may be therapeutic";
6. "how do we decide on how much and when."

(Maroda, 1998, p. 122, italics added)

Unfortunately, the title of the Maroda paper, "Why Mutual Analysis Failed," I believe, encouraged a very negative tone to the evaluation of the analysis, and disregards its pioneering, experimental nature. Maroda said: "Ferenczi's work with R.N. in psychoanalysis proved our worst fears that indulging a demanding patient will only result in greater demands and malignant regression" (Maroda, 1998, p. 122). As will be discussed in latter chapters, Severn's recovery and personal growth after the analysis indicate a more positive picture. What is more, Ferenczi and Severn's analysis was not about mutual analysis, but about pioneering an analysis of trauma.

Ferenczi's clinical experiments in need satisfaction and mutual analysis raised the issue of balancing gratification with analytic understanding in the treatment of trauma disorders. During the analysis of Severn, Ferenczi introduced a new, liberal concept of clinical functioning in psychoanalysis:

> I encouraged my colleagues to train students to a greater liberty and a freer expression in behavior of their aggressive feelings toward the physicians … I urged analysts to be more humble-minded in their attitude to their patients and to admit the mistakes they made, and I pleaded for *a greater elasticity in technique even if it meant the sacrifice of some of our theories.*
>
> *(Ferenczi, 1988 l, p. 113, italics added)*

This new clinical philosophy lead Ferenczi to develop the concept of *nachgiebigkeit*, originally translated as "indulgence." I have suggested this Ferenczian term's truer meaning is captured in the above-cited quotation, namely *elasticity* rather than indulgence (Rachman, 1997a, pp. 301–302). Ferenczi's innovation was to elasticize analytic response to meet the analysand's need and not be imprisoned by theoretical dogma. He believed in changing the compulsion to respond with interpretation. Interestingly enough, this clinical attitude of flexibility was shared by Kohut, who is credited with saying: "Wear your theory lightly." The idea was that responding in the direction of the analysand's needs was preferable to imposing a preconceived direction on how to respond to an analysand based on a preconceived theoretical framework. Balancing gratification with understanding remains an important issue in clinical psychoanalysis.

Ferenczi shared the analysis with Severn, as it was unfolding, with his closest colleague, student, and successor to the Hungarian Society of Psychoanalysis, Michael Balint. Balint (1992/1968) understood that the analysis was a clinical experiment in treating a severe trauma disorder. He said that Ferenczi was aware of the enormous difficulty that Severn presented as an analysand. As Ferenczi outlined in his *Clinical Diary* (Ferenczi, 1988), he first tried traditional analytic methods such as interpretation and dream analysis. Not only did these methods have limited effect, but Severn severely criticized Ferenczi for bombarding her with interpretations. Severn felt the interpretations interfered with her need to explore her inner space to contact her childhood traumas. As will be discussed in Chapter 22, Ferenczi had to work on understanding Severn's idea of a "semi-trance session," which she developed to retrieve her childhood traumas. Severn's protests against interpretation took the form of expressing feelings of frustration and anger in such a dramatic way that Ferenczi felt he needed to stop his interpretative behavior, listen carefully to Severn's subjective experience, and contemplate re-evaluating his clinical functioning. This process led to an important change in the analysis. Ferenczi came to believe empathic understanding of Severn's expressed need to explore her trauma took precedence over interpreting her resistance. Balint (1992/1968) was told by Ferenczi that he devised the analysis with Severn with the idea of it being a "grand experiment." As Balint observed, the experiment was successful but not complete. Balint concluded that Severn improved significantly but was not cured. (How many analysands, including those who have gone through training analysis, can be considered to be fully cured?) Moreover, the new data in the present volume indicates that Severn made a positive recovery after termination of the analysis (see Chapter 20).

Traditional psychoanalysis has wrestled with Ferenczi's introduction of activity and non-interpretative measures from their inception (Rachman, 1997a, b, 2003a). Freud accepted Ferenczi's introduction of activity and clinical empathy (Rachman, 1997a). But it was the use of non-interpretative measures in the analysis of Severn that caused controversy. A traditional analyst, Kurt Eissler, first became a mediator for a rapprochement between Ferenczi's innovations and traditional psychoanalysis. In his now famous parameters paper, Eissler tried to integrate Ferenczi's innovative work with difficult cases into traditional psychoanalysis by making the following declaration:

> for most patients the treatment can be carried out without any special activity on the part of either doctor or patient, and even in those cases in which one has to proceed more actively the interference should be restricted as much as possible. As soon as the stagnation of the analysis, the only justification for the only motive of the modification, is overcome, the expert will immediately resume the passively receptive attitude most favorable for the efficient cooperation of the doctor's unconscious.
>
> *(Eissler, 1953, p. 198)*

Eissler formulated four principles that must be followed if a parameter is to be employed in a psychoanalysis.

1. A parameter is introduced only when interpretative psychoanalysis has been used and is insufficient.
2. The parameter should only contain a minimum level of activity.
3. A parameter must be self-eliminating. It should not exist during the final phase of an analysis.
4. The parameter must be able to be eliminated by interpretation.

(Eissler, 1953, p. 198)

It is clear that Eissler was making a minimal concession to the difficulties of analyzing a difficult case like Severn. Freud was more understanding of such difficulties than Eissler, when he endorsed Ferenczi's introduction of activity into psychoanalysis (Rachman, 1997a). It was clear to analysts who were regularly working with narcissistic, severely neurotic, character disorder and borderline cases that Eissler's idea of parameters was too restrictive a clinical perspective to analyze difficult cases.

Stone (1954), realizing this deficiency, developed the idea of *widening the scope of psychoanalysis*. He reasoned:

> [There] are very sick personalities who, to the very end of analytic experience, may require occasional and subtle or minimal emotional or technical concessions from the analyst in the same sense that they will carry with them into their outside lives, vestiges of ego defects or medications, which, while not completely undone, are – let us say – vastly improved.
>
> *(Stone, 1954, p. 576)*

Stone realized that there were very special considerations in the treatment of borderline conditions. Evoking Ferenczi's original ideas, Stone understood the emotional strain on the analyst:

> [T]he decisive factor is the ability to stand the emotional strains of the powerful tormentor and tormenting transference and potential countertransference situations which such cases are liable to present over long periods, without giving up hope, or sometimes, alternatively, the severe acting out which borderline patients may exhibit on the other alternative to intercurrent clinical psychosis.
>
> *(Stone, 1954, p. 587)*

As if Stone was talking about working with Severn, he said:

> Another consideration in our field is the analyst himself ... a therapist must be able to love a psychotic or a delinquent and be at least warmly interested in the borderline patient ... for the optimum results ... their 'transferences' require new objects, the only ones having been destroyed or permanently repudiated.
>
> *(Stone, 1954, pp. 592–593)*

Although, the post-pioneering perspectives in psychoanalysis integrated the modifications of the Ferenczi/Severn clinical experience, it was usually not acknowledged. The Object Relation perspective was developed with Balint as the conduit from Ferenczi. Winnicott in his clinical work and theorizing believed:

> [M]any patients cannot dare to express their hurts or their needs until some part of these needs are in some symbols.
>
> *(Winnicott, 1958, p. 132)*

Kohut (1977) had expressed some interest in the issue of gratification and its role in building self-structure. His idea of *transmitting internalizations* is a form of providing recognition of the analysand's need for fulfilling development needs. The problem with Kohut's formulation and the colleagues who try to clarify or explain it is that they wrapped the idea in Freudian terms, so that Kohut will not appear to be a dissident like Ferenczi. Additionally, Kohut is revered as a psychoanalytic pioneer who introduced a new contemporary framework. Many of his followers repeat his omission by not acknowledging that Kohut had antecedents in the evolution of psychoanalysis that were not acknowledged, such as Ferenczi (Rachman, 1989). Nevertheless, Kohut can be seen as acknowledging that the analysis of severe neurosis and borderline disorders needs to address the issues of emotional deficits and subsequent gratification. Miller (1985) illustrated Kohut's clinical empathic approach in supervision.

Although the Severn/Ferenczi analysis had been characterized as an example of the imbalance between gratification and understanding, which does not allow for personal growth (Maroda, 1998), the data from Severn's recovery after the termination of her analysis with Ferenczi showed positive findings (see Chapter 20). In Severn's assessment of her analysis, she did not criticize Ferenczi for any clinical behavior (Eissler, 1952). Severn indicated that she was ready to leave Ferenczi, when she was prematurely terminated because of his illness. She felt emotionally exhausted and financially strapped. Her desire to terminate from Ferenczi indicates she was in touch with the reality of the difficulty in the therapeutic relationship and its limitations. She did not cling to Ferenczi, as if, the termination would mean she could not go on with her life without him. What is more, after leaving Ferenczi, she recovered from the malignant regression experience, publishing a book shortly after arriving in Paris to live with her daughter. She returned to a clinical practice, gave lectures, and enjoyed a social life with her daughter, Margaret, and friends. At the time of the Eissler/Severn Interview in December of 1952, she seemed to be a thoughtful, emotionally sound, assertive individual who discussed her experiences with Ferenczi, her consultations with Freud, and her understanding of psychoanalysis with clarity and insight. These positive changes in her functioning do not substantiate Maroda's idea that the Ferenczi/Severn interaction was an example of a failed analysis. Although I would agree that the issues of malignant regression and countertransference analysis are valid (see Chapters 15, 16, 17, and 22). Severn's recovery after termination indicates the analysis with Ferenczi did provide a therapeutic vehicle for her to recognize, work on, and resolve some important aspects of her trauma disorder.

Ferenczi pointed the way to the analysis of what were originally called difficult cases, which then were identified as narcissistic, character, borderline psychotic disorders. The analysis with Severn helped clarify that these difficult cases were trauma disorders. Ferenczi and Severn pointed the way toward the analysis of trauma and the necessity for the use of non-interpretative measures (Rachman, 2014a, b, 2015a, b, c). Balint (1992/1968) integrated Ferenczi's clinical experiment with Severn into the theoretical framework of the Object Relations perspectives. Balint and other analysands and students of Ferenczi, such as Clara Thompson, modified Ferenczi's experimental idea of gratification (Green, 1964; Thompson, 1964).

Of course, we need to clearly acknowledge and believe that an analyst can never become the agent for the full satisfaction of unfulfilled childhood needs. This would not be psychoanalytic therapy. The focus of an analysis is *good enough gratification*, so that a deprived trauma survivor can experience a process of empathy, trust, and necessary fulfillment. A relief from deprivation allows for the possibility of analyzing the childhood traumas. In infancy before separation and individuation an infant needs to have basic needs fulfilled before a sense of self and mastery develops. A parent needs to be experienced as a nurturing figure, so that they can know someone will be their *cry for help*. If a child approaches individuation from an experience of deprivation, parental deprivation will be incorporated into the self. In seriously deprived individuals an expressed need for fulfillment should not automatically be seen as a resistance to working through conflicts. What Severn and Ferenczi gave us from their interaction is the two-person experience in the psychoanalytic encounter. Analyst and analysand negotiate the issue of need gratification so that recovering from trauma is balanced with empathy and understanding.

14

THE RULE OF EMPATHY

Ferenczi and Severn's contribution

With the following words, Ferenczi formally introduced clinical empathy into psychoanalysis:

> I have come to the conclusion that it is above all a question of psychological tact whether or when one should tell the patient some particular thing, when what he has produced should be considered sufficient to draw conclusions, in what form these should be presented to the patient, how one should react to an unexpected or bewildering reaction on the patient's part, when one should keep silent and await a further associations and at what point the further maintenance of silence would result only in causing the patient useless suffering, etc. As you see, using the word 'tact' has enabled me only to reduce the uncertainty to a simple and appropriate formula. *But what is 'tact'? The answer is not very difficult. It is the capacity for empathy.*
>
> *... This empathy will protect us from unnecessarily stimulating the patient's resistance or doing so at the wrong moment ... But its tactless infliction [pain] by the analyst would only give the patient the unconsciously deeply desired opportunity of withdrawing himself from his influence.*
>
> All these precautions give the patient the impression of good will on the analyst's part, through the respect that the latter shows for the former's feelings ...
>
> *(Ferenczi, 1980h, pp. 89–90, italics added)*

I believe it is important to clearly establish Ferenczi's contribution in introducing clinical empathy into psychoanalysis. Traditional psychoanalysis has ignored Ferenczi's pioneering contribution to empathy (Pigman, 1995), and successfully practiced *Todschweigen* (see Chapter 7), so that the concept of clinical empathy, as developed by Ferenczi, was removed from the analytic literature. There has also been an additional, more subtle version of *Todschweigen*, which was initiated by Heinz Kohut (Rachman, 1989). In Kohut's ignoring Ferenczi as a progenitor, he added to the neglect of Ferenczi in the same way as the practice of *Todschweigen* had accomplished. But, when I asked John Gedo (1988), an early collaborator of Kohut, whether Kohut was acquainted with Ferenczi's work, he told me Kohut had read all of Ferenczi's work. In fact, Gedo said that Kohut was asked in the 1960s, to review Ferenczi's work for the German journal, *Psyche*, which he turned over to Gedo (Gedo, 1968). Did Kohut give the Ferenczi article to Gedo because he didn't want to be associated with Ferenczi, a dissident? I asked Gedo why, if Kohut knew Ferenczi's work so well that he was asked to write a review, Kohut didn't ever refer to Ferenczi's Elasticity Paper as a precursor to his work on empathy? Gedo said this was an issue for him, that Kohut did not give credit to others and claimed ideas for himself. This speculation and opinion about Kohut further fueled my desire to contribute to the undoing of the *Todschweigen* experience for Ferenczi, that Kohut had developed by creating the impression that he alone had introduced empathy into psychoanalysis. However, there were some attempts during Kohut's lifetime to appreciate Ferenczi in the Psychology of the Self-Perspective. Michael Basch (1984) made a heroic attempt to acknowledge Ferenczi as a precursor to self-psychology. Robert Stolorow (1976), clearly stated that Kohut's work on empathy had its roots in Carl Rogers' earlier work in the 1940s and 50s. Unfortunately, neither article seemed to make an inroad in changing the accepted idea in psychoanalysis and self-psychology that empathy in psychoanalysis began with Ferenczi, rather than Kohut.

In 1988, I was a participant in a panel on empathy with Anna Ornstein at the American Academy of Psychoanalysis Conference in New York City. My panel contribution was that Kohut and the followers had completely overlooked the contributions of Ferenczi, creating the impression that Kohut had introduced clinical empathy into psychoanalysis. When I outlined the data in Ferenczi's 1928 Elasticity Paper (Ferenczi, 1980h), which I believe demonstrated that Ferenczi had introduced clinical empathy, there was a very positive reception to this idea. The analysts who represented the American Academy felt that the self-psychology perspective had usurped empathy, as if they were the only analysts who believed in empathy. The publication of my presentation (Rachman, 1989) also brought a very positive response. Analysts who contacted me appreciated the enunciation of Ferenczi's contribution to empathy for psychoanalysis, the field of which encompassed all analytic perspectives.

After Kohut's death, an opening up occurred in the self-psychology community, which produced a book, which included a group of authors with a variety of theoretical perspectives that contributed to Self Psychology (Detrick & Detrick, 1989). This book included essays by Esther Menaker (on Rank) and myself (on Ferenczi), which seem to indicate that a group of Kohut's followers realized, to their credit, that their perspective had become a closed system with only Kohut and his original followers as sources of reference. There was another positive change in the Self Psychology perspective. Joseph Lictenberg, MD, the editor-in-chief of the journal *Psychoanalytic Inquiry*, opened up Self Psychology further by inviting guest editors to produce editions of *Psychoanalytic Inquiry* for all meaningful perspectives and to express ideas from the entire psychoanalytic spectrum. He generously invited me on three occasions to edit an edition of this journal on Ferenczi and The Budapest School of Psychoanalysis (Rachman, 1997b, 2014b, 2016b). Lichtenberg's openness, flexibility, and creativity was nourished by his analysis with the late Lewis Hill, MD, an analysand of Ferenczi and the late medical director of Sheppard and Enoch Pratt Hospital in Maryland. When Hill held this directorship, Lictenberg was chief of the hospital's psychiatric clinic.

Severn's contribution to clinical empathy

The analysis between Ferenczi and Severn naturally became a hallmark in understanding the importance of empathy in a therapeutic relationship. Their relationship, as has been emphasized, readily became an outstanding example of the pioneering development of a two-person psychology (see Chapter 17). Severn asked for an ongoing voice in the conduct and meaning of her analysis. Ferenczi analyzed his personal reaction to Severn's assertion that he was unaware of his countertransference reaction. As he was to discover in their mutual analysis, he had an underlying hatred toward women that was rooted in his negative feelings toward his emotionally unavailable mother and his childhood sexual trauma with a nursemaid. In a show of emotional strength, Severn put pressure on Ferenczi to confront and analyze his negative feelings toward her. Eventually, it became clear to Ferenczi that there could be no meaningful analysis unless he would listen to Severn's ideas and integrate them into their clinical interaction. This kind of emotional/interpersonal crisis that occurred between Severn and Ferenczi is at the heart of empathy. Ferenczi needed to discontinue the one-person psychology he learned from Freud. It was crucial to change the clinical focus from his trying to analyze Severn's resistance to free associate and accept his interpretations. This only came about when Ferenczi was willing to entertain a two-person psychology, which, in this instance, meant giving and respecting the ideas and experienced feelings, and behavior of the analysand. It was no longer a doctor analyzing a patient. The Ferenczi/Severn dyad became analyst and analysand involved in a co-created democratic relationship, where the analyst attunes and responds to the analysand's subjectivity, and the analysand is affirmed by responding to the analyst's subjectivity. An analysis of mutual subjectivities became the narrative of the analysis. What is more, empathy became the emotional/interpersonal glue of the analysis, particularly in the analysis of trauma disorders.

Severn was credited by Ferenczi as being influential in the development of clinical empathy. He realized that Severn taught him to become more flexible so he could respond with empathy instead of interpretation:

> *A patient of mine* [E.S.] *once spoke of the 'elasticity of analytic technique' a phrase which I fully accept. The analyst, like an elastic band, must* yield *to the patient's pull,* but without ceasing to pull in his own direction, so long as one position or the other has not been conclusively demonstrated to be untenable.
>
> *(Ferenczi, 1980h, p. 129, italics added)*

This statement from Ferenczi is contained in his 1928 paper, "The Elasticity of Psychoanalytic Technique," which was an address given before The Hungarian Psychoanalytic Society in 1927 (Ferenczi, 1980h). In presenting their paper before his Hungarian colleagues, Ferenczi tested his report of the empathic encounter before a receptive audience. His fellow members of The Hungarian Psychoanalytic Society, like Ferenczi's successor, Michael Balint, not only supported their leader's pioneering studies but integrated his findings into their work, beginning an alternative perspective to the Freudian School, namely The Budapest School of Psychoanalysis (Rachman, 2016a). Ferenczi wanted his colleagues to listen closely to the expressed needs of an analysand and not see it as a resistance. What is more, the analyst should be willing to respond, when appropriate, to the analysand. An analyst's unwillingness to respond can be not only a sign of an inflexibility in clinical response, but, potentially non-therapeutic behavior. Ferenczi, with Severn's help, was asking analysts to come out of the realm of interpretation and development of insight into a new awareness of becoming an empathic partner in the analysis, allowing the analysand to influence their thinking and behavior. Bending toward the analyst was a remarkable idea. Ferenczi used the German concept of *nachgiebig-kiet*, which was poorly translated as "indulgence" (Rachman, 1997a). A more exact meaning would be *to elasticize the analyst's response, to be flexible* so that a clinical response is neither an indulgence nor a frustration, but *an empathic response to the developmental needs of the individual*. Here is Ferenczi's idea of what he meant:

> I recall, for instance, an uneducated, apparently quite, simple patient who brought forward objections to an interpretation of mine, which it was my immediate impulse to reject; but on reflection, *not* I, *but the patient, turned out to be right*, and the result of his intervention was a much better general understanding of the matter we were dealing with.
>
> *(Ferenczi, 1980k, p. 94)*

Elizabeth Severn's analysis and the development of empathy

Ferenczi's introduction of the rule of empathy occurred as a result of his clinical experiences as Severn's analyst, which evolved from his earlier groundbreaking work on introducing the role of activity in the analysis of difficult cases. This innovation, which was endorsed by Freud, contained the belief that there were analysands for whom the traditional method of psychoanalysis needed to be amended because these analysands could not follow the rule of free association. Ferenczi realized that a change in methodology was needed not only because the patient population was changing, but also because there was a narrow focus on the Oedipal issue, which eliminated consideration of trauma, severe neurosis, and borderline conditions.

It was, however, the challenge of the Severn analysis that brought Ferenczi's capacity for empathy to the fore. Her emotional disorder, intelligence, assertiveness, and dedication to finding a cure, pushed Ferenczi to experience and understand that clinical empathy was an essential dimension in treating a trauma disorder.

Severn entered analysis with Ferenczi with three unsuccessful analyses behind her and a feeling of intense depression and suicidal ideation. These factors led her to feel she had one last chance at a cure with a responsive analysand like Ferenczi. Convention, in her analysis with Ferenczi, would be totally overturned. Three dramatic interactions in the Ferenczi/Severn analysis illustrate the co-created development of clinical empathy, semi-trance session, and mutual analysis. Severn entered her analysis with Ferenczi unaware that the origin of her emotional problems was a series of childhood traumas imposed upon her by her father (see Chapter 12).

Severn had experimented, as early as 1916, with a self-hypnotic trance state, where she was able to emotionally return to an earlier period in her life (see Chapter 22). Severn naturally turned to using this device in the analysis with Ferenczi. She was trying to find a way to emotionally connect to the flood of memories that emerged in their trauma analysis regarding the sexual, emotional, and physical abuse by her father. On several occasions, Severn attempted to enter into a semi-trance state so that she could begin to integrate her repressed feelings with the thoughts contained in the emerging memories. But Ferenczi was unaccustomed to a session that began with a period of prolonged silence. He became increasingly anxious as Severn maintained her silence while she attempted to enter into a form of trance. Ferenczi's anxiety expressed itself in the bombardment of Severn with interpretations so she would begin to speak. Severn finally became exasperated in one of these semi-trance sessions and yelled at Ferenczi to "shut up" (Ferenczi, 1988). This was a remarkable moment; Ferenczi and Severn turned it into psychoanalytic history. Instead of becoming angry at Severn for telling him to shut up, Ferenczi reassessed his use of interpretation, analyzed his own subjectivity, and responded with empathy. Ferenczi, from then on, allowed Severn to enter into her semi-trance state and, rather than provide interpretations, provided *a hovering empathic presence*, which provided a safe environment to reach and explore her traumas. Ferenczi adopted this method as part of his trauma analysis.

The empathic response to Severn's employment of the semi-trance method became an important avenue for analyzing her trauma disorder, because it focused on actual, childhood trauma rather than the tradition of analyzing the Oedipal conflict. Ferenczi, it must be remembered, was a dedicated Freudian analyst when he began his psychoanalytic career. The trajectory of his clinical behavior changed as he specialized in working with non-Oedipal cases. From the time he began to use activity to help difficult cases until the clinical interaction with Severn, Ferenczi became dedicated to elasticizing the analytic encounter, so that the *voice of the analysand informs the analysis. The analysand becomes a partner in determining the analytic narrative as it becomes a two-person experience. A two-person experience requires the analyst to maintain an empathic compass attuning to the subjective state of the analysand.* Becoming attuned to the childhood traumas of Severn allowed Ferenczi to help her identify her father as the abuser and delineate the series of abusive experiences he inflicted upon her. When Ferenczi switched from interpretation to empathy, he was able to accept her repressed memories of childhood abuse as Severn's narrative truth (see Chapter 21). He did not question whether her retrieved memories were authentic.

Rather than fantasies, Ferenczi's empathic attitude was based upon believing that Severn's report of her childhood traumas was what she believed happened to her. Affirming Severn's belief in her own traumas was not validating Severn's recall of childhood abuse (see Chapter 21) but an affirmation of her as a traumatized human being who needed to have her experiences understood and accepted.

The most challenging moments for empathy in the analysis between Severn and Ferenczi occurred during the intense struggle over mutual analysis. When the struggle over mutual analysis began, Severn and Ferenczi were worlds apart on the issue of his negative countertransference feelings toward her. Ferenczi was aware that he possessed negative feelings about Severn from the onset of their therapeutic relationship. But it wasn't until Severn forced Ferenczi to confront that their analysis had come to a serious impasse because of his negative feelings toward her that he realized that his negative feelings caused the impasse. What is more, she said that he needed her to help him to work through his negative feelings toward her (see chapters 13 through 18). This was the moment when Ferenczi's capacity for empathic understanding would be most tested. He struggled with the dilemma of allowing an analysand to analyze him (Ferenczi, 1988). Besides overthrowing a universally accepted tradition in psychoanalysis of the analyst always being in charge of the clinical experience, Ferenczi had to analyze his negative countertransference. Ferenczi discovered, when he finally allowed Severn to analyze him, that he had hatred toward women. Ferenczi was not able to acknowledge or analyze his negative countertransference until Severn began her turn in analyzing him. As it turned out, Severn's clinical talent proved to be substantial. It was the first time that an analysand analyzed her analyst. She was correct in her diagnosis that their therapeutic impasse was due to Ferenczi's negative feelings towards her. In turning his attention to Severn's analysis of his emotional issues, Ferenczi demonstrated that he could work through his emotional defensiveness and became attuned to Severn's analysis of him. Ferenczi then could empathize with Severn's experience of her feeling rejected and criticized by him. The co-created countertransference analysis allowed the impasse to be sufficiently reduced so the trauma analysis could proceed.

A dramatic and unexpected result of the countertransference analysis was that Ferenczi produced retrieved memories of his childhood sexual abuse by his nursemaid (Rachman, 2012b, 2014a, b). When Ferenczi fully analyzed his childhood memories, his associations also included retrieved memories of sexual abuse with a nursemaid. Ferenczi was able to both enrich his analysand's subjective experience and the meaning of their emotional issues as a result of his integration of his own childhood abuse. We also have to note that Severn's capacity for empathy may have been the equal of Ferenczi. Although Ferenczi railed against her interpretation that he had intense negative feelings towards her and women, her insight was correct. In their mutual analysis, Ferenczi, with Severn's help, was able to uncover the genetic origin of these feelings and connect them to their therapeutic relationship, and then they both changed their behavior so that their impasse was altered.

Severn's special capacity for empathy was demonstrated by her accurate empathic understanding. She was able to attune to Ferenczi's unexpressed negative feelings toward her. Her assessment was accurate that he did harbor intense, hateful feelings toward her. She was able to interact with him as an analysand/clinician helpful in helping Ferenczi retrieve and analyze a significant emotional issue in his personality. Severn's initiation of confronting Ferenczi's unresolved negative countertransference and helping him successfully resolve the problem indicated that she had the capacity to be both an analysand and analyst in their clinical interaction. As an analysand she showed herself to be a seriously needy traumatized individual who tested Ferenczi's capacity to be empathic. As an analyst, she showed herself to be an empathic clinician who could analyze an individual's unexpressed countertransference and help him retrieve his trauma disorder.

Freud's affirmation of Ferenczi's introduction of clinical empathy

Freud was not only approving of Ferenczi's 1928 Elasticity Paper, but was grateful that he had introduced clinical empathy because he knew his own recommendations for clinical behavior had become taboos for psychoanalysts:

> ... the 'Recommendations on Technique' I wrote long ago were essentially of a negative nature ... the most important thing was to emphasize what one should not do, and to point out the temptations in directions contrary to analysis. Almost everything positive that one should not do, I have left to 'tact', ... the result was that the docile analysts did not perceive the elasticity of the rules I had laid down, and submitted to them as if they were taboos. Some time all that must be revised, without, it is true, doing away with the obligations I had mentioned.
>
> *(Jones, 1953, p. 241 – Letter from Freud to Ferenczi, January 24, 1928)*

Freud, however, showed some concern about psychoanalysis adopting the use of empathy. His major concern was that empathy as a clinical attitude would move psychoanalysis into a mystical, subjective realm. He was correct that this new form of clinical attitude would move psychoanalysis away from only using interpretation, since empathy is a response that favors an emotional response to the analysand's subjective experience. As has been discussed, *Freud was wedded to interpretation, described by Ferenczi and Rank (1925) as a kind of fanaticism* geared toward analyzing the Oedipal complex. At a more personal level, Freud may have been also expressing his own discomfort with an experiential approach, which encouraged the analyst to be more human in the therapeutic relationship. Freud added his concern in the same letter that praised Ferenczi's contribution of clinical empathy into psychoanalysis:

> All that you say about 'tact' is assuredly true enough, but I have some misgivings about the manner in which you make those concessions. All those who have no tact will see in what you write a justification for arbitrariness, *i.e.*, subjectivity, the influence of their un-mastered complexes.

What we encounter in reality is a delicate balancing for the most part on the preconscious level of the various reactions we expect from our interventions. The issue depends, above all, on a quantitative estimate of the dynamic factors in the situation. One naturally cannot give rules for measuring this; the experiences and the normality of the analyst have to form a decision. But with beginners, one therefore has to rob the idea of 'tact' of its mystical character.

(Jones, 1953, p. 241 – Letter from Freud to Ferenczi, January 24, 1928)

Carl Rogers, the founder of client-centered psychotherapy (Rogers, 1942, 1959), was in the tradition of Ferenczi, in that he saw himself as a clinician trying to treat troubled individuals and who was open to being responsive, flexible, and empathic. As an academic/clinician practicing in a college counseling center, he arrived at a similar understanding about the importance of empathy in the therapeutic process. Rogers did not recognize Ferenczi as the founder of clinical empathy, although there was a professional connection. Rogers had contact with social workers who worked with Otto Rank. It is likely that the *Todschweigen* experience concerning Ferenczi's ideas and work (see Chapter 7) was successful in removing them from psychology as well as psychoanalysis. Rogers' training occurred in the early 1930s, at the time when Ferenczi's work on empathy with Severn was just coming to a crescendo. After Rogers' training, the *Todschweigen* experience fully descended upon Ferenczi's work. Rogers' work and his writing shared with Ferenczi a fundamental positive view of people who are emotionally troubled and a belief that such people possess the capacity to employ their own natural resources to work on their emotional issues. They also shared a focus on the experimental dimension of the therapeutic encounter. Rogers also believed, as did Ferenczi, that an individual's conscious communication contains an essential truth.

Rogers' ideas about empathy (Rogers, 1951, 1959, 1967, 1975, 1986) helped clinical empathy become a significant dimension of humanistic psychotherapy in the following ways:

1. A focus on the subjective experience as a major source of data about the individual.
2. Attention is paid to the manifest level of communication as providing essential truth about the individual.
3. Empathy as the major force for conveying a sense of understanding of the individual's subjective world.
4. Empathy is the vehicle that communicates to the individual that he/she is understood.
5. Empathy is the life blood of a therapeutic relationship.

The following quotation describes Rogers' fundamental belief in empathy as a necessary dimension of interpersonal contact and as a vehicle for human growth:

> The state of empathy, or being empathic, is to perceive the internal frame of
> reference of another with accuracy and with the emotional components and
> meanings which pertain hereto as if one were the person.
>
> *(Rogers, 1980, p. 40)*

There is a dimension of similarity between Ferenczi and Rogers that I can add to
the discussion, based on personal experience. In 1986, I was privileged to attend an
extended-time experiential workshop, which Rogers conducted at the American
Psychological Association Conference in Philadelphia. This was one of the last
opportunities to have personal contact with and experience Rogers' way of being as
a clinician and thinker. To an group of 40 or so who had flown over, Rogers showed,
in person, the empathy, kindness, compassion, and gentleness that were so evident in
his many writings. This kind of humanism, I believe, characterized Ferenczi's way of
being, based on how he came across in his writings (Ferenczi, 1988). We also have
reports of individuals who worked with him, such as Balint (1992/1968); De Forest
(1954); Dupont, (1988); Severn (1933); and Thompson (1964) that verify Ferenczi's
humanism. I believe Ferenczi and Rogers shared the above-mentioned personal
qualities, and that these contributed to their interest in and capacity for empathy.

Heinz Kohut, it can be said, verified Ferenczi's original findings without ever
mentioning his progenitor as introducing clinical empathy into psychoanalysis. For
that matter, Kohut never mentioned other figures who made significant contributions to empathy, such as Carl Rogers. But Robert Stolorow corrected this error by
paying tribute to Rogers (Stolorow; 1976). As a result of Kohut's personal contribution to the *Todschweigen* experience for Ferenczi, the analytic community believed
that Kohut had invented empathy (Kohut, 1971, 1977, 1978, 1984). In actuality,
Kohut and Ferenczi's work had significant parallels: they were concerned with the
quality of relatedness between parent and child; they shared the idea that the individual feeling unloved, unappreciated, and misunderstood interfered with normal
personality development; they were concerned about re-traumatizing the patient
in the analytic situation by un-empathic behavior; they wanted to provide a reparative therapeutic experience in the psychoanalytic situation; they were aware of the
analysand's unconscious reaction to the analyst's manner of relating to them and
how this affected the analysand's transference and associated resistance; they viewed
the relationship as a mutually influencing interpersonal system, or a two-person
psychology, rather than the analysand endowing the neutral analyst with archaic
transference projections.

Any criticism I have offered about Kohut does not mean he did not make significant contributions to the understanding of empathy. Kohut clearly understood
the importance of empathy in clinical behavior and in the relationships between
human beings:

> Empathy is not just a useful way by which we have access to the inner life
> of man – the idea itself of an inner life of man, and thus of psychology
> of complex mental states, is unthinkable without our ability to know via

introspection – my definition of empathy – what the inner life of man is, what we ourselves and what others think and feel.

(Kohut, 1977, p. 300)

Empathy and this contemporary analysis of trauma

The legacy of the Ferenczi/Severn development of clinical empathy is an important contribution to the contemporary analysis of trauma survivors. The longer I attempt to successfully analyze trauma survivors, the more I realize that a co-created empathic interaction is the essential dimension of establishing and maintaining a therapeutic relationship and providing the necessary ingredient for change and personal growth. There has never been an instance in analyzing an incest survivor where empathy has not been a central issue. I will go further with my statement and say: if you do not believe in empathy as an essential clinical dimension to interact with a trauma survivor, you cannot successfully treat incest survivors. I also believe that most analysts do not treat incest survivors because widening the scope for analysis makes significant demands on the analyst for empathy. A false idea has been institutionalized in the analytic community that you can only perform analysis with analysands who have Oedipal or neurotic conflicts. As has been mentioned, building the foundation of psychoanalysis on interpreting an individual's Oedipal complex to develop insight into his/her emotional issues can be seen as a limited theory and treatment. Furthermore, a statement can be made that some of the pioneering cases that underline psychoanalysis can be analyzed as having been trauma disorder cases (see Chapter 8). My own experience in analyzing incest and trauma survivors has been that the ideas and methods of Ferenczi and Severn have laid the foundation for a contemporary analysis of trauma (Rachman, 2000; Rachman & Kleet, 2015).

15

THE CLINICAL IN-VITRO EXPERIMENT IN INTERSUBJECTIVITY BETWEEN FERENCZI AND SEVERN

The Severn/Ferenczi analysis

One of the significant contributions the Severn analysis with Ferenczi made was the awareness that analyzing subjective experience of both the analysand and analyst was essential to understanding the therapeutic relationship. Understanding the subjective experience of the therapeutic dyad became important for opening up the contribution of the analyst's functioning. Severn shared herself as fully as possible with Ferenczi. She readily responded to Ferenczi's therapeutic interventions, whether they were interpretative or non-interpretative. A good example of Severn's receptivity to Ferenczi and her willingness to fully disclose her own subjectivity was the uncovering of her childhood trauma (see Chapter 12). Severn intellectually understood that the emotional disturbances that hung over her like a black cloud were the result of her life experience. But, she had no idea what those experiences were. In consort with Ferenczi, she was guided toward emotionally exploring her childhood. As *the analyst of difficult cases*, Ferenczi had developed the perspective that non-Oedipal issues were involved in these cases. In their joint explorations, it became clear that Severn's father was the traumatogenic agent. When the father's sexual, physical, emotional, and interpersonal abuse was uncovered Severn openly self-disclosed those experiences to Ferenczi. This led to an analysis of her childhood traumas.

Negative countertransference therapeutic impasse

As the Severn/Ferenczi analysis passed through many difficult stages during the last year or so of the analysis, one of the most difficult phases emerged. During this last period in the therapeutic struggle, little or no progress in the analysis was made. Ferenczi did not have any answers to the difficulty. Severn was convinced she knew the basis of the difficulty (Eissler, 1952; Ferenczi, 1988). She felt that Ferenczi harbored negative feelings towards her that he did not express or confront. However, she experienced these negative feelings intensely. Severn did not hesitate to confront Ferenczi with her interpretation of the difficulty (Rachman, 2014a, b). What is more, Severn initiated an interaction, which was to become an *in-vitro clinical experiment in intersubjectivity*. She made what was an outrageous statement to Ferenczi. She said that he needed to examine his subjectivity in their relationship. Ferenczi did not turn to his first analyst, Freud, or his second peer analyst, Groddeck, (Rachman, 1997a) to understand and analyze his negative countertransference reaction to Severn. What happened was unique and revolutionary. *Severn told Ferenczi he should let her analyze his countertransference reaction to her.* She felt she was in a unique position to do so. She believed she had become an analyst by virtue of her training analysis with Ferenczi. Their analysis was focused on the emotional experience of Severn's childhood trauma. But Ferenczi and Severn also had theoretical discussions about empathy, countertransference analysis, and non-interpretive measures (Ferenczi, 1988; Rachman, 1998). As has been noted in previous chapters, Severn became a student of psychoanalysis before she entered analysis with Ferenczi (Severn, 1920), and by the time of her termination, she and Ferenczi identified her as an analyst (see Chapter 5). She knew Ferenczi well enough and had the technical skill to analyze his negative countertransference. What is more, she had a vested interest in helping him resolve the impasse so she could get the therapeutic help she needed from him to resolve her childhood traumas. I also believe she had empathy for her analyst. In the experience of shared subjectivity, Severn became finely attuned to Ferenczi's inner self. She became acquainted with his vulnerabilities. Severn knew Ferenczi needed help with his negative feeling about women.

Severn's diagnosis of Ferenczi's antipathy

Severn, as it turned out, was absolutely correct in her analysis of Ferenczi's subjective experience. He did have hateful feelings toward women and, consequently, towards her. She did not know how profound her interpretation actually was until Ferenczi, with her help, fully analyzed his feelings toward women. It is a tribute to Severn's analytic capacity that she was so clear in her perception and feelings that Ferenczi was not fully aware of his emotions towards her. Ferenczi did harbor feelings of dislike, viewing her as aggressive, masculine, having an imperial attitude, and not being a typical, compliant analytic patient. It must have been obvious to Ferenczi, from his first consultation session with Severn, that she was not a typical analysand. She had a challenging combination of qualities, which included severe psychopathology, alongside exceptional intellect, clinical observation, assertiveness, her own experience as a therapist, and a driving motivation to get better. In Freud's preface to his case of the Wolf Man, who I have compared to Ferenczi's case of Severn (see Chapter 8), he realized that such difficult cases are very valuable for the analyst and psychoanalysis. Difficult cases force the analyst to become aware of their own subjectivity and the difficulties in the analytic relationship.

Severn was a difficult case who sought out the analyst of difficult cases because Otto Rank had convinced her that Ferenczi had the capacity to analyze her. Severn was the rare analysand who could voice her dissatisfactions directly to her analyst. In Freud's case of the Wolf Man, Sergei Pankejeff, he was not able to voice his dissatisfactions to his analysts, either Freud or his second analyst, Brunswick. In his discussions of his analyses, sixty years later, with a reporter/investigator, however, he made it clear he was very dissatisfied with both of his analyses (Obholzer, 1980). But unlike Severn the therapeutic atmosphere in these analyses did not encourage the free expression of dissatisfaction with the analyst. Neither did he have an opportunity to have a discussion about Freud's assessment that the analysis was successful. The Freudian method did not provide for a two-person psychology. Sergei Pankejeff was not invited by Freud to express his negative feelings or explore them. It was an important change in the nature of the analytic encounter that Severn was not only allowed but encouraged to criticize Ferenczi's functioning. Her diagnoses of his contribution to their therapeutic impasse turned the analysis in the direction of a democratic, two-person, shared-subjectivities, mutual-analytic encounter.

Ferenczi's struggle to accept Severn's analysis of his functioning

Severn outpaced Ferenczi in the idea of a mutual interchange as an integral part of the analytic encounter. Let us not forget, Freud had set the standard for clinical psychoanalysis in his theory and clinical attitude for the analytic encounter. This standard was a one-person experience, the analyst analyzing the analysand. In the one-person experience the analysand did not analyze the analyst. In fact, one can say, analyzing the analyst was entering a taboo area of functioning. The traditional attitude would see an interest in analyzing the analyst as a resistance to being analyzed. If you analyze the analyst, you are resisting analyzing yourself. Introducing the idea that the analysand was in resistance can be seen as a criticism of the analysand's functioning. It blames the analysand for the difficulties: "You are not being a good analysand. You should concentrate on analyzing your own functioning. Analyzing my functioning is a diversion from analyzing yourself. Analyzing yourself is your only mandate."

Analyzing the analyst in the pre-Severn/Ferenczi clinical encounters meant that criticizing the analyst was interpreted as an acting out in the transference. In other words, any negative feelings toward the analyst were projections of neurotic feelings derived from childhood experiences in the family. These negative feelings toward the analyst, therefore, had no place in the reality of the analytic encounter. Such feelings are a delusion, if you wish, that the analysand has developed. The analyst's job, then, is to help the analysand analyze his/her decision, return to reality, and get on with the analysis of the individual's complexes. This may sound like an exaggeration, but it can be experienced in this way by a vulnerable, traumatized analysand.

Clearly Severn did not accept this traditional view of analyzing resistance. Ferenczi, although trained by Freud as a traditional analyst, had by 1932 contributed to the widening scope of psychoanalysis through his development of active and non-interpretative clinical measures (Rachman, 1998, 2007a; Rachman & Hutton, 2006). But as the analyst of difficult cases, he struggled with Severn's invitation for him to further elasticize the psychoanalytic encounter by allowing her to move from an active analysand to becoming a collaborator of Ferenczi. In his *Clinical Diary*, Ferenczi stated that he struggled for most of the year of 1932 with the idea that he would allow Severn to analyze him (Ferenczi, 1988). Never before in psychoanalytic history had an analyst allowed an analysand to formally contribute to the understanding of her own clinical experience. After all, Ferenczi's innovations had never included such mutuality. The struggle toward mutuality and the sharing of subjectivities involved: sharing of power, control and status (Rachman, 2000b); fear of dependency (Rachman, 2000b); the anxiety of self-disclosure (Rachman, 2004a); capacity for emotional expression (Rachman, 2003a); and belief in mutuality (Rachman, 2007a, b).

In order for Ferenczi to agree to mutuality, he needed to examine the meaning that power, control, and status had for him. Fortunately, Ferenczi had never been caught up in the rivalries and politics of psychoanalysis; he was willing to sacrifice the presidency of the International Psychoanalytic Association in order to pursue his own work (Rachman, 1997a, b). However, he still needed to work through his personal issues of letting go of the need to be *the authority* in the analytic encounter. But modifying tradition does not mean handing over the analysis to the analysand. Ferenczi had to struggle with these kinds of thoughts whispering in his ears, in Freud's voice. Certainly, Ferenczi was concerned about what would happen to the therapeutic relationship if he let Severn—a seriously disturbed, aggressive, and controlling individual—became his analyst. Would he be able to be the analyst in the relationship ever again? Would Severn become lost in being the analyst and abandon her own analysis? Would Severn respond empathically to Ferenczi's self-disclosure? Would Ferenczi be able to be sufficiently emotionally open, so that he could reach the depths of his negative feelings towards a woman? Would disclosing these kinds of feelings be helpful to Severn. Would they become lost in a *folie à deux* of disturbed feelings, transference/countertransference reactions, and unresolved childhood trauma. It is understandable that Ferenczi struggled with these kinds of questions and a host of anxieties and insecurities before he was able to resolve the dilemma of mutuality:

> Two days in a row of only being analyzed: depressing feeling of having handed over the control, the reins. Disquieting idea that the patient had succeeded in escaping from analysis entirely, and in taking me into analysis instead … telling myself that real analysis can come about only when relaxation takes place as in the child-parent relationship, that is to say, total trust and the surrender of all independence. Thus, the superiority of the analyst became first mutuality, being on equal terms, and then total subordination.
>
> (Ferenczi, 1988, pp. 73–74)

Ferenczi surrenders to Severn

As we can see in the above quote, Ferenczi was aware that his emotional struggle with Severn involved surrendering to her. In essence, he had to believe that he could trust her with his emotional life. This is no easy matter to settle in an analytic mind. I am aware in my own clinical practice with trauma survivors the difficulty one can have in entering into any form of mutuality and sharing your subjectivity. With the previously mentioned analysand who read my aura, I was never fully convinced I should enter into an analytic encounter of shared subjectivities. It was her anger and its volatility that made me question whether I could trust her with my inner self. I felt she could turn on me in an instance, expressing a deep-seated rage, as if I were her abuser. My transparency, therefore, was only expressed in a limited way, when absolutely necessary, to maintain empathic contact. But in clinical contacts with an analysand I could trust, I was more open (Rachman, 2004a).

As the analysis between Severn and Ferenczi unfolded (see Chapter 12), Severn did express directly her frustrations and criticisms towards Ferenczi. However, Severn had a great deal of affection for Ferenczi (Eissler, 1952; Ferenczi, 1988), as he did for her (Ferenczi, 1988; Rachman, 2016d). I believe Ferenczi's awareness of Severn's affection for him was a factor in his being able to surrender to her:

> I was very pleased with what I was learning from him [Ferenczi] ... I had chosen him [Ferenczi] because I thought he was more of a physician than Freud was ... he [Ferenczi] was more interested in the patient ... and I was not sorry that I had chosen to work with Ferenczi.
>
> *(Eissler, 1952, pp. 1–2)*

Ferenczi's affection for Severn was demonstrated in a gift he gave her. In the first year of their analysis, Ferenczi gave Severn a photographic portrait of himself with an affectionate inscription (see Image 1, p. v).

You can only willingly surrender to someone you trust and have feelings of love or affection toward; these sentiments characterized the Severn/Ferenczi relationship. When Ferenczi surrendered to Severn, a remarkable emotional event occurred. The shared subjectivities of Severn and Ferenczi allowed Severn to analyze Ferenczi. Severn was convinced that Ferenczi had repressed his childhood negative feelings toward women. This repression was causing the impasse in their relationship. When Severn took turns analyzing Ferenczi, she helped him to emotionally focus on his early childhood and helped retrieve his negative childhood feelings, fantasies, and dreams about his nursemaid and mother (see Chapter 21). Severn helped Ferenczi associate to the retrieved childhood trauma data through creating the semi-trance sessions with him that she had used to retrieve and analyze her own childhood traumas. What emerged was a series of associations that indicated Ferenczi was, as was Severn, a victim of childhood sexual abuse by an adult. A nursemaid involved him in sexual experiences, which frightened, stimulated, and later produced a series of repressed negative feelings (see Chapter 12). It was these negative feelings of childhood seduction by a nursemaid, as well as his negative feelings toward his mother (Rachman, 1997a), and his father and grandfather's feelings of misogyny (Ferenczi, 1988), that produced Ferenczi's angry feelings toward women. Severn then helped him develop the insight that these repressed negative feelings towards women were expressed as antipathy towards her in their clinical encounter.

When Ferenczi was able to emotionally admit his anger toward women and his lack of empathy toward Severn, it eventually allowed him to reduce his negative feelings toward Severn. This change allowed him to become more empathic and emotionally connected to her. What is more, Severn changed her behavior in a significant way by reducing her emotional demands on him. The therapeutic impasse was resolved. For all the limitations that the Ferenczi/Severn analysis had, I believe that Severn helped Ferenczi reach a level of therapeutic depth and analysis in their relationship that was not present in his formal analysis with Freud or his peer analysis with Groddeck. Severn was Ferenczi's third analyst and, it can be said, his best.

Contribution of shared subjectivities in the analytic encounter

The clinical experiment in mutual analysis that Severn and Ferenczi shared in the final year of their analysis became a laboratory experience for observing the effect sharing subjectivities can have in enhancing the analytic encounter. Severn helped pioneer the analysis of the analyst and countertransference analysis. This new method pioneered the idea that the analyst needed to examine his/her own feelings when an impasse occurred in the therapeutic relationship. Ferenczi's willingness to surrender to Severn's insistence and analyze his subjectivity in their clinical encounter initiated a new perspective in theory and method for the psychoanalytic encounter. In Ferenczi's contribution of his own subjectivity to Severn's analysis of her trauma disorder, we have the beginnings of what has been termed a two-person psychology for psychoanalysis (Aron, 1990, 1992). This theoretical adjustment introduced the idea that the analytic encounter is a relational one where both the analyst and analysand are contributors to the understanding and analysis in the therapeutic encounter. It is no longer a matter of a doctor analyzing a patient. The new clinical philosophy initiated a democratic interchange where authority, status, and control boundaries became elasticized, as Ferenczi had pioneered in his previous clinical innovations (Rachman, 2000b). Severn moved Ferenczi beyond his previous functioning, expanding the boundaries of analyst activity and clinical empathy towards mutuality. The subjectivity of the analyst became as important as the subjectivity of the analysand. This was a revolutionary change from the traditional view of what has been termed a one–person psychology, that is to say the entire focus of the analytic encounter was on the analysand's subjectivity. The analysts' inner world was invisible in the therapeutic relationship. In fact, Freud, when he identified the countertransference reaction (Freud, 1957, 1958), made it clear this discovery was not to be shared with analysands or, for that matter, with the analytic community (McGrath, 1974). Severn and Ferenczi broke this taboo that Freud instituted about countertransference. Freud saw the countertransference reaction as a negative event in the analytic encounter. It was an indication that there was a negative process occurring in the transference relationship. Freud saw it as a hindrance. He believed countertransference reactions should be analyzed out as soon as possible. Only then can the analysis proceed. Countertransference, in this view, was a retardant to analysis, a sign that the analysis was not going well, and the relationship was flawed. The Ferenczi/Severn relationship helped contribute to a positive, functional view of countertransference.

Severn helped Ferenczi become aware that his antipathy to her was causing the impasse in their relationship. Only by confronting the countertransference reaction and analyzing it thoroughly, down to what Ferenczi had previously termed *rock bottom* could the analysis proceed. Prior to the Ferenczi/Severn analysis, it was not a tradition for the analyst to examine his/her subjectivity. Ferenczi/Severn urged the analyst to become fully acquainted with it, to embrace it, to make it an integral part of the analysis. The analyst's subjectivity was as valuable as the analysand's. In fact, it is only through the sharing of subjectivities that an analysis can reach the emotional depth necessary to uncover trauma. From our discussion of their mutual analysis, Ferenczi's negative countertransference reaction was fully analyzed by what can be termed a countertransference analysis (Rachman, 1997a, 2003a). The analyst uses his/her countertransference reaction to fully understand and analyze his emotional reaction to the analysand. The analyst applies the same motivation, energy, emotionality, and intellect that the analysand is expected to use to analyze his/her emotional issues. Countertransference reactions become a very important part of an analysis. The influence of this approach to countertransference became integrated in contemporary therapeutics (Searles, 1979; Wolstein, 1959, 1988). Countertransference analysis is now part of the therapeutic thinking in the cultural, interpersonal, Object Relations, relational analysis and Self Psychology perspectives.

16

THE CONFUSION OF TONGUES BETWEEN SÁNDOR FERENCZI AND ELIZABETH SEVERN

The Confusion of Tongues theory of trauma can be seen as Ferenczi's commentary on the theoretical and clinical implications of the Ferenczi/Severn analysis. This formulation was Ferenczi's understanding of the intellectual, emotional, and interpersonal issues involved in performing a trauma analysis with a severely disturbed analysand. It includes his challenges, successes, and limitations in analyzing Severn. A full description of the Confusion of Tongues theory of trauma has been outlined (Rachman & Klett, 2015). The present discussion will focus on the Ferenczi/Severn analysis contribution to the development of the theory and its clinical methodology. Ferenczi's clinical experience as the analyst of difficult cases helped prepare him to analyze Severn, but, Severn was not the only trauma case. In Ferenczi's *Clinical Diary* he discussed a series of trauma cases which contributed to the emerging Confusion of Tongues theory. For example, in the case of Dm, a pseudonym for Clara Thompson who had a previous analysis with which she was dissatisfied, the analysand was able to retrieve and explore with Ferenczi, her incest trauma with her father.

The analysis with Severn, because of her input of ideas and technique, helped highlight the issues involved in this first alternate to the Oedipal theory (Gedo, 1986). The Confusion of Tongues theory introduced an alternate framework for psychoanalysis to help analyze cases of narcissistic, character, borderline, and psychotic disorders, whose origins were actual physical, emotional, and sexual abuse (Rachman & Klett, 2015). Severn was the epitome of such a non-Oedipal case. As has been discussed (see Chapter 12), she was physically, emotionally and sexually abused by her father, during, at least, three periods of her childhood. Freud by the time Ferenczi began to develop the Confusion of Tongues theory, had firmly established The Oedipal Theory of neurosis as the cornerstone for psychoanalysis. When he heard about Ferenczi's new theory he not only severely criticized it, but worked with Jones and others to condemn and suppress it, as has been discussed as the *Tödschweigen* experience (see Chapter 7). Freud, Jones, and other orthodox followers were successful in removing the Confusion of Tongues theory and Ferenczi's Relaxation Therapy from mainstream psychoanalysis for over 50 years (Rachman, 1997b).

When Ferenczi's *Clinical Diary* was first published in French (Ferenczi, 1985), it struck a chord in psychoanalysis, which, by then, had begun to go beyond tradition, with the Object Relations, Interpersonal Self Psychology, and Relational perspectives. It provided a theory and treatment of psychological disorder beyond neurosis (e.g., trauma and borderline and psychotic disorders) which were geared to fit the patient population that analysts and psychotherapists were encountering in the post–pioneering psychoanalysis. What is more, Ferenczi's contributions were able to be studied without the atmosphere of condemnation and suppression from the traditional analytic community. This poisonous atmosphere in psychoanalysis, which previously prevented the analytic community from appreciating the significance of Ferenczi's work, is clearly illustrated in an exchange of letters between Freud and Jones after Ferenczi died. First, Freud sent a letter to Jones seven days after Ferenczi's death on May 22, 1933:

> for years Ferenczi was not with us, in fact, not even with himself. … at the center was the conviction that I did not love him enough, that I did not want to recognize his works and also that I had badly analyzed him. His innovations in technique were connected to this sense he wanted to show me how lovingly one must treat one's patients in order to help them.
>
> In fact, these were regression to the complexes of his childhood, the chief pain of which was the [alleged] fact that his mother had not loved him, a middle child among eleven or thirteen others, passionately or exclusively enough. He would himself become a better mother, and in fact found the children he needed.
>
> *Among them was a suspect American woman to whom he devoted four or five hours a day (Mrs. Severn?).* When she left, he believed that she could influence him through vibrations sent across the ocean. He said that she analyzed him and thereby saved him (so he played both roles, was both the mother and the child.)
>
> *She seems to have produced in him a pseudologic phantastica, since he believed her accounts of the most strange childhood traumas, which he then defended against us.* In these disorders was snuffed out his once so brilliant intelligence. But let us preserve his sad exit as a secret among ourselves"
>
> *(Masson, 1984, p. 181 – Letter Freud to Jones,*
> *May 29, 1933, italics added)*

Jones response to Freud's May 29, 1933 letter indicated that he agreed with Freud's assessment of Ferenczi's and Severn's so–called psychopathology:

> *I will of course keep secret what you told me about the American lady, but I am afraid the paranoia is public news: it was sufficiently obvious to all analysts from his last Congress paper* [Ferenczi's COT paper].
>
> *(Masson, 1984, p. 181 – Letter from Jones to Freud, June 3, 1933,*
> *unpublished letter, Jones archive, italics added)*

Jones believed that Ferenczi showed signs of emotional illness because he believed in the so-called love–cure. Jones was also telling Freud that, at the 12th International Psychoanalytic Congress in Weisbaden, Germany, where Ferenczi presented his Confusion of Tongues Paper, the audience of analysts gave him a negative reception. They did not accept his idea of actual childhood sexual trauma as a factor in the development of neurosis (Masson, 1984; Rachman, 1997a, b).

Why did Freud, Jones, and members of the orthodox analytic community feel the need to suppress The Confusion of Tongues theory and condemn Ferenczi's analysis of Severn? The answer is, that Freud thought that treating Severn and falling under her influence by seriously deviating from the Oedipal theory and espousing the Confusion of Tongues ideas and non-interpretative measures was a sign of regression. Ferenczi, he believed, showed regression in thought, a sign of personality disorder. As we examine the ideas and practices in the Confusion of Tongues, it will be evident that these were thoughtful, innovative, and clinically sound tools developed to treat trauma disorder. What is more, this change was not a regression, but the opposite, an evolution in psychoanalytic thinking and practice (Rachman, 1998, 2007a). Ferenczi developed the Confusion of Tongues theory not as a personal attack on Freud to replace the Oedipal theory, but to contribute to an analytic understanding and treatment of trauma (Rachman, 1997a). Ferenczi wanted The Confusion of Tongues paradigm to stand, side by side, with the Oedipal Complex theory.

Identify and retrieval of childhood trauma

Severn's analysis was a landmark in psychoanalytic history because its focus was understanding and retrieving her childhood traumas. Focusing on trauma as the cause of emotional illness was an important change in analytic thinking. Indicating that trauma was the origin of psychological disorder meant that actual or real experiences of childhood are significant factors, if not essential dimensions, in understanding and analyzing the individual. In addition, the nature of the analysand's interpersonal interaction with his/her family was significant to understanding and treatment. Sole concentration on the unconscious Oedipal drama in the unconscious mind of the analysand completely omits the exploration of childhood trauma due to parental abuse. Freud considered an analysis built upon the real experience of childhood seduction of the analysand as regressive, returning psychoanalysis to its repudiated origin (Rachman, 1997a, b). Masson (1984) argued that rejecting Ferenczi's idea of a Confusion of Tongues theory of actual sexual traumas as a significant factor in psychological disorder would mean that traditionally analyzed individuals should submit themselves to a re-analysis to determine if childhood trauma was a factor in their psychopathology. The clinical application of the Confusion of Tongues theory was to conduct an analysis, in an atmosphere where an analysand can freely focus and explore their childhood traumas. The analytic attitude is not solely focused on collecting unconscious data, making interpretations and the development of insight.

Clinical empathy

The introduction of clinical empathy, which Ferenczi initiated with the help of Severn (see Chapter 14), provided a new avenue for clinical interaction in treating trauma. The Confusion of Tongues theory encouraged attuning to the subjective experience of the individual, instilling an atmosphere of openness, safety, and trust, allowing for the free expression of needs, as well as feelings, toward the analyst. This was Ferenczi's desire when he introduced clinical empathy into psychoanalysis—that the emphatic response stands, side by side, with interpretation (Rachman, 1997a, 2007a). Trauma survivors need to have their real experiences of abuse be responded to with empathy. Interpretation can only come after a period of extended empathic understanding (Rachman & Klett, 2015). What needs to be understood is that interpretation can be experienced by a trauma survivor as being unempathic, rejecting, and hurtful (Rachman & Klett, 2015).

Therapeutic need fulfillment

The Severn/Ferenczi analysis emphasized the importance of trauma caused by parental abuse. The abusive experiences produce shame, fear, confusion, anxiety, depression, interpersonal withdrawal, and a host of other symptoms (Rachman & Klett, 2015). It is not unusual that these symptoms can lead to borderline adaptation. The trauma can produce a phobic-like reaction to parental figures. Negotiating an analytic relationship under these conditions, mean practicing Ferenczi's principles, like the Rule of Empathy, clinical responsitivity, flexibility and experimentation (Ferenczi, 1980h; Rachman, 1997a, 2003a; Rachman & Klett, 2015). As Ferenczi was able to do with Severn, he changed his clinical method from the Oedipal/interpretative to the Trauma/Empathic mode because she suffered from actual childhood trauma, not from an Oedipal disorder. She suffered from sexual, physical, and emotional abuse by her father (see Chapters 10 and 12). *What she needed was an experience, which is reparative of childhood traumas,* with an emphatic, responsive and flexible analyst who understood and accepted the difference between Oedipal and Trauma disorders.

Re-traumatization in the psychoanalytic situation

The psychoanalytic situation in the Confusion of Tongues theory becomes a critical dimension for understanding and treating trauma. The clinical interaction through the transference relationship becomes the avenue for the analysand to reveal and express the childhood abuse in the parental relationship. The manifestations of the abusive relationship are contained in the clinical interaction of the therapeutic dyad. In fact, the analyst needs to be alert to childhood traumas being enacted in the psychoanalytic situation. Severn enacted her childhood sexual trauma with Ferenczi. She developed an erotic transference, which was an enactment of her childhood sexual abuse with her father. My colleagues and I believe the manifestation of an erotic transference can be an indication of childhood sexual trauma (Rachman, Kennedy, & Yard, 2007, 2009). Analysis of the analysand's childhood sexual traumas can bring the erotic transference into focus (Rachman, Kennedy, & Yard, 2007, 2009). The erotic transference can be an enactment in the transference of the childhood sexual abuse. If the analyst has created an empathic atmosphere where the analysand experiences safety, trust and caring, he/she can express the childhood trauma. It is only in such an empathic, accepting, and caring atmosphere can a trauma survivor explore their deep–rooted feelings of parental abuse. Of course, this two-person psychology is only relevant if the analyst has the theoretical perspective that childhood trauma is a relevant psychodynamic in the etiology of personality disorder (Rachman, Kennedy, & Yard, 2007, 2009).

The Ferenczi/Severn analysis produced a very important issue in the psychoanalytic situation. Both Ferenczi and Severn observed that the clinical interaction between them produced remnants of the original trauma relationship. In their therapeutic interaction Severn observed Ferenczi's negative feelings toward her, which she experienced as abusive and lacking empathy. Under such conditions of sensing hateful feelings and a lack of empathy by Ferenczi she realized that the psychoanalytic situation must be a safe, accepting place, where abusive behavior, whether real or transferential, is recognized and confronted. The problem Ferenczi presented for Severn was he did not recognize his negative countertransference reaction to Severn. It was necessary for Severn to help Ferenczi to become aware he needed to examine his own subjectivity, to analyze himself, not just Severn. As we have seen, he was finally able to accept that Severn knew something that he did not know. The period when Ferenczi was not able to admit he harbored negative feelings towards Severn was a period of re-traumatization in the psychoanalytic situation for Severn, as she experienced him as the negative father who did not show empathy. She saw Ferenczi as abusive. Severn/Ferenczi translated their relationship into an understanding of the Confusion of Tongues, emphasizing the analyst must pay an ever-hovering attention to the possibility of re-traumatizing the analysand who was originally traumatized within the family. The analyst must pay attention to his/her conscious clinical behavior as well as the shadowy parts of the interaction which exists in the unconscious or the subconscious. The analyst must develop sensitivity to the analysand's verbal and non-verbal behavior, which indicates the manifestation of trauma. Ferenczi's pioneering work on non-verbal behavior in the analytic situation was used to understand the manifestations. Manifestation of trauma in the psychoanalytic situation is evident in the nature of the analysand's behavior toward the analyst. By observing and exploring these manifestations the analyst can help to introduce the issue of trauma into the analysis. By attuning to his/her own subjectivity, the analyst can discern, by projective identification, the analysand's expressing elements of a trauma background. By noting the trauma manifested in the transference, the analyst can often begin the analysis of the trauma disorder. The purpose of becoming aware of the re-traumatization process in the psychoanalytic situation, is to maintain the *therapeutic relationship as a passion-free experience*. The analyst must take pains not to act out any seductive or erotic thoughts, feelings, or behavior toward the analysand. A passion-free atmosphere in the psychoanalytic situation can prevent re-traumatization.

The notion that the analyst creates a passion-free emotional atmosphere is central to the Confusion of Tongues theory. In the analysis with Severn there is no evidence that there was actual sexual contact. It was in the analysis with Severn that Ferenczi developed the idea that a passion-free atmosphere was essential. Severn's childhood traumas produced a damaged individual who needed a reparative therapeutic experience (Rachman, 1998). When Freud reproached Ferenczi for the alleged acting out with analysands, in the famous "kissing letter" (Falzeder, Brabant & Giampiere–Deutsch, 2000, pp.421–423, December 13, 1931), Freud assumed that Ferenczi's trauma analysis incorporated active erotic interaction such as kissing. As has been discussed (see Chapter 8), this notion was conveyed to him by Clara Thompson who bragged that Ferenczi allowed her to kiss him. This relaxation of the standard analytic procedure was allowed in Thompson's case, because Ferenczi accepted her need to create a cherishing love relationship with him as a reparative paternal figure (Rachman, 1998). Ferenczi believed his behavior with Thompson was empathic and passion-free, although, it had erotic overtones for Thompson. It would have been preferable that Ferenczi indicated in his *Clinical Diary* that he analyzed the erotic transference in this experience.

In Ferenczi's response to the kissing letter he clearly states that his *Confusion of Tongues theory and trauma analysis alterations to traditional theory and treatment seriously cautions against erotic transference interactions*:

> I consider your fear that I will turn into another Stekel unfounded. 'Youthful sins', misdemeanors, they have been overcome and anatically worked through, can even make one wiser and more careful than people who did not go through such storms. My extremely ascetic 'active therapy' was surely a pre–cautionary measure against tendencies of this kind, for that reason, in their exaggerations they took on an obsessional character. When I gained insight into this, I relaxed the stiffness of the prohibitions and avoidance to which I condemned myself (and others). *Now, I believe I am capable of creating a mild, passionless atmosphere, which is suited to incubate also what has hit hereto been concealed. But since I fear the dangers just as much as you do,* I must and will, now as before, keep in mind the warnings that you reproach me with, and strive to criticize myself harshly.
>
> *(Falzeder, Brabant & Giamperi–Deutsch, 2000, p. 424–Letter from*
> *Ferenczi to Freud, December 27, 1931, italics added)*

Countertransference analysis

The analysis of the analyst is one of the major mechanisms that allows the analyst to maintain a passion–free atmosphere in a trauma–analysis. By believing in clinical psychoanalysis as a two-person experience, the analyst is mandated to examine his/ her personal reactions to the analysand as they emerge in the clinical interaction.

The analyst provides an ongoing avenue for detecting any sexual content in the interaction, as well as any thoughts, feelings or behavior that can be interpreted by the analysand as creating an abusive experience. All clinical interactions in the analysis of trauma present opportunities for transference manifestations of the childhood trauma and the countertransference reactions to them. In fact, another important aspect to the Confusion of Tongues theory, is that the psychoanalytic situation is the vehicle by which the childhood trauma is revealed. This, of course, is the beginnings of an important departure from the Freudian perspective. The Confusion of Tongues perspective uses the relationship which is created between the analyst and analysand as important data for the analysis. In this departure, the analyst analyzing the analysand is supplemented by the analyst analyzing the analyst. In Ferenczi's analysis of Severn, psychoanalysis went from a one-person to a two-person psychology, perhaps, in its most dramatic form.

Clinical hypocrisy

One of the most important lessons Ferenczi learned from the analysis with Severn was that emotional honesty by the analyst was curative for the Confusion of Tongues trauma (Rachman & Mattick, 2012). From their joint struggle to resolve the intense therapeutic impasse in their clinical relationship, it became clear that the analyst needs to be judiciously self-disclosing (Rachman, 1982) in order to cure the Confusion of Tongues between an analyst and analysand. Severn was convinced that Ferenczi had intense negative feelings toward her, which, initially, he could not successfully address. It was only when she convinced him to examine his subjectivity that the impasse could be examined. With her help, he confronted his negative feelings. Then he took another step towards analytic history by disclosing his feelings toward her. Ferenczi, from these kinds of clinical interactions with Severn and other trauma survivors, realized that the tradition of *a one-person psychoanalysis, where only the analysand is examined leads to a clinical hypocrisy.* If the analyst hides his/her emotionality from the analysand the analysis is not emotionally open and honest, and, therefore, limited.

Ferenczi attempted to redefine the nature of the analytic relationship. Emphasis is now placed on the nature of the relationship rather than diagnosing the person's psychopathology. The analytic encounter becomes a laboratory for working on, and through, the transference and real relationship in the here-and-now of the psychoanalytic situation. A schema for acknowledging and working through the clinical hypocrisy is the Confusion of Tongues between an analysand and analyst can be outlined as follows:

1. The analyst admits there is a disturbance in the relationship.
2. This disturbance, mistake, or error is a result of a contribution by the analyst.
3. The analyst self–discloses his/her contribution to the disturbance in the clinical interaction.

4.   The analyst does not blame the analysand for the difficulty by referring to the concept of resistance, transference, or suggesting that only the analysand's functioning contributed to the difficulty.
5.   Analyst and analysand enter into a dialogue about the clinical issue searching out the intrapsychic, interpersonal events that fueled the emphatic break.
6.   The analyst is willing to take responsibility for his/her contribution to the difficulty, judiciously disclosing the contribution.
7.   The analyst is willing to change his/her behavior after taking responsibility for the difficulty.

Severn taught Ferenczi that being emotionally open and honest with an analysand helps create a reparative experience (Rachman, 1998) where empathy, tenderness, non-erotic affection and understanding is an antidote for the abusive experience of childhood which caused trauma.

From suppression to inspiration

The Confusion of Tongues paper which Ferenczi presented at the 12th International Psychoanalytic Congress in Weisbaden, September 4, 1932, immediately caused a controversy which is still alive in contemporary psychoanalysis (Rachman, 1997a, b). Freud believed Ferenczi was acting out against him and wanted to supplant him and the Oedipal theory (Gay, 1984). Although there is no doubt that Ferenczi was angry at Freud (Ferenczi, 1988), his alternate theory of psychological disorder was a contribution, which he believed would supplement, not replace the Oedipal theory (Rachman, 1997a). However, Freud was so threatened by the Confusion of Tongues theory that he, Jones and other traditionalists, practiced *Todscheweigen* and removed Ferenczi's ideas from mainstream psychoanalysis (Rachman, 1997b, 1999). It is only with the publication of Ferenczi's *Clinical Diary* (Ferenczi, 1985, 1988) that a rediscovery of Ferenczi's contributions to the psychoanalysis can be appreciated in contemporary psychoanalysis.

Fromm (1959), at a time when Ferenczi's work was being suppressed, was a courageous voice in the wilderness announcing that the Confusion of Tongues Paper was one of the most important publications in the history of psychoanalysis. From contemporary research and scholarship we know that his Confusion of Tongues paradigm has relevance for contemporary psychoanalysis by providing a blueprint for studying and treating trauma (Harris & Kuchuck, 2015; Masson, 1984; Rachman, 1997a, 2003a, 2016b; Rachman & Klett, 2015; Roazen, 1975).

17

A TWO-PERSON PSYCHOLOGY FOR PSYCHOANALYSIS

Severn and Ferenczi's analytic partnership

Freud's one-person psychology

Freud's wish was to develop and maintain a standard procedure for analyzing the Oedipal Complex which he felt further generations of psychoanalysts would preserve. He was very successful in accomplishing this goal, as traditional and contemporary psychoanalysis preserved Freud's legacy both theoretically and clinically (Ellman, Grand, Silvan & Ellman, 2000; Mills, 2012). The very interesting and puzzling phenomenon that runs through Freud's clinical functioning is that he seemed to ignore clinical data that did not validate his theory. Freud experienced moments as a clinician which challenged the idea of a fixed standard procedure. As early as the Case of Dora, Ida Bauer (Freud, 1955d), Freud did not acknowledge the sexually seductive event that occurred between Ida Bauer, a 14-year old girl and Herr K., a 40-year old married man, as a psychodynamic in the development of her emotional problems (Rachman & Mattick, 2009, 2012). In fact, Freud suggested that it was a sign of her Oedipal problem that Ida Bauer rejected the sexual advances of the 40-year old Herr. K. Besides a kind of fanaticism to prove his Oedipal theory correct, Freud was expressing his paternalistic and chauvinistic beliefs, that a young girl should be inherently flattered by a man approaching her for sexual contact. Of course, Freud, as he would later be critical of Ferenczi, believed revisiting the issues of sexual seduction as a factor in the development of psychological disorder was *regressing* to his original seduction hypotheses (Rachman, 1997b). I have suggested that Freud's neglect of the incest trauma as a psychodynamic in emotional disorder has a personal component (Rachman, 2016b).

Psychoanalysis continued to neglect the incest trauma and criticize Ferenczi for attempting to bring attention to it:

> I am afraid that some of the recent interest in Ferenczi's late work may be a byproduct of the current popularity of the idea that sexual abuse is frequently

overlooked, even by therapists. I do not doubt that this contention about sex abuse is, in fact, valid; I am certain, however, that facile and arbitrary methods of reconstruction also lead to the confusion of fantasy and reality. In other words, there is no substitute for careful analytic work, by way of repetition in the transference, to establish the history of significant experiences in early childhood.

(Bacon & Gedo, 1993, p. 135)

Ferenczi's two-person psychology

The history of Ferenczi's clinical functioning indicates an inherent attitude toward viewing the therapeutic process as a joint endeavor between the two participants. In his pre-analytic days, Ferenczi's interaction with a patient named Rosa K. (Rachman, 1997a), was informed by the patient's expressed needs. He wrote a letter for her, indicating she was a cross–dresser, had a psychiatric condition, and should not be treated, therefore, as a criminal. What is more, Ferenczi asked this patient to create a diary about her life, so he could use it to more fully understand her psychology. After this initial psychiatric practice, Ferenczi's clinical work involved a progressive development where the analysand contributed to the analyst's understanding of the analysis. As has been described, in Ferenczi's active analytic approach (see Chapter 8; Rachman, 1997a), he invited the analysand to join him in activity in the psychoanalytic situation, which would address the analysand's inability to maintain the free association method. This kind of generic mutuality came naturally to Ferenczi, both as a person and as a clinician. Inviting an analysand to be your clinical partner indicates an openness to sharing authority control and status in the relationship. An identity as a healer was prominent in Ferenczi's personality. He did not have a special need to be the authority. What is more, Ferenczi had an intellect and personality which was flexible, responsive, and experimental in nature (Rachman, 1997a).

Ferenczi, it can be said was searching for mutuality when he met Freud in 1908. His family experiences had left him with these yearnings. Being one of 12 children, he suffered from maternal deprivation (Rachman, 1997a). He was emotionally close to his father, who died when he was 15-years old (Rachman, 1997a). Ferenczi's adulthood was marked by his unconscious yearning for a close nurturing relationship with a paternal figure. It was an emotional bonanza for Ferenczi when he became Freud's favorite son, looking forward to fulfilling his need for ongoing emotional contact with a father figure. Unfortunately, he was to be dramatically disappointed.

Ferenczi's search for mutuality with Freud

The Freud/Ferenczi relationship started on an emotional high. On Sunday, February 7, 1908, shortly before the Salzburg Congress, Ferenczi met Freud. Jones noted this important emotional event:

> Dr. F. Stein of Budapest … who, through an introduction from Jung, induced Ferenczi [to meet] Freud … *the effect was electric.*
>
> *(Jones, 1955, p. 34, italics added)*

Freud had recently come out of the difficult ending of his relationship with Wilhem Fliess and did not, at the time of the Ferenczi meeting, have a close male friend-ship (Rachman, 1989b). Freud was struck by Ferenczi's willingness to enter into a relationship, even though the negative experience with Fleiss was reverberating in his mind. Ferenczi, in his first encounter with Freud, was attempting to create an interpersonal closeness, and emotional intimacy with the person who was to become his teacher, analyst, and dear friend.

Ferenczi's need for mutuality with Freud became an emotional crisis early in their relationship. Freud asked Ferenczi to accompany him to Italy to work on writing the Schreber Case (Freud, 1911). Freud had read the account of Daniel Paul Schreber, a German judge who suffered from what was previously known as dementia praecox (later known as paranoid schizophrenia). He never interviewed or treated this case but was fascinated with reading Schreber's memoir (Schreber, 1955). Freud was interested in writing a paper on the case because he believed it provided a new understanding of psychosis, homosexuality, and paranoia. Freud thought that Schreber's emotional disturbances were the result of the repression of homosexual desires, which in his childhood were oriented toward his father and brother. Freud believed that repressed drives were projected onto the outside world, which led to intense hallucinations. Freud used his interpretation of the Schreber case to intro-duce a new classification of mental disturbances which he named, *paranoid dementia.*

Freud invited Ferenczi to take a trip with him to Sicilly, Italy to work on writing up the Schreber Case. In the so-called Palermo Incident, which occurred on this trip to the city of Palermo, there was a Confusion of Tongues experience between the two men, which erupted into an emotional/interpersonal crisis. Ferenczi was under the false assumption that he was asked to participate in the joint venture of writing the Schreber paper. However, it became clear, early in their interaction that Freud had a different plan for their meeting. On the first evening of the Sicily trip, Freud asked Ferenczi to take his dictation on the Schreber case, not to contribute his own thinking, about the material. When Ferenczi realized what was happen-ing, he became angry, rebelled and refused, if you will, to become Freud's secretary (Grosskurth, 1991). Not only was Ferenczi's dreams about being Freud's collabora-tor dashed, but Ferenczi's desire to become a mutual partner of Freud was crushed. The emotional disappointment may have been the greater loss, because this desire for mutuality became a vehicle that was used by Jones to attack his personality. Jones used this difficulty between Freud and Ferenczi as an indication of Ferenczi's severe emotional problems (Jones, 1955), which he was later to expand in his trea-tise that Ferenczi's emotional disturbance was connected to his deviations from Freud's work (Rachman, 1997a). In a contemporary critique on Ferenczi's desire for mutuality with Freud, Aron & Starr (2016) think that Ferenczi did not realize that mutuality was both his desire and innovation, but, was not a part of Freud's personal desire. What is more, they interpret this need as a homoerotic longing. A desire to have a closer and collaborative partnership by Ferenczi with Freud may have had neurotic components, since Freud was not available for such a relationship.

After the emotional crisis of the Palermo Incident Freud rebuked Ferenczi for his emotional neediness and personal immaturity. He wrote to Ferenczi on October 6, 1910, in response to an apologetic letter from Ferenczi after his returning to Budapest from Sicily.

Dear Friend:

> You not only noticed but also understood, that I no longer have any need to uncover my personality completely, and you correctly traced this back to the traumatic reason for it. Since Fliess's case, with the overcoming of which you recently saw me occupied, that need has been extinguished. A part of homosexual cathexis has been withdrawn and made us of to enlarge my own ego, I have succeeded where the paranoia fails. So when you look at it more closely you will find that we haven't so much to settle between us as perhaps you thought at first. I would rather turn your attention to the present.
>
> *(Jones, 1955, pp. 83–84)*

Freud made it clear that he could not share Ferenczi's desire for mutuality. This need was clearly expressed by Ferenczi in a series of statement in a letter sent to Freud on October 3, 1910, after the Palermo Incident (Balint, Falzeder & Giampieri–Deutsch, 1993). In the first statement, Ferenczi made it clear how important his need for mutuality was:

> I strive for absolute mutual openness.
>
> *(Brabant, Falzeder, & Giampieri–Deutsch, 1993, p. 218)*

Ferenczi pushed for a *psychoanalytic/peer* relationship with Freud, where they would exchange personal feelings, intimacies, emotional needs, as well as ideas, political gossip, and interpersonal experiences. He yearned for a full emotional friendship with Freud, but, Freud clearly did not have this same need.

Ferenczi wanted more than a professional relationship with Freud, he continued to long for an emotional connection, an open and intimate relationship with a peer, a mutual relationship.

> I was longing for personal, uninhibited, cheerful companionship with you and I can be cheerful, indeed, boisterously cheerful, and I felt perhaps unjustified-forced back into the infantile role.
>
> *(Brabant, Falzeder, & Giampieri–Deutsch, p. 217)*

> [they] *are not ashamed in front of each other, keeping nothing secret, tell each other the truth without risk or result.*
>
> *(p. 220 italics in the original)*

Freud's rejection of Ferenczi's invitation for a peer-oriented analytic relationship and his pathologizing Ferenczi's desire, had a negative effect on Ferenczi, encouraging him to question his own motives. The relationship with Freud, being a one-person experience, always seemed to encourage Ferenczi to recount his own assertions. Ferenczi was always vulnerable to Freud's negative view of him, until he was able to separate from him, and develop his own friendships with Georg Groddeck, as well as his Hungarian colleagues and concentrate on his own theoretical and clinical ideas and methods (Rachman, 1997a, b).

Ferenczi could not make it clearer that, in spite of Freud's concerns about his homoerotic feelings and abandonment from Fleiss, what he wanted from Freud was not neurotic, but befitting for two mature analysts, to develop.

> Do you know which hours of our trip retain the most pleasant memories for me? The ones in which you divulged to me something of your personality and your life. It was then, and not during the scientific conversations that I felt free of inhibitions, like a 'companion with equal rights', as you always wished me to be and as I so much would like to have him.
>
> *(Brabant, Falzeder & Giamperi–Deutsch, 1993, p. 218)*

Freud was accurate in his observation of a pathology in Ferenczi's need to have an intimate relationship with him, but, not because Ferenczi was expressing a neurotic need to fulfill an infantile wish, rather, because it was a quest for a mutuality with an unobtainable figure. Falzeder's (2010) astute observation about the Freud/Ferenczi relationship, underlined the difficulty for Ferenczi to gain mutuality with Freud.

> Freud did not even dream of giving Ferenczi some of this love. No, Ferenczi should get a grip on himself, stop acting like an obnoxious child, and should, as Freud admonished him … leave the island of dreams which you inhabit with your fantasy children and mix in with the struggle of men.
>
> *(p. 401)*

Groddeck and Ferenczi's mutuality

Ferenczi's struggle toward mutuality with Freud as we have seen, was filled more with pain than satisfaction. It led him to continue to search out opportunities for mutuality, most notably with his friend, Georg Groddeck. Groddeck was the physician who was the first to apply Freud's discoveries to organic medicine (Groddeck, 1928). As has been mentioned, Groddeck ran the sanitarium at Baden-Baden, where he pioneered the combined use of psychotherapeutic treatment, such as diet and massage, with psychoanalytic understanding (Grotjahn, 1966). He is considered the father of psychosomatic medicine. Ferenczi was a visitor to Groddeck's sanitarium, going for the cure as much as to maintain contact with his kindred spirit. Both Ferenczi and Groddeck were linked together by their identity as doctors who wished to treat difficult cases, and in their belief that they could be agents for cure. They were also both daring and experimental. They both argued that doctors should not try to fit their patients into a theory, but, search to respond to their needs. Both were very aware of the personal factor in the analytic cure and that they needed to examine their own contribution to the therapeutic process (Rachman, 1997a).

Ferenczi shared a friendship with Groddeck from 1921–1933, one that provided him with a mutuality he valued. In 1921, Groddeck became Ferenczi's friend with a heartfelt letter he sent, praising Groddeck for his openness.

> Never before have I talked so openly to a man ….
>
> *(Ferenczi & Groddeck, 1982, p. 55)*

Then he revealed the intimacy of his hurt with Freud:

> On several occasions I let myself be analyzed by him [Freud] (once for three weeks, another for 4-5 weeks, and for years we've travelled together every summer.) But I never felt free to open myself totally to him. He had too much of this prudish respect; he was too important for me, too much of a father. The result: in Palermo, where he wanted to do this famous work on paranoia (Schreber) with me, I had a sudden attack of rebellion. I jumped to my feet, on the first evening of work because he wanted me to take down his dictation. I told him that to have me simply take down his thoughts was not writing a paper together.
>
> *(Ferenczi & Groddeck, 1982, p. 55)*

Ferenczi was able to open up to Groddeck about many personal issues, including his negative feelings about Freud. In this letter, Ferenczi's need for a more open, mutual relationship is clearly shared with Groddeck. He recounted the exact nature of his disappointment with Freud. How mistreated he felt. How he yearned to share this with a peer. This letter to Groddeck is a remarkable document of emotional honesty and engagement, which indicated Ferenczi's search for mutuality with a peer. Ferenczi wrote to Freud praising Groddeck, mentioning that he was doing a little self-analysis in the presence of and with the help of Groddeck. He also said his relation to Groddeck is pleasant and refreshing (Dupont, 1984).

Severn and Ferenczi's mutuality

The remarkable clinical experiment in mutual analysis that occurred in the last phase of the Ferenczi/Severn analysis, as has been detailed, grew out of a transference/countertransference issue. Severn was keenly aware of the importance of the unconscious dimension of the therapeutic relationship. In her second consultation session, she had with Freud, Severn shared an insight about the transference relationships:

The trouble was the early students of Freud had not been thoroughly analyzed. They had been analyzed in an intellectual manner, and I don't think the
transferences had been worked out fully, and this limitation did not appear to
Freud to be a limitation.

(Eissler, 1952 p. 3)

Ferenczi was aware of deficiencies in their therapeutic relationship with his analyst
Freud (Ferenczi, 1988). There is no question that Ferenczi's analysis with Freud was
seriously flawed, not only because the method of transference/countertransference
analysis was in its infancy, but because Freud could not provide the trauma analysis
Ferenczi needed.

Severn's desire to enter into a mutual analysis grew out of her insight that
Ferenczi had developed a severe negative transference reaction to her that was
interfering with the analysis. This is how Severn described the issue:

that Ferenczi had these feelings against me, and he finally admitted with my
prodding, that he hated intelligent women, and naturally that made it a little
difficult for my analysis to proceed.

(Eissler, 1952, p. 2)

Although, Ferenczi was emotionally open and self-examining, he had a great deal
of difficulty responding to Severn's interpretation that he had a negative transference reaction to her (see Chapter 12). Severn initiated a new kind of therapeutic
interaction between Ferenczi and herself, which included some new emotional
dimensions in an analytic encounter, such as, authenticity, mutuality, vulnerability,
and surrender. These dimensions were part of what they named mutual analysis
(Ferenczi, 1988). Mutual analysis in psychoanalytic therapy became one of the most
controversial methods in the history of psychoanalysis. In the controversies which
surround the introduction of mutual analysis, the fundamental innovation it introduced was neglected, which were the issues of the boundaries of clinical empathy
and a two-person psychology (see Chapters 14 through 17).

Mutual analysis was Severn's invention. It was an invention of necessity. As has
been mentioned, Severn sought out Ferenczi as the analyst of last resort. As she told
Eissler in their interview in 1952, she was in a desperate emotional state, severely
depressed struggling toward suicide (Eissler, 1952). Severn gathered her strength,
resources, and knowledge, which combined with Ferenczi's willingness and capacity to respond to her, to create a historical moment in psychoanalysis. Severn asked
her analyst to recognize his own emotional difficulties in the therapeutic relationship. It was his responsibility to own them as his own issue and *not to blame the analysand* for the therapeutic difficulty. Just as the analysand is asked to analyze his/her
emotional issues, the analyst is asked to analyze his/her own personal issues. In the
special case of the Severn/Ferenczi analysis, the analysand was more attuned to her
analyst's emotional issues that contributed the difficulties in therapeutic relationship than was the analyst. This is not how Freud and other analysts who followed

his system developed psychoanalysis. According to tradition, it is the analyst, who is, not only in charge of diagnosing, but, creating the therapeutic relationship.

Ferenczi believed that the analyst should strive to have the personal awareness to discern their own contributions to the analytic encounter.

> the rule by which anyone who wishes to undertake analysis must be ana-lyzed himself. Anyone who has been thoroughly and has gained complete knowledge and control of the inevitable weaknesses and peculiarities in his own character will inevitably come to the same objective conclusions in the observation and treatment of the same psychological new material and will consequently adopt the same tactical and technical methods in deal-ing with it. I have the definite impression that since the introduction of the second fundamental rule differences in any analytic technique are tending to disappear.
>
> *(Ferenczi, 1980h, p. 89)*

Countertransference analysis

Of course, we know Ferenczi did not have an analysis that reached the depths of his childhood traumas. He complained in his *Clinical Diary* (Ferenczi, 1988), of the limitations in his analysis with Freud. Because his analysis was incomplete, he had personality weaknesses and blind spots. He was usually vigilant to his weakness, but, the analysis of Severn made him more vulnerable, pushing him to the limit. The Severn/Ferenczi relationship helped develop a methodology to aid the analyst who has difficulty recognizing and analyzing his countertransference. This innovation combined with the focus on intersubjectivity, a two-person psychology, clinical empathy, the Confusion of Tongues theory, as well as the introduction of non-interpretative measures constituted a paradigm shift for psychoanalysis, a focus on a two-person psychology and empathic understanding (Rachman, 2016a).

Severn and Ferenczi brought the issue of countertransference into prominence in psychoanalysis. Traditionally, it was argued that countertransference interfered with the analyst's capacity to interpret the analysand's functioning which took intellectual concentration and knowledge. An emotional reaction meant the analy-sand was throwing the analyst off the path to interpretation. The Ferenczi/Severn analysis helped reveal that the analysand's emotional reaction to the analyst, and the analyst's neglect of attending to this emotion reaction was not, as Freud taught, an annoyance or hindrance to the analysis, but, as Severn taught Ferenczi, *it was the analysis*. There was no analysis without working through the countertransfer-ence reaction Ferenczi had toward Severn, which were his own negative feel-ings towards an abusive nursemaid and his neglectful mother. The Ferenczi/Severn analysis reversed the idea that the countertransference reaction was an unnecessary contaminant.

Both Ferenczi and Severn were aware they had reached a therapeutic impasse. Not only was there no positive changes in her functioning, but she had developed a serious dependency. Ferenczi did not fully understand the impasse. Initially, he viewed the impasse as a one-person experience. Severn had severe psychopathology, which was difficult to heal. She also had an eroticized transference reaction to Ferenczi, based upon the childhood seduction by her father. She viewed Ferenczi as the idealized father figure to who she turned to repair her childhood trauma. Because Ferenczi had not analyzed his countertransference reaction, they became immersed in a dependency therapeutic impasse.

Severn was acutely aware of Ferenczi's countertransference and challenged him to confront it. Ferenczi did not approach the confrontation as resistance or acting out in the transference. Severn told Ferenczi that their analysis had reached an intractable impasse because of his countertransference issue. Imagine, an analysand when psychoanalysis was in its classical period, behaving in such a manner as to not only challenge the analyst, but, criticize his functioning. We must understand that traditional analysis did not encourage such active and direct expression of criticism toward the analyst. The analyst was the one to determine the clinical format. As have been pointed out, Severn was no more a traditional analysand than Ferenczi was a traditional analyst. Mutual analysis developed out of this unconventional therapeutic dyad, e.g. the difficult analysand with the analyst of difficult cases. Severn's genius and her assertiveness moved her to introduce the next step in the development of mutual analysis. She had no compunction to tell Ferenczi that he was the cause of their therapeutic impasse. What is more, she was convinced she knew how to resolve the impasse. The resolution would come from Ferenczi allowing her to analyze him. He listened to her criticism and did not retaliate against her. Of course, he was confused, angry and scared. He believed that the function of an analyst was to hold and understand all the feelings and thoughts of the analysand, including those about his own functioning. They were both motivated to remove the therapeutic impasse.

Then, Severn made the most audacious statement to Ferenczi. She said that, in essence, *she was the only one to solve the issue of the therapeutic impasse.* Severn told Ferenczi he should let her analyze him. It was not so much an offer as it was an insightful observation. Of course, she could have told him to seek out an analyst in his Hungarian colleagues. But Severn believed she was best suited to the task. Severn believed she had a particular insight into Ferenczi's unconscious. Their sharing of subjectivities helped her become attuned to her analyst's inner functioning. Severn was also correct that a therapeutic encounter regarding Ferenczi's antipathy toward her was long overdue (Rachman, 2014a, b, 2015a).

It took Ferenczi about a year, struggling with his anxiety, confusion, power, and control issues before he could allow Severn to analyze him, before he could let go, and share authority in the relationship. Eventually, he was able to surrender and allow Severn to become an analyst with him. They developed a method of taking turns in being the analyst and analysand. The analysis with Severn was the most successful of the three analyses, in which Ferenczi participated. Ferenczi's formal analysis with Freud, was not only incomplete but seriously criticized by Ferenczi for not reaching deep enough into the emotional issues in his relationship with Freud

(Ferenczi, 1988). The peer-to-peer therapy relationship with Georg Groddeck allowed Ferenczi to develop the mutual relationship he wanted to accomplish with Freud. It was the mutual analysis with Severn, however, that reached the emotional depths of Ferenczi's childhood trauma.

In clinical interaction with Severn, Ferenczi was able to reach a depth of uncovering that allowed Ferenczi to confront his own childhood sexual abuse, apparently an issue he had repressed (Rachman, 2014a, b, 2015, see Chapter 12). Ferenczi analyzed his antipathy towards Severn by uncovering his negative experience of sexual abuse with a nursemaid in the following manner:

1. With Severn's prompting, Ferenczi disclosed his negative feelings to Severn, whose transference reaction reminded him of his mother.
2. Severn encouraged Ferenczi to go deeper and explore his countertransference reaction. Ferenczi immersed himself in his childhood experiences, as Severn had taught him to do; during the Semi-Trance Session a vague image of a female servant girl emerged.
3. Focusing on this emerging image, recovered memories appeared. One was: "[a] mad fantasy of being pressed into this wound in the corpse ...a housemaid probably allowed me to play with her breasts but then, pressed my head between her legs" (Ferenczi, 1988, p. 61, Clinical entry – March 17, 1932).
4. As Severn pressed the countertransference analysis, Ferenczi developed an insight: "my hatred of females. I want to dissect them ... to kill them". (Ferenczi, 1988, p. 61, Clinical entry – March 17, 1932).
5. Ferenczi then disclosed the emotional connection between his mother and Severn:

> The patient's demands to be loved corresponded to the analogous demands on me by my mother. I did hate this patient, in spite of all the friendliness, I displayed.
>
> *(Ferenczi, 1988, p. 99 – Clinical entry, May 5, 1932)*

Severn's capacity to be an analyst and analysand, allowed the mutual analysis to be productive. She was also able to express her empathy toward Ferenczi in his difficulty with his countertransference reaction.

> I gradually got the feeling that he was hampered in spite of a very brilliant mind and a very responsive personality, that he was hampered by a lack of a complete analysis in his own case, that there was certain feelings that he had applied to patients in spite of himself. He theoretically knew that he shouldn't have any personal reactions and he didn't for a long time admit that he had any, but through my dream life they were revealed and they were largely of an aggressive and critical nature against me.
>
> *(Eissler, 1952 p. 2)*

Ferenczi reported that the therapeutic impasse was resolved by the mutual analysis. The analysis was then able to proceed. However, he recommended mutual analysis only as a last resort, particularly, in the case of an intractable therapeutic impasse, when the traditional analytic procedures were employed. Unfortunately, the analysis was prematurely terminated (see Chapter 19) because of Ferenczi's illness.

We need to understand why the Severn/Ferenczi clinical experiment in mutual analysis was meaningful. First, it was Ferenczi, with Severn's cooperation who uncovered and analyzed Severn's childhood sexual trauma, a precursor for her pushing so hard for Ferenczi to analyze his own issues. Severn before she entered analysis knew there was something mysterious and dark lurking in the shadows of her mind, which was relevant for her depression and suicidal ideation. But, she had no idea what the issues were. It was the trauma analysis that Ferenczi and Severn developed together that helped uncover Severn's childhood traumas with her father (Rachman, 2014b; Severn, 1933, see Chapter 12). This clinical interaction developed the insight that the dark shadows, threatening to overwhelm her were specific childhood traumas. The analysis of her childhood traumas gave Severn an understanding that her emotional problems were the abuse she suffered as a child. Severn knew this form of therapeutic exploration was not only helpful to her, but she adapted it as a therapeutic method in her development as an analyst (see Chapter 25). Severn believed Ferenczi should practice what he preached; he should use the principles of trauma analysis they discovered to analyze his own emotional issues. By allowing Severn to penetrate his professional and personal facades, Ferenczi joined his analysand in a mutual analytic encounter. It is not often that one individual allows that kind of penetration by another. Ferenczi described it in this way in a March 13, 1932 Clinical entry in his *Clinical Diary* which he titled, "A two-children analysis":

> Certain phases of mutual analysis give the impression of two equally terrified children who compare their experiences, and because of their common fate, understanding each other completely and instinctively try to confront each other. Awareness of the shared fate allows the partner to appear as completely harmless, therefore as someone whom one can trust with confidence.
>
> *(Ferenczi, 1988, p. 56)*

Mutual analysis as reflected in the interchange between Elizabeth and Margaret Severn

An important lens through which to view the controversial issue of the clinical experiment of mutual analysis is Margaret Severn's reaction to this issue. In a series of letters she sent to her mother, Margaret Severn was very critical of Ferenczi. From December, 1932 to February, 1933, Margaret Severn's letters to her mother expressed her discontent with her mother's report of the mutual analysis experiment. In response to Elizabeth Severn telling her daughter she had negotiated with Ferenczi the issue of joint payment for mutual analysis, Margaret said:

That's a very bright idea of Ferenczi to pay you for analysis. Would you remain if he did?

I suppose it would be best, for then you would be better too when you did come …

Love and kisses to my darling.

(Letter from Margaret to Elizabeth Severn.
December 8, 1932 – Paris. In Rachman, 2016d)

Ferenczi paying E. Severn for her analysis of him, became a factor in whether she would be able to remain with Ferenczi rather than return to her daughter, because more money would be available for their household. Margaret would continue to tour as a dancer, providing some of the necessary funds necessary to maintain a joint living situation for the Severns, when her mother came to live with her daughter in London, after leaving Ferenczi in Budapest.

if … you should see fit to accept Ferenczi's offer to pay for the analysis you give him, … it might be best for you to remain in Buda until you are better yourself and not make the terrific effort of changing just yet … If on the other hand you do come … in February or March, I would naturally have to be there to help you.

Margaret went on, in this same letter, to tell her mother she was in good shape emotionally and could continue on without her analysis of her.

my dose of analysis has given me enough equilibrium that I could go on quite well for some time now alone if it seems necessary.

(Letter from Margaret to Elizabeth Severn.
December 10, 1932 – Paris. In Rachman, 2016d)

Margaret also wrote a long letter to her mother, expressing her anger towards Ferenczi, believing Ferenczi was doing her harm. Margaret didn't realize that her mother's struggles with Ferenczi were not an indication of a negative relationship, but, of an analytic struggle towards change:

I do not wish to do any harm to Fer., but after all it isn't my fault that he has made such a failure of his cases and neither you nor he told me that his analysis with you was to be regarded as a secret.

I am sorry for Fer., but the situation is the result of his own illness which he wasn't bright enough to see or admit before.

Well it's a good thing for Fer., that I'm not in Buda now for if I were I would light a bomb under him. The more I think of his attitude to you and its inadequacy either as doctor or friend the more furious I become.

(Letter from Margaret to Elizabeth Severn. December 14, 1932.
In Rachman, 2016d)

Margaret was befuddled by her mother's continued affection for Ferenczi, while she was angry at him. Elizabeth was struggling, in her analysis, with the difficult experiment of mutual analysis. Margaret was so aligned with her mother perhaps, in a pathologic way, as if, she herself, was being hurt by Ferenczi's behavior. Margaret' symbiotic relationship with her mother (see Chapter 9) and her problem with anger (see Chapter 9) exaggerate Margaret's negative response to Ferenczi. After all, Margaret was an incest survivor. She may have perceived Ferenczi as being an abuser of her mother in their emotional struggles to find a therapeutic cure.

> I am glad that your letter today is more hopeful again but it seems rather like your old tricks of oscillating back and forth as I am about to agree with you that Fer. is a terrible demon and ought to be slain at once. I get at letter saying he's really such a sweet little thing after all. If he really is just such a little darling underneath you'll just have to make up your mind not to be hurt by what's on top. I guess because it's awful for you to keep on going through this torture. But that you really felt 'free' for a few hours is splendid news and if it can happen once it can happen again and MUST ....
>   So long, angel. Merry Christmas Mag.
> *(Letter from Margaret to Elizabeth Severn. December 22, 1932 – Paris. In Rachman, 2016d)*

Elizabeth Severn was more forgiving of Ferenczi's shortcomings than her daughter. E. Severn not only benefitted emotionally from their analysis, but also professionally. She, in essence, told her daughter, that she would be the judge of her own analysis with Ferenczi:

> I think it was Ferenczi who first said: The patient is always right.
> *(Severn, 1933, p. 61)*

Severn discussed the changes in the nature of the analytic relationship that she and Ferenczi had developed in their analysis:

> these two people [analyst and analysand] ... must be on equal ground plus a lenient, sympathic and completely unselfish attitude from the analyst... the relationship should be anything but a pedagogic one, ... the (I know more than you do attitude is not successful... The patient is a human being needing endless understanding, and Einfühlung (empathy)... To do this requires ... great liberality of thought, [and] great humanness of feeling ... in its highest sense, Love.
> *(Severn, 1933, pp. 61–62)*

Severn realized that using the concept of love was a form of blasphemy for an analyst. In 1933, empathy, much less, the concept of love, were not, yet, adapted by psychoanalysis although Ferenczi had introduced clinical empathy in 1928 (Ferenczi, 1980h; Rachman, 1989). Severn benefitted from Ferenczi's capacity to extend his emphatic capacity to respond with what was called *cherishing love*. Severn clarified the concept of non-erotic cherishing love, she received from Ferenczi:

> when I speak of love, I do not, of course, mean being 'in love' ... I mean love which is tolerant all-merciful ... such as a wise mother, gives her children ... as a spontaneous and natural gift... only this can bring about a real healing ....
>
> *(Severn, 1933, p. 62)*

The experience of the analysis of the negative countertransference experience with Ferenczi helped Severn develop the following idea about the personal qualities of the therapeutic relationship:

> *respect for the patient* is absolute necessity... *Nor can it be done without liking him,* ... *being more intimate and human,* and *less distant...* [being an analyst requires certain gifts and qualities] ... which are rare....
>
> ... being analyzed ... be very thorough, going deeply into the character traits and *removing* all personal bias, all 'blind spots', and all unconscious phantasies and impulses which would obscure the clear light of reason and muddy the warm spirits that flow from the heart ... a person who is already gifted and of a high grade quality-in short, *a Healer.*
>
> *(Severn, 1933, p. 63, Italics added)*

The analysis of countertransference which was pioneered in the mutual analytic experience of the Ferenczi/Severn analysis has found its way into contemporary psychoanalysis in the Object Relations (Casement, 1985; Little, 1951; Winnicott 1949, 1960); Interpersonal (Searles, 1975; Wolstein, 1959); Relational (Maroda, 1991; Rachman, 2003a) and Self Psychology (Stolorow, Brandschaft & Atwood, 1983) perspectives.

Phenomenology, empathy, surrender, and judicious self-disclosure in mutual analysis

The clinical interaction between Ferenczi and Severn in their struggles to analyze the therapeutic impasse through mutuality can be understood through the lens of phenomenology. As a philosophical tradition developed by Edmund Husserl (1962), it was introduced into American philosophy by Marvin Farber (1943). I was introduced to phenomenology by Farber, while I was an undergraduate student at the University of Buffalo in the late 1950s. During that period the fields of psychology and psychotherapy were integrating the study of phenomenology for understanding of the clinical relationship. This approach introduced a new focus on the subjective experience between the therapeutic dyad. During my clinical studies at the University of Chicago in the early 1960s at the Counseling and Psychotherapy Research Center, where Carl Rogers (1961) and his associates developed

Client-Center Psychotherapy, the integration of phenomenology, psychology, and psychotherapy was fundamental.

The underlying assumption to this phenomenological view of psychotherapy emphasized that understanding the essence of an individual is founded in the relation between the object and the perceiver. Attention is directed toward the nature of the immediate experience as it unfolds in thinking, feeling, and interpersonal functioning of the therapeutic participants. Focusing on the actual experience of the clinical interaction directs attention not only to what the patient, client, or analysand is saying, but, to what is being experienced. If one concentrates on this immediate experience, a natural attunement ensues about what is the nature of the experience that the individual is having with the therapist. Attention shifts from focus on the unconscious, symbolic communication of the individual and formulating this understanding into psychodynamic explanations, to understanding how the individual experiences the therapeutic interaction, conveying this as the essence of the therapeutic experience.

The mutual analysis experiment, I believe, first opened up psychoanalysis to considering the value of analyzing the subjective experiences of the analysand and analyst. Severn helped consider that the analysand's understanding of the psychoanalytic situation needs to be considered in order to fully understand the analytic process. The introduction of mutual analysis actually pushed empathic understanding to its outer boundaries. The beginning of introducing an empathic focus in psychoanalysis began with Ferenczi's declaration of the need to establish a more experiential foundation for psychoanalysis (Ferenczi & Rank, 1925), then towards introducing clinical empathy as the second rule of psychoanalysis [after interpretation (Ferenczi, 1980h, Rachman, 1989)] and Ferenczi and Severn's attempt to establish a new category of treatment in trauma analysis (Ferenczi, 1988; Rachman, 2014a, b, c). The further evolution of empathic understanding resides in the clinical experiment of mutual analysis.

Once clinical flexibility, responsiveness, and empathy were established, Ferenczi was challenged by Severn to extend his clinical innovations to the fullest. She was not attempting to influence him to lose his personal or professional footing, but, correctly interpreting his difficulty in understanding their transference/countertransference relationship. At that moment, Severn realized that Ferenczi's negative feelings about her were harming her and the analysis. When *she became the analyst in the relationship and Ferenczi became the* analysand, something meaningful happened. What is more, one can say, that any moment when an analysand observes and reports his/her idea that the analysand has a thought, feeling or behavior about the analyst that is relevant to the therapeutic process, he/she becomes an analyst or partner in the analytic process.

When the analyst becomes the analysand, can the analyst maintain his/her empathic capacity or will the analyst regress to a transference interpretation and convey that the analysand is behaving neurotically by attempting to explore their relationship? Ferenczi's experiment in entering into a mutual analysis with Severn can be seen as an empathic attempt to fulfill her need to have a responsive father figure who would admit his abusive behavior in their relationship. At that moment, she needed a father who acknowledged that he was abusing her by harboring negative feelings about her, that he did not own. She needed Ferenczi to examine and admit to these harmful feelings, which were causing a re-traumatization in their therapeutic relationship. Ferenczi's empathic contribution was the capacity to push himself to understand this rather than analyze her negative father transference, as if, she was to blame for the therapeutic impasse they had reached.

Ferenczi was able to use this kind of experience with Severn to reformulate the concept of transference in relational analytic terms as outlined in this clinical entry in his *Clinical Diary*:

13 August 1932

A catalogue of sins of psychoanalysis

Reproaches of a woman patient [? E.S.]: (1) Psychoanalysis lures patients into 'transference' ... interpreted as a sign of a profound personal friendship, indeed tenderness ... they become blind and deaf to ... how little *personal* interest analysts have in their patients (2) Meanwhile the unconscious of the patients perceived all the negative feelings in the analyst ... (3) the analysis provides a good opportunity to carry out unconscious, purely self-seeking, ruthless, immoral, ... a sense of power over a succession of helplessly devoted patients ... tax payments for life.

(Ferenczi, 1988, p. 199)

Ferenczi in this passage was acknowledging his debt to Severn in helping him realize that a Confusion of Tongues theory and trauma analysis method are necessary when you analyze a trauma survivor. In analyzing Severn, she was teaching him that not all transferences are manifestations of the analysands's unresolved, unconscious infantile Oedipal neurosis. In analyzing trauma-induced psychopathology, Ferenczi learned about the analyst's contribution to the analytic encounter. Analyzing a trauma survivor means creating a two-person therapeutic experience. The analyst must be willing to analyze his/her own contribution to the analytic encounter. This passage expressing Ferenczi's anger at himself from conducting his analysis of Severn with a limited analytic perspective, may have also been his expression of anger toward Freud for not being able to analyze his traumas of childhood, confining the analysis to an Oedipal Conflict analysis.

What healed the deep-seated childhood traumas Severn suffered at the hands of her psychopathic father? Ferenczi suggested the relational experience with an empathic parental figure:

Being Alone leads to splitting.

The presence of someone with whom one can share and communicate joy and sorrow (love and understanding) can HEAL the trauma. Personality is reassembled 'healed' (like 'glue').

(Ferenczi, 1988, p. 201 – Clinical entry, August 13, 1932)

Continuing on with the cause for trauma based upon a two-person psychology, Ferenczi discussed that *forgiveness* was a part of working through the experience for both analyst and analysand:

> That it was all *possible* to arrive at insight and communion with oneself spells the end of general misanthropy. Finally it is also possible to view and *remember* the trauma with *feelings of forgiveness* and consequently *understanding the analyst who is forgiven* enjoys in the analysis what was denied him in life and hardened his heart.
>
> *(Ferenczi, 1988, pp. 201–202 – Clinical entry August 13, 1932)*

The emotional issue of surrender

Ferenczi's year-long struggle to accept Severn's idea of a mutual analysis, besides being an intellectual/theoretical struggle to embrace a radical idea at the outer boundaries of psychoanalysis, was also an intense struggle to surrender power, control, and status to a woman analysand (Rachman, 2000a). Allowing a woman to become the authority in the analytic relationship was very difficult for Ferenczi as the retrieval of his childhood trauma revealed his fear and anger towards women (see Chapter 12). He was also a person of his time, in that women were not considered the intellectual or emotional equals of men. He seemed to generally transcend this prejudice in his clinical work, as his early empathic work with Rosa K. illustrated (see Chapter 8). But, Severn, in addition to these other considerations, was a woman he perceived as aggressive, masculine, and imperial. She became someone with whom Ferenczi had angry and fearful feelings.

Severn, however, was an analysand who was asking him to let her analyze him. This meant he had to emotionally put aside his need for power, control, and status in a relationship. This is never an easy emotional task for any analyst, assuming that allowing an analysand to analyze an analyst may have its merits. By surrender, I mean relinquish the need to be in control of the relationship, to need to be in a higher, stratified position in the relationship, and to maintain the power in the relationship. As has been discussed, the relationship with Severn made Ferenczi acutely aware of how the method of psychoanalysis he was taught, and Severn wished to change, was inherently positioned in an undemocratic way, to favor the power, status, and control of the analyst. It was not an easy task to go against his analyst, teacher, friend and father figure, Sigmund Freud, and allow a disturbed individual to diagnose and treat him for his negative countertransference reactions. He needed to relinquish his need to be *the authority*, to determine the process and course of the analysis, and to accept the role of being an analysand. Ferenczi was able to surrender to Severn because his personality was not solely based upon being an authority who needed to control analysands, colleagues, and maintain a high-status profile. Ferenczi had indicated that he could forgo the power, control, and status of being the president of the International Psychoanalytic Society, which Freud offered and Ferenczi turned down (Rachman, 1997a). Ferenczi sacrificed this opportunity to pursue his own interest in understanding and treating trauma disorder.

Ferenczi's surrender to Severn, meant having a certain faith that your analysand is someone you can trust with your inner life. Although he had negative feelings about Severn, their mutual analysis, helped him to retrieve the origin of these feelings and transform his negative feelings into empathy. No doubt, Severn helping him to reach the depths of his negative feelings toward women made him realize he was in good hands with her as his analyst. Ferenczi was able to formulate the kind of surrender which was involved in mutual analysis, into a theoretical idea that could be useful in the less dramatic and necessary forms of clinical interaction with trauma survivors.

Surrender was related to Ferenczi's concept of *nachgiebigkeit*, a clinical flexibility derived from the German verb, *nachgeben*, to yield, to be flexible, pliable (Rachman, 1997a, p. 303). It is a further development of his concept of *the elasticity of psychoanalytic technique* (Ferenczi, 1980h). In other words. mutual analysis can be seen as the furthest extension of the elasticity principle, rather than emerging solely from a personal defect in his functioning, as Freud and the traditional analytic community believed (Jones, 1957).

Judicious self-disclosure

An important means to encourage analytic understanding in the experience of mutuality is to respond with judicious self-disclosure (Rachman, 2003a). The distinguishing characteristics of such disclosing to the analysand involves the analyst disclosing only those aspects of their own functioning which will aid the analysand in the examination of their emotional issues. It is not necessary or helpful to reveal all of the analyst's subjectivity when it can harm, discourage, or cause an empathic failure. In actuality, the analysand does not want to know every single detail of the analyst's subjectivity. What the analysand needs is *a good enough response*, so that provides the necessary empathic understanding and repair to the injured/traumatized child-in-the-adult. The countertransference disclosure should not overwhelm, frighten or create an attitude of an *all knowing, all loving analyst*. There is no mother in a child's experience, and no adult/analyst who can function as the *all-loving parental figure who cures emotional disorder*. Ferenczi may have been caught in a megalomania fantasy of becoming Severn's savior. As it turned out, he was a significant contributor to her emotional recovery, but, Severn was a significant contributor to her own recovery (see Chapter 20). There is no room for unbridled narcissism in analytic encounters. Mutuality also means both members of the therapeutic dyad contribute to the success of the analytic encounter. An anlysand is not solely being analyzed by an analyst. Two individuals are both analysand and analyst with each other, becoming analytic partners. Judicious self-disclosure acknowledges the two-person psychology in the analytic encounter (Rachman, 2004a).

Commentaries on mutuality

Wolstein (1993) believed that Ferenczi's *Clinical Diary*, where the account of mutual analysis was outlined was a significant contribution to psychoanalysis because it focused on the dialogue of the unconscious between analyst and analysand defining the experimental field of clinical interaction. In the issue of mutuality, Wolstein saw it as a shared inquiry into the transference/countertransference relationship. As such, he saw the clinical experiment in mutuality as an important attempt to evolve psychoanalysis toward fulfilling Ferenczi and Rank's (1925) thesis: "what the patient needs is an experience, not an interpretation ..." (Wolstein, 1993, p. 182).

Aron (1993) made an important distinction in understanding mutual analysis. Mutuality and asymmetry should not become fusion. Ferenczi did not analyze his countertransference, until Severn convinced him to do so. When the analysis was in difficulty he *redoubled* his efforts to analyze his countertransference efforts (see Chapter 22). Fortune (1996), has a balanced assessment of the mutual analysis:

> in the best spirit of early psychoanalysis, Ferenczi's experiments in mutual analysis was an inspired–albeit, therapeutically flawed–act of following, and learning from the patient.
>
> *(p. 171)*

Commentary on mutual analysis

One of the most vehement criticisms of Ferenczi's clinical experiment in mutual analysis has been made by John Gedo. As a well-respected theoretician and once, Ferenczi scholar Gedo's severe criticism, not only of Ferenczi's clinical functioning, but demeaning his personal functioning, is puzzling. Gedo suggested that mutual analysis was a function of Ferenczi's psychopathology, namely an expression of sadomasochistic tendencies, his inability to maintain a traditional analytic framework with difficult analysands, his inability to understand the transference implications of his clinical interactions, and his focus on reconstructing the childhood traumas of his analysands. Gedo seemed to find no meaning in Ferenczi's later work on trauma analysis, attributing this to a deviation from Freudian psychoanalysis and a personal deterioration in functioning (Bacon & Gedo, 1993). What is so puzzling, is why would Gedo take the time and energy to politically assassinate Ferenczi, as a modern–day Ernest Jones?

Judith Dupont (1988) has provided a very thoughtful and insightful discussion about the recognition of confronting the reality that the analytic encounter contains a built in mandate for self examination:

> It has often been said that the analyst throughout his life pursues his own analysis with the assistance of his patients. In general, this means the self-questioning induced by the analytic sessions with patients obliges him to engage in permanent self-analysis.
>
> *(Dupont, 1988, p. xx)*

In her wisdom, Dupont accepts the mandate, that in psychyoanalysis, there is a place to consider the method of learning from the patient:

> Mutual analysis is designed to illuminate those shadowy corners, so that each protagonist can locate himself in relation to the other with greater assurance.
>
> *(Dupont, 1988, p. xxi)*

Contemporary view of a mutual analytic encounter

The Severn/Ferenczi clinical interaction in mutual analysis is seen a daring experiment, born of a desperate attempt to resolve an unanalyzable transference/countertransference impasse, which produced a meaningful enough result to resolve the impasse. Due to the premature termination of the analysis, Severn left the experience not fully recovered. She developed an emotional dependency upon Ferenczi, in his attempt to respond to her expressed need for a non-abusive, loving father figure. We know from theoretical clinical developments since Severn and Ferenczi's clinical journey in the 1930s that narcissistic, trauma, and borderline cases respond positively to extensive periods of empathic understanding, before the analysis of the basic faults can be accomplished (Balint, 1992/1968; Kohut, 1984; Rachman & Klett, 2015; Searles, 1975; Winnicott, 1965).

It is of particular importance that the enactments of trauma within the transference and real relationships are maintained at a level of emotional regression that does not encourage a complete acting out of the childhood pathology (see Chapter 22). The therapeutic relationship must elasticize so that it can provide an experience of fulfillment and repair (Rachman, 1998), while being monitored for any indication of an emergence of new pathology, loss of contact with reality, intense dependency, or a loss of ability to analyze one's functioning, becoming lost in the transference (Rachman & Klett, 2015). As we shall see in Chapter 22, regression must be maintained at a therapeutic level.

18

NON-INTERPRETATIVE MEASURES IN THE ANALYSIS OF TRAUMA

Anna O./Bertha Pappenheim as a founder of psychoanalysis

In order to gain a perspective on the trailblazing development of non-interpretative measures introduced by Ferenczi and Severn, we need to examine how psychoanalysis became so wedded to interpretation from its onset. There is an interesting similarity to Bertha Pappeheim's co-creation with Josef Breuer of the psychoanalytic method of free association and Severn's co-creation of non-interpretative measures with Sándor Ferenczi. Bertha Pappenheim's case became known as the case of Miss Anna O., published jointly by Breuer and Freud (Breuer & Freud, 1895). The case was presented as a study of hysteria where the symptoms of the disorder were revealed through verbal discussions with the patient. Pappenheim's method of chimney sweeping became known as free association and the therapy contributed to the development of psychoanalysis. The collaborative clinical interaction between Breuer and Pappenheim can be outlined as follows:

1. Beuer began the treatment using hypnosis.
2. Breuer observed that Pappenheim experienced moments that he called *absences*, that is, a change in functioning, characterized by confusion. These were dissociative moments when she would talk to herself, muttering words or phrases, which seem to induce a kind of hypnosis. Breuer observed that these words were melancholy fantasies which had poetic qualities.
3. There came a time when Pappenheim wanted to end the hypnotic session which Breuer had initiated as the basic form of treatment. In a spirit of mutuality and democratic functioning *Breuer accepted Pappenheim's suggestion to talk rather than maintain a hypnotic trance.*
4. Pappenheim led the way in the clinical interaction by *her desire to talk directly to Breuer, without any other additional methods.*

Breuer once again agreed with this new convention, introduced by his patient. Thus *talk therapy began.*

1. Thereafter, Pappenheim began to talk freely to Breuer, saying anything that came into her mind. She referred to this kind of freely talking about her emotions as *chimney sweeping.*
2. *Freud described Pappenheim in generous terms as the founder of psychoanalysis.*

(Breuer & Freud, 1895)

Although there are those who believed that Breuer and Freud misdiagnosed Pappenheim's symptoms as a neurosis (Macmillian, 1996, p. 631), the treating of psychological disorder by talking freely about one's experiences in order to understand them was a turning point in the treatment of human behavior. One could say that Breuer, Pappenheim, and Freud should have been nominated for a Nobel prize for the discovery of psychoanalysis. The question still lingers: Why didn't Freud win a Nobel prize for the development of psychoanalysis? The establishment of the Talking Cure still remains the central dimension of clinical psychoanalysis.

Freud's emotional blindness to the importance of trauma

In order for me to discuss the sacred role of interpretation in traditional psychoanalysis, I need to confess my difficulty with the Oedipal theory of neurosis. I have never fully understood, accepted, or valued Freud's Oedipal theory of neurosis, nor the dependency on interpretation as the golden means to treat emotional disorder. I firmly believe that Freud "got it right the first time," that is to say, in the beginning he correctly formulated that actual childhood seduction leads to psychological disorder (Freud, 1954). Sexual, physical, and emotional abuse account for an important dynamic in the development of a trauma disorder. Freud's emotional blindness to the existence and importance of real events causing psychological disorder was a result of his unidimensional theory of the Oedipal complex. The insistence on the psychodynamic of the child's unconscious romance with the parent blinded him to considering other factors. I have postulated that a significant personal issue was also a factor in Freud's emotional blindness: Freud's childhood seduction by a nursemaid was not fully integrated into his understanding of his personality development and functioning (Rachman, 2016b). Although the childhood seduction was part of his self-analysis, it did not seem to inform his understanding of child abuse in Ferenczi's thinking and treating of the Incest Trauma. Freud's personal experience with incest did not inform his theorizing. He made no room in his Oedipal theory for the Incest Trauma (Rachman, 2012a). In fact, his view of psychoanalytic theory set a precedent for ignoring actual trauma in the development of psychological disorders.

Freud needed to find, I believe, an explanation for neurosis which bypassed sexual abuse of a child, as this allowed him to maintain his repression of his own childhood seduction. As Marianne Krüll (1986) has pointed out, Freud's father had established an ethic of maintaining secrecy about family matters. Freud was willing to discuss his own seduction as an intellectual matter, as part of his self-discovery, as an explanation for hysteria, but not as a personal issue to be worked through analytically. If one accepts a trauma explanation for sexual seduction, one is free to introduce therapeutic measures which go beyond interpretation. In the analysis between Severn and Ferenczi, it became clear that sexual seduction and physical and emotional abuse could lead to a trauma disorder necessitating the employment of non-interpretative measures.

Why was Freud not amenable to the idea of a trauma disorder and the modification of analytic technique to successfully treat actual trauma? There are some possible explanations. Freud was most comfortable using his intellect rather than expressing his emotions. Freud had every right to be proud of his intellect, since his intellect provided the genius to discover psychoanalysis and build a theory to understand human behavior. But Freud was always more naturally connected to theory than technique. He was the theory builder. Freud knew this about himself (Roazen, 1975). When Ferenczi was introduced to him, in the first years after conceptualizing the basic tenets of psychoanalysis. Freud found his clinical alter ego. Ferenczi, it can be said, was the clinical genius of psychoanalysis to Freud's theoretical genius (Rachman, 1997a). We have validation of this when Freud made a special attempt to endorse Ferenczi's clinical innovations (Rachman, 1997a, b). Freud welcomed Ferenczi's introductions of clinical empathy, praising himself as a mature clinician with no peer (Freud, 1933; Rachman, 1997a). Freud, in his response to Ferenczi's introduction of clinical empathy, self-disclosed that his own contributions to clinical practice had been to establish taboos. He realized that he made only negative suggestions. The rule of abstinence was a good example of Freud's tendency. Freud formulated the rule of abstinence to warn young analysts *not to indulge female analysands* by satisfying their emotional demands (Freud, 1915, 1914).

Abstinence referred to *not giving in* to an analysand; *withholding a response.* Traditional psychoanalysis became wedded to the rule of abstinence, the use of silence, and withholding of a response for fear that fulfilling a need would encourage neurosis. In order to cure neurosis, according to the philosophy of treatment, the analysand had *to give up* their neurotic needs. As long as the fiction continued that Freud's theory of psychoanalysis was based on his only treating neurotic disorders, there was no need to consider changing the analytic standard of interpretation and the development of insight. However, the analysands in Freud's iconic cases can be seen as having problems other than neurotic issues. In the case of the Wolf Man, Sergei Pankejeff, the analysand can be seen as a victim of childhood sexual abuse. It is possible he was the victim of his sister's sexual abuse (see Chapter 8).

The case of Dora, Ida Bauer, can also be reconsidered as an instance of childhood seduction rather than an Oedipal complex case (Rachman & Mattick, 2012). In analyzing Bauer's emotional issues, Freud completely ignored instances of childhood sexual abuse. For example, Herr K., a friend of the Bauer family, was clearly interested in sexual contact with Ida Bauer and attempted to seduce her. In one instance, the 42-year-old Herr K. tried to force a kiss on the 14-year-old Bauer. Freud not only ignored this data in formulating his theory of the analysis, but he insisted that the only relevant data to be considered was his forced interpretations of her so-called Oedipal complex (Rachman & Mattick, 2012).

Oedipal theory and interpretation

Although Ferenczi was formally trained as a Freudian analyst, he always had a more open, flexible, and empathic approach to the analytic encounter (Ferenczi, 1902). In his work with difficult cases he developed a non-interpretative approach. This approach allowed him to observe the experience of the analysand and to attune to his/her own experience in the psychoanalytic situation. In 1919 Ferenczi (1980c) noticed that as an analysand was lying on the couch, she indicated a sense of rest-lessness by moving her body and constantly changing her position. *Ferenczi changed the focus of the analytic session from being attuned to the spoken word to becoming aware of non-verbal communication in the analytic encounter.* The addition of the attunement to the non-verbal interaction was in addition to the focus on verbal behavior. Ferenczi noticed that during the changing of body positions, the analysand was rubbing her legs together. It occurred to him that the rubbing of her legs may have been a symbolic masturbatory gesture. Furthermore, Ferenczi thought this masturbatory equivalent was syphoning off psychic energy and motivation needed to explore the unconscious fantasies underlying the reported sexual difficulties. The observation of the non-verbal behavior and its possible interpretative meaning led to a change in clinical therapeutics. Rather than interpret this behavior, Ferenczi introduced active intervention. He developed the idea of prohibiting the analysand from continuing to cross her legs while she was lying on the couch. The analysand cooperated with the suggestion. Then, Ferenczi suggested she uncross her legs as she functioned in her daily life. This active approach produced a change in the analysand's functioning. The change in behavior led her to recall some childhood experiences. Ferenczi used interpretation to analyze the child experiences. This led to a change in the analysand's functioning.

Ferenczi was experimenting with the idea that being active in the therapeutic interaction was necessary when associations dry up, so to speak. Being active in the relationship was an expression of a natural personal tendency of his. What Ferenczi was able to do is combine intellect with activity. The analysis of non-verbal behavior opened the door for the use of non-interpretative measures in clinical psychoanalysis. As in the above-cited case, he combined interpretation with the activity, which led to an analytic exploration of the emotional issue. Eventually, Ferenczi realized that prohibition of behavior and too vigorous use of activity led to negative transference reactions and abandoned the practice (Rachman, 1997a). The negative transference reactions became a resistance and contributed to a lack of associative material.

Ferenczi and Rank's *Development of Psychoanalysis* was a turning point on the road to the development of non-interpretative measures. Ferenczi and Rank re-evaluated the nature of the analytic encounter (Ferenczi & Rank, 1925). In the second decade since the founding of psychoanalysis, Ferenczi and Rank, who were part of the original group that surrounded Freud, felt it was necessary to discuss *elasticizing the boundaries of analytic functioning* (Ferenczi & Rank, 1925). This reevaluation occurred before the Ferenczi/Severn analysis, and after Freud and Ferenczi had earlier collaborated on re-assessing the exclusive use of interpretation for phobic and obsessive disorders (Rachman, 1997a). At this point in their personal and professional relationship they were in accord. They both agreed that interpretation needed to be implemented by active means (Rachman, 1997a). The Ferenczi and Rank thesis took the change in clinical therapeutics to a new level. Their focus on the experimental dimension of the analytic encounter was a turning point. It signaled that an intellectual/cognitive approach, that is, maintaining a solely interpretative interaction in a therapeutic relationship was not sufficient for working through emotional issues. This meant a necessary change in the functioning of the analyst.

Gedo (1986) believed that the Ferenczi and Rank book, *The Development of Psychoanalysis* was a psychoanalytic classic, which aimed to change the focus on the intellectual focus of interpretation and development of insight.

> the novel stress on the crucial importance of affective experience in the here and now of the analytic transference ... to enunciate ... analysis must be understood as a process ... symptom-analysis and complex analysis had become outdated. An adequate analytic process must promote affective relieving ... resistance ... must not be treated as undesirable or worst, sinful.
>
> *(Gedo, 1986, p. 44)*

The issue of resistance was also an important part of the changes that Ferenczi and Rank discussed. Resistance was the original idea that explained an analysand's difficulties in responding positively to the interpretation/insight paradigm. This explanation emerged from a perspective which viewed the relationship between analyst and analysand as a power struggle. When their analysand had difficulty in analytic encounter, the analyst saw the difficulty as a defect in the analysand's functioning. *Resistance became a theoretical way to institutionalize blaming the analysand for the therapeutic difficulty.* This so-called one-person psychology perspective for the analytic relationship was embedded in Freud's iconic case studies. As was discussed in Chapter 8, the analysis of the Wolf Man, Sergei Pankejeff, was focused entirely on Freud's interpretation of the dream of wolves. There was no attempt to develop an interpersonal two-person discussion of Pankejeff's so-called resistance or emotional issues. Freud presented his interpretations as if they were the truth. What is more, Freud acted as if there was no truth in what the analysand believed or felt. The Ferenczi and Rank recommendations laid the foundation for a focus on the analytic process in the here-and-now interaction between analyst and analysand, with the affective dimension taken into account. As the Ferenczi/Severn analysis began, Ferenczi had been defining clinical psychoanalysis as a relationship between analyst and analysand where both are partners in co-creating the analytic experience. In this new approach, the analysand's contribution would be valued, and the analyst would be asked to contribute his/her own affective reactions.

The Ferenczi/Severn analysis of trauma and the development of non-interpretative measures

One of the central objections by Freud to the Ferenczi/Severn analysis was his belief that Ferenczi was rejecting his Oedipal theory, and, thusly rejecting him professionally and personally. There was some truth in Freud's motion. But Freud's reaction to the meaning of the Ferenczi/Severn's analysis was more personal, political, and authoritarian than intellectual or scientific. Freud, fueled by his orthodox follower's criticisms and denouncements of Ferenczi, was disappointed, angry, and alienated from his once-favorite student, because he felt Ferenczi had left him and psychoanalysis behind to concentrate on studying and treating trauma (Rachman, 1997a, b). Freud was correct in that Ferenczi did withdraw to protect himself from Freud and the orthodox community by concentrating on his relationship with his Hungarian colleagues who supported his trauma studies. Ferenczi was also protecting himself from the denouncements that the orthodox analytic community made about his person and work (Rachman, 1997b). Freud correctly perceived that his once-cherished friend was drifting away from him theoretically and clinically. He was incorrect in that Ferenczi was not rebelling against him (Gay, 1984), but struggling to find his own identity as a psychoanalyst (Rachman, 1997a).

When Ferenczi agreed to see Severn for analysis, it changed both their lives. Ferenczi's analysis with Severn encouraged his ability to be empathic, flexible, responsive, and creative. In fact, all the developments in theory and method from 1925–1933 that became part of the Budapest School of Psychoanalysis (Rachman, 2016a) were first developed in the Ferenczi/Severn analysis.

Ferenczi's identity as a healer and his clinical ethos/Severn's identity as a healer and her clinical innovations

Why did Freud turn to Ferenczi at the Budapest Congress and declare that the future of psychoanalytic therapy will be in his hands? *Freud clearly passed the mantle to Ferenczi* during that Congress (Rachman, 1997a). Freud was well aware that Ferenczi had the desire, the talent, and the motivation to initiate change in the analytic method. Although Ferenczi was a student and adherent of psychoanalysis, he was never a blind follower of Freud. Early in their relationship Ferenczi attempted to assert his independence and own identity. In the famous Sicily incident, Ferenczi complained to Freud that he did not want to be Freud's secretary when they were going over the Schreiber case (Grosskurth, 1991). Ferenczi thought that they were going to collaborate and Freud thought that Ferenczi would help him by taking his dictation. Freud counted on Ferenczi being a company man (Fromm, 1954). Freud's original group of students and colleagues seem to divide themselves into different groups: the disciples who accepted his ideas and protected their master from criticism (Grosskurth, 1991) and the dissenters. Abraham, Eitingon, and Jones were the loyal, unquestioning followers; Adler, Jung, and then Rank developed different perspectives from Freud and had to leave the fold. Freud needed to have company men (Fromm, 1959), adherents, rather than colleagues who entertain new ideas and perspectives to broaden or extend the boundaries of psychoanalysis. What is more, students who wanted to develop their own identity could not find a welcome father in Freud. Being with Freud meant to be part of a unified movement (Fromm, 1954). Introducing a new perspective, such as Ferenczi attempted to do, in the study and treatment of the Incest Trauma, was misunderstood by Freud as aggression against the father (Gay, 1984; Jones, 1957) rather than a son's attempt to find his own identity (Rachman, 1997a). We shall see how much a part of Ferenczi's identity it was for him to develop a perspective which was different, but, not opposed to his teacher, Freud. A theory of psychoanalysis which incorporates a view of human behavior developed through the life cycle views a son's development of a perspective different from the father as a psychological step toward personal identity formation (Erikson, 1950). Ferenczi was a respectful student of Freud and psychoanalysis, but he was an independent thinker and innovative clinician. As Thompson has pointed out (Green, 1964), Ferenczi was wedded to pleasing Freud and needing his approval. Ferenczi was not able to break away from Freud and found his own perspective. Ferenczi never left the field of psychoanalysis, nor did he condemn Freud for the mistreatment he received. Severn, it can be said, followed her teacher Ferenczi in this way. Although she had three unsuccessful analyses, was disappointed by her personal contact with Freud, and toward the end of her analysis with Ferenczi was dissatisfied with him, she never condemned Ferenczi nor psychoanalysis.

Ferenczi's personality was suited for his desire to be a healing psychoanalyst. He was a warm, outgoing, and responsive individual. He was interested in, and attracted to, interpersonal contact. When he entered a room of colleagues, he would greet them with a hug and kiss. This embracing behavior even extended to the dour Jones (Rachman, 1997a). It was generally considered that Ferenczi was the warmest and most likeable of the early pioneers of psychoanalysts. It was a natural development that Ferenczi would integrate his positive personality into his clinical behavior.

Ferenczi identified himself as a healer. He was motivated to analyze in order to cure, to help an individual work through his/her emotional difficulties. His clinical functioning was colored by his personality and identity. He believed he could help anyone who was genuinely interested in being helped. He exuded confidence, compassion, and hope. His type of analytic encounter was not an exercise in an intellectual conversation; it was an emotional and interpersonal experience. Analysands knew they were engaged with a passionate, empathic person who was interested in helping them. *He had a therapeutic presence.* If the analysis did not proceed as planned, the analysand became aware he had a clinical partner to work through any difficulties. In the free association process, or in the relationship, Ferenczi would not automatically interpret the difficulty as the analysand's resistance. He would offer new perspectives where non-verbal, active, non-interpretative measures were entertained. The burden of solving the clinical difficulties, therefore, was not only the responsibility of the analysand, but also the analyst. The clinical difficulty became an opportunity for analyst and analysand to cooperate and co-create a solution to the difficulty.

If one traces the history of Ferenczi's training and functioning as a clinician, they can see his capacity for innovative functioning as a young psychiatrist at St Rokus Hospital in Budapest, as well as his work with the underprivileged and transgendered patients. The trajectory of Ferenczi's innovations once he joined the analytic community became a blueprint for clinical innovation in psychoanalysis (Rachman, 1997a, 2003a). The stages in the expanding of Ferenczi's interpretative clinical behavior can be described as follows:

1. He encouraged the analyst to go beyond interpretation toward introducing the use of activity in responding to an analysand's difficulty with free association (Rachman 1997a, 2004a).
2. The nature of the analytic encounter was changed. Although analysis remained the talking cure, it evolved by becoming an experiential and interpersonal interaction (Ferenczi & Rank, 1925; Thompson, 1914).
3. The language of the psychoanalytic dialogue is expanded to include non-verbal communication (Ferenczi, 1980b, c).
4. The introduction of the role of activity in the psychoanalytic encounter and the identification of non-verbal communication laid the foundation for a Two-Person Psychology for psychoanalysis. Ferenczi invited the analysand to join him in co-creating the analytic encounter. Ferenczi illustrated a new direction for the analytic encounter, which he called "Nachgiegkeit," *a leaning toward, or in the direction of, the analysand* (Rachman, 1997a). When the analysand could not adhere to the basic rule of free association, Ferenczi deviated from tradition. He observed that some analysands' inability to adhere to the rule of free association was not due solely to resistance or any other negative behavior toward the analyst or the analytic process. The issue was the analysand's emotional difficulty or incapacity. The traditional idea involves an emotional struggle, in any analytic encounter between the analysand's motivation to get well and the analysand's receptivity to analyzing his/her difficulties. The formulation of a power struggle as an inherent dimension of an analytic relationship skewed the therapeutic encounter toward the analyst as the authority and the analysand as the subordinate. This therapeutic philosophy is now considered a one-person psychology.

(Aron, 1992)

Expanding the boundaries of analytic functioning through the Ferenczi/Severn analysis

Ferenczi's analysis with Severn brought into perspective the pre-Oedipal emotional issues which she suffered in during childhood (see Chapters 10 and 12). This case was not an indication of an Oedipal complex, but a case where actual traumatic experiences had occurred as paternal sexual, emotional, and physical abuse. Once it was established that trauma was the origin of Severn's disorder, two basic issues needed to be considered. First, the establishment of trauma as Severn's emotional disorder meant that Oedipal theory and clinical interaction geared toward interpretation and the development of insight needed to be reevaluated. Secondarily, clinical interactions which addressed the analysis and working through of actual childhood trauma needed to be developed. Criticisms of the Severn/Ferenczi analysis as deviating so drastically from tradition that this analysis cannot be considered to be psychoanalysis do not take into account Freud's dictum, which he arrived at from working with his difficult cases such as The Wolf Man/Sergei Pankejeff. Freud stated that only the most difficult cases force new understanding and functioning upon the analyst. Freud believed that only when we face such difficulties can we fully understand the true depths of psychoanalytic functioning. In Elizabeth Severn as an analysand, Ferenczi was faced with an individual who presented such difficulties. She was a clinical innovator and a veteran psychotherapist. Her unsuccessful analyses left her with negative feelings about being analyzed. She had given great thought to what was not helpful in her failed analyses. She had her own ideas about treatment and what she needed from her analyst and the therapeutic process with Ferenczi.

Another important factor in this analysis was Severn's challenge to Ferenczi to be a different kind of analyst, one who would be true to his reputation as being *the analyst of difficult cases* (Rachman, 1997a). Severn had superior intelligence and significant emotional understanding of herself and others. Her intelligence and emotional understanding led to self-confidence and belief in herself. Her own clinical work from 1908–1925, before she met Ferenczi, was innovative (see Chapter 11) Ferenczi called her a colleague (Rachman, 2016d). Severn had many important positive qualities that were admirable and outstanding. She was totally dedicated to overcoming her emotional difficulties. As has been mentioned, she suffered from severe depression and struggled with suicidal ideation and despair. Yet, when she heard about Ferenczi's work with difficult cases from Otto Rank, she was motivated to move from New York City to Budapest in order to dedicate herself to her recovery. When the analysis prematurely terminated, she was able to continue working on her emotional issues by herself, recover, and go on to develop her clinical practice as a psychoanalyst (see Chapter 20 and 25).

I believe that Severn shared with Ferenczi a certain kind of clinical genius. Her functioning as a clinician, before she met Ferenczi (1908–1925) and in the 26 years after the termination of the analysis (1933–1959), show a successful clinical practitioner who was able to deal with a variety of individuals using flexible and innovative clinical methods. Severn had, as did Ferenczi, superior clinical intuition that she employed in her clinical practice as well as in her clinical interaction in her analysis with Ferenczi (see Chapter 11). Severn felt the following clinical dimensions were necessary to successfully resolve her severe emotional issues:

1. Emotional responsiveness by the analyst.
2. Active clinical interaction.
3. Willingness to experiment with the clinical method.
4. Going beyond interpretation to non-interpretative measures.

5. Analyst's willingness to invite the analysand to be a clinical partner in the analytic encounter.
6. An analyst who is emotionally attuned to his/her reactions and willing to enter into a countertransference analysis of them.
7. An analyst who does not have a strong need for power, control, or status.
8. An analyst who can create a democratic and mutual relationship.
9. An analyst who admits that he/she can make mistakes.
10. An analyst who fundamentally believes in emphatic understanding.

Non-interpretative measures in the analysis of trauma

In the pioneering analysis of trauma, the Ferenczi/Severn relationship can be seen as a pioneering study in the use of non-interpretative measures (Rachman, 2014b). Some observers saw the introduction of non-interpretative measures as experimental, that is, non-traditional procedures initiated to deal with difficult cases, that may never become standard procedures (Balint, 1992/1968; Lorand, 1966). It is likely, that Ferenczi and Severn thought the non-interpretative measures were necessary for the treatment of trauma. In Chapter 13 an examination is made of the efficacy of these measures. Trauma analysis, as developed by Severn and Ferenczi, concerned itself with focusing on the emotional disorder whose origin was found in actual childhood trauma, not unconscious, fantasized events. Of course, there were unconscious and fantasy issues that were operative in a traumatized analysand. But, in order to reach the deepest level of the analysis, the trauma and how it affected the individual needed to be addressed. As Balint (1992/1968), Searles (1975), and Winnicott (1965), verified, there are psychological disorders which need extended periods of therapeutic interaction in an empathic holding environment where interpretation is not the sole method of response. It is when the analysand has built up a sense of safety, trust, and empathy that the analyst can contemplate *the judicious use of interpretation*. Interpretation used prematurely does not provide trauma disorder analysis with the necessary experience of being with a compassionate, empathic figure a trauma survivor so desperately wants and needs. As a clinician who has worked with trauma survivors for over 40 years, I have never had a traumatized individual ask for an interpretation. On the other hand, there have been many instances of trauma survivors who asked for gentleness, kindness, warmth, empathy, responsiveness, emotionality, and activity (Rachman & Klett, 2015). However, interpretation can become a significant part of trauma analysis when it is employed after a prolonged experience of empathy. All trauma survivors know what they need based on their abusive experiences within their family as well as surrogate parental figures (including therapists, analysts, teachers, clergy, family, friends, and relatives. Not all trauma survivors have the capacity to ask for what they need. In such instances, the experienced analyst may introduce non-interpretative measures. Severn was not, as has been mentioned, hesitant to voice her needs. The spectrum of non-interpretative measures that were developed during the Severn/Ferenczi analysis can be listed as follows:

1. Lengthening the duration of a session.
2. Lengthening the number of sessions, either scheduled or spontaneously arranged.
3. Reducing the duration of silence in an analytic session.
4. Responding to the expressed needs of the analysand.
5. Creating a semi-trance state during a session to encourage therapeutic regression.
6. The development of countertransference analysis.
7. Mutuality in the therapeutic relationship.
8. Use of extramural contact, such as arranging sessions outside of the consultation room.
9. Clinical empathy as a primary mode of clinical observation and responding.
10. Dramatizing interaction in an analytic session by focusing on the emotional and subjective experience of the relationship.

Uses and misuses of non-interpretative measures

One must consider the clinical experimentation concept when introducing non-interpretative measures. There is no doubt that some non-interpretative measures revolutionized the analytic encounter, the introduction of clinical empathy being one such innovation. I have attempted to correct the perception in contemporary psychoanalysis that Kohut was the author of clinical empathy (Rachman, 1989a). I believe this occurred because Kohut did not credit any pregenitors such as Ferenczi, or Carl Rogers, the distinguished humanistic psychotherapist, who was an early proponent of clinical empathy [Rogers, 1951, 1957, 1959, 1961, 1975]. Kohut, in his writings, did not refer to other theoreticians as precursors (Rachman, 1989a). Several generations of psychoanalysts were, therefore, trained to believe Kohut invented clinical empathy and seemed to be a cult of followers of Kohut. There has been, however, a group of Self Psychologists who have pioneered the integration of a variety of analytic perspectives with Kohut's insights (Bacal, 1985; Basch, 1984; Detrick & Detrick, 1989; Lichtenberg, 2016; Stolorow, 1976).

Severn demanded empathy because it was not only absent in her three previous analyses, but, more importantly in her childhood. In my attempt to understand Severn's need for empathy I will speak in her voice to Ferenczi about her trauma:

> Do not tell me that my emotional problem is that I have the unconscious fantasy that I want to sleep with my father. And, of course, do not add the fantasy of being a rival with my mother for my father. You have helped me to realize that it was no fantasy. My crazy, psychopathic father actually did have sex with me when I was a child.
>
> I do not have an Oedipal Complex, I have a Trauma Complex. Do not interpret my childhood for me. What I need is someone to understand what happened to me, not what I imagine had happened to me. I need you to

understand *how I feel as an abused child*. Can you feel what I feel? *Do you believe me*, when I say, I was sexually abused by my father? After all, you were taught by Freud. He taught you and all other psychoanalysts that parent/child sexuality is a figment of a child's imagination. Do you think I imagined that my father actually had sex with me? Do you think I am, in resistance to exploring my unconscious wishes for a romance with my father? Can you understand my abused child-in-the-disturbed adult? *Can you felel with me without needing to tell me what I am thinking?*

Severn's demands for empathy were met by Ferenczi, although she was right that Ferenczi was taught to think of the Oedipal complex as the cornerstone of clinical psychoanalysis.

The first notation in Ferenczi's writings listed the introduction of empathy (Ferenczi, 1980h) as an indication of a Ferenczi/Severn collaboration (see Chapter 14). Apparently, Ferenczi was being flexible and empathic in their interaction, and she helped name the form of clinical behavior as *elasticizing the analytic situation*. It was also Severn's need for empathy, which Ferenczi observed she needed, that influenced his developing this mode of non-interpretative measures as a fundamental method of therapeutic responding (Rachman, 1988a, 1989a). Once introduced, Ferenczi influenced by Severn, continued to expand the boundaries of empathic functioning in the use of non-interpretative measures. Their relationship solidified the development of an alternate theory, the Confusion of Tongues (Ferenczi, 1980k, 1988); a new form of therapy, trauma analysis (Ferenczi, 1988) and the use of non-interpretative measures (Ferenczi, 1980h - k; 1988). These developments can be seen as a widening the scope for analytic functioning in the direction towards understanding and responding to the subjective experience of the analysand.

One of the dramatic developments in non-interpretative measures was Severn's development of the *Semi-Trance Session* (Severn, 1916). Severn, as early as 1916 would be able to induce in herself an altered state of consciousness, where she was able to retrieve and explore her early childhood experiences (see Chapter 22). Ferenczi was not familiar with this method and did not have a positive view of regression. He had the traditional analytic view of regression, that is, emotional connection to an earlier or primitive mode of psychological functioning was considered undesirable, and labelled regressive (Freud, 1990). This is the view Ferenczi was taught, and an orientation he had when he began to work with Severn. Ferenczi, consequently, had a confused and anxious reaction to the semi-trance experience. Severn, without asking Ferenczi, introduced her method into their analysis. Without warning, she would close her eyes and remain silent while she induced the semi-trance state. Unprepared for such interaction he became concerned and anxious when Severn did not speak. He interrupted the silence by offering interpretations. Severn's silence also made Ferenczi anxious. Severn erupted into an angry outburst, telling her analyst to be quiet. His interpretations were interrupting her attempt at reverie. Ferenczi struggled to understand Severn's semi-trance method; although it was foreign, confusing, and anxiety-provoking, Severn was not about to abandon a method she felt had been helpful to her. Interestingly enough, Ferenczi did not view her behavior as resistance. Consequently, he did not enter into a power struggle with Severn, trying to convince her she was resisting his interpretations or putting herself in emotional danger. He did not demand that she should let him be in charge of clinical innovations. As we shall see in an upcoming chapter (Chapter 22), her semi-trance session can be seen as a precursor to Balint's idea of therapeutic regression (Balint, 1992/1968). By struggling to accept Severn's new methodology, Ferenczi contributed to the development of therapeutic regression.

Mutual analysis

The development of mutual analysis grew out of Severn's insistence that Ferenczi needed to analyze his negative countertransference toward her. She had correctly diagnosed that he had negative feelings toward her, of which he was unaware. These unanalyzed negative countertransference feelings produced the therapeutic impasse. Was asking Ferenczi to analyze his countertransference a meaningful request? Did the mutual analysis that ensued contribute to our understanding of the use of non-interpretative measures? Severn's demand for Ferenczi to analyze his countertransference was a remarkable event. According to Ferenczi's own description of her struggle to be open and self-disclosing, he was very reluctant to disclose his emotional struggle to resolve his negative countertransference reaction to Severn. Ferenczi found the courage to analyze his countertransference reaction with Severn, not because he was frightened to say no to her for fear she would be emotionally damaged by his rejection. He was able to enter a mutual analysis, I believe, because Severn helped him confront his disavowed negative feelings and he found the courage to analyze them so he could continue to be a therapeutic agent for his analysand.

In Ferenczi's description of his experience of mutual analysis (Ferenczi, 1988, see Chapters 12 and 13) he was able to analyze his countertransference down to, what he called *rock bottom*. With Severn's capacity to analyze, he was able to uncover his childhood sexual abuse by a nursemaid which Ferenczi linked to his negative feelings toward women. He also added that maternal deprivation contributed to hateful feelings toward women, which were transferred to Severn. Ferenczi's description of his analysis with Severn indicates an emotional depth and development of insight that he did not find in his analysis with Freud (Ferenczi, 1988), taking into account the Freud/Ferenczi analysis took place about 15 years before the Severn/Ferenczi analysis. After then, the Ferenczi/Severn analysis was focused on childhood seduction and mutuality. Severn and Ferenczi may have been a better fit for an analysis than Freud and Ferenczi. As has been discussed, Severn and Ferenczi were compatible intellectually, emotionally, and clinically (see Chapter 10). What is more, they moved toward being peers before the mutual analysis.

Ferenczi claimed that the mutual analysis with Severn helped resolve the former intractable negative transference by providing her with an empathic response for her desperate attempt to be heard about his abusive feelings towards her. Whatever criticisms one can raise about the efficacy about mutual analysis (see Chapter 13), the idea of attuning to the analysand's subjective experience of the analyst and provide an opportunity to contribute to resolving a therapeutic impasse is an important development for clinical psychoanalysis. It provided a vision for expanding the empathic method to encourage a co-created analytic encounter. It deconstructed the one-person psychology of traditional psychoanalysis, where the analysand was a supplier of psychological data about oneself and the analyst was the sole instrument of change through interpreting the prescribed data. Responding to the analysand's need to enter into the analytic process as a collaborator was a daring request by Severn. Analysands were required, in the pioneering era of psychoanalysis, to follow the blueprint of the standard procedure that defined the analytic relationship between analyst and analysand (Rachman, 1997a, p. 131). As has been mentioned, Freud realized the standard procedure had to be altered, because as clinical experience expanded, analysands didn't fit the standard theory (see Chapter 8). Freud with Ferenczi's help, introduced the role of the active analyst (Rachman, 1997a). But, the Ferenczi/Severn analysis pushed the already expanded boundaries of clinical psychoanalysis to levels which Freud and traditional psychoanalysis found unacceptable.

I believe that the most egregious problem in mutual analysis is questioning the analyst's power, control, and status in an analytic relationship (Rachman, 2000b). Individuals in positions of authority are very reluctant to yield power, status, and control in a relationship. Analysts argue that changing the dimensions of power, control, and status will lead to a diminution in being a therapeutic figure. Clinical psychoanalysis, as has been discussed, was developed as a procedure to be administered by the analyst. The analyst, in this framework, is the agent of change. Mutual analysis was developed on the premise that both analyst and analysand can contribute to the therapeutic process of change. It is a shared responsibility, empowering the analysand to be part of the change experience. Not all analysts are as willing to be a partner, rather than the sole authority, in the therapeutic relationship, as was Ferenczi. Fromm (1959) discussed Freud's functioning as being the head of a movement, not willing to share power, status, or control. Ernest Jones was also characterized as the prototypical company man, dedicated to protecting and carrying out the wishes of the head of the movement.

Clinical psychoanalysis also is based upon a doctor administering a cure to a disturbed patient. You cannot, therefore, relinquish control to an analysand who is not capable of being a therapeutic agent. Only a fully analyzed individual who has received professional education as a physician and training as an analyst can be trusted to have the capacities to be a therapeutic agent. The Ferenczi/Severn analysis can be used as a laboratory in viewing the contribution that an analysand can make to the therapeutic experience. Severn demonstrated that an analysand has the capacity to analyze her analyst's countertransference reaction to her and help him analyze the genetic meaning of this negative reaction.

Mutual analysis, however, as Ferenczi clearly stated, only should be used as a last resort. Ferenczi reported that the therapeutic impasse did improve (Ferenczi, 1988;

see Chapter 12). However, he decided to discontinue the clinical experiment when it became clear Severn was using mutual analysis as a resistance which created a new impasse. She began to believe her function in the analysis was not to contribute to her own analysis, but to help Ferenczi improve his therapeutic skills.

Mutual analysis can be transformed into a meaningful therapeutic procedure. Individuals can be faced with crises throughout the life cycle, where one can believe that personal growth is preferable. An ideal use of mutual analysis from the aforementioned perspective would be mutual analysis between analytically and therapeutically trained individuals who wish to provide an opportunity for continued personal growth after formal analysis. I have used this perspective in three experiences.

In recent years, I have been engaged in three examples of mutual analyses; one was with a group of colleagues, and two were with two different individuals. The mutual analysis in a group experience was conducted for about two years with four members (Rachman, 2003a). The group members were graduates of two different analytic institutes, about ten years post-analytic training. The members were interested in exploring emotional and interpersonal issues, but were not interested in entering into a formal analytic relationship. All the members had established a friendship with one another before beginning the mutual analysis. There was no formal leader of the group. The protocol agreed upon had the following elements:

1. A member with a crisis has precedence to begin the session.
2. Members were free to introduce their own issues or issues with each other in the group experience.
3. There was the ethic of openness, emotional honesty, and compassionate confrontation.
4. Everyone was responsible to look out for members by encouraging responsiveness and inquiring about silence or withdrawal.
5. Empathy was the primary method of therapeutic response.

All members were able to discuss their issues and felt they received meaningful help. The interaction was more open, emotionally alive and friendly than formal analytic treatment. The positive atmosphere in the group did not prevent confrontation or the expression of angry feelings. Interpretations and other standard analytic responses did not predominate. All members felt they were able to work toward their desired change. When there was an issue that a member introduced for another member to explore and it was rejected, the member's right to repeat the issue at a later session was respected. There was no campaign instituted to convince the member that it was imperative to work on an issue. It was as perfectly acceptable to respond to or refuse to work on problems. Unfortunately, a variety of scheduling problems arose after two years of meeting and the group dissolved. The mutual analytic experience was so valuable that two members who had compatible schedules were able to continue to meet for individual sessions of mutual analysis.

Peer-to-peer mutual analytic experiences were very satisfactory. The two members were good friends, shared a liberal analytic framework, and had respect for each other's clinical functioning. They readily established a therapeutic working relationship. They continued the exploration of some of the issues that they had begun in the mutual analytic group. In particular, one of the mutual analytic dyad had a longstanding issue with a family member with which had never been worked through in two formal personal analyses. The analysis regarding the family matter continued over a period of six months, on a once-a-week basis. The other member of the dyad was able to focus on the member who wanted to finally work through his long-lasting issue with a relative. The member was able to explore his issues fully, with no interference due to negative transference issues, which had been an issue in the past personal analysis. He fully disclosed his intense hurt and feelings of rejection by a family member whom he saw as unable to empathize with him regarding a family conflict. He needed his family member to be an emotionally active and responsive agent on his behalf to provide a necessary alternative to his passive, emotionally absent father, to whom he could not turn for help. It was a natural part of the relationship between these two mutual analytic partners to respond to each other with empathic understanding. The mutual analytic partner's capacity to provide empathy was very powerful. It was both the absence of any underlying negative transference in the mutual analytic relationship and the capacity to respond with empathy that allowed the analysis of the family conflict to be successful. The individual was able to work through his emotional issue, which haunted him for over 20 years. His feelings of hurt and rejection were significantly reduced. In fact, he volunteered that the mutual analytic interaction, regarding his family matter was more helpful than he had ever received in any previous formal analysis.

Extramural contact

Psychoanalysis has been traditionally defined as a clinical activity within the confines of a consultation office. This is so because the transference relationship is valued as a vehicle for exploring the childhood neurosis through the unconscious manifestations in the relationship to the analyst. Consequently, the psychosocial field between the analyst and analysand, needed to be maintained clear of contaminants. Contact outside the controlled environs of the analyst's offices, therefore, is rarely, if ever, considered desirable.

Extramural contact is a form of a non-interpretative measure, which involve analyst/analysand contact outside of the consultation office. Therapies which do not rely on transference analysis as a procedure are less likely to prohibit extramural contact. Before Severn became an analyst, during the period she developed her clinical practice as a therapist (see Chapter 11), she used extramural contact as a therapeutic procedure. She visited patients in their home and, while they were in the hospital, accompanied them on a behavior-therapy procedure. Severn employed extramural in a very natural way, as she would verbal interaction. The results were reported as being successful (see Chapter 11). What is more, Severn did not report any complications in employing extramural contact. With these positive conditions, it does not seem unusual that the Ferenczi/Severn analysis involved the incorporation of extramural contact. One of the most dramatic and controversial employment of an extramural contact was Severn joining Ferenczi and wife, Gazella on a vacation trip. As discussed in Chapter 8, Ferenczi and his wife travelled to Madrid in 1928, accompanied by Severn (see Image 13).

It is likely that Severn initiated the idea of accompanying the Ferenczis on their vacation. If we examine Severn's evaluation of her analysis, she indicated that a significant dependency had developed with Ferenczi (Eissler, 1952). She experienced him as the ideal parental figure based upon his empathic approach. This reaction was complicated by an eroticized transference reaction, which emerged from the exploration of Severn's childhood trauma experiences with her sexually abusive father. During this pioneering period, there was the idea that separations between analyst and analysand were considered undesirable. Analysis was scheduled on a six-day-a-week basis. The intense transference relationship was a fixture of the analysis. It is no wonder that a dependency developed for Severn as her

IMAGE 13 Dr. and Mrs. Ferenczi and Elizabeth Severn, Spain, 1928

emotional problems matched the dependency created by the analytic procedures. Accompanying Ferenczi during his vacation period, I believe, was undesirable for both Severn and Ferenczi.

Severn would have benefited from separation from her analyst. The idea that separation is undesirable does not acknowledge that separations in a human relationship when based on empathic understanding of the analysand's developmental needs. Severn developed the concept of extra-office contact, on her own, as she did a host of clinical procedures in her self-educated, self-taught clinical methodology (Rachman, 2015a).

Ferenczi's active approach to psychoanalysis (see Chapter 8) laid a foundation for changing the structure and process of the analytic encounter in clinical psychoanalysis about the time Severn was mid-way through her second decade of her clinical practice. During his introduction of the active role for the analyst, he did not stress extramural contact. Activity occurred within the analytic session. When Ferenczi and Severn entered into their joint analytic relationship, it brought together Severn's idea of therapeutic behavior outside the clinical sessions, and Ferenczi's flexibility, responsiveness, activity, and empathic understanding to include a non-interpretative measure in their therapeutic contact which was, and continues to be, controversial.

Ferenczi's agreement to allow Severn to accompany him on vacation with his wife does seem to suggest a countertransference reaction. As can be seen in the Ferenczi/Severn analysis countertransference reactions were prevalent (see Chapters 12 through 16). In these instances, Ferenczi was aware of his negative feelings toward Severn, but, did not analyze them. It was only when Severn confronted him about them, and analyzed his countertransference, that his behavior became therapeutic. In the issue of the Madrid trip, neither Ferenczi nor Severn confronted his clinical behavior as a countertransference reaction. Neither member of the therapeutic dyad confronted the reinforcing of Severn's dependency on Ferenczi with this non-interpretative measure.

Periods of separation in a therapeutic relationship are an important agent of change. Such separations are similar to the growth inducing separations that need to be part of a parent/child relationship. Such separation should occur after attachment between mother and infant is developed (Bowlby, 1988). Then individuation and separation of the child and mother must take place (Mahler, Pine, & Bergman, 1973).

Ferenczi should have referred Severn to Groddeck's therapeutic facility at Baden-Baden, which was generally considered a short-term psychoanalytic facility. Severn could have been treated by another analyst, during Ferenczi's vacation period, returning to analysis with him, when he returned. Referring Severn to Groddeck at Baden-Baden, by its very nature, would mean Ferenczi was willing to separate from Severn. Ferenczi may have had his own issues separating from Severn. Was he, for example, dependent on Severn's need for him? Separation cannot occur in a codependent relationship. As Severn reported post-analysis, Ferenczi struggled with feelings of failure, at times, because he felt he wasn't doing enough to make the analysis a success.

This was amplified at the last phase of the analysis when Severn was in a malignant regression.

It is important to note that Ferenczi's Confusion of Tongues theory (see Chapter 15) does not encourage extramural contact. When Severn confined herself to her bed, Ferenczi continued the analysis by visiting Severn and conducting the sessions in her apartment. The individual separation process had broken down by that time. Ferenczi was, by that time, dramatically trying to maintain Severn as a functioning individual. The lesson from this extramural contact, especially in a trauma survivor who develops a severe dependency transference, is such contact should be limited (Gutheil & Gabbard, 1993). There are, however, reports of extramural contract, which did not indicate that negative results are inevitable when they are judiciously employed (Zur, 2010).

Judicious use of extramural contact, that is, therapeutic interaction outside the formal conditions of mainstream practice, can be helpful with trauma survivors. Affectionate hugs, handshakes, and shoulder pats, especially initiated by the analysand, can aid the sense of caring and affection that trauma survivors crave. Visiting an analysand who was part of an analytic therapy group, confined to her apartment because of an orthopedic operation, was very helpful to her maintaining her and the group's therapeutic relationship. Telephone contact has been important for the analyses in instances of illness and physical confinement. Kohut, who came out of the closet about non-interpretative physical contact with an analysand, was described in his last lecture about treating a suicidal analysand as follows:

> Once he was even spontaneously moved to ask if she would like to hold on to his fingers while she talked. "Maybe that would help you," he said to her … he was desperate. The patient clasped Kohut's fingers tightly. It made him think of the "toothless gums of a very young child clamping down on an empty nipple …"
>
> *(Strozier, 2001)*

Although I have been critical of Kohut for not acknowledging Ferenczi as a precursor for the idea and clinical practice of empathy (Rachman, 1989), recent revelations indicate that his neglect of Ferenczi and a more liberal approach to clinical functioning were based on a need to remain in good standing within mainstream psychoanalysis. Strozier (2001) reported that Kohut was rejected by most of his peers:

> Anna Freud and Heinz Hartmann, who had been close friends, … turned their back on him … combined with Kohut's own allegiance to traditional doctrine.
>
> *(p. 133)*

What is more, these factors contributed to disavowing Ferenczi's alternative to traditional psychoanalysis. According to Bacal and Carlton (2010), a confidant of Kohut told him that:

> Ferenczi had the right idea! That is, Kohut, like Ferenczi; believed that there was a good deal to be said for responding to a patient in the ways that the patient experienced as therapeutic, even if these ways would not be endorsed by the prevailing tenets of psychoanalytic practice.
>
> *(p. 134)*

19

SEVERN'S TRAUMA OF PREMATURE TERMINATION

Ferenczi's termination trauma with Freud

Severn's premature termination by Ferenczi was a result of his growing physical weakness due to the onslaught of pernicious anemia. During his last year of 1933, Ferenczi first went to Vienna in late August of 1932, to meet with Freud and present his "Confusion of Tongues" paper for Freud's approval. It can be said that this meeting evoked an emotional, intellectual, and interpersonal trauma for Ferenczi (Rachman, 1997a, b), but we need to note that Freud also emotionally suffered from their meeting. First, we need to explicate the emotional trauma Ferenczi experienced with Freud during this Vienna meeting of August 29, 1932. It was customary for the members of Freud's inner circle, The Society of Rings, to share their ideas with Freud before presentation or publication. This would be accomplished by sending a *Rundbriefe*, a circulating letter between Freud, Ferenczi, Abraham, Etingon, Sachs, Jones, and Rank (Grosskurth, 1991). Ferenczi knew that his Confusion of Tongues paper (Ferenczi, 1980h) was controversial. However, he wanted to present it, in person, to Freud. He hoped against hope that Freud would accept his new work on trauma analysis. The Confusion of Tongues paradigm was not intended, as Freud and the analytic community thought, to replace the Oedipal theory, but to stand alongside of it, to help psychoanalysis study evolve toward the treatment of trauma disorders (Ferenczi, 1988).

By late August of 1932, Freud and Ferenczi's relationship was strained to breaking point (Rachman, 1997b). One can imagine the emotional strength and courage it took Ferenczi to directly face Freud and present this controversial theory to him for his mentor's approval. Izette De Forest (1942, 1954) was a Ferenczi student and analysand with whom he shared his emotional experience with Freud in presenting the Confusion of Tongues paper to him. She, in turn, shared Ferenczi's ordeal with Erik Fromm (1959). According to Izette de Forest's report, Ferenczi nervously presented his Confusion of Tongues paper to Freud in the face of icy silence. Freud gave no overt response, either during or after the presentation. When it became clear it was time to end the emotional torture, Ferenczi held out his hand to say goodbye. Freud did not shake his hand, turned his back on Ferenczi, and walked away (Fromm, 1959).

This was not just an Oedipal drama, but an actual trauma between two beloved friends, one colleague harshly rejecting his best friend and favorite son. Of course, one can outline the psychodynamics of a failed symbolic father/son transference relationship. But, that will only distance us from this emotional tragedy that so devastated Ferenczi's sense of self:

He has been profoundly shaken by his meeting with Freud in Vienna.

(Dupont, 1988, p. XVII)

Balint, an eyewitness to Ferenczi's last year, suggests that the Vienna meeting may have proved to be fatal.

[Ferenczi] suffered a shattering blow during the last meeting with Freud (and by subsequent illness which one does not know – was a coincidence or a consequence).

(Balint, 1969, p. 222)

Balint's hypothesis suggested that the Freud rejection was emotionally catastrophic for Ferenczi, which combined with the physical crisis of his fatal illness of pernicious anemia to produce a termination trauma with Freud. Freud failed to inquire about his closest friend's state of mind either during or after the trauma. Freud interpreted Ferenczi's attempt at independence and theoretical evolution as a negative transference, acting out. An Oedipal interpretation was offered, which suggested Ferenczi raised an unconscious fantasy to kill the father. Why didn't Freud engage in some form of an empathic dialogue with Ferenczi, to work on Ferenczi's rebellion, alienation and anger? Ferenczi having negative feelings about his mentor and closest friend and colleague was not a psychoanalytic crime. Ferenczi needed a moment of empathic understanding. Freud needed to try to understand his friend's intellectual and clinical excursions from traditional psychoanalysis rather than react as an angry father.

Balint's description of the Confusion of Tongues Vienna meeting of 1932 causing Ferenczi to suffer a "shattering blow" (Balint, 1969, p. 222) and Dupont saying this last meeting between the two analytic giants caused Ferenczi to be "profoundly shaken" (Dupont, 1988, p. XVII), gave rise to the idea that Freud died of a broken heart. Ferenczi's failing health and his loss of Freud's friendship, no doubt, gave rise to a depressive reaction. Severn, who had terminated before the Vienna meeting, was aware of Ferenczi's despondency. She had her own version of the psychological aspects to Ferenczi's death, hypothesizing that his despondency over feeling like a failure because their analysis was not completed fully successful was a factor (Eissler, 1952).

After the difficulty with Freud in August, Ferenczi had to endure the negative experience of presenting his Confusion of Tongues paper at the 12th International Psychoanalytic Congress in Wiesbaden on September 4, 1932. The reaction to his paper was generally negative (Masson, 1984). One of the exceptions was Balint, who was a loyal follower of Ferenczi. Unfortunately, Balint's lone voice was not enough to quiet Ferenczi's hurt and rejection. After Wiesbaden, Ferenczi attempts to recover from the trauma of Freud and the analytic community's rejection by first attending Groddeck's sanatorium in Baden-Baden and then going on vacation to the south of France. His physical illness became a prominent factor in his life, (Balint, 1969; Dupont, 1988). Ferenczi wrote to Freud that, at this time, his "life was a series of treatments" (Falzeder, Braband & Giaperi-Deutsch, 2000; letter from Ferenczi to Freud, September 27, 1933).

In spite of injections his condition worsened. During the period of 1932–33 he was "forced to give up his practice, became bedridden chiefly because of the degeneration of his spinal cord …" (Balint, 1969 p. 222). Ferenczi never recovered from his illness. He died on May 22, 1933 of pernicious anemia and was buried in the Jewish Cemetery of Budapest on May 24, 1933. Severn, who was in the last days of her analysis with Ferenczi, was emotionally shaken by Ferenczi's termination trauma with Freud. Nineteen years after this event, she expressed to Kurt Eissler that she believed this emotional trauma with Freud had a shattering, perhaps a fatal effect on Ferenczi (Eissler, 1952). I also raise the question as to whether Ferenczi's trauma with Freud impaired his capacity to create a therapeutic termination experience for Severn.

The *Clinical Diary*

The *Clinical Diary* (Ferenczi, 1988), provides the richest source of self-disclosing data of Ferenczi's functioning with Severn. One of the experiences in the Severn/Ferenczi relationship that needs greater clarification is the termination process that occurred between them when the analysis ended. There are almost no formal reference to the termination process. Can we infer that the sparsity of data about termination reflects an analogous reluctance on the part of Ferenczi and Severn to have discussed this issue of termination between them? Sometime in late 1932, during the final months of the analysis with Severn, Ferenczi began to accept his failing health as a reality, adjusted his working schedule, and realized the analysis with Severn would have to end. In the *Clinical Diary*, Ferenczi hints at the idea of termination with Severn with this statement:

> I released R.N. from her torments by rejecting the sins of her father, which then I confessed and for which I obtained forgiveness.
> *(Ferenczi, 1988, pp. 213–214 – Clinical Entry October 2, 1932 [last entry])*

This clinical entry seems to reflect Ferenczi's attempt to resolve the negative paternal transference in their relationship. Before the analysis ended he used clinical empathy in an attempt to work through the negative father transference: "she had a great deal of aggression and resistance against me as a father surrogate" (Ferenczi, 1988, p. 214 – Clinical Entry August 24, 1932). Although Severn left analysis with some dissatisfaction, she believed Ferenczi had done his best to help her (Eissler, 1952). The above-quoted statement of Ferenczi's shows his attempt to empathize with her need to work through her anger and criticism of him as the analysis drew to an end.

There is another aspect to the ending of the Ferenczi/Severn relationship that we need to discuss. I believe their ending was a *traumatic experience* that contributed to Severn's feeling of desperation and disturbance (Eissler, 1952). In the letters of Margaret Severn to her mother, we have a note about the ending of the analysis:

> the fact that you say he now avoids the subject of your imminent departure. As much as possible shows a selfishness and lack of consideration either as a patient or friend or analyst.
>
> *(M. Severn, 1932 – Letter from Margaret to Elizabeth Severn,*
> *December 1932, Paris)*

We can infer that by December of 1932, Severn knew the analysis with Ferenczi would end. But, it is still not clear whether there was any therapeutic discussion between Ferenczi and Severn about the premature termination.

It seems likely that Ferenczi did not allow himself to accept his illness. He did not want to accept his demise. His clinical work, writing relationship with analysand and colleagues, and his relationship with his wife Gizella were his intellectual, emotional, interpersonal lifelines. Denial of his illness allowed him to create a life-saving fantasy (Rachman, 1967) that he would continue on, as if there would be no end. Ferenczi's denial, his need to maintain his self-esteem for an analysis that made him feel like a failure (Eissler, 1952), and Severn convincing him she could only get better if she became his analyst combined to drain his emotions, intellect, and capacity to maintain his usual vitality and clinical acuity. The premature (but, necessary) termination of the analysis with Severn produced a traumatic experience which was not confronted or analyzed. Termination from an analysis has aspects of a traumatic experience even if the termination is bilateral. An agreement by both parties to end the analysis because the therapeutic goals have been reached is not without emotional issues that both analysand and analyst need to examine. There are the issues of dependency, separation anxiety, development of new or previous existing psychopathology, and feelings of loss, abandonment, and depression. The analysand wants to separate, be independent, shed the identity of a disturbed individual who cannot function without another person attending to him/her. But there is also the reaction of the child-in-the adult, who has become accustomed to being in a therapeutic relationship and has developed a dependency upon the treatment process and the analyst. This dependency needs to be respected and understood. The analysand needs to go through a termination process in order for personal growth to be the final stage of an analysis (Rachman, 1980, 2015c).

The basic issue is that unilateral or premature termination, whether it is induced by the analysand or analyst, has even greater possibilities for trauma, which must be turned into a therapeutic experience. Termination by the analysand can stimulate for the analyst issues of anxiety, anger, dependency, separation, abandonment, and loss. One of the most destructive termination interchanges I have ever heard about is the analyst attacking the individual for a unilateral termination. This analysand said this to me, about the termination:

> When I told the analyst that I was dissatisfied with the experience, he launched into a scathing criticism of me. He said I was a difficult case, who was having difficulty forming a working relationship. What is more, he said I had serious problems and I will take my problems with me. I should think twice about quitting because I will be harming myself.

The analyst, I believe, was furious with the analysand for leaving him, and tried to frighten the analysand by appealing to his guilt and anxiety in order to keep him in analysis. There was no empathy expressed to the analysand for wanting to terminate or any working through of the analysand's emotional problems. Analysts are not at their best in the termination phase of an analysis (Rachman, 2015c).

Sudden, unilateral termination of the analysis by the analysand that is a one-person experience needs to be turned into a two-person, co-created experience. This means the analyst turns the sudden termination from a disturbance into a therapeutic experience. It must be understood that termination is a process and a formal part of the analysis. The analyst can, whether he/she agrees with the termination, help the analysand express their feelings and receive empathy. Only then can the analysis move toward a bilateral termination process.

If the analyst and analysand disagree, a co-created process of analyzing the issue should occur. The analysand would be asked to share his/her ideas about what the basic issues are in wanting to end the analysis and demonstrate a willingness to fully explore the emotional issues involved in termination, such as transference, dissatisfaction, anxiety, etc. If the analyst disagrees with the analysand's idea of termination, he/she first needs to examine their possible countertransference reactions. These issues could include anger, anxiety, control, domination and status issues, separation anxiety, and, of course, the anxiety about the loss of income. Any emotional issue the analysand can experience regarding termination can also be experienced by the analyst. The disclosure of the analyst's countertransference analysis of his/her personal issues occurs in a judicious way focused on termination, not as an opportunity for the analyst to work through their unresolved neurotic conflicts.

The analyst, when necessary, has an obligation to share a divergent idea about termination. In one dramatic example, an analysand's desire to unilaterally terminate was turned into a discussion of her unfinished business about working through her childhood sexual trauma (Rachman & Klett, 2015). I suggested to an analysand that she had unfinished business. After I presented her with what I considered the evidence, I asked her to join me in continuing the exploration, to which she agreed. The unilateral desire to terminate was turned into a bilateral experience.

If at all possible, the analyst should contribute to a positive termination by working on empathically understanding the analysand's desire to terminate. A desire to terminate should not be seen as a rejection of psychoanalysis or the analyst. As difficult as termination may be, it is an opportunity for the analyst and analysand to further the analysis. The concept of resistance gives way to empathic understanding. If termination is inevitable, the analyst strives to turn the moment into a therapeutic one. The goal is to leave the individual with a positive feeling about psychoanalysis and the analyst, so that the individual can return to analysis in the future when necessary.

Unfortunately, Ferenczi was not his best during the ending of the analysis with Severn. It was due to the inability to analyze his countertransference or understand his negativity toward Severn. Ferenczi had initiated the termination because of failing health. What is more, as Severn revealed in her interview to Kurt Eissler, she felt it was time for her to terminate (Eissler, 1952). But neither member of this therapeutic dyad was emotionally able to have a therapeutic discussion about termination.

Of course, a co-created termination would have been helpful to both Severn and Ferenczi. Severn was in the midst of a malignant regression during the last year of her analysis with Ferenczi (Eissler, 1952, see Chapter 22). As I have indicated, Ferenczi needed to help Severn with the emotional crisis by sending her to Groddeck's Sanatorium at Baden-Baden for an emotional rest, reducing her anxiety and sense of chaos. When she returned from the Sanatorium, Ferenczi could have begun a discussion of his pernicious anemia, his growing weakness, and his plans to stop working on a particular date.

Another consideration in the termination process could have been transferring Severn to continue analysis with Balint, Ferenczi's successor. Balint was an intimate of Ferenczi as well as an eyewitness to the analysis with Severn (Balint, 1992/1968). After a period of therapeutic rest at Groddeck's sanatorium, Severn could continue on with the analysis with Balint until she could move from a malignant stage to a stage of therapeutic regression. Ferenczi, I believe, was caught in a personal struggle to prove that trauma analysis was successful, as exemplified by the Severn case. He wanted to prove this to Freud, the orthodox analytic community, and, of course, himself. Severn believed that Ferenczi was struggling with a sense of failure about their analysis (Eissler, 1952). Ferenczi's personal and professional struggles enveloped Ferenczi so that he was not intellectually or emotionally free to consider a plan for Severn's termination.

Severn suffered from a premature termination trauma because of actual and intrapsychic issues. Ferenczi losing his physical and emotional capacities, particularly at a time when the analysis was in crisis, stimulated the feeling of a loss of her positive parental figure, a sense of abandonment, a loss of support and affirmation, and a regression to primitive levels of functioning. She could no longer contribute as a partner in the therapeutic process. She felt alone, frightened, and abandoned. In the

Ferenczi/Severn analysis the issue of dependency also complicated the premature termination trauma. In an attempt to successfully treat Severn's childhood traumas, Ferenczi introduced a series of non-interpretative measures which were intended to help her reduce unfulfilled developmental needs of childhood, which were interrupted by parental abuse (see Chapter 12). These non-interpretative measures, which were co-created between Ferenczi and Severn, often had significant positive therapeutic effects. For example, Ferenczi's introduction of clinical empathy into psychoanalysis helped Severn gain a sense that Ferenczi understood her emotional issues from her subjective frame of reference. With this new way of responding, Severn developed a sense of trust, safety, and affirmation, something she had not felt in three previous analyses. There were, however, uses of non-interpretative measures that can be said to have interfered with therapeutic progress and created a severe dependency experience. The Madrid trip was an instance of a non-interpretative measure that created dependency (see Chapter 18).

The negative father transference trauma

As has been outlined in Chapter 7, Severn was severely abused by her father as a child. In fact, it was Ferenczi who helped Severn retrieve her childhood traumas, which were not in her consciousness. When she began the analysis she suffered from the feeling of dread that enveloped her emotional life, but could not identify the cause of the emotional darkness in her consciousness. One of the successes of the analysis was the focus on the childhood traumas, with the father being a trau-matizing agent through severe sexual, emotional, and physical abuse. He also threw her out of their home. He was characterized as a psychopath or criminal (Ferenczi, 1988). The Confusion of Tongues theory (Ferenczi, 1980h) introduced the idea of re-traumatization in the psychoanalytic situation, which cautioned analysts to become aware of their countertransference reactions, which could stimulate enact-ments of childhood traumas. In the Severn analysis, Ferenczi needed to become aware of how his behavior in the psychoanalytic situation could stimulate an abu-sive father transference for Severn. In fact, during the analysis, Ferenczi created an emphatic atmosphere where he created a passion-free atmosphere (see Chapters 12–15) but, I believe, in the premature termination phase, Ferenczi was unwittingly involved in an enactment of a negative father transference, namely, the original abusive father. I say unwittingly, because he was so preoccupied with his sense of failure in the analysis, as well as with his physical deteriorations due to previous anemia, that toward the end of their relationship he was not able to emotionally concentrate on the formal requirements of analysis. In addition, the development of the trauma analysis model that Ferenczi was creating with Severn had dramatically elasticized the boundaries of a traditional analysis. What was missing therefore, from the ending of the analysis was Ferenczi's analytic awareness that prematurely end-ing his analysis would cause Severn an emotional disturbance and that the analytic meaning of that disturbance needed to be therapeutically explored as a condition to terminating the analysis.

The ideal termination process for the Ferenczi/Severn analysis to be outlined as an analytic experience would involve the following:

1. Ferenczi emotionally confronted the details of his pernicious anemia for himself, and decide to share and work through the implication of his fatal illness and terminating of his relationship with Severn.
2. At least, one to three months of sessions are set aside for Ferenczi to help Severn with her emotional reactions to the premature termination. Ferenczi explores Severn's confusion, depression, and anger, and feelings of abandonment and abuse.
3. At the center of the termination would be developing the awareness that a premature termination of an analysis for Severn would stimulate a severe negative father transference. Severn, it is argued, by the premature termination suffered from the experience of feeling that Ferenczi abused and abandoned her, since the analysis did not focus on her feelings and its implications for her emotional well-being. Ferenczi prematurely terminating Severn could have been experienced by her as her father throwing her out of their home, abusing her, and not caring about her. In other words, he was more concerned with his well-being than with her. It would have benefitted Ferenczi's feeling of a sense of failure and anxiety about his illness, if there was an analysis of the premature termination. Both Severn and Ferenczi would reduce their emotional disturbances by analyzing the termination as a process within the analysis, sorting out the neurotic from the real.

Margaret Severn's anger at Ferenczi for the difficulties in the analysis of her mother

The emotional difficulties of the Ferenczi/Seven analysis came to a crescendo in the year of 1932, when Ferenczi wrote his *Clinical Diary* (Ferenczi, 1988). As discussed, mutual analysis was to be the remedy that Severn suggested to resolve the therapeutic impasse. However, the remedy then became the problem. We do not have Elizabeth Severn's letter to her daughter, Margaret, so we do not know what Elizabeth told Margaret about the difficulties in her analysis. Fortunately, however, we do have Margaret's letters to Elizabeth, which clearly state the daughter's view of the difficulties in the analysis. What we need to do is sort out Elizabeth's view of the analysis from her daughter's. Margaret's reaction seems to be one of an angry child, over-identified with her mother's personal functioning. As has been discussed in Chapter 7, Margaret and Elizabeth developed an intense symbiotic like relationship, which did not leave much psychological space between them. In just over a week before Christmas in 1932 and just two months before termination, Margaret expressed her outrage in a letter to Ferenczi:

> Well, the cat is out of the bag. I have told Neder that you are no longer being analyzed by Fer., but that he is being analyzed by you. She called me up to

unload her worries about Nat and further she feels that F. has not only done Nat no good but has harmed her and that the process is likely to go on for year if he has his way.

On the whole her remarks showed such insight and were so accurate that I did not feel when asked a direct question that I was called upon to be in his defense after what he has caused you to go through intentionally or unintentionally.

… I did not feel it was up to me to conceal certain facts such as his present analysis with you especially when there are other people there like Lowel and Clara who know it.

Neder says he is tearing Nat to pieces without giving her anything to hold onto as this is exactly what happened to you. How could I do otherwise than admit this possibility? I did try to say that I thought he was changing but she said 'yes', maybe, but he is an old man now or acts like one and by the time he has changed, Nat would be finished completely. I do not wish to do any harm to Fer., but after all it isn't my fault that he has made such a failure of his cases and neither you nor he told me that his analysis with you was to be regarded as a secret. Neder cited the instance of his allowing Nat to take Chloroform daily as outrageous and of course it is. I told Neder that this information was confidential and that she couldn't even tell you that I had told her and that no doubt Nat would hear of it one way or another in Buda.

But I am to see them again before they leave. Saturday night and I think I will withdraw the veil of secrecy because I see no real reason for it. I am sorry for Fer., but the situation is the result of his own illness which he wasn't bright enough to see or admit before. And I am not satisfied with his half-hearted behavior to you now either.

I don't wonder that feeling as she does Nat hasn't paid him, although I know her tendency in general in this respect. I bet she'd pay you. Although Neder is pretty strong in her accusations she comes damn near the truth.

After Tea

Well it's a good thing for Fer., that I'm not in Buda now for if I were I would light a bomb under him. The more I think of his attitude to you and its inadequacy either as doctor or friend the more furious I become.

His pigheadedness is not admitting your ability as an analyst more fully and his manner of taking his analysis as if it were doing you a favor, an attitude which I couldn't avoid remarking in my stay there, for it was always you who strained a point to make the appointments and never he together with his absolute feeblemindedness in suggesting that you study anatomy and what not is TOO disgusting. In addition the fact that you say he now avoids the subject of imminent departure as much as possible shows a selfishness and lack of consideration for you either as a patient or friend or analyst that is insufferable. The sooner you get away from there the better. You have analyzed him enough to discover his injustice to you. And if he doesn't want it for himself enough to even discuss the possibilities of continuing it he isn't worth the trouble. Your courage and strength of character in this impossible situation are simply superhuman in their grandeur and he doesn't give you the least recognition of this. Awful.

(Letter from Margaret to Elizabeth Severn, December 14, 1932, Paris, In Rachman, 2016d)

Margaret who was a non-professional, a bystander to the analysis of her mother by Ferenczi, reacted as a child whose mother was being hurt. She was receiving the information about the experience during the most difficult period of the analysis when her mother was in a regression, struggling to separate from Ferenczi (Eissler, 1952) and Ferenczi struggling with terminating the analysis in February of 1933, months before his death of pernicious anemia on May 22, 1933 (Rachman, 1997a). Elizabeth Severn was struggling with her emotional life, Ferenczi struggling with his physical life. Under such crisis situations, neither analysand nor analyst can function at an optimal level.

Margaret Severn was like a symbiotic child connected to her mother. Margaret was a child angry at the person she believed was trying to destroy her mother. Even as an adult, she felt she could not live without her mother. She suffered the childhood experience of abandonment of both mother and father, as well as the survivor of her grandfather's sexual abuse. She was surprised when her mother did not share her anger toward Ferenczi. He was the enemy; he was the abuser, as were her father and grandfather. Margaret wanted to hurt Ferenczi. He was the transferential male abuser of her childhood.

Michael Balint, who was an observer to the Severn analysis, as Ferenczi's closest colleague, student, and analysand (Balint, 1992/1968; Rachman, 1997a) understandood its pioneering contributions to treating trauma disorders. In fact, he was to use his observations of the Severn analysis and his theoretical discussions with Ferenczi to develop the concept of therapeutic regression, which distinguished stages in the attempt to retrieve and analyze childhood trauma by titrating the analysand's anxiety, so that it does not lead to further pathology. He realized, as an analyst, what Margaret Severn could not: that there are vicissitudes in the process of the analysis of a trauma disorder in a severely disturbed individual where the analysis can be viewed as harmful. Margaret's analysis was unconventional, conducted by her mother and, at times, at a distance. She did not experience or understand this process. She did not have a third party who was an analyst not involved with her mother to whom to turn for understanding.

In another aspect of her anger toward Ferenczi, Margaret did not understand Ferenczi's struggle to enter into a mutual analysis with her mother, as well as the fact that this technique was initiated by her mother:

I am sorry to see there has been such an upset about the Fer. business, but I wasn't surprised to see that his sweetness didn't last till the next letter. If he is so ashamed of being analyzed by you, what does he do it for? And you are not only swallowing all that but are preparing all that to go bravely forth and tell the world you're cured, whether you are or not. Humbug I call it, just to protect him. He's made a mess and you are trying to shoulder the responsibility. Well, you won't get any thanks for it. Here you are trying to protect him after he's made a mess out of you and he hasn't even got the guts to appreciate it. I give up. If he is mad that you tell people, why did he not first stipulate as a condition that you shouldn't. It surely isn't considered ordinary analytic for the analyst to go around denying that he has any patients I didn't really say.

(Letter from Margaret to Elizabeth Severn, Friday,
December 23, 1932, Paris. In Rachman, 2016d)

Margaret's anger about her mother's analysis with Ferenczi diminished when it became clear that the analysis was going to terminate. Ferenczi told her mother they would discontinue their work together because Ferenczi was too ill to work. He would soon be confined to bed and needed help to feed himself:

Dearest, so delighted that it now appears that you can leave Buda in a happier frame of mind. Thank God that Fer. is coming to his senses. Your courage in this matter has been simply about him. I should have given up long ago. ... And Hooray for the book and everything [The 1933 book] ....

(Letter from Margaret to Elizabeth Severn, February 13, 1933,
Paris. In Rachman, 2016d)

20

SEVERN'S RECOVERY, 1933–1959

"To Work, To Love" (Freud)

Analysts have often referred to Freud's standard of 'To Work, To Love' (Erikson, 1950), as an indication of the success of an analysis. If we examine this standard in the light of Severn's functioning from 1933 until 1959, the 26-year period from the ending of her analysis until her death, we may be able to throw new light on the Ferenczi/Severn analysis as well as Severn's contribution to psychoanalysis. In the first year of her recovery, Severn wrote the last of her three books, entitled *The Discovery of the Self* (Severn, 1933). It is a testimony to her resilience that she was able to write this book as she was recovering from her trauma. This book is a psychoanalytic treatise on trauma disorder, the book Ferenczi and Severn intended to write together. Masson (1984) was critical of Severn's 1933 book as being amateurish and non-scientific, implying it did not deserve serious attention. Nancy Smith (1998, 1999, 2001) had a positive assessment of Severn's book, concluding that it reflected a meaningful view of trauma analysis contribution to psychoanalysis, clinically and theoretically. It is a subjective report of an analysand's experience in, as well as her ideas about, trauma analysis (Rachman 2015a). Her experiential report and her ideas about the analysis of trauma, the need for empathic understanding, the need for the analyst's responsiveness and flexibility and capacity for tenderness and affection have been incorporated into contemporary psychoanalysis. I believe *The Discovery of the Self* warrants re-examination. Consideration should be made to re-issuing this book, which has been out of print since the 1930s. This book is historically important and establishes Severn and Ferenczi's analytic partnership in a pioneering study and treatment of trauma disorder.

Severn was able to resume her clinical practice, after the termination of the analysis, but this time she considered herself a psychoanalyst, no longer a metaphysician or psychic healer (see Chapter 25). Ferenczi stated that Severn had a training analysis with him (Ferenczi, 1988; Severn, 1932, 1933). As has been mentioned,

Severn believed in psychoanalysis even after her difficult termination with Ferenczi. In her interview with Eissler, he appeared to be interacting with her as she was an analyst, including calling her Dr. Severn (1952).

After her recuperation in Paris, she moved to London, where she had developed a following from her earlier clinical practice and the positive reception of her two earlier books (Severn, 1913, 1920). Sometime in the 1940s, Elizabeth and her daughter Margaret moved to New York City. Her daughter had retired as a modern dancer to run a dance teaching program. Severn practiced at 87th Street and Park Avenue until her death in 1959. A testimony to her success can be found in letters of her analysands (Rachman, 2016d). In a series of photographs from 1935 until 1950 (see Images 14, 15, and 16), Severn's appearance changes dramatically, from the overweight and disheveled look of 1933 when she terminated with Ferenczi to her recovered look thereafter. The later photographs in the series show an individual who is well groomed and well dressed. Her visage seems to indicate contentment and happiness.

IMAGE 14 Photograph of Elizabeth Severn, December 14, 1933, London

IMAGE 15 Photograph of Elizabeth Severn, New York City, 1935

When I first inspected the interview that Kurt Eissler conduced with Severn on December 20, 1952, when she was 73 years old, I was surprised. The previous negative assessment of Severn's functioning reported in the analytic literature referred to her as a dysfunctional fringe individual. The Eissler interview shattered this negative view. As I read the 24 pages of typed manuscript, a different picture of Severn emerged. She came across as very intelligent, thoughtful, assertive, and an analytically informed individual. She was open and non-defensive in her responses to Eissler. However, there were moments in the interview when Eissler pressed Severn with questions about a particular area of interest to Eissler. Severn would not let herself be intimidated into saying anything negative about her analysis with Ferenczi. At no time, did Severn indicate any non-analytic boundary violation by Ferenczi. What is more, she said that he did a credible job as her analyst. In fact, she felt Ferenczi had done everything he could to help her. Her recovery period demonstrated that, although this pioneering analysis had faults, it contributed to her recovering from a trauma disorder.

Severn left Budapest in early 1933, in a state of near collapse and despair. She told Eissler:

IMAGE 16 Photograph of Elizabeth Severn, 1950

> [I felt] … a complete wreck. That was my personal experience.
>
> *(Eissler, 1952, p. 7)*

One would think Severn would have been angry with Ferenczi and psychoanalysis for being in an emotional upheaval at the end of the analysis. But in 1952, Severn said with clarity.

> it [the analysis] didn't lessen in any way my belief in analysis or its usefulness.
>
> *(Eissler, 1952, p. 7)*

But Severn's daughter was not so generous in her evaluation of the analysis with Ferenczi. According to Fortune (1993, p.112), Margaret Severn wrote a letter of protest to Ferenczi complaining about his treatment of her mother. After Budapest, Severn went to stay with her daughter to recuperate. Margaret's dance career brought her, at that time, to Paris. Although Elizabeth Severn had analyzed her daughter Margaret, whatever difficulties that analysis may have caused Margaret did not interfere with helping her with her mother's recovery. Their loving relationship predominated.

To love, to work: Freud's standard for analytic success

Although Severn's analysis with Ferenczi ended on a negative note, and has been criticized by some as unsuccessful, the data from her 26-year recovery period, 1933–1959, indicates a more positive picture. Is there a way to look at the effects of the Ferenczi/Severn analysis with new eyes? Why not use the most traditional analytic standard for a successful analysis? Freud's standard was outlined by Erik Erikson:

> Freud was once asked what he thought a normal person should be able to do well. The questioner probably expected a complicated answer, but Freud in the curt way of his old days, is reported to have said, "Lieben und arbeiten" (to love and to work).
>
> *(Erikson, 1950, p. 229)*

Severn's recovery, as has been discussed, involved improved mental health. She reported that her suicidal ideation was no longer a preoccupation (Eissler, 1952). She was functional in her career as a teacher and lecturer. She had the emotional energy necessary to have loving relationships and to work successfully as a clinician.

To love

Severn showed meaningful functioning in her capacity to love after her analysis with Ferenczi. All through her adult life, Elizabeth Severn maintained a close, loving relationship with her daughter, Margaret. Perhaps, one could say their relationship was pathologically close. Severn did analyze her daughter and the psychological space between them was narrow. But, Margaret Severn adored her mother, writing letters to her, sometimes on a daily basis, for about 20 years, while she toured the United States and Europe as a dancer (Rachman, 2016d). When the two moved to New York City, they had regular social contacts with friends and colleagues. On Sunday afternoons, they would invite friends and colleagues for tea and cakes. An eyewitness to these social gatherings reported that Elizabeth Severn was an excellent, friendly, and responsive host (Lysova, 2007).

A letter from Karen Horney, who later became the founder of the Cultural School of Psychoanalysis, illustrated Severn's capacity to form and maintain friendships during her years of recovery (see Image 17):

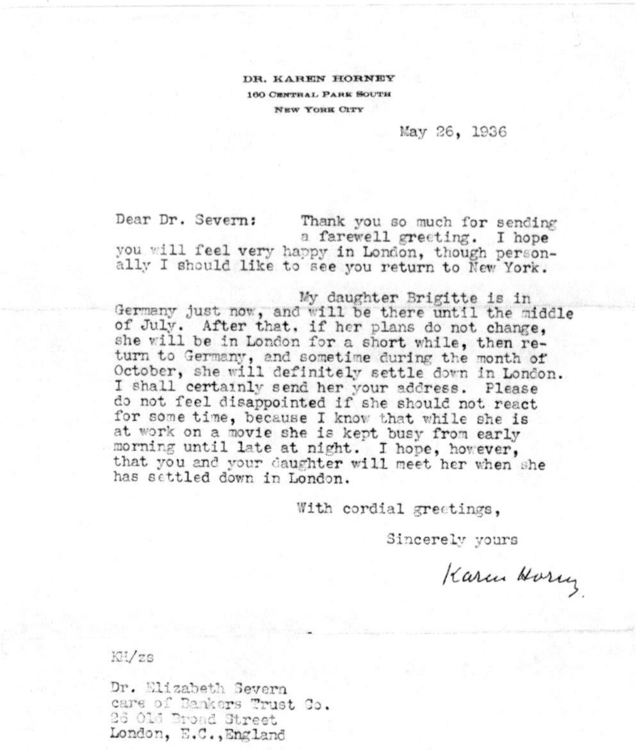

DR. KAREN HORNEY
160 CENTRAL PARK SOUTH
NEW YORK CITY

May 26, 1936

Dear Dr. Severn: Thank you so much for sending
                     a farewell greeting. I hope
you will feel very happy in London, though personally I should like to see you return to New York.

                     My daughter Brigitte is in
Germany just now, and will be there until the middle
of July. After that, if her plans do not change,
she will be in London for a short while, then return to Germany, and sometime during the month of
October, she will definitely settle down in London.
I shall certainly send her your address. Please
do not feel disappointed if she should not react
for some time, because I know that while she is
at work on a movie she is kept busy from early
morning until late at night. I hope, however,
that you and your daughter will meet her when she
has settled down in London.

                     With cordial greetings,

                          Sincerely yours

                          Karen Horney.

KH/zs

Dr. Elizabeth Severn
care of Bankers Trust Co.
26 Old Broad Street
London, E.C.,England

IMAGE 17   Dr. Karen Horney's letter to Dr. Severn, May 26, 1936

Thank you so much for sending a farewell greeting. I hope you will feel
very happy in London, though personally I should like to see you return to
New York.

(Letter from Dr. Karen Horney to Dr. Severn,
May 26, 1936. In Rachman, 2016d)

Karen Korney goes on to tell her she is referring her daughter Brigette because
her daughter is going to move from Germany to London. It is not clear if Horney
is introducing her daughter to Severn as a potential analysand or as a social contact
for the Severns. In any event, Horney had sufficient positive feelings about Severn
to trust her with her daughter for friendship or analysis.

To work

Severn's career began being a clinician with a metaphysical perspective, then with a psychological perspective, and finally with a psychoanalytic perspective (see Chapters 11 and 25). In what seems like a remarkable achievement, Severn published her third book in 1933, shortly after the termination of her analysis. Either Severn was writing *The Discovery of the Self* (Severn, 1933) during her last year of analysis with Ferenczi or she wrote it shortly after the termination. In either event, it indicates that Severn had the emotional and intellectual capacity to conceive, write, and publish her major work during a period of emotional turmoil. This work was completely ignored by the traditional analytic community when it was published, and has been out of print for over 50 years. The book represented her attempt to integrate her own dissident ideas about psychoanalysis, the meaning of her analysis with Ferenczi, and her ideas and experience of trauma analysis.

If one carefully examines the Eissler interview (1952), and listens to not only the words, but also the music of the Eissler/Severn interaction, Severn appears to be an intellectual and interpersonal match for Eissler. Eissler attempted on several occasions to pressure Severn into revealing improprieties in Ferenczi's relationship with Severn. She never said anything that would imply unethical or unprofessional behavior by Ferenczi and not because she was protecting her analyst. She gave the distinct impression that nothing sexual happened. Previously, I had attempted to disprove the myth of sexual contact in the Ferenczi/Severn analysis (Rachman, 1993). Severn's written word in the Eissler (1952) interview verifies the previous research. She never let Eissler intimidate her in any way. She also spoke respectfully of Freud, admiring his theoretical and intellectual capacity, but was critical of his experience-distant clinical approach. Clearly, she felt Ferenczi was the healer and Freud the theoretician. Severn was Eissler's intellectual and interpersonal equal. What is more, Severn offered many insightful statements about psychoanalysis, Freud, Ferenczi, Rank, and her own functioning. This interview showed Severn to be a person who had recovered from her illness and was functioning at a high level of emotionality and intellect.

In 1943, 10 years after the termination of her analysis, Severn's recovered functioning is revealed in a letter she wrote to an ex-patient, answering his letter to her while he was serving in the armed forces:

> I still recall with pleasure the hours you and I spent together in an effort to remove some of the distractions to a good adjustment in your life and I hope that you may have found some benefits available in the year intervening. Your account of your present activities and feelings is, a special satisfaction to me and I hope you will write more fully, about it another time.
>
> With affectionate good wishes,
> Yours sincerely,
> Manning.
>
> *(Letter from Manning to Elizabeth Severn, October 26, 1943. In Rachman, 2016d)*

This letter described an analyst who is free to be self-disclosing and show appropriate affection. A further level of self-disclosure, which some could see as problematic, was as follows:

> My own work goes on about as usual although I have very little direct contact with the war. Anxiety states in general are increased owning, mainly, to extra work (all kinds of help, services, etc., are hard to get) financial strain, etc., but the problems presented to me are mostly those of people wishing to increase the usefulness and peace of mind through self-understanding such as your good patients are doing.
>
> *(Letter from Manning to Elizabeth Severn, October 26, 1943.*
> *In Rachman, 2016d)*

The letter seems to indicate a fully functioning analyst, who enjoyed a mutually positive relationship with an analysand. While he was away serving in the war, Severn was seeing his parents for analysis. This is an indication of Severn's philosophy of boundary permeability.

An interesting article was among Severn's personal library of books, newspaper clippings, and documents (Rachman, 2016d). It was published in 1935, two years after Severn ended her analysis with Ferenczi. On the one hand it indicates her interest in maintaining contact with the popular culture, as the article was written for the lay public about a new kind of inpatient psychiatric facility. Saving the article may have indicated a continued thinking through of her own psychological treatment. The article described the transformation of the famous psychiatric facility in Hartford, Connecticut, referred to as *The Retreat* (now known as *The Hartford Retreat*. Before the transformation, the facility was known as an insane asylum. The transformation involved removing the bars from the windows, creating community groups, and introducing activities that parallel life in the real world. The changes transformed *The Retreat* from a Victorian mausoleum-type building to a cheerful, positive, modern clinical atmosphere. They produced greater enrollment and more positive rehabilitation. Was Severn thinking that she could have benefitted by a stay at *The Retreat*, either during or after her analysis? Or, did she see the development in *The Retreat*'s treatment philosophy as an application of psychoanalysis to be inpatient treatment:

> In its mental treatment *The Retreat* uses suggestion and psychoanalysis.
> *(Fortune Magazine, "A sane asylum," 1935, p. 1240)*

Severn's own assessment of her analysis with Ferenczi suggested recovery:

> As to my own analysis, some of the worst of my symptoms were allayed or disposed of, including the suicidal compulsion and the devastating headaches, though I was emotionally exhausted and still subject to the devitalizing nightmarish dreams – and from these I have never fully recovered.
> *(Eissler, 1952, p. 24)*

Severn's statement on recovery seems to match Michael Balint's assessment of the Ferenczi/Severn analysis. Balint assessed the analysis in the following way:

> The patient, a talented but profoundly disturbed woman, improved con-siderably ... *but could not be considered as cured* ... when we discussed his experiments – the case ... [which] *was the grandest, but by no means the only one* – Ferenczi accepted that, in a way, he failed, but added that *he himself learned an immense* amount, and perhaps even others might benefit from his failure if he realized that this task, in the way he tried to solve it, was insoluble.
>
> *(Balint, 1992, p. 113, italics added)*

Is an analysand with the type of profound childhood trauma from which Severn suffered completely curable? Aren't there always psychological scars that result from a disorder caused by severe childhood traumas created by parental abuse? Can an analyst completely cure such pathology with a therapeutic relationship? As Balint and Severn reported, it was a good enough cure. Freud found the analysis of the Wolf Man, Sergei Pankejeff, to be as difficult as Severn, and one can question as to whether Freud's analytical effort showed any success, as evaluated by Pankejeff himself, (see Chapter 8).

My own experience with analyzing incest trauma survivors over 45 years echoes Ferenczi's experience with Severn (Rachman & Klett, 2015). But, after analyzing an incest survivor for about 10 years, with what seemed great success, she initiated a unilateral termination. We then kept in touch subsequently through mail, the analy-sand sending me articles about incest. Then, all of a sudden, she became angry and broke off contact. When I tried to discuss the matter, she never responded.

Ferenczi's wise words seem to be a fitting final evaluation to his analysis of Severn:

> I do not know of any analyst whose analysis I could declare, theoretically, as concluded (least of all my own). Thus we have, in every single analysis, quite enough to learn about ourselves.
>
> *(Sándor Ferenczi, 1988 – Clinical Diary entry 8 August, 1932, p. 194)*

21

SEVERN AND FERENCZI'S RECOVERED MEMORIES OF CHILDHOOD SEXUAL ABUSE

An appraisal

As has been emphasized, over and over again, Severn helped introduce an alternative clinical method for psychoanalysis, trauma analysis (see Chapter 12). This method combined the alternative theoretical framework, The Confusion of Tongues paradigm (see Chapter 15) with the clinical innovations of relaxation therapy (see Chapters 14, 16, and 17). One of the controversial dimensions to this new method was the belief in the retrieved memories of childhood trauma as being authentic, not fantasy productions of a conflicted mind. In Chapter 12, "Trauma analysis: Stages in the Ferenczi/Severn analysis," and Chapter 13, "Analyzing the Ferenczi/Severn analysis," the retrieved memories of childhood sexual abuse were reported. In Severn's analysis with Ferenczi, she recalled horrific childhood abuse by her psychopathic father, which Ferenczi labeled as *traumatic shocks*. These abusive experiences were a very significant part of the analysis. As Severn reported, before her analysis with Ferenczi, she felt she was *living under a black cloud during her adult life*, haunted by emotional disturbance. She had no idea where the emotional disturbance originated or how to reduce its negative effect on her life (Eissler, 1952). In her previous three analyses, there was no relief from her emotional disturbances (see Chapter 10), or any indication that childhood abuse was a factor in her personality development.

Central to Severn's trauma analysis with Ferenczi was the retrieved memories of childhood abuse by her father, reported by Ferenczi, in his *Clinical Diary* (Ferenczi, 1988). The abuse in childhood ranged from one and one half to 11 years old. There is a need to discuss the issue of retrieved memories of childhood in the Ferenczi/Severn analysis in the light of contemporary analytic thinking, which has strongly favored the fantasy and unconscious conception of childhood trauma (Lichtenberg, 2016c).

Freud's view of psychoanalysis as the study of imagination

In Freud's analysis of the Wolf Man/Sergei Pankejeff (see Chapter 8), he made it clear that early childhood recollections of sexuality are the product of a child's imagination, as he noted in this case:

> I have remarked ... that it will certainly be considered improbable, firstly, that a child at the tender age of one and a half could be in a position to take in the perceptions of such a complicated process and to preserve them so accurately in his unconscious; secondly, that it is possible at the age of four for a deferred revision of this material to penetrate the understanding and finally, that any procedure could succeed in bringing into consciousness coherently and convincingly the details of a scene of this kind which had been experienced and understood in such circumstance.
>
> *(Freud, 1955d, p. 192)*

Freud raised two important issues in this statement. First, he believed that a child's memory of abuse cannot be trusted as evidence of sexual abuse in the analysand's history. These memories in the early period of a child's life also raised an issue as to their authenticity for Freud:

> scenes, like this one in my present patient's case, which date from such an early period and exhibit a similar content, and which further lay claim to such an extraordinary significance for the history of the case, are as a rule not reproduced as recollections, but have to be divined – constructed gradually and laboriously from an aggregate of indications.
>
> *(Freud, 1955d, p. 194)*

Freud's concerns, so clearly expressed in the Pankejeff case, established a tradition where *reconstruction of an analysand's childhood data by the analysand was valued over the self-report of the analysand*. In actuality, Freud produced a remarkable intellectual reproduction in the Pankejeff case. The reproduction became, in my opinion, evidence for Freud's intellect and creativity rather than an indication of the analysand's actual early childhood recall of sexual abuse. Freud needed to impose his own understanding on the analysand's data because he did not inquire about the childhood sexuality, because he didn't believe it was possible that the analysand's self-report had any reality. This skepticism about the analysand's recollection helped establish an institutional skepticism in psychoanalysis regarding the reality of repressed memories and the validity of the childhood sexual abuse as a psychodynamic in the development of psychological disorder. We need to examine the issues raised by this tradition that Freud established and that has been maintained by mainstream psychoanalysis. A contemporary relational perspective can aid our understanding in re-evaluating the reality of repressed memories and their meaning for analyzing trauma disorder.

The reality of repressed memories

There has been considerable controversy over the last two decades or so about the recall of childhood abuse. Poorly trained and over-zealous therapists have contaminated the therapeutic encounter by suggesting that patients, clients, or analysands need to make contact with the unrecognized origins of their adult psychopathology by vigorously encouraging retrieval of childhood abuse. This has led to what some authors have claimed to be a *false memory syndrome*. This claim is open to question, since The False Memory Institute was developed as a reaction to a daughter claiming that her father sexually abused her. The mother of the abused daughter, who was a psychologist, defended her husband by suggesting that their daughter, who was also a psychologist, was, in essence, suffering from a delusion (Freyd, 1996; Freyd & Birrell, 2013). Research during the past two decades has firmly established the reliability of the phenomenon of recovered memory. The advocates of the false memory syndrome claimed they had discovered a new syndrome involving iatrogenic-created false memories of childhood sexual abuse. A critical examination of the empirical and epidemiological evidence suggested that the existence of such a syndrome lacks general acceptance in the mental health field, and that the construct is based on a series of faulty assumptions, many of which have been scientifically disproven (Dallam, 2001).

Although there has been a controversy about the way childhood abuse has been reported by survivors or retrieved by some therapists, we cannot question that childhood sexual abuse is common and existed in Freud, Ferenczi, and Severn's clinical lifetimes. As I have attempted to demonstrate in several publications (Rachman, 1997a, 2003a, 2016b, c; Rachman & Klett, 2015), Freud was the first to reveal the importance of childhood abuse as a factor in the personality development. Those of us who have devoted our careers to working with survivors of childhood sexual abuse (as well as survivors of physical, emotional, and interpersonal abuse) know the phenomenological truth that is evident in the narratives they report to their therapists and analysts. Often, trauma survivors experience their recall of childhood abuse as labeled as unconscious, not a narrative event happening in the reality of their own consciousness or, even worse, a product of fantasy, not the actual experiences which haunt their waking life. As Loftus, a leading expert on the reality of repressed memories, has declared:

> I do not question the commonness of childhood sexual abuse itself but ask
> … about how the abuse is recalled in the mind of adults.
>
> *(Lofton, 1993, p. 520)*

In the present discussion of repressed memories of childhood sexual abuse, I am specifically referring to an analytic process where these memories emerge in the context of a psychoanalysis which is geared to work through the basic fault of the individual's personality, within an empathic framework (Rachman & Klett, 2015). A trauma analysis is conducted as a co-created, two-person experience so that the unfolding of the recall of childhood memories is not imposed on the analysand. This standard was established by Ferenczi and Severn in their analysis (see Chapter 12).

Historical vs. narrative truth

How should we approach the recovered memories of abuse by Elizabeth Severn, which were reported to have occurred in her earliest childhood? Severn's first childhood trauma, recovered in her analysis with Ferenczi, and unknown to her in three previous analyses, was reported to have occurred at one and a half years old. What was also recovered was that her father was her horrific abuser (Ferenczi, 1988). Her father, who was described as a psychopath and criminal, was involved not only in deviant behavior with his daughter, but in the community (Lipskis, 2011). The question arises as to whether we can accept the report of a retrieved memory of sexual abuse of a child during the first or second year of life. There are several ways to approach this issue, e.g. empirically, philosophically, and clinically.

In an attempt to add some empirical data to the discussion, we can turn to a study reported by the National Center for Juvenile Justice. The data includes the National Incident-Based Reporting System (NIBRS). This information includes demographic information on all victims, the level of victim injury, and the victim–offender relationships. From 1991 through 1996 NIBRS master files contain reports from law enforcement agencies in 12 states. The FBI's offense coding structure classifies sexual assault into four separate offense categories, from most to least serious. These crimes are forcible rape, forcible sodomy, sexual assault with an object, and forcible fondling. If more than one of these offenses occurred, the most severe sexual charge was used to classify the sexual assault. The sample from which this study draws was over 100,000 victims and victim offenders. The detailed age distribution of the victims of sexual assault emphasizes the high proportion of juvenile victims. *There were more victims in such individual age groups between three and 17 than in any individual age group over age 17 (any adult age group) and more victims age two than in any age group above age 40.* For victims under age 12, *four-year-olds were at greatest risk of being the victim of a sexual assault. Females were more than six times as likely as males to be the victims of sexual assaults* known to law enforcement agencies. Specifically, *86% of all victims of sexual assault were female, 69 % of victims under age six were female, and one of every seven victims was under the age of six* (Snyder, 2000). This study indicated that *female children are commonly the victim of sexual abuse, at as young as two, four, or seven years old.*

We need to add Spence's distinction between narrative and historical truth, which is very relevant to our discussion (Spence, 1982). Severn's descriptions of her childhood abuse from one and a half to 11 years old was accepted by Ferenczi as narrative truth. It was a clinical affirmation of Severn as someone who was valiantly attempting to discover the origins of her severe emotional disturbance. In a co-created therapeutic regression experience that she called a Semi-Trance Session, she emotionally returned to her early childhood where Ferenczi created a holding environment so Severn could feel safe enough to reduce her anxiety and defenses to allow her repressed memories to emerge. *These memories of abuse are Severn's narrative truth.* They are the emotional story of her abuse, which is her truth. Because of his clinical genius, Ferenczi could realize that validating her narrative truth was the key to helping her to unravel the darkness of mood and functioning. By understanding and affirming her retrieved incident of childhood abuse, Ferenczi provided the empathic understanding that allowed Severn to retrieve and explore her shadows of abuse and come into the light of analytic understanding and personal growth. This process has helped survivors of such incidents reclaim their lives (Rachman & Klett, 2015).

In over 40 years or so of analyzing incest survivors, there have been instances where repressed memories of sexual abuse had been reported as occurring during the first two years of life. A particularly dramatic example of very early childhood abuse retrieved by an analysand was the Case of Winston, reported in Rachman and Klett (2015). This analysand retrieved memories of maternal sexual abuse dated to the first or second year of life. Winston retrieved a series of memories which depicted a repeated scene of his mother bathing him in a bassinet. During the bathing of him as a very young child, a period which Winston assigns to his first and second year of life, his mother would interrupt the bathing to include an interlude where she used him as a sexual object. In his associations to these retrieved memories, he described his mother as being sexually aroused by washing his penis. Once aroused, she developed an action for her sexual satisfaction. She held her infant son as if he were a penis, rubbing him against her vagina. With both the contents of this retrieved memory and its occurrence reported to be so early in the analysand's life, it is natural to question the authenticity of the data. But then, there are other considerations. Winston as an adult showed exceptional capacities for intellectual memory and recall of events. He possessed eidetic imagery. Winston demonstrated to me his capacity to remember the written word on a specific page, including the line, and even place in the line, in which it appeared. He could describe an event in such detail that you could imagine yourself being there. These descriptions were enlivened by the use of metaphors, references to mythology, and historical figures and events. His intelligence level was tested to be at the very superior level. Taken together, all these special personal capacities seem to give some validity to Winston's retrieved memories and their associations. In the analysis they were reported by an individual who was there and could bring you into the experience. Winston also showed the same unusual capacity for remembering regarding non-abusive events in the earliest period in his life. He described the memory of lying in a large object, high off the ground, with the sun shining down on him through what seemed to be a covering of gauze. When we reconstructed the memory together we agreed to the possibility that he was recalling a scene where a young child was placed in a large perambulator, covered by a gauze coverlet, and put in the direct sunlight, perhaps during the first or second year of life.

22

THE DEVELOPMENT OF THERAPEUTIC REGRESSION

Severn, Ferenczi, and Balint

Anna O./Bertha Pappenheim hypnosis, talk therapy and regression

Regression, as a theoretical and clinical concept, was involved in the founding of psychoanalysis. Although I have discussed this case in Chapter 8, we need to expand our understanding because regression was used in the hypnosis in Breuer's Case of Anna. O./Bertha Pappenheim (Breuer & Freud, 1895). She was an Austrian–Jewish feminist and the founder of the League of Jewish Women. In 1954, The West German government issued a postage stamp in honor of her contributions to the field of social work. She became a patient of Josef Breuer in November 1880, referred by a friend of the Pappenheim family. Bertha became ill, as a result of her father's deteriorated physical condition. While attending her father as he grew weaker, she developed hallucinations and states of anxiety. Later on, she developed a variety of symptoms:

1. Language disorders (aphasia); sometimes, she could not speak, sometimes she spoke only English, French, or Italian. She could always understand her native language of German. The aphasia could last for days.
2. Paralysis and numbness in the limbs of one side of her body.
3. Neuralgia, facial pain treated with morphine and chloral hydrate, which led to addiction. The condition was so painful surgery was considered.
4. Visual impairment; she squinted and perceived objects as larger than they were.
5. Mood swings between anxiety and depression.
6. Amnesia; she could not remember when she was in a state of anxiety or depression.
7. Eating disorder. When in crisis, Pappenheim refused to eat. One summer she only ate fruit.

The development of her intensive psychopathology as a response to her father's serious illness and subsequent death, meant Bertha Pappenheim was a very difficult case for Josef Breuer, equivalent to Freud's Case of The Wolf Man/Sergei Pankejeff and Ferenczi's Case of R.N., Elizabeth Severn. Breuer was one of the most distinguished physicians of his time. He was also an eminent neurophysiologist. Sigmund Freud, as a young man, had worked in Breuer's laboratory. It was Freud who eventually managed to persuade him to publish the details of Bertha's illness and treatment (Breuer, 1955; Breuer & Freud, 1895). Hearing about this case, Freud believed that Breuer had demonstrated that hysteria (neurosis) could be cured by a cathartic method, which involved *talking about an individual's emotional experiences*. This, he reasoned, had never been done. Although they cooperated on compiling this case along with other cases (Breuer & Freud, 1895), they did not agree on a unitary theory of sexuality, as Freud would later expound.

The stages in Papenheim's treatment are of most interest in the present discussion because it involved forms of regression. Initially, Breuer began the therapeutic contact with Pappenheim considering her symptoms to be a manifestation of hysteria. By inducing a light hypnotic trance during their morning therapy sessions, Breuer helped Pappenheim regress to an earlier emotional period, hoping to elicit lost memories. Stewart (1993) believed that: "Hypnosis is a form of regression" (p. 249). What is so interesting about this case was that Freud considered it as the beginning of psychoanalysis, in that the analysand, Bertha Pappenheim changed the nature of the therapeutic activity of psychotherapy, leading to the development of psychoanalysis. Pappenheim first asked Breuer to give up putting her into a hypnotic state in exchange for *talking to Breuer about her symptoms and their origins*. In essence, she asked for a more natural method of therapy. She wanted to eliminate a physician-developed method and introduce a patient-formed method. Breuer showed courage and foresight in accepting Pappenheim's request to change the method of clinical interaction. The new method moved toward what Pappenheim called her *chimney sweeping*. She talked freely to Breuer, saying whatever came into her mind. Breuer called what she experienced as *absences*, a change of personality functioning accompanied by confusion. Pappenheim would talk to herself, muttering words or phrases which seem to induce a kind of self-hypnosis. Then, in this new state of the Breuer/Pappenheim's co-created interaction, the *analysand's induced regression* occurred when she was able to remember experiences connected to her psychopathology.

The therapy with Pappenheim was laborious for Breuer and he became intensely anxious. He seemed to be unaware of a possible erotic reaction in the relationship. Breuer has been criticized by both the traditional analytic establishment, as well as by members of contemporary analytic perspectives such as Object Relations (Stewart, 1993), as having unsuccessfully treated Pappenheim. Stewart believed that Breuer's countertransference had diminished the treatment. Recently, Breuer's therapy behavior has been re-evaluated in a more positive way:

> When Breuer approached Anna's bedside with an apparently obsessive interest in the tiniest details of her behavior, he was *displaying the most objective and*

enlightened stance available to a medical man of his time, not to mention *a great deal of patience and devotion.* What Breuer did *was utterly original,* in relation to any form of mental distress: *he listened not only in order to establish a diagnosis, but also to effect a treatment.* Freud, for all his reservations about the case, *drew on it for the basis of his own talking cure.*"

(Launer, 2005 p. 465–466, italics added)

However, Breuer's difficulties in the treatment of Pappenheim seemed to be connected to transference/countertransference issues. Pappenheim was sent to a sanatorium on occasion, after Breuer terminated their clinical interaction. Pappenheim eventually recovered and made significant contributions to society. *Freud thought Pappenheim's idea of chimney sweeping or free association was the beginning of psychoanalysis.*

Recollecting, remembering, and talking it out

The plausible sexual feelings that were present in the Breuer/Pappenheim relationship were also present in Freud's early hypnotic cases. A dramatic example of Freud experiencing a very uncomfortable sexual feeling in a hypnotic relationship is as follows:

> Freud, in his turn, having hypnotized a female patient, found that she threw her arms round him in great passion, whereupon he called for his maidservant to remove her. He recognized the sexuality but was not too disturbed by its manifestations [Freud seemed very disturbed by it]. It is this kind of behavior we would call acting out or else describe as formal regression. The patient acts or repeats or regresses rather than remembering and recollecting.
>
> *(Stewart, 1993, p. 250)*

It was the behavior displayed by female patients with Breuer and Freud that came to be seen as regression and acting out. Traditional analysis as it developed under Freud's basic analytic principles believed the analysand's task was to recollect, remember, and talk about the repressed memories, which were the origins of the emotional disturbances. The traditional attitude was created when the analysand was not encouraged to talk about or physically express sexual feelings toward their analyst. The established standard was to only allow remembering, recollecting, and the intellectual exploration of clinical feelings. The attitude was intended to keep acting out to a minimum. Also, Freud and the orthodox community maintained that regression was a negative dimension in the psychoanalytic situation when they rejected Ferenczi's attempt to understand and treat non-Oedipal psychological disorders where freer emotional expressions were necessary to reach the underlying trauma.

There has been some attempt in traditional psychoanalysis to reconfigure regression as having a positive quality. Rothenberg and Hausman (1976) discussed Ernst Kris's idea of *regression in the service of the ego* as:" … the specific means whereby preconscious and unconscious material appear in the creator's consciousness" (p. 10). Kris's formulation laid a foundation for ego psychology to take a more positive view of regression. Regression was no longer solely a matter of acting out. Blos (1962) believed that regression during adolescence advances the cause of personality development.

Stewart (1993) described a clinical case where he used a new view of therapeutic regression (which he learned from Michael Balint, his teacher). He created a therapeutic atmosphere with a borderline analysand where the individual could *act in* her fantasy about the dead soul of a friend, who needed to be put to rest, so the torment of suffering could end. Stewart made no interventions about the analysand's behavior as regression. He accepted the person's need to perform prayers for the dead at a cemetery. This non-interpretative clinical behavior is consistent with the revisions that Ferenczi, Severn, and Balint made in the understanding and the clinical practice of therapeutic regression.

"The Subjective or Trance State by E.S.": Severn's contribution to the development of therapeutic regression

Among the materials that I found among *The Elizabeth Severn Papers* (Rachman 2016d), was an interesting and previously unknown document, entitled, *Dictated in a Subjective or Trance State by E.S., Friday morning, June 14th 1916.* The document has a handwritten title by Severn and a typed two-page description of what can be labeled as a clinical experiment in therapeutic regression. This method was chronicled in her book, *Psychotherapy of Behavior* (Severn, 1920; see Chapter 11). Her clinical behavior at this period was characterized by her empathic and flexible clinical capacity to respond to a wide variety of disturbed individuals. There was, however, another dimension to her personal and clinical behavior: she had a unique desire and capacity to examine her own functioning. In fact, she developed the *Subjective/ Trance State* in 1916 to find such a means for self-examination.

At the same time, around 1916, Freud was establishing the basic principles of psychoanalysis, and Ferenczi was experimenting with the introduction of activity into the psychoanalytic method. When Freud introduced the concept of the countertransference reaction in 1910 (McGrath, 1974), he realized that the analyst's emotional reaction had an important influence on the therapeutic experience. But he was unsure if he wanted to integrate countertransference as an essential part of the analytic encounter. In actuality, he wanted to keep countertransference as a secret from analysands, analysts, and perhaps from the outside therapeutic community, as he wrote to Jung (McGrath, 1984). Ferenczi, during this same time period, was not as actively involved in analyzing his countertransference as he was in the analysis of Severn. Severn, to her credit, can be viewed as being in advance of both Freud and Ferenczi during the first decade of psychoanalysis. One can conclude that her *Trance and Subjective State* method demonstrates her willingness to examine her own functioning, showing her insight, talent, and clinical understanding of psychoanalysis.

Severn (1916) began her report of the trance session by saying she saw, "another world, space untrammeled by the physical" (p. 1). She felt there were no limits on conventional depth or horizon in the altered state. In this subjective state of consciousness, she reported being more aware of "my own self that consciousness I should always have but rarely do" (p. 1). She complained that she was vulnerable to the demands of others. The demands of others appear to close the door to greater self-awareness; more importantly, in the demands of others, Severn said, "I lost my personality" (p. 1). She asked: "Why have I such a passion for the lives of other people, when I know that my self has a life of its own?" (p. 1). In her own analysis with Ferenczi she was able to create an interaction with him which did not suppress her own sense of self. In the unfolding of the analysis between Ferenczi and Severn she was able, perhaps for the first time, to create a more democratic and mutual encounter. Giving expression to her own sense of self, not allowing another to define it for her sense of self, was crucial for Severn to overcome her crippling childhood traumas. We shall also understand how Severn used her own capacity to develop a method to access her own subjectivity. The trance state began for Severn as a means to access her subjective experience.

Severn was able to create new images in her trance state so that she could reduce her anxiety and examine her functioning. On additional issues she examined in this session was, "the sacrifice of the self" (p. 1). She is referring to her tendency to suffer emotionally when she feels she cares so deeply in her work with others that it becomes her own issue: "We should aim to help suffering, but not by suffering" (p. 1). This principle can be seen as a fundamental dimension of the need for countertransference analysis. The idea of suffering as a clinician, which Severn notes in the 1916 trance session, later emerges in Ferenczi's *Clinical Diary* (Ferenczi, 1988) as the issue of the "terrorism of suffering" (p. 211). Severn in this trance session was struggling with the difficulties of the emotional demands of being a therapeutic agent. In allowing herself the time, space, and silence to contemplate her inner struggles, she came to the insight that she characterized as follows: "hear the voices of the silence" (p. 2).

Severn also indicted that one can either consult a "spiritual Master" or speak to you in your own "personal God" in order to gain self-understanding (p. 2). The significance of Severn's subjective, trance state is that she developed an ongoing methodology for self-examination. In 1916, when Severn developed her method, there was no methodology introduced in psychoanalysis to integrate the countertransference reaction and a clinical behavior for the psychoanalyst. As Freud wrote to Jung during this period, he wanted to keep the idea of the analyst's emotional response a secret (McGrath, 1974). Ferenczi *was the first analyst to translate Freud's discovery of the countertransference reaction into an ongoing methodology, which he called the analysis of the analyst* (Ferenczi, 1988). Ferenczi used self-observation and self-analyses to create a hovering attention to his empathic attitude toward an analysand (Ferenczi, 1980h; Ferenczi & Rank, 1925). This kind of *empathic compass* allowed Ferenczi to work meaningfully with difficult cases like Severn. It was in the clinical work with Severn that two major aspects of self-analysis were highlighted: (1) Severn's use of the new subjective trance method to retrieve her childhood traumas; (2) Severn's insistence that her analytic cure was tied to Ferenczi's capacity to analyze his negative countertransference reaction to her (see Chapters 12, 14, and 16).

Severn's subjective/trance sessions in the analysis with Ferenczi

During the last year of the analysis, which I have indicated was the most tumultuous in the eight-year experience, Ferenczi (1988) described his difficulty in accepting Severn's trance session as a meaningful part of the analysis when he said:

> when she fell into a semi-trance, I usually disturbed this very early on by pressing for an explanation or clarification and by providing interpretation.
> *(Clinical entry – February 4, 1932, p. 30)*

Severn was comfortable with the regressive experience by 1932, having practiced it regularly for 17 years. But Ferenczi was definitely uncomfortable with this practice:

> I used to be similarly prompted by alarming symptoms – shortness of breath, interruption of pulse and breathing, pallor, coldness and cold sweat ....
> *(Clinical entry – February 4, 1932, p. 30)*

These behavioral symptoms, which Severn displayed during the subjective trance session, frightened Ferenczi. In previous sessions of this kind, Ferenczi would show his anxiety of Severn being in a trance-like state by offering her a host of verbal interpretations. He felt her silence meant Severn was suffering in the analysis. Ferenczi thought he was trying his best to help her. In reality, it was a moment where greater understanding of the issue of therapeutic regression was needed. Severn was helpful in gaining this understanding. In an attempt to teach Ferenczi the positive functions of therapeutic regression, she interrupted his bombardment of interpretations by telling him to shut up:

> whereas at other times I had the objectionable habit, with this patient especially, of engaging her occasionally in conversation or discussion, from which *she sometimes had to defend herself with an energetic "shut up"* .... Even when she fell into a semi-trance.
> *(Ferenczi, 1988 – Clinical entry, February 4, 1932,*
> *italics added, pp. 29–30)*

By the time the trance session quoted above by Ferenczi occurred in 1932, Severn was not only comfortable with her own method, but, was expert in using it. Ferenczi was not only a novice in its use, but had to overcome his traditional psychoanalytic training, which viewed regression as a negative experience. Analytic tradition believed in the regressive experience was an expression of an emotionally immature state because the analysand was acting out, rather than talking out, the core personal issues. Ferenczi and Severn were analytic partners, perhaps even analytic peers. It is clear from the above quotes that he learned how to integrate Severn's method into their trauma analysis, which Ferenczi and Severn eventually developed to treat her trauma disorder (Ferenczi, 1988; see Chapter 12).

From abstinence to responsitivity

Although Severn was developing her clinical method to include a form of therapeutic regression, psychoanalysis had to go through important theoretical and clinical developments to be able to integrate therapeutic regression. It is worth mentioning that in 1916, psychoanalysis was under the influence of Freud's mandate, the *Rule of Abstinence* (Freud, 1958b). Originally, the *Rule of Abstinence* was introduced by Freud in the following way:

> The treatment must be carried out in abstinence. By this I do not mean physical abstinence alone, nor yet the deprivation of everything that the patient desires, for no sick person could tolerate this.
> … the patient's need and longing should be allowed to persist …, in order that they serve as a force impelling … to do work and make changes … we must beware of appeasing those forces by means of surrogates. … the patient's condition is such that, until her repressions are removed, she is incapable of getting real satisfaction.
>
> *(Freud, 1958b p. 165)*

Freud believed he was trying to help young male analysts not to respond to female analysands' attempts to seduce them by responding to their erotic needs. Such responses produce complicated, un-analyzable erotic transferences. Unfortunately, the rule of abstinence became for traditionalists a mandate to be emotionally withholding, depriving, inactive, and distant (Rachman, 1997a).

I would also suggest that Ferenczi possessed a quality which Breuer and Freud lacked. Ferenczi had personality and professional qualities which allowed him to be more comfortable with analysand's emotional expressions of affection, love, and sexuality. Contrary to what is thought about his clinical functioning, he did not encourage physical or sexual contact (Rachman, 1993). In fact, he did not easily deviate from standard psychoanalytic practice, always being aware of Freud's criticism about any new developments with which Ferenczi might begin experimenting (Rachman, 1997a). What is more, in both the cases of Clara Thompson and Elizabeth Severn, he reluctantly entered into the deviations that both these analysands, it can be said, forced upon him (see Chapter 8). In all instances of experimentation, Ferenczi was searching for therapeutic means to respond to trauma disorders, when traditional methods of clinical intervention were ineffective.

Two issues became clear in the second and third decades of psychoanalysis. First, both Freud and Ferenczi's client population were not necessarily neurotic or suffering from an Oedipal complex. Rather, many analysands actually were severe neurotics, character and narcissistic, or borderline disorders. Secondarily, these individuals, some of which had childhood trauma experiences, did not respond well to privation, silence or the use of interpretation. Freud was aware that Ferenczi had reported a series of cases of the so-called difficult analysand who had problems adhering to the rules of abstinence and free association. They were better able to respond to non-interpretative measures (Rachman, 1997a; see Chapter 18). In demonstrating his proficiency in treating non-Oedipal disorders, Freud passed the mantel of clinical psychoanalysis to Ferenczi at The Budapest Congress in 1918, when he endorsed his introduction of activity in clinical psychoanalysis (Rachman, 1997a).

In essence, Ferenczi began to view the psychoanalytic situation as a stage where the original childhood trauma was reenacted with the analyst. He questioned the traditional view that analysands act out their childhood experiences in a vacuum, that is, without the emotional participation of the analyst. In actuality, the use of the rule of abstinence and interpretation encouraged regression.

Trauma analysis and regression

The Ferenczi/Severn analysis became the vehicle for introducing the concept of *therapeutic regression* into psychoanalysis. Throughout this manuscript, Severn's ideas and clinical methods have been described as influencing Ferenczi in his conduct of their analysis. It can be said that Severn's *Subjective/Trance State* was the origin of therapeutic regression, in that she developed this method in order to become emotionally connected to, and understand, her subjective experience. This allowed her to eventually use this method to retrieve her childhood trauma. Severn's 1916 document detailed her example of a clinician using a method to reach their own subjective experience. This is an early sign that Severn believed in a two-person psychology, in that she was developing an ongoing method to maintain an awareness of her own functioning. In so doing she was practicing an early version of countertransference analysis. She was becoming aware of her own functioning and how it related to maintaining a therapeutic relationship. When Severn asked Ferenczi to examine his own functioning with her, she was applying her subjective/trance state method to her own personal analysis. She correctly observed that Ferenczi had negative feelings toward her that were impeding the relationship. She also knew from her own experience that examining one's own functioning was essential to reaching the depths of one's emotional issues. In the clinical analysis of trauma, however, it became clear it was absolutely necessary. In fact, *the examination of the countertransference reaction became the analysis of countertransference*. The development of Severn's intense erotic transference reaction in the relationship and Ferenczi's intense negative countertransference reaction to her illustrated how volatile and emotionally demanding a trauma analysis can become. Ferenczi and Severn's trauma analysis incorporates the idea of retrieving, re-experiencing and reliving the original emotional trauma, not just remembering and repeating it (Rachman

& Klett, 2015). Severn never became a historically important figure in psychoanalysis because Freud declared she was an *evil genius*. This negative condemnation relegated her to obscurity. The "genius" part was ignored, even though methods like the Subjective/Trance Session helped transform psychoanalysis through her idea of therapeutic regression. This was evident in her attempt to inform Ferenczi of the value of an analysand using a form of introspection to retrieve childhood trauma. This changed the analytic encounter into a two-person experience, as the analysand uses his/her capacity to add intellectual and emotional material from their own perspective. Clinical interaction added the analysand's willingness and capacity to contribute to the analytic process. Severn follows in the footsteps of Anna O./Bertha Pappenheim, who taught Josef Breuer and Sigmund Freud the curative function of creating a conversation between a therapist and a patient that focuses on free association and abreaction (see Chapter 8). It is puzzling to see how astute and prophetic Freud was in his assessment of Pappenheim's contribution to psychoanalysis, and how critical and prejudicial he was about Severn's contribution.

Ferenczi developed a new perspective about the analysand's functioning in the psychoanalytic situation, which was informed by Severn's interaction with him. In an evolutionary statement he introduced a new way of being for a therapeutic dyad:

> I encouraged my colleagues to train their patients to a greater liberty and a freer expression in behavior of their aggressive feelings toward the physician –
> … I urged analysts to be more humble-minded in their attitude to their patients and to admit the mistakes they made, and I pleaded for a greater elasticity in technique, even if it meant the sacrifice of some of our theories.
> *(Ferenczi, 1980k, p. 113).*

Freud, Ferenczi: regression or emancipation

When Freud became aware of Ferenczi's analysis of Severn through the rumors circulating through members of the analytic community, such as Clara Thompson, he thought the analysis was regressive in nature. Thompson reportedly characterized the analysis as breaking the rule of abstinence and encouraging gratification of needs. Thompson was most likely jealous of the attention Ferenczi paid to Severn, as she became aware of them and later reported on their trauma analysis, and Ferenczi described the gratifications he offered when they were both in analysis with him (Ferenczi, 1988). Thompson's acting out by spreading rumors about Ferenczi was a dramatic example of an enactment of an erotic transference. Neither Ferenczi nor Thompson fully understood the nature of this experience because the theory and treatment of trauma was in development. However, when discussing her bragging about her kissing disclosure to the analytic community, Ferenczi did not analyze Thompson's behavior. Basically, he expressed dissatisfaction with Thompson for misunderstanding his empathic response for her need to have a passion-free therapeutic relationship (Ferenczi, 1988). Thompson was elated at having her need for an affectionate experience with a non-abusive father fulfilled. She was unaware that her disclosure that she could kiss Ferenczi anytime she wanted would anger Freud and bring severe criticism to her analyst. Freud used Thompson's disclosure to diagnose Ferenczi as functioning at a regressive level in using trauma analysis to treat his difficult cases. Freud did not understand the nature of Ferenczi's Relaxation Therapy, which employed clinical empathy, non-interpretative measures, and countertransference analysis (see Chapters 12 through 18), and was being used to treat trauma rather than an Oedipal disorder. What Freud did not understand or accept was that Ferenczi had begun an alternate treatment for an alternate disorder. He was not being angry or rivalrous with Freud. Ferenczi was trying to accommodate a neglected group of individuals who suffered from trauma disorders. Thompson as well as Severn was one of such neglected individuals. Ferenczi's alternative method was not regressive, but, a form of an emancipated evolutionary, alternative method (Rachman, 2007a).

Ferenczi in developing the Confusion of Tongues theory and Relaxation Therapy was following his own research and clinical experience (Ferenczi, 1988). Freud reacted with frustration, anger, and condemnation, as if Ferenczi was in a state of rebellion toward him that was leading to a pathologic professional and personal regression. There were instances when the Ferenczi/Severn analysis was flawed and even questionable. But it must be emphasized that Ferenczi's basic motivation in developing an alternative to the Freudian psychology and method was to successfully understand and treat individuals who suffered from abuse due to childhood trauma. The present volume attempts to demonstrate that Ferenczi's alternate analysis with Severn was useful, helpful, and revolutionary. Although I have criticized Ferenczi's analysis of Thompson, several members of the William Alanson White Institute said they noticed significant positive changes in Thompson's personal functioning after returning from Budapest and her analysis with Ferenczi. In particular, people noticed Thompson was less schizoid and related to men in a more positive way (Mihacy, 1993).

Ferenczi's emancipation from Freud came with a bitter price. He separated in a way that seemed like a renunciation of Freud and traditional psychoanalysis. For his last years, Ferenczi maintained contact with his Hungarian colleagues, and devoted himself to his clinical work with trauma disorders. He rejected Freud's attempts to involve him in the governance of the International Psychoanalytical Association because he wanted to protect himself from criticism and condemnation of his new work. Ferenczi knew Freud and the analytic community would not approve of the trauma analysis with Severn, since he had received, the so-called *Kissing Letter* from Freud. Ferenczi was right to be protective of himself and his reputation, as he found out, when during his last days, Freud personally and professionally rejected him over his Confusion of Tongues presentation (Rachman, 1997b).

Ferenczi was not being regressive in his new theory and clinical methods; he was becoming independent of Freud's theory and technique. He was being a dissident not a regressive. Being a dissident has a negative connotation in psychoanalysis, as if Ferenczi was doing something undesirable or regressive (Jones, 1957). I prefer to think of Ferenczi's differences from Freud as *a form of emancipation*, a search for finding his own identity as a psychoanalyst. Ferenczi was no longer solely trying to please Freud, the master. He moved from an adolescent identity crisis with Freud (Erikson, 1950; Rachman, 1975) to becoming an adult and finding that he had differences with his mentor. Ferenczi, in pursuing his own thinking, was fulfilling his own identity needs. He was finding his own voice, but Freud did not help Ferenczi with his identity crisis. Freud wanted Ferenczi to continue to maintain his interest in his view of psychoanalysis. He even went so far, in consort with Jones, as trying to suppress Ferenczi from expressing his own ideas, both in presentation and in print (Rachman, 1997b, 1999). As Paul Roazen (1975), pointed out, Freud and Ferenczi were talking about psychoanalysis form the vantage point of treating different kinds of cases, Freud the so-called neurotics and Ferenczi, the non-Oedipal, difficult trauma cases (Roazen, 1975). Freud believed psychoanalysis should be sole province of treating neurotic disorders. Ferenczi wanted psychoanalysis to evolve towards treating difficult cases, e.g., severe neurotic, borderline, and psychotic disorders where a traumatic origin was evident.

The core issue in the Ferenczi/Severn analysis was not the issues of regressive theory and technique. I believe the *most distinguishing and controversial issue in the Ferenczi/Severn Analysis* was the issue of *therapeutic regression* in clinical psychoanalysis. Ferenczi's clinical interaction with Severn initiated the therapeutic use of regression in the analytic encounter. Prior to this first formal analysis of trauma, tradition had dictated that regression was a negative phenomenon to be avoided in an analytic experience. If an analysand showed signs of regression, that is to say, behaving, as if their thinking and feeling were in early phases of development, it was thought of as a danger sign. The danger being that the analysand was psychologically deteriorating due to the inability of the analyst to properly analyze the case or control the countertransference. Regression was not desirable or necessary. It was not therapeutic, but sounded an alarm that the therapy was off course. It was with this traditional attitude toward regression as a negative clinical experience that the Ferenczi/Severn analysis was originally evaluated.

The uniqueness of the Ferenczi/Severn analysis was that it was not a traditional analysis of a traditional analysand. It was analysis of a trauma disorder. Orthodox analysts wanted to maintain the so-called analytic purity of psychoanalysis as a cure for neurotic illness. Elizabeth Severn was not a traditional analysand. Freud was also disheartened that Rank left the Society of Rings (Gay, 1984) and espoused a new theory, the Birth Trauma Theory of Neurosis (Rank, 1994). Rank apparently continued to believe in his view of psychoanalysis and the kind of psychoanalysis that Ferenczi practiced (Rachman, 1997a).

The Severn/Ferenczi analysis asked psychoanalysis to consider the idea of *regression in the service of trauma analysis*, or, as Balint, later termed it, *therapeutic regression* (Balint, 1992/1968). Severn and Ferenczi believed that in order to work through the psychological damage of actual childhood trauma the analysis had to reach, to what Ferenczi termed *rock bottom*, the full emotional depth of the original trauma. Severn insisted the Ferenczi allow her to use the analytic session in a different way, not for Ferenczi to interpret what she was revealing as to demonstrate that she was suffering from an Oedipal conflict disorder. Severn knew better. The dark cloud that hung over her head and caused her debilitating depression was ignited by some real events of her childhood. But, she could never find out, what those events were in her three previous analyses. When Ferenczi began to realize that Severn's *Subjective/ Trance Method* was more relevant to her trauma analysis than was interpretation of Oedipal material, *they co-created a therapeutic experience where Severn could confront her own traumatized child in her adult personality*. By doing so, Severn became aware of the emotional damage the abusive experiences with her father had caused. It was then that Severn and Ferenczi realized that the depression and suicidal thoughts that threatened to engulf her were the result of the physical, emotional, and sexual abuses she was subjected to by her psychopathic father.

This early form of therapeutic regression that Severn created with Ferenczi's help developed a therapeutic process: in order to have meaningful change, one must be willing to face the deepest level of the analysand's subjective experience. Severn created chaos by turning the analytic session upside down. My dear friend Robert Kennedy, S.J., PhD, Jesuit Priest, Zen Buddhist Roshi and psychotherapist, believes that a change agent, a teacher, must be willing to have the student overturn the teacher. He is fond of using Thomas Mann's saying, which encourages overthrowing authority to create change:

> Any method of teaching as it humanizes, refines, undermines authority and makes slaves ripe for freedom and any teaching method is bad insofar as it blocks action.
>
> *(quoted in Kennedy, 1995)*

Ferenczi saw the emotional intelligence of allowing Severn to actively confront him and create chaos in the psychoanalytic session, by introducing a two-person psychology for psychoanalysis. Before Ferenczi saw Severn he was known as the *enfant terrible of psychoanalysis* (Dupont, 1988). Ferenczi was the member of Freud's inner circle who created chaos by treating difficult cases deconstructing the analytic method. In order to be successful in treating difficult cases, Ferenczi also introduced the role of activity, clinical empathy, and elasticizing the clinical methodology, which also disrupted the tradition of analytic functioning (Rachman, 1997a, 2003a; Rachman & Klett, 2015). When Severn joined forces with Ferenczi, two dissident forces blended together to cause great chaos and controversy, such as the development of therapeutic regression to retrieve and treat trauma. It was encouraging analysands to relive the original childhood trauma as if it were happening again, but with the ability to view the experience not as a traumatized child, but as a surviving adult. Retrieving, remembering, and reintegrating is very different from analyzing resistance, transference, dreams, and early recollections (Rachman & Kleet, 2015). Treating trauma through the employment of therapeutic regression creates a co-created emotional therapeutic experience where the analysis is geared to reaching the full depths of an emotional disorder.

Development of therapeutic regression

Two issues become clear in the second and third decades of psychoanalysis. First, both Freud and Ferenczi's client population were not necessarily neurotic or suffering from an Oedipus complex. Rather, many analysands were themselves severe neurotics, with character, narcissistic, or borderline disorders. Secondarily, these individuals, some of which had childhood trauma experiences, did not respond well to privation or did not feel gratified by the analyst's silence or the use of interpretation. The difficulties in the clinical interaction varied from the analysand's silence to intense demands for physical contact (see Chapters 8 and 12–17). As has been discussed, Freud was aware that Ferenczi had published a series of these cases, his so-called difficult cases (Ferenczi, 1980a–g) who had serious problems adhering to the rule of free association, but responded better to non-interpretative measures (Rachman, 1998). In demonstrating his proficiency in the treating of non-Oedipal disorder, Freud passed the mantle to Ferenczi (Rachman, 1997a).

As a result of focusing on the analysis of difficult cases, Severn being the most difficult of his difficult cases, Ferenczi began to view the psychoanalytic encounter as a stage where the original childhood disturbances were reenacted with the analyst. He questioned the traditional view that analysands act out their childhood experiences in a vacuum, that is, without the emotional participation of the analyst. In actuality, the traditional use of the rule of abstinence and interpretation encouraged regression, but was not recognized as iatrogenic or causing regression even when a silent, minimal intervention analyst responds with intellectually oriented interpretations. This encouraged a kind of emotional regression in an atmosphere of emotional distance or coldness, further pushing the analysand into the childhood trauma, but without the feeling that the analyst is there as a therapeutic presence.

In the analytic change that Ferenczi developed in the analysis with Severn, the therapeutic use of regression was an important part of the method. The analyst created an empathic atmosphere in the psychoanalytic encounter, so that the analysand could naturally return to confront and analyze their childhood traumas. Trauma was deconstructed to mean actual experiences in the interpersonal interactions between the child and parents (and parental figures). By focusing on the subjective experiences of both analyst and analysands, using empathic understanding as the therapeutic compass, a co-created psychoanalysis developed. The therapeutic dyad assesses whether there was over- or under-stimulation by parental figures, to respond with appropriate need gratifications, and help the traumatized individual to integrate and analyze the need for responsiveness.

Therapeutic regression returns to contemporary psychoanalysis

The campaign to suppress Ferenczi's work, which began the view of regression as a negative experience, was so successful that the idea of therapeutic regression virtually disappeared from psychoanalysis (Rachman, 1997a, b, 1999, 2003a). During the post-pioneering period of psychoanalysis, 1949–1960s, certain members of the British Psychoanalytic Society, namely, the Middle or Independent Group returned to the idea of therapeutic regression. Primarily, Michael Balint (1992/1968), Harold Stewart (1993), Christopher Bolas (1987), Masud Khan (1958), Margaret Little (1951), and D.W. Winnicott (1958). As the Independent Group returned to the issue of therapeutic regression, Balint and Stewart in particular showed renewed interest in Ferenczi and Severn's work with therapeutic regression. Unfortunately, the Independent Group generally did not recognize Ferenczi as a progenator. In fact, Winnicott deliberately disregarded Ferenczi, to Balint's dismay (Rachman, 1997a, 2003).

As Ferenczi's analysand, student, colleague, and friend, Michael Balint was in a unique position to experience first hand the issue of therapeutic regression as he observed and discussed with Ferenczi his analysis with Severn. Balint described the Ferenczi/Severn analysis as *the Grand Experiment* in the following way:

> I was privileged to witness, fairly closely, an experiment ... on a grand scale – perhaps the first of its kind analytic history. It was carried out by Ferenczi who, agreed with one of his patients, [Elizabeth Severn] to fulfill this role, [of satisfying traumatic-based needs] as far as it was in his power ... this got as much time from him as she asked for, several sessions per day and, if necessary were considered undesirable, she was seen during the weekends and was allowed to accompany her analyst on his holidays. ... The experiment went on for some years. The results were still inconclusive when Ferenczi, owing to his illness, had to give up analytical work only before he died.
>
> *(Balint, 1992/1968, pp. 112–113)*

Balint's development of therapeutic regression

Balint (1992/1968), developed a theory of therapeutic regression which was a valiant attempt to integrate Freud's Oedipal theory of neurosis with Ferenczi's Confusion of Tongues paradigm in order to integrate the new perspective into mainstream psychoanalysis (Rachman, 2003a). This analytic perspective was one of the few attempts to both integrate an understanding of neurotic and the more severe disorders, such as the borderline condition. What is more, Balint, like his mentor Ferenczi, incorporated the issue of trauma as an important dimension of analytic theorizing. Balint extended Ferenczi's concept of the Confusion of Tongues trauma to include emotional trauma in the individual's childhood experiences with parental and authority figures. Balint became the conduit for the Budapest School of Psychoanalysis in the Object Relations perspective (Bacal & Carlton, 2010).

In Balint's theory of therapeutic regression he attempted to integrate the traditional theory of Freud's Oedipal complex as the source of neurosis with the aforementioned developments in the study and treatment of the more severe psychological disorders. Balint's knowledge of the Severn analysis opened up his thinking to the necessity to consider that borderline, trauma, and psychotic disorders need the modification in theory and technique that Ferenczi pioneered. But Balint also re-evaluated Ferenczi's ideas, and attempted to bring them into the mainstream of analytic thought. Unfortunately, he was not successful in doing this in his lifetime (Balint, 1992/1968). Traditional analysis has never fully appreciated Ferenczi's or Balint's pioneering ideas about pre-Oedipal conditions (Rachman, 1997a, b, 2003a).

Balint delivered a theory of the psychology of human behavior which attempted to integrate Freud's Oedipal view of neurosis with Ferenczi's Confusion of Tongues paradigm, and the analysis of Severn in the aforementioned description of the Grand Experiment. Balint (1992/1968) described three levels of human functioning. The *area of the Oedipal Conflict*, is the fundamental level, characterized by the conflict that originates on an unconscious level in the mind of the individual. It operates on the basis of a one-person psychology. The second level of mind is the *basic fault*, which operates on a very different level. It involves two individuals, one of which has experienced a fault, or, serious trauma in their personality development. The traumatized individual functions at a primitive level. What is necessary for the analysis is the establishment of a relationship where one individual, an analyst, has to become involved in contributing to the therapeutic relationship. The third level of functioning is the *area of creation*. There is no outside object and no transference. The individual in this sphere needs to make something of him/herself. He/she creates something or is capable of creating a relationship, or develops the capacity to deal with illness.

Realizing that Ferenczi's attempt to satisfy as many of Severn's unfulfilled needs as possible was a serious flaw in his trauma analysis, Balint (1992/1968) developed *an important distinction between therapeutic and malignant regression*. In 1968, he reappraised Ferenczi's work and helped integrate it into mainstream psychoanalysis:

> more than thirty years ago [1933], … the general view … was that Ferenczi's experiments had shown that responding to a regressed patient's cravings was a mistake; it caused endless and useless troubles both for the patient and the analyst, and was anyway condemned by Freud … What I asked for was a critical reappraisal – not an uncritical acceptance – of what was valuable in the ideas development in Budapest under Ferenczi's leadership. There was no response. Having failed, the only policy remaining to me was to continue with my clinical work and test ideas by further experience. In recent years, I think there have perhaps been some signs of a change in the general attitude, though I may be mistaken. So I am trying again.
>
> *(Balint, 1992/1968, p. 133)*

On the basis of continued clinical work with individuals needing gratification rather than interpretation, Balint concluded that there are moments in the analytic relationship that gratification can be satisfied: "but, *the satisfaction did not replace interpretation, it was in addition to it*" (Balint, (1992/1968, p. 134). Therapeutic regression was creating *a new beginning* in that it freed individuals from oppressive forms of relating to objects of love and hate. *This change moved regression from an intrapsychic to an intrapersonal experience. It also changed the role of the analyst:*

> He must be there; he must be pliable to a very high degree; he must not offer much resistance; he certainly must be indestructible, and he must allow his patient to live with him in a sort of harmonious interpenetrating mix-up.
>
> *(Balint, 1992/1968, p. 136)*

Balint was suggesting that relationship is as essential to human existence as the air we breathe. It is a substance which is always there, from which an individual can use, depend upon, from which one can live one's life. As such it is essential to an analysis. Kohut believed that the *empathy* in the relationship was as essential to human existence as the air we breathe (Kohut, 1984). Both Balint's and Kohut's views were first developed by Ferenczi (1980h) and Severn (1933).

Balint recognized that the issue of therapeutic regression needed to be differentiated into the *benign and malignant forms of regression*. Benign regression is characterized by easily forming a therapeutic relationship, which is similar to a mutually trusting experience with a primary object. A regression occurs, leading to a new beginning, ending in a new discovery. The regression is for the purpose of understanding of the analysand's internal problems, moderating the intensity of demands or needs, and modulating severe hysterical symptoms or regressed transferences. Malignant regression is characterized by: desperate clinging development; unsuccessful attempts at reaching a new beginning, an unending spiral of demands or needs, addiction; regression is aimed at gratification by external action; a high intensity of demands, expectations or needs; severe hysteria. It is the analyst's job to modulate the therapeutic regression so that it is maintained at the level of a benign regression. Balint saw first hand in the analysis between Ferenczi and Severn, the difficulty in managing a malignant regression. Balint's tripartite theory of mind was a valiant attempt to integrate and expand Ferenczi's Confusion of Tongues paradigm, so that Ferenczi's clinical work with Severn's work on trauma could be integrated into mainstream psychoanalysis.

Winnicott (1958a) regarded therapeutic regression as one of the most important unfinished issues in psychoanalysis. He felt regression meant dependency on the mother and her management of the relationship. There was mutuality in the interaction between analyst and analysand. What is more, the standard response of interpretation was suspended during the therapeutic regression stage, to be reinstated afterwards. Although Winnicott did not recognize Ferenczi or Balint's influence, his own clinical behavior, which was described by another member of the British Middle Group, Margaret Little (1951), was similar to Ferenczi's clinical behavior in the therapeutic regression with Severn. Little described Winnicott's clinical behavior with her, who diagnosed herself as a borderline disorder, as being dissident because he would increase the length of sessions on a regular basis. What is more, he would hold Little's hand or head for long periods of time. There is no evidence that Ferenczi used this kind of physical touch as a regular method (Rachman, 1993,

1997a). I find it strange that Winnicott would use physical touch with an analysand in a therapeutic regressed state, a method as controversial as Ferenczi's mutual analysis, yet, distanced himself from Ferenczi and Balint as progenitors.

The contemporary use of therapeutic regression in treating trauma disorders has been experimented with (Rachman, Kennedy and Yard, 2005, 2009; Rachman & Kleet, 2015). The results have been meaningful in trauma disorders which originate in childhood abusive experiences, especially when the trauma has been somatized and early childhood verbal activity is limited.

Stewart, a student of Balint, believed that the traditional structure of the analytic session lends itself to a version of a dream-like or regression state:

> The use of the couch, a quite warm room lit not too brightly; frequency of sessions, an attentive therapist (a basically silent or infrequently responsive analyst, whose emotional distance is intended to encourage the analysand to respond to his/her own subjective experience) are all, in fact, aids in promoting regression in the patient.
>
> *(Stewart, 1993, p. 250)*

23

SEVERN'S ORPHA FUNCTION

Resilience and recovery from trauma

Freud's, Ferenczi's, and Jung's interest in mysticism, spirituality, and the occult

Severn's interest in the occult was shared by the founders of psychoanalysis. Freud had some interest in the occult, but he did not want psychoanalysis to be linked with mysticism. Ferenczi had his own interest in this area, which he both explored himself and was able to emphatically respond to in Severn's belief system. In 1909, early in psychoanalytic history, Freud, Ferenczi, and Jung, after they returned from the Clark University lectures in America, visited a female medium in Berlin whom Ferenczi knew. Freud was intrigued by her performance, stimulating his interest in thought transference. Realizing that he could not be associated with the occult as the leader of psychoanalysis, Freud encouraged Ferenczi and Jung to explore the area (Rachman, 1997a). Jung in 1911, wrote to Freud of his interest in the occult:

> Occultism is another field we shall have to conquer with the aid of the libido theory … I am looking into astrology, which seems indispensable for a proper understanding of mythology. There are strange and wondrous things in these lands of darkness. Please don't worry about my wanderings in these infini- tudes. I shall return with rich booty, for knowledge of the human psyche. For a while longer I must intoxicate myself on magic perfumes in order to fathom the secrets that lie hidden in the abysses of the unconscious.
>
> *(McGuire, 1974, p. 421)*

Clearly, Jung, in this letter, expressed his own personal, broad interest in all forms of knowledge. Freud, at this period, limited his interest in the occult, as shown when he wrote to Ferenczi on May 11, 1911.

Jung writes to me that we must conquer the field of occultism and asks for my agreeing to his leading a crusade … I can see that you two are not to be held back. At least go forward in collaboration with each other; it is a dangerous expedition and I cannot accompany you.

(McGuire, 1974, p. 421)

Freud and Ferenczi's interest in the occult were still evident in the mid-1920s. Ferenczi noted in 1925 in a *Rundbrief* [circulating letters between the Society of the Ring members (see Grosskurth, 1991) that Freud and Anna were involved in thought transference experiments (Gay, 1988):[1]

It should interest you to know that we made a series of rather unsuccessful thought transference experiments in Vienna with Professor and Fraulein Anna.[2]

Freud, Ferenczi, Jung, and Anna Freud's interest and participation in the occult indicate that there was once room to experiment with mysticism, the paranormal and the occult to see if they could contribute to psychoanalysis. It also provides an intellectual and clinical zeitgeist for Severn and Ferenczi's discussion of the Orpha function.

Severn's belief in the mystical

Mysticism was, in Severn's time, defined as becoming one with God or the absolute as well as to any kind of ecstasy or altered state of consciousness. In contemporary thinking it is more popularly used as a label for anything esoteric, occult, or supernatural (Moore, 2005). Severn believed in forms of Western esotericism and modern spirituality, such as Gnosticism, Transcendentalism, Thesophy and the Fourth Way (Magee, 2016). Modern Western spirituality and transpersonal psychology combine Western psychotherapeutic practices with religious practices like meditation to attain transformation. Severn was part of the development of secularizing mysticism. This is the separation of mystical ideas and practices from their traditional use in religious ways of life to only secular ends of purported psychological and physiological benefits. This is best seen in Severn's application of esoteric thinking to clinical practice of therapy (see Chapter 11).

Severn revealed a variety of responses during the analysis with Ferenczi that could be seen as being mystical, or spiritual. She was a spiritually minded person before she entered analysis with Ferenczi. Severn studied the Christian Science movement, which she used as a personal ideology as well as an inspiration for her clinical practice. The attraction to spirituality is also a characteristic of incest survivors. As a survivor of parental abuse, she lost faith in traditional belief systems, e.g., family and church. Severn lost faith in family and church when she struggled to understand and heal her childhood abuse. She may have turned toward spirituality as she became angry and disenchanted with traditional authority. The abuse may have added another dimension to Severn's turn toward a non-traditional belief system (Rachman, 2016d; see Image 18).

In my clinical practice with incest survivors, there have been individuals, who, like Severn, became emotionally connected to spirituality because they lost their faith in traditional authority. One individual told of her belief in auras. She firmly believed she could read people's auras, that she had visions and believed in past

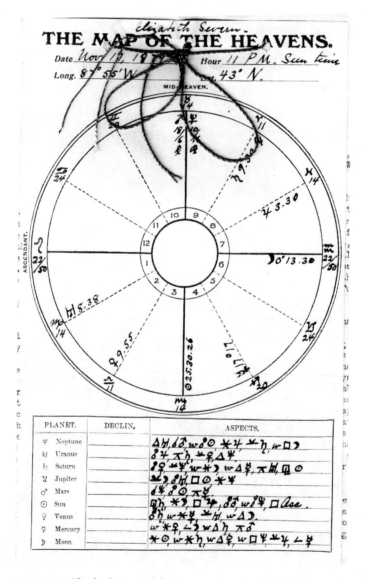

IMAGE 18   Elizabeth Severn's horoscope done by J. Wallington

lives. One day, this person, who knew about my interest in Ferenczi, told me the following:

> Last night an image of Ferenczi came to me. He had such a kind face. He was very happy with your work with me. I've studied your aura. You have the aura of a healer. You are a natural born healer, like Ferenczi.
>
> *(Anonymous, 1991)*

Elizabeth Severn's horoscope

One of the most interesting items that I found in the Elizabeth Severn Papers is a copy of her horoscope (Rachman, 2016d; see Image 19). The document is typed on three pages of onion-skin paper, with an illustrated diagram of the planets as they apply to Severn's horoscope reading. The notations on the chart of the planets are in astrological code. There is no indication of when Severn's horoscope was completed. The horoscope was based upon a reading by J. Wallington, based on her birthdate, November 17, 1879, 11 p.m. A summary of the typed manuscript indicated the following evaluation:

> magnificent endowments, the highest qualities of intellect and character … Happily the hardest time, the greatest difficulties and obstacles, appear to be the first half of life. Later things straighten themselves out, and the close of life, probably at a good old age is successful and happy. … strong clashes that may develop at times between intellect and emotions, … Individuality and personality pull together for the same ends, … the conflicts, … come from events and disturbances on the other plane, rather from different phrases of the nature working against each other. This is great strength here, pride, loyalty, high honor, keen sensitiveness, intense determination, combined with great energy that will push through to successes regardless of obstacles.
>
> … great resistances is indicated to any suggestions of change that come from outside, … is capable of originating and pushing through changes of the greatest, perhaps or revolutionary character. There is great organizing and executive ability, broad human sympathy, subtlety, tact, and great power in handling and directing others.
>
> The most striking feature of the endowment is the comprehensive, profound, and powerful mind, with its deep insight, keen powers of analyses, breadth and height of vision, broad humanitarian, and deep philosophical and scientific nature. Here is a born searcher after hidden things, drawn … to the study of the mystical and occult, with great psychic possibilities, yet never losing the grip on science and law. Her opinions are her own … and are a strongly held, … the mind is very practical, … great common-sense … a far-reaching grasp of the things of the spirit …
>
> There is very great personal magnetism, and rare charm, a fine power of companionship, and of adaptability to the minds of others in all spheres…

Passions run strong ... a life filled with storms and conflicts, with great fluctuations of happiness and fortune ...

There are better clashes with the parents, particularly with the father, trouble and suffering coming from parents, ... probable separation from them, and danger of a separation from of loss of a child.

There will be sudden and startling changes of circumstances and environment, ... the latter part of life will see a competence amassed, and be generally filled with prosperity and happiness.

As to the profession, the horoscope shows only one possibility if the inner nature is followed out, and that is the combination of teacher and healer. Ordinary teaching would never serve. The humanitarianism, the interest in and intense desire to help the sick and suffering, are strong ... leaning to and understanding of metaphysics and the deeper and higher powers of the mind, ... the healing and straightening out of human tangles has to be worked out in that may instead of by medical or material means ... there is an intense desire for service, services to humanity ...

Decided popularity and many warm friendships and associates ... great deal of travel show, long journeys, and much changing of residences ...

One of the great handicaps in the life, is ill-health. There is naturally a strong constitution, and great vitality, but much sickness is shown.

(Wallington [date unknown], E. Severn's Horoscope.
In Rachman, 2016d)

A horoscope is an astrological chart or diagram representing the positions of the sun, moon, planets, astrological aspects and sensitive angles at the time of an event, such as the moment of a person's birth. There have been no scientific studies to demonstrate the accuracy of a horoscope. The methods used to analyze the horoscope are pseudo-scientific (Carlson, 1985). There is no scientific framework which verifies a meaningful influence between an individual and the position of stars in the sky at the moment of a person's birth.

With these reservations in mind, we can comment on the astrologist's evaluation of Severn's personality and functioning. The evaluation points to Severn's intelligence, strong personality, intuitiveness, pride, determination, and sensitivity, which were characteristic of her. The horoscope made two very significant evaluations: the first was about Severn's background and the other was her choice of a vacation. The astrologist said Severn had great difficulties in the first half of her life, where there were clashes with her father. There was also notation of a separation or loss of a child. Regarding a choice of a profession, Severn's horoscope said that there was only one path that she would follow, that of being a healer and a teacher. Severn, according to this evaluation, had a strong desire to heal the sick and suffering, to be of service to humanity. There were other evaluations that seemed to be on the point about Severn. The horoscope said that she would be handicapped throughout life with ill-health. There will be conflicts and storms with which she would have to deal. Passions run strong, with great fluctuations of happiness and fortune. The

astrologist also predicted there would be a great deal of changes in living arrangements, including changing residences. Finally, the horoscope said she was a searcher
of hidden things, mysticism, the occult, yet someone who stays close to science.

Severn's Orpha function

One of the most unique and dramatic events in the Ferenczi/Severn analysis was the
discovery of Severn's capacity to cope with severe trauma. During the last year of the
analysis in 1932, Ferenczi described a life-sustaining capacity Severn revealed during
their mutual analytic experience. Ferenczi described this capacity as Orpha, which
was likely a co-created term with Severn, derived from the Greek myth of Orpheus,
who was a legendary poet and musician who could experience power over people,
animals, and nature. Furthermore, he was one of the handful of Greek heroes who
visited the Underworld and returned. His capacity for music and song had power
over Hades (Miles, 1999). My interpretation of using the Orpheus mythology for
Severn's *Orpha function* is the symbolism of the power Severn had in creating a new
origin, and that she had been to hell and back emotionally and survived.

Ferenczi first described Orpha in the following way:

> The enormity of suffering plus helplessness and despair of any outside help,
> propped her towards death; but as conscious thought is lost, or abandoned,
> *the organizing life instincts (Orpha)* awaken, and in place of death allow insanity
> to intervene.
>
> *(Ferenczi, 1988, p.8, italics added)*

Ferenczi goes on to elaborate that Orpha's sole purpose is to preserve life, at all cost.
He believed that Severn possessed this capacity from the time of her first trauma
at the age of one and a half years old. The Orpha fragment was Severn's guard-
ian angel, providing her with a positive functioning part of her personality which
could cope with trauma by anesthetizing the self from unbearable sensations. It
also produces fantasies, hallucinations that allowed Severn to restore her emotional
equilibrium. At moments of severe trauma, when Severn felt she was on the verge
of suicide or insanity from which she could not return, the Orpha function of
her personality split itself off from the traumatized self with a fragment as a life-
enhancing mechanism.

What is remarkable about this emotional functioning is that Ferenczi described
the Orpha function as a kind of bodily organ that Severn created to cope with
and conquer trauma and maintain emotional equilibrium. In what seems like a
neo-Lamarckian mechanism, Ferenczi described the acquired characteristic
development of the Orpha organ in Severn:

1. The process begins when Severn is faced with unbearable sensations or pain
    (physical, emotional, sexual) and her personal resources have been exhausted; a
    period of physical reaction sets in.

2. A series of psychosomatic mechanisms occur. Breathing is difficult. There is a shortage of oxygen to the heart. Both the bladder and the bowels are emptied. Vomiting may occur. As the body is being overwhelmed by the traumatic experience, Severn's "physical powers" takes over. Ferenczi described this part of the psychosomatic process: "… the hallucination of breathing can maintain life, even when there is the total somatic suffocation."

(Ferenczi, 1988, p. 117)

Ferenczi suggested that the psychosomatic process is an attempt to delay Severn's personality disintegration and a prelude to the development of an "ad hoc organ" (Ferenczi, 1988, p. 117).

3. While Severn was in utter distress, gasping for her emotional existence, an organ forms in the shape of a bladder at the back of her head. This organ absorbed the pain and negative affect which could not be tolerated. The area where this organ is formed coincides with the site where Severn's father had injected her with either narcotics or poison. Injections of poisons were administered by Severn's father at the nape of her neck, which led to an inflammation of the mastoid area (mastoid bone sits behind the ear, which consists of air spaces that help drain the middle ear). During the analysis with Ferenczi, Severn reported a recurrence of this inflammation. When she visited an ear specialist no medical explanations was given for the inflammation. Although the phantom bladder is described as expandable, continued trauma can burst the organ. In the case of this crisis, it is the analyst's function to psychologically help repair the Orpha function.

Orpha as a hallucination

Ferenczi used the concept of hallucination (Ferenczi, 1988, p. 117) in discussing Severn's development of the Orpha function. In another clinical entry Severn was listed as schizophrenic. This suggests that he had some thoughts about Severn as being psychotic, or he believed Severn's Orpha organ to be a sign of severe psychopathology. There is some connection to severe emotional disorders. The concept of "tactile hallucination" is defined as a "false perception of tactile sensory input that creates a hallucinatory sensation of physical contact with an imaginary object (Berrios, 1982, p. 285). When schizophrenia is the diagnosed disorder, there is a 20% incidence of some sort of tactile hallucinations (Lewandowski, 2009). Feinchel (1999) believed that tactile hallucinations were symptoms of schizophrenia. In schizophrenic individuals who have tactile hallucinations, the most common sensation is one in which their skin is stretched elastically across their head (Pfeifer, 1970). If one views Severn's functioning as one as a schizophrenic individual, then the Orpha power can be seen as pathology. The diagnostic impression discussed in Chapter 10 suggested Severn had a borderline disorder caused by severe childhood abuse.

Ferenczi's experience of Severn's Orpha function

The disturbing experience of Severn's development of the Orpha function occurred in the analysis with Ferenczi when he focused on exploring her childhood trauma:

> Accordingly the analyst's aim has been to discover and eliminate all tendencies toward flight and evasion in the patient, in order to force them through the one remaining passage: that of the trauma.
>
> *(Ferenczi, 1988, p. 106)*

As Severn was directed by Ferenczi to explore her childhood traumas, she became emotionally distraught and as she entered the zone of re-traumatization. As Ferenczi outlined in his Confusion of Tongues paper (Ferenczi, 1980h), exploring childhood trauma can, and often does, re-traumatize the analysand, as the repressed feelings become liberated. Severn's re-traumatization was an *emotional holocaust* as she became emotionally connected to the horrific abuse of her father. At these moments of emotional panic, Severn would turn to Ferenczi for help, pleading with him to alleviate her suffering, saying: "take it away, take it away" (Ferenczi, 1988, p. 106). At first, Ferenczi was confused; he did not know what to do. In order to become educated as to what he could do, he turned to Severn. She told him to affirm her Orpha function, to empathically attune to her capacity to use her emotional strength and resiliency. In the most basic therapeutic terms, she asked him to affirm and accept her capacity to maintain emotional equilibrium and conquer her traumatic experiences. In a remarkably touching description, Ferenczi revealed the empathic response Severn needed:

> The painful part of the psyche in representation in this instance materially, as a substance, and I am required to surround this matter with a strong, impenetrable covering, or to present the reset of the psyche which is located in the head, from collapsing by erecting suitably placed, solid, supporting beams. Furthermore it is asked of me that even when I go away I leave a part of myself with, or in, the patient as a guardian.
>
> *(Ferenczi, 1988, p. 107)*

Ferenczi disclosed that being empathic during these moments of intense reliving of the trauma did not come easy. He felt embarrassed to affirm Severn's Orpha function, since he questioned the reality of her ad hoc organ. These kinds of crisis moments became a test for Ferenczi's capacity to move from his Freudian training as an interpreter of analytic data to provide empathic understanding. Those who have been critical of Ferenczi for indulging Severn's needs, rather than interpreting them, may have never faced the emotional depths of a severely disturbed analysand who is on the verge of disintegration. There were instances in the analysis when Ferenczi mistakenly supported Severn's emotional dependence (see Chapter 13), but his empathic response to affirming her Orpha function was not an indulgence, but clinical genius. Ferenczi struggled with Severn's need for full empathic attunement. She would request that he give her the support she needed, repeating her words, over and over again. Practicing his elasticity principle, he complied without feeling dominated or controlled, patiently listening to her nightmares, emotional outbursts, and pleas for help. Ferenczi's empathy was essential for Severn. Ferenci had a special capacity to provide the empathy that Severn needed so badly. Ferenczi's understanding of this need, and his capacity to struggle to provide it, set the stage for a new way of being for an analyst, an empathy/reparative philosophy as an alternate to the interpretative/insight philosophy.

Orpha as a restorative or resilient fantasy

As Mészáros (2014) points out that Ferenczi described the process of resilience in his now-celebrated, long-neglected paper, the Confusion of Tongues (Ferenczi, 1980k) where he discussed the growth which can occur after trauma:

> a surprising rise of new facilities after a trauma, like a miracle that occurs with the wave of a magic wand, or like that of the fakir [bird] who are said to rise from a tiny seed, before our very eyes, a plant, leaves and flowers. Great need, and more especially mortal anxiety, seem to possess the power to wake suddenly and to put into operation latent dispositions which, un-cathected, waited in deepest gratitude for their development …
>
> One is justified as opposed to the familiar regression to speak of a *traumatic progression*, of a *precious maturity* … not only emotionally but also *intellectually*, can the trauma bring to maturity a part of the person.
>
> *(Ferenczi, 1980k, pp. 164–165)*

This is a trauma that naturally occurs in nature between an animal and a plant. The fakir bird pecks at the seed, forcing the seed to open. Surprisingly, the bird's forced opening of the seed temporally traumatizes the seed by opening it prematurely. Ferenczi used this analogy to illustrate that an organ can recover from premature stimulation. The seed that is attacked by the bird opens up to produce a living, flowering plant. Did Ferenczi develop this analogy and the idea of recovering from trauma through the clinical experience with Severn over her Orpha function? Severn demonstrated to Ferenczi how she was able to cope with her traumas by developing a mechanism to not only cope with severe trauma but conquer trauma. This is the capacity of resilience to positively respond and recover from trauma.

The modern concept and study of resilience began in the 1970s, with a study by Emmy Werner (1971). In an area of disadvantaged children in Kauai, Hawaii, where children grew up with many parents who were alcoholic or mentally ill, there was a group of these children who were called *resilient* who did not exhibit destructive behavior, later in life. The study introduced a new focus, where the study of human behavior turned from a study of the psychopathology of behavior to the study of the adaptive, positive, resilient functioning of human behavior. The Severn/ Ferenczi analysis opened up the consideration of viewing trauma in a new analytic perspective. An individual who has severe emotional problems with actual trauma as its origin can, with the empathy and affirmation of his/her analyst, use their capacity to rebound from depilating trauma. Although Ferenczi has been credited with introducing the idea of resilience in psychoanalysis (Mészáros, 2014), Severn has not received credit for her contribution.

Viewing it as having a positive value, Severn's Orpha function can be seen as a restorative or resilience fantasy. It was a narrative story about what she needed to maintain emotional stability in the growing awareness of how her father's horrific abuse of her damaged her personality development and hampered her functioning. She was a fiercely independent person who needed or wanted to be able to use her own power to recover from her defects. She used her fantasy to restore her emotional health. According to Lichtenberg (2017), we must seek out what we need to fill in what is missing. Between Severn's own capacity to rally her own emotional and intellectual forces and Ferenczi's capacity to empathize with and affirm them, she was able to maintain her resilience. As has been discussed, Severn not only showed resilience during her analysis, but after leaving Ferenczi she continued to demonstrate her resilience in enjoying a happy and productive life in the 26 years after her termination of the analysis with Ferenczi, (see Chapter 20).

Margaret Severn's conversations with Orpha

In a letter to her mother, Margaret mentioned that she used the idea of Orpha to feel better, as she was concerned about her own health and her mother Elizabeth's:

> *Darling – Wed, mom in Bed*
>
> I have been very worried about you – your writing that someday you felt you just wouldn't be able to pull yourself together around my old fear of losing you … I had a bad night. Fever, I guess, for I was burning hot and couldn't sleep … the cough which became uncontrollable. So I appealed to Orpha but she seemed weak and far away and this frightened me as I felt you must surely be ill, in fact, all during the night I had this fear. So I told Orpha that only *part* of you was sick and part of me, that my well part was full of strength to help you and vice–versa. So she came but remained very high up and said she couldn't come down and I should come up. So I did, … with some difficulty.
>
> *(Letter from Margaret to Elizabeth Severn, June 16, 1937, Czechoslovakia. In. Rachman, 2016d)*

It is clear from this communication with her mother that Margaret had integrated the concept of the Orpha function as part of her own functioning. Her mother was living in England and had communicated with her daughter that she was ill and in bed with illness. Elizabeth Severn's illness, which came four years after her termination from the analysis with Ferenczi, evoked a basic fear for Margaret. Since her childhood abduction by her father, which separated her from her mother for two years, Margaret developed a fear of losing her mother. When her mother was confined to bed because of illness (it was unclear if it was for physical or emotional illness), it aroused Margaret's lingering fear. As has been discussed, they were emotionally inseparable (see Chapter 9). Margaret learned to deal with physical emotional issues for her mother. You gather your strength, you emphasize your positive qualities, you empower yourself to cope with the difficulty. Apparently, in this instance, Margaret was partially successful because she was trying to help her mother and herself, at the same time when she was physically ill with a serious cough and emotionally distressed by the fear her mother might emotionally collapse or die from a physical illness. Evoking the Orpha function gave Margaret hope that both their illnesses could be conquered.

Orpha as a life-saving fantasy

There are catastrophic emotional events in an individual's life which can be developed to reduce overwhelming anxiety and provide an alternative to psychosis (Rachman, 1967). My formulation of this concept grew out of a clinical experience with an adult female analysand who described her seriously disturbed childhood with a psychotic mother. Her mother never left their apartment in Brooklyn, wearing tattered clothes during her interpersonal isolation, as she spent her days by herself. When they interacted she was overly critical, distant, and unloving. She was depressed and overweight. The analysand would cry in response to her mother's aggression.

The analysand's mother had a completely different, but very disturbing relationship with her son. As soon as the husband and daughter would leave for work in the morning the mother would enter into sexually seductive, symbiotic-like interaction with the son. This was characterized by entering the son's room and initiating a particular disturbing interaction, which the mother called "The Canarsie Roll." When the father left for work, the mother would wake up her son by joining him in his bed, and repeatedly roll over him with her body. This son was completely under the emotional domination of the mother, succumbing to her seductions.

In spite of the mother's damaging behavior with the son, the female analysand seemed to be surprisingly emotionally intact, given her mother's disturbed interactions. The daughter was a well-functioning adult, in a relationship with plans for marriage. She developed a successful working career. When I asked her to reflect on her positive functioning as an adult given her disturbing childhood, she said: "I always believed that I was not from this family." This woman sincerely believed in a variation on the *Changeling Fantasy* (Briggs, 1976). In our discussion of her fantasy family, she also realized it was a wish to have had a normal family, not the disturbed one from which she originated. What was so fascinating about this description of an analysand's valiant attempt to survive a trauma-ridden childhood moved me to consider her fantasy as *a life-saving attempt* to cleanse herself of the emotional poison of her traumatogenic mother. This analysand created a restorative fantasy to cope with the trauma, depression, and rejection of a disturbed mother by creating a loving, affirming family. Severn's creation of the Orpha function was more complicated because she created an ad hoc organ to deal with her traumas. But both analysands developed a unique way to cope with trauma, so as to maintain emotional equilibrium and enhance their resilience.

Notes

1   Fer, Rank, Eittington, Jones.
2   "Ferenczi was with us for a Sunday. We talked about many things and the three of us did experiments on thought transference, which came out remarkably well, especially the experiment in which I myself played the medium and then analytically extended the thoughts that came to my mind. The thing is getting more and more under our skin" (Ferenczi's *Rundbrief*. March 15, 1925. In Falzeder, Braband, & Giamperi–Deutsch, 2000, p. 206).

24

FERENCZI'S CASE OF R.N., ELIZABETH SEVERN

A landmark in psychoanalytic history

In the history of psychoanalysis there have been a series of clinical cases which are cited in the literature as being landmark events because they illustrated theoretical or clinical breakthroughs. They are assigned to analytic candidates to study. A group of these iconic cases will be reviewed to show their value in contributing to the evolution of psychoanalysis. I have critically examined these cases and tried to point out that they do not always illustrate their iconic value. The present volume has attempted to show that the case of Elizabeth Severn qualifies to be considered as a landmark case in psychoanalysis. Yet this case has not enjoyed this status because both Ferenczi and Severn were silenced in the analytic community through the traditional analytic practice of *Todschweigen* (see Chapter 7). I will review the contributions that Severn made to Ferenczi's theoretical and clinical innovations in the period of 1928–1933, when Severn was being analyzed by Ferenczi (Rachman, 1997a), which suggest that Severn was a contributor to the innovations developed during this period. It can be argued that these innovations contributed to psychoanalysis by widening the scope of its functioning to include the post-Freudian perspectives in contemporary psychoanalysis (Rachman, 2007a, 2014c).

Psychoanalysis' iconic cases: the case of Anna O./Bertha Pappenheim

Josef Breuer's case of Bertha Pappenheim (Breuer & Freud, 1895) has been considered the most fundamental origin of psychoanalysis, the so-called *beginning of talk therapy*. This landmark innovation involved therapeutic contact to deal with hysteria (neurosis) by verbal interaction with a therapist that allows for emotional release and intellectual understanding (Breuer, 1955). Unfortunately, Breuer's efforts with Pappenheim have been criticized by the traditional analytic community, because he gave up on the treatment and was not aware of the psychodynamics evolved in the treatment.

Freud became acquainted with Breuer's treatment of Pappenheim in 1882, as they worked together and became friends (Berger, 2009). Freud was fascinated with the case, as was his fiancée at that time, Marha Bernays. From Freud's early conversations with Breuer, and then with Martha, the issue of sexuality in Pappenheim's treatment was raised. Martha was a friend of Bertha Pappenheim. The treatment by Breuer raised several issues. The therapy by Breuer was not sufficient for cure. Pappenheim was repeatedly admitted to the Bellevue Sanatorium at Kreuzlingen, where Robert Binswanger was the physician in charge. The Kreulinger doctors favored their own methods, e.g., exercise, baths, and isolation from the family. Breuer described the treatment as arduous. These feelings by Breuer, as well as an experience that has been characterized as a sexual interaction between Breuer and Pappenheim, led to an end of their therapeutic relationship. Martha knew something unspeakable must have happened to end so abruptly Breuer's treatment of Bertha. She suspected that something erotic had happened and this gave rise to hurt feelings on Fran Breuer's part.

Breuer, in writing up the case of Pappenheim, did not comment on Pappenheim's sexuality or any so-called erotic experience in the therapy. Freud referred to the issue as the presence of a strong positive transference of a sexual nature, which was unanalyzed. Breuer was very uncomfortable with the mixing of the personal and professional, encouraging him to withdraw from the treatment. Breuer described this experience:

> I was engaged in relieving … the suffering of one of my most acquiescent patients … by tracing back her attacks of pain to their origins. As she woke up on one occasion, she threw her arms round my neck. The unexpected entrance of a servant relieved us from a painful discussion, but from that time onwards there was a tacit understanding between us that the hypnotic treatment should be discontinued. I was modest enough not to attribute the event to my own irresistible personal attraction, and I felt that I had now grasped the nature of the mysterious element that was at work behind hypnotism. In order to exclude it, or at all events to isolate it, it was necessary to abandon hypnotism.
>
> *(Berger, 2009, pp. 84–85)*

Breuer's difficulties in the Pappenheim treatment should not exclude the emotional courage, empathy and intelligence he exemplified in pioneering what is considered the origins of the *talking cure*, the forerunner of psychoanalysis. Breuer and Pappenheim co-created the talking cure. Pappenheim wanted to verbally explore her underlying emotionality. He agreed to change their method from hypnosis to talking about feelings in each other's presence—Pappenheim's *chimney sweeping*, as she called her verbal interaction. Breuer not only made room for his patient's idea of how to create therapeutic interaction, but affirmed it. Although it was Breuer's case, Freud realized the meaning and importance of Pappenheim's contribution. His recognition of her as forerunner of psychoanalysis is an outstanding recognition of how a patient can be a contributor, a partner, if you will, in their own therapy.

Breuer's and Pappenheim's collaboration make this case one of the landmark cases in the history of psychoanalysis. This case moved the treatment of emotional disorder into the twentieth century. The Pappenheim/Breuer method moved away from nineteenth-century ideas of treatment of the use of restraints, drastic use of hydrotherapy, etc. Talk therapy set the stage for Freud's development of psychoanalysis and the modern understanding and treatment of emotional disorders.

Case of the Wolf Man/Sergei Pankejeff

Freud had, at least, five iconic case studies: Little Hans/Herbert Graf; The Rat Man/Ernst Lanzer; Dora/Ida Bauer; Daniel Paul Schreiber; and The Wolf Man/ Sergei Panjekeff. He used these clinical experiences to advance his Oedipal theory and the preferred clinical intervention of interpretation toward the goal of curing neurosis (hysteria). The case of Sergei Pankejeff (Wolf Man) was Freud's intellectual tour de force to demonstrate his cherished Oedipal theory and interpretive technique. In addition, this case would play a major role in Freud's theory of psychosexual development. The dream of wolves upon which Freud built his famous primal scene interpretation was one of the most important dreams in the development of Freud's theories. This case was the first detailed case study used by Freud to prove the validity of psychoanalysis, bringing together the main aspects of catharsis, the unconscious, sexuality, and dream analysis.

As important as this case was seen by Freud and the traditional analytic community there has been criticisms offered. Perhaps, the most significant evaluation of Freud's analysis was made by the analysand Sergei Pankejeff. In Chapter 8, I discussed the remarkable data that has been collected by a journalist who interviewed Pankejeff in his later years (Obholzer, 1982). Pankejeff said that he did not accept Freud's view of his emotional difficulties, and felt the interpretation of his dream of wolves was inaccurate. What is more, he felt the treatment by Freud, and subsequently, by Ruth Mack Brunswich, was a failure. I have also suggested that the issue of childhood sexual seduction was a significant factor in Pankejeff's analysis, which was totally neglected.

The renunciation by Freud's analysand, Pankejeff, of his treatment and the possibility that the analysis does not reflect Freud's theoretical conclusions have not discouraged the traditional analytic community from maintaining this case as a landmark in the history of psychoanalysis.

Case of Sabrina Spielrein

While Jung was an assistant to Eugene Bleuler at the famous mental hospital Burghölzi in Zurich, Switzerland, he was assigned to treat an 18-year-old patient, Sabrina Spielrein. She had been admitted for an emotional breakdown in 1904. She told Jung that her father had often beaten her and was preoccupied by masochistic beating fantasies. Jung used his word association tests with her and some rudimentary psychoanalytic techniques (Minder, 2001). Jung reported that she made a rapid recovery.

Spielrein decided to become a physician and excelled academically. Subsequently, she became a psychiatrist. Her doctoral dissertation on schizophrenia became the first to appear in a psychoanalytic journal and the first written by a woman. Because her study was one of the first to focus on schizophrenia, the need for more research begun and led to more people focusing on mental illness. Freud referred to her work in the postscript to the Schreiber case. She left medical school resolved to be a psychoanalyst.

Spielrein had a complicated relationship with Jung (Kerr, 1993). She developed strong feelings toward him as she was his patient, was his assistant in his laboratory, and was seeing him socially (Launer, 2014). Spielrein voiced her love for Jung and apparently expressed her desire to have a baby with him. Whether these internal feelings consummated in Spielrein and Jung having intercourse has been doubted (Launer, 2014; Lothane, 2003; Owens, 2015). Although popular depictions of their relationship, as in the movie made from Kerr's *A Most Dangerous Method* (Hampton, 211), suggest Spielrein and Jung had sexual relations, Spielrein's own words suggest they did not (Owens, 2015), as is reinforced by Lothane's (2003) assessment.

In 1929, Spielrein presented a paper, while living in Russia, defending Freud and psychoanalysis, at a time when psychoanalysis was being marginalized in Russia. She also included sympathetic comments on the work of Ferenczi and his more emotionally engaged role on the part of the analyst (Launer, 2014). Spielrein was a talented, intellectually gifted individual who made a pioneering contribution to psychoanalysis, and who is a forgotten figure. Spielrein and Jung suffered from the same *Todschweigen* experience as did Severn and Ferenczi.

Case of Ellen West

The case of Ellen West, a patient of the founder of Dasein analysis Ludwig Biswanger, has often been quoted in the literature as a classic case of an eating disorder (Jackson, Davidson, Russell & Vandereycken, 1990). Since she was a child, Ellen West was preoccupied with her weight and eating. She had strong cravings for food, yet she had an extreme fear of gaining weight. These thoughts led to depression. She became addicted to laxatives. What started out as anorexia nervosa morphed into bulimia nervosa and possibly schizophrenia. She also developed a death obsession. Feeling she was imprisoned in thoughts about what to eat, or not to eat, death was the only way out of her self-imposed prison. To West, her life felt empty and food made her feel worse (Jackson, Davidson, Russell & Vandereycken, 1990). Unfortunately, she ended her life with poison.

Binswanger's (1975) treatment reflected an existential approach to analysis. He felt that West's bulimia was an expression of an existential vacuum to fill her needs. He was pessimistic about her condition, because she never seemed happy and peaceful, fearing she would commit suicide. Carl Rogers (1980) was critical about Binswanger's thinking and treatment of West. He felt Binswanger's pessimistic view of West's condition was adapted by her. Rogers felt she should have been helped to open her thinking to be attuned to her own experience of herself and allow interaction with others to inform her thinking and feeling.

Case of Miss F.

The premier clinical case for defining the development of the Self Psychology perspective is considered to be Kohut's clinical interaction with Miss F. (Kohut, 1971). Much like Ferenczi's interaction with Severn, there were moments of difficulty with Miss F. which led to change. In the tradition of Ferenczi's use of analyst self-disclosure, Kohut reported that as the analysis with Miss F. became protracted, he became bored. He also wanted to argue with her when she rejected his interpretations. Miss F. became violently angry if Kohut became silent. He could calm her down by summarizing what she said. But, if he went beyond the summary to an interpretation, she would fly into a rage. She would accuse Kohut of:

> "wrecking the analysis" [she] demanded a specific response to her communications, ... she completely rejected any other.
>
> *(Kohut, 1971, p. 285)*

If Kohut were more willing to credit and explore Ferenczi's work (Rachman, 1989) or Roger's (Stolorow, 1976), he would have seen his struggle was first experienced by Ferenczi and Rogers. The present volume has chronicled Severn's negative reactions to Ferenczi's need to interpret her silence so she could reach her childhood trauma (see Chapter 22). While I was a graduate student at the University of Chicago, there was a classic story passed around about Roger's difficult interaction with a client, *who demanded he remain silent.* A female client sought Rogers for psychotherapy in the first years of his practice as a client-centered psychotherapist, a perspective he had developed. The client-centered thinking about responsiveness is informed by the client's need for a response by attuning to his/her subjective experience. In the case under consideration, Rogers began to respond in his usual manner, but, each time he did, the client interrupted him by, in essence, asking him to remain silent. Rogers heard what the client had said, but felt it was natural for him to try to contribute to a client's understanding of his/her emotional issues. However, each time he offered a response, she suggested he was interrupting her flow of associations and interfered with her attempt to understand herself. Finally, she said to Rogers that she did not need his feedback; she needed him to remain silent so she could use his presence to work on herself, by herself. As difficult as it was for Rogers to accept the prohibition on his responding to this client, he finally *accepted the client's expressed need for a silent empathic presence.* Subsequently, Rogers used this example to illustrate the central role of empathic understanding in client-centered, now called person-centered, psychotherapy.

Returning to Miss F., she was not interested in and rejected Kohut's interpretations related to Oedipal issues. Miss F. needed a mirror function. By this he believed, his analysand needed him to be an extension of herself. She wanted him to mirror her thoughts and feelings. Looking for a precedent in psychoanalytic theory, Kohut turned toward his first analyst, August Aichorn. Aichon had the capacity to work with adolescents and narcissistic patients by providing the needed *narcissistic echo* (Aichorn, 1935). Kohut realized, to his credit, that Miss F. was not repeating a rejecting maternal or brother transference, but asking, no, demanding, approval and confirmation. If the mirror response rather than the interpretative function was sustained then, Kohut began to believe, it would serve to facilitate the development of something that was missing in the analysand's nuclear self. The analyst, in this way, was not an interpreter of the Oedipal complex, but an empathic responder to the analysand's need for empathy. Kohut rediscovered what Ferenczi and Rogers had originally discovered, without ever crediting his progenitors.

Besides mirroring, Kohut postulated that his new approach to Miss F. also served as a self-object function. The analysand was using the analyst as a vehicle to both reflect and satisfy a need. Basch (1995), felt Kohut's self-object concept was in the Freudian tradition: "… is the significant and truly original extension of Freud's work" (Basch, 1995, p. 370).

I believe Kohut's work was in the tradition of Ferenczi. The presentation of the cases of Bertha Pappenheim, Sabrina Spielrein, Ellest West, Ernst Lanzer, and Miss F. indicate that an analysand can help produce a change in the analyst's thinking and functioning, so that an evolutionary step develops in psychoanalysis. The clinical interaction between Elizabeth Severn and Sándor Ferenczi, as this volume has outlined, deserves to be considered in the same designation as a landmark case in the history of psychoanalysis, because it contributed to an evolution in analytic technique and theory.

Ferenczi's landmark cases

In my research on Ferenczi's clinical career, I believe there are three cases of his that can be considered as significant contributions to psychoanalysis. In his pre-analytic days, when he was a psychiatrist and not yet a psychoanalyst, Ferenczi demonstrated a pioneering capacity to function as an empathic presence rather than an interpreter. One of his first case studies was the case of Rosa K., reported in 1902 (Ferenczi 1902; see Chapter 8). Rosa K. was a female transvestite (in contemporary terms, gender dysphoric), who was regularly harassed by the Budapest police for dressing in men's clothing. She had been arrested for this proclivity, which was against the law in the early years of the twentieth century in Hungary. Ferenczi was engaged in a unique, non-traditional clinical interaction when he first began treating patients at the turn of the twentieth century (Rachman, 1997a). The Case of Rosa K. utilized Ferenczi's unique intellectual and clinical talents. Rosa K. was a female who was sexually interested in females and regularly dressed as a man. She called herself Robert. He wrote Rosa K. a letter on his physician stationary.

This indicated that as a psychiatrist, he had diagnosed her as a transvestite, which meant she suffered from a psychiatric disorder. Furthermore, Rosa K. was under his care for the disorder. Under those circumstances, which he outlined in the letter for Rosa K., she should not be arrested for a criminal offense. In essence, he provided her with a life-saving document (Rachman, 1967), which allowed her to live a more meaningful life. This letter was a remarkable intervention based upon empathy. This letter freed her from the threat of being incarcerated for being true to her identity. In these pre-historic days before sexual liberation, Ferenczi demonstrated his empathy, concern, and compassion for his patient, rather than being an authority for the state's inhumane treatment of a transvestite or homosexual.

There was another innovative clinical experience which also demonstrated an early empathic approach. Ferenczi asked Rosa K. to write a diary of her child-hood and adult experiences, in order to more fully understand her subjective experience as a transvestite. It is unfortunate that we do not have a copy of this historically important document. When I was writing my first Ferenczi book (Rachman, 1997a), I contacted Judith Dupont, who had sent me a Xerox copy of the original Hungarian version of the Rosa K. case study. She said she did not know of the existence of the Rosa K. diary (Rachman, 1997a). I believe Ferenczi's empathic treatment of a gender dysphoric individual at a time when medicine and society's attitudes toward homosexuality and cross-dressing were medieval and his capacity to respond to Rosa K. with an empathic perspective make the case of Rosa K. a landmark for the Budapest School of Psychoanalysis (Rachman, 2016a).

During Ferenczi's introduction of the active method in psychoanalysis (Ferenczi, 1980a–g), there was a landmark case of active psychoanalysis, the case of the Female Croatian Musician (Ferenczi, 1980b). A female opera singer sought out Ferenczi for analysis because she was suffering from what we now would call *stage fright* or *performance anxiety*. She could not rehearse for her performance because she would become overrun with anxiety. The groundbreaking clinical interaction of this case involved creating a role-playing scenario where the female musician was asked to recreate the rehearsal situation, e.g., playing the piano, conducting the orchestra, attempt to sing her song. Ferenczi had used the non-verbal observation of her symbolic sexual behavior to inform the analysis, so that the analysand was helped to become aware that her crippling anxiety was connected to a childhood sexual anxiety with her brother. These clinical innovations furthered our understanding of the analytic encounter, in the following way: (1) non-interpretative measures are helpful and necessary with difficult analysands in difficult situations; (2) the here-and-now of the psychoanalytic situation can be employed for recreation of the original trauma; (3) non-verbal communication was a new area of understanding about human behavior; (4) interpretation of non-verbal behavior became a new avenue for analytic understanding; (5) an active role for the analyst was established in the psychoanalytic situation; (6) co-created, two-person clinical interaction was developed (Rachman, 1997a).

Case of R.N./Elizabeth Severn

Although the cases of Rosa K. and the Female Croatian Musician can be seen as iconic cases, the Severn case was the highlight of Ferenczi's clinical contributions to psychoanalysis. The Severn analysis became the first formal analysis of the Incest Trauma (Rachman & Klett, 2015).

This idea that the Severn/Ferenczi analysis was the origin of trauma analysis (Ferenczi, 1988) is a significant landmark in the history of psychoanalysis. This clinical case was an attempt to establish actual trauma, whether sexual, physical, or emotional, as a distinct psychological disorder with its own theory and techniques. Trauma analysis was based upon the clinical experience of their analysis (Rachman, 2014a, b, e) and the theoretical perspective of Confusion of Tongues paradigm (Ferenczi, 1980k; Severn, 1933). These evolutionary changes in psychoanalytic theory and technique were the result of a co-created analysis by Severn and Ferenczi. In actuality, the concept of trauma analysis likely developed out of Severn's insistence that her emotional disturbance be analyzed beyond the Oedipal conflict. What is more, she developed the method of therapeutic regression in order to retrieve her childhood experiences of trauma. This is a very important part of her contribution because she sensed the emotional connection between childhood trauma and adult personality disturbance. This contribution expands analytic understanding to include actual traumatic circumstances as causal in emotional disorder. Severn discussed this idea in her book published after the termination of the analysis (Severn, 1933; Chapter 25; see Image 9).

A new psychology for psychoanalysis emerged from what has been called a two-person psychology and empathic perspective for psychoanalysis (Rachman, 2016a). These changes developed from *Severn's insistence that she contribute to her own analysis.* Of course, the most dramatic example of this was the mutual analysis that she initiated with Ferenczi. For the first time, the psychoanalytic situation was reconfigured so that psychological space was provided for the analysand's thoughts, feelings, and interpretations becoming significant in the analytic encounter. In the Ferenczi/Severn analysis, the analysand was not only allowed to have her voice heard about how to conduct the analysis, express what difficulties the analyst was providing in the clinical interaction, but she was invited to express herself freely when she felt she could contribute to overcoming the difficulty in the clinical interaction.

Freud's one-person struggle with Dora compared to Ferenczi's two-person struggle with Severn toward empathy

In Freud's struggle to understand why Dora was prematurely terminating from him he initially acted like the analyst/interpreter, trying to understand her contribution to the negative act of rejecting the treatment. In his criticism of his analysand, he went as far as to say Dora's termination was an act of vengeance on her part. Yet, Freud I believe, was on the edge of discovering clinical empathy when he reflected on Dora's dissatisfaction in their interaction.

No one who, like me, conjures up the most evil of those half-tamed demons that inhabit the human breast, and seeks to wrestle with them, can expect to come through the struggle unscathed. *Might I perhaps have kept the girl under my treatment* if I myself had acted a part, if I had exaggerated the importance to me of her staying on, *and had shown a warm personal interest in her* – a course which, even allowing for my position as her physician, would have been tantamount *to providing her with a subsititute for the affection she longed for, I do not know.*

(Freud, 1953, p. 109, italics added)

In his self-reflection he noted that perhaps he could have given Dora what she wanted, which was a more maternal or tender transference relationship. To his credit, he questioned whether he should have showed her empathy rather them interpretation (Rachman & Mattick, 2009, 2012). Freud's personality, scientific interest, and clinical attitude favored his attention to demonstrating that neurosis was caused by the drama of the Oedipal struggle. Freud thought that The Case of Dora provided this historically important opportunity. Freud focused on Dora's experience as much as he focused on his own need. In the end, this is one of the characteristic differences in the theoretical and clinical research between Freud and Ferenczi. Freud contributed a comprehensive framework; Ferenczi contributed a new understanding of clinical interaction which expanded the boundaries of psychoanalysis.

Severn and Ferenczi

Severn and Ferenczi made a significant contribution to providing a new narrative for the analytic encounter. The nature of the issue of status, power, and control in an analytic encounter was fundamentally changed. These dimensions of therapeutic relationship are generally under-evaluated in an analytic encounter, where the focus is on the analyst as interpreter. The nature of the psychoanalytic encounter became a more democratic and mutual experience when Ferenczi responded to Severn's need to be a clinical partner in her analysis. In fact, she could not tolerate, as she reported to (Eissler, 1952), any analysis which did not respect her intelligence and clinical acumen. She had several unsuccessful experiences with analysts who did not understand her or could not empathically attune to her. Her interaction with Ferenczi created a democratic attitude in the clinical interaction. Actually, she fought for—and, because Ferenczi was especially empathic and emotionally courageous, won—the right to be a clinical partner in the analysis. Again, compare Severn's contribution to her own analysis with Dora's inability to give voice to her emotional/interpersonal needs. Dora, who was a trauma survivor, lost her voice after the attempted molestation by Herr K. (Rachman & Mattick, 2009). She was not helped to untie her tongue in her analysis, because her trauma experiences were not deemed significant data in the analysis.

Ferenczi struggled to change his clinical functioning with Severn so that he could become in harmony with her. He may have begun the analysis with a flexible variation on the Freudian ethic of being the analyst who provides the clinical direction to the analysis. But, Severn made it clear, she wanted to be a contributor to the content and direction of the analysis. As Ferenczi reported, she contributed to his understanding of clinical empathy (Ferenczi, 1980h/k), non-interpretative measures (Ferenczi, 1988), role of childhood trauma (Ferenczi, 1980k, 1988), and mutuality (Ferenczi, 1988). Severn significantly influenced the change in status for an analysand. Before the Ferenczi/Severn analysis, an analysand was viewed as a patient, a disturbed individual who needed to be treated by a physician who had the superior knowledge, training, and clinical experience to provide the necessary diagnosis and therapy for their emotional problems. It does not take a genius to figure out that allowing a change in status, control, and power to an analysand would completely alter the Freudian clinical attitude. It was, and still remains, an emotional threat to the analytic community, who wants to maintain the position of the analyst as the authority. Traditional psychoanalysis is built upon the analyst maintaining the position of diagnostician and treatment expert. Even a so-called dissident point of view, like Interpersonal Psychoanalysis, maintains the attitude of the analyst as expert (Sullivan, 1947). The Relational Perspective, which acknowledges Ferenczi as a forerunner (Aron & Harris, 1993; Harris & Kuchuck, 2015) has integrated Severn and Ferenczi's new clinical attitude.

The maintenance of power in the analytic relationship has not been easily relinquished. Freud set the standard of maintaining the authority of the analyst. He would not relinquish his stature as the ultimate analytic authority when first Jung, then Ferenczi, offered to analyze him when he was having emotional difficulty. They were ceremoniously turned down (Rachman, 1997a). The early pioneers who followed Freud were also individuals who seem to be interested in power, control, and status. As Fromm (1959) has suggested, they were interested in maintaining Freud as the Master and protecting him from any threat from analytic dissidents or society. Ferenczi seemed to be someone who had no great interest in political or clinical power. He turned down the Presidency of the International Psychoanalytic Association. Ferenczi knew he was functioning in a clinically dissident manner and, therefore, could not be a spokesperson for analytic tradition. His personality was so configured that his need for affection and tenderness, his willingness to enter into non-status oriented relationships, and his capacity to give and receive love combined to focus his attention on empathic relationships rather than ones marked by control, status, or power.

There is the *dimension of surrender* that is necessary if power does not dominate in a relationship. Ferenczi surrendered to Severn, which, clearly, she had requested. The surrender was part of their relationship from the beginning. She made it clear she was dissatisfied with former analysts. The inability of her former, well-known analysts, some of whom were trained by Freud, fueled Severn's desire to have a completely different analytic experience. Most probably this is why Rank, after he failed with Severn, referred her to Ferenczi (Eissler, 1952). Rank was familiar with

Ferenczi's clinical talent from their work together (Ferenczi & Rank, 1925). Severn could not tolerate an analyst who was either caught up in his own theory, as she reported Rank was, or unable to show empathy, or who demonstrated counter-transference issues he/she was not able to address (Eissler, 1952). Severn brought her unfilled needs, her frustrations, and her criticism of psychoanalysts, as well as a desire to have her crippling traumas successfully addressed. Ferenczi was able to fully engage with Severn because he was able to surrender to her, while maintaining his capacity for empathy, understanding her traumas, showing flexibility in responding, and indicating a willingness to extend the boundaries of clinical behavior to respond to her developmental needs (Ferenczi, 1988).

The willingness for the analyst (or analysand) to surrender is, by definition, a dimension of mutuality. Severn had initiated mutual analysis. She accused Ferenczi of not analyzing his negative countertransference reaction to her. She felt he was causing the stalemate in their analysis. What is more, she had the audacity to claim that she could help him analyze his problem. This was an audacious claim for an analysand to make. Severn had in mind that she would help analyze Ferenczi's countertransference, while Ferenczi continued to analyze Severn's traumas. Ferenczi struggled for about a year before he surrendered to Severn's idea. Once he did, with Severn's help, he was able to successfully analyze his countertransference. Ferenczi's willingness to allow an analysand to analyze him down to his basic fault, his fundamental traumas (Balint, 1992/1968), was unprecedented. In other words, Ferenczi became an analysand in Severn's clinical interaction with him. It is not likely that Ferenczi had an inkling of how emotionally meaningful was Severn's clinical intervention in offering to help him analyze his negative countertransference to her. He couldn't possibly have known that he would not only emotionally retrieve his negative feelings toward women, as well as his mother, but, remarkably, his childhood sexual trauma with a nursemaid (Rachman, 2014a, b, 2015a). Would it be fair to conclude that Ferenczi's emotional capacity to retrieve his childhood sexual trauma was, in part, a function of Severn's clinical expertise? Of course, another element was Ferenczi's surrender to her. Surrender altered the perception of an analysand as only a disturbed individual who was not able to contribute to an analysis.

Ferenczi surrendered to Severn's mutual analysis because it was surrender or no analysis. Ferenczi throughout his clinical career, was able to rise to the occasion with difficult cases. Ferenczi was able to change his clinical functioning for Rosa K. and the Female Croatian Musician before he changed for Severn. But, Ferenczi's mutual analysis with Severn *was a clinical experiment, and should be remembered as an experiment.* However, there are elements of mutual analysis that have relevance in contemporary psychoanalysis. The ethic of mutual analysis, which Severn pioneered, is part of the foundation of a Relational Perspective (Aron, 1990, 1992; Aron & Harris, 1993). Mutuality as a relation dimension of therapeutic interaction integrates a democratic clinical attitude (Rachman, 2006, 2007a, b), listening to the patient (Casement, 1985), placing empathy in the forefront of clinical understanding and interaction (Ferenczi, 1980h/k; Kohut, 1984; Rogers; 1975; Searles 1979; Winnicott 1958), analysis of countertransference (De Forest, 1954; Ferenczi

1988; Severn, 1933), and an analysand's view of analysis (Casement, 1985; Severn, 1933). I have, for years, involved myself in a peer mutual analysis, both in group (Rachman, 1997a) and more recently, individually (Rachman, 2003a), which has been very helpful. One individual found it more helpful than the individual's personal analysis.

Severn was influential in the development of psychoanalytic technique. Severn influenced Ferenczi to expand his innovative clinical functioning to new heights as she encouraged him to integrate her own clinical innovations (Severn, 1913, 1920, 1933), as well as her own understanding of what she needed to successfully analyze her own trauma disorder (Eissler, 1952). As Ferenczi chronicled in his *Clinical Diary* (Ferenczi, 1988), in order to establish therapeutic relationships and treat Severn's trauma disorder, he needed to attune to her subjective experience. This was dramatic and revolutionary. Analytic technique was no longer solely dependent on traditional methodology, such as analysis of resistance, transference, fantasies or dreams, or interpretation and the development of insight. Severn helped Ferenczi to reconfigure the technology of psychoanalysis. During their eight-year analysis, the following new techniques were introduced: extending the traditional time of an analytic session; conducting a session outside the consultation room; development of clinical empathy; therapeutic regression; analyst self-disclosure; dramatic and emotional enlivenment in the psychoanalytic situation; mutual analysis; analysis of countertransference; analyst self-disclosure.

For a considerable time after the post-pioneering psychoanalytic period, the Severn/Ferenczi methodological changes produced a schism in psychoanalytic circles under the controversy of fulfilling needs or interpretation of a need (Bacal, 1985). Two mainstream psychoanalysts tried to integrate the Severn/Ferenczi innovative clinical ethic. First Eissler then Stone developed criteria or the integration of non-interpretative measures into mainstream psychoanalysis. Eissler (1953) suggested that character disorders, delinquency and non-neurotic disorders may need a more flexible, analytic method, which can introduce *parameters* to meet some of the needs of analysands. However, Eissler's parameters must be dissolved by the termination of the analysis. It was the beginning of traditional psychoanalysis broadening the clinical method to include non-interpretative interventions. But, Eissler's recommendations did not address the issue of lingering emotional disturbance in trauma disorders and severe non-neurotic disorders. Stone (1981) was more astute in his analytic thinking and clinical acumen. He realized that there were emotional disturbances that could not be successfully analyzed by traditional means. What is more, it was not realistic in treating difficult cases, that Eissler's rule of eliminating parameters should prevail. Stone argued that non-interpretative measures may have to be part of an analysis with difficult cases and not be eliminated before the analysis is terminated. Contemporary psychoanalysis, especially those perspectives which integrate a Relational Perspective, regularly accept a methodology which includes non-interpretative measures.

The pioneering analysis of trauma that Severn helped develop also gave rise to a new theory of psychoanalysis, the Confusion of Tongues paradigm (Ferenczi,

1980k, 1988; Severn, 1933). It was the first alternate to the Freudian theory of psychology (Gedo, 1986). In that sense, it is of great historical importance. But the Confusion of Tongues was not considered of great theoretical and clinical importance when it was introduced. Severn and Ferenczi collaborated in developing the idea that actual sexual childhood training produces a unique psychological disorder with unique psychodynamics and treatment methodology. The Confusion of Tongues concept is often misunderstood. It was officially set forth by Ferenczi in 1932 (Ferenczi, 1980k, also 1988), and included in Severn's long out-of-print and forgotten book, the *Discovery of the Self* (Severn, 1933). Basically, the Confusion of Tongues is a theory of how to understand and treat sexual trauma and psychological trauma. Neither Ferenczi or Severn wanted to supplant the Oedipal theory with The Confusion of Tongues theory. They wanted to extend the boundaries of psychoanalysis beyond the Oedipal conflict, to include the study and treatment of trauma (Rachman, 1997a, b, 2003a; Rachman & Klett, 2015). Severn and Ferenczi were prophetic, as the study and treatment of trauma is an important part of psychotherapy and psychoanalysis and hopefully will gain greater acceptance (Rachman, 2010b, 2012a, c, 2014e, 2016b).

The removal of Ferenczi and Severn from psychoanalysis

Toward the latter part of Ferenczi's analysis with Severn, when he distanced himself from Freud and the orthodox community, and the negative rumors about the Severn analysis and Ferenczi's "non-analytic" behavior were being circulated (Rachman, 1997a, b), the mainstream establishment began the practice of *Todschweigen* (see Chapter 7). Ferenczi's retreat from Freud and the Circle of Rings was a defensive maneuver to protect himself and Severn from the onslaught of criticism and condemnation that did eventually come (Rachman, 1997b). Ferenczi's Confusion of Tongues presentation unleased the criticisms and sent the *Todschweigen* experience in full motion, so that both Ferenczi and Severn were *silenced to death*, disappearing from psychoanalytic literature, study in approved analytic institutes, and recognition in the analytic community.

There were valiant attempts to return Ferenczi as a significant figure of psychoanalysis in the post-pioneering period. Balint (1949) first published the Confusion of Tongues paper in English previously denied by Freud, Jones, and others (Rachman, 1997b). De Forest (1942, 1954), was one of Ferenczi's first American analysands and students who attempted to explain the significance of Ferenczi's ideas and methods for psychoanalysis. De Forest was an enthusiastic student of Ferenczi, in whom Ferenczi confided and discussed his feelings about being rejected by Freud (Fromm, 1959). Thompson (1942) was the second of the triad of American women analysands (the third being Severn), who helped promulgate Ferenczi's ideas after his death (Severn, 1933; De Forest, 1942, 1954; Thompson, 1942, 1943, 1944, 1950). A shining light in the darkness of the *Todschweigen* experience of removing Ferenczi and Severn from mainstream psychoanalysis was Erich Fromm. There were, at least, three contributions that Fromm made to the

Ferenczi Rennaissance. Fromm's understanding of Ferenczi's suffering, Freud's mean-spirited treatment of him, and his willingness to stand with Ferenczi were courageous and opened up a positive alternate evaluation of Ferenczi, searing a hole in the darkness of the *Todschweigen* barrier. Fromm did this in three ways: (1) discussed Freud's authoritism as a leader of psychoanalysis who needed to discourage dissidence. Fromm had the courage to examine Freud's functioning and criticize it at a time when the hero worship of Freud was rampant, in part, due to Jones' hero-worshiping Freud biography (Jones, 1953-1957); (2) the presentation of De Forest's one-person account of Ferenczi's account of his last meeting with Freud when the Confusion of Tongues paper was condemned and Freud mistreated Ferenczi; (3) Fromm's remarkable statement that the Confusion of Tongues paper should be considered as one of the landmark ideas in the history of psychoanalysis. Fromm praising one of Ferenczi's most maligned contribution as one of psychoanalysis' most important theories was a courageous act that demonstrated his independent thinking and functioning as an analytic pioneer. Fromm's book, *Sigmund Freud's Mission* (Fromm, 1954), was the important container for these ideas. Fromm identified with Ferenczi's spirit.

There were some attempts to maintain interest in Ferenczi in the period 1960–1970. Sándor Lorand, the first European analyst to immigrate to the United States and a Ferenczi analysand, published a chapter on Ferenczi in a 1966 book on psychoanalytic pioneers (Lorand, 1966). In paying tribute to Ferenczi as one of the outstanding pioneers in psychoanalytic history, Lorand helped maintain interest in Ferenczi during a period when he was being ignored in mainstream psychoanalysis.

In 1968, John Gedo wrote an article for the German journal *Psyche* entitled "Noch einimal der Gelentre Saugling" (The wise baby reconsidered), which was his idea of a comprehensive review of Ferenczi's contributions to psychoanalysis (Gedo, 1968, 1976). Gedo told me the story how he came to write this review, which clarified some important revelations about Kohut and Gedo. *Psyche* first contacted Heinz Kohut to write an updated evaluation of Ferenczi's work. At this time in the 1960s, Gedo was one of Kohut's early collaborators. Kohut passed the assignment onto Gedo. If Kohut was contacted by *Psyche* to write a review about Ferenczi's ideas it meant Kohut was considered a Ferenczi scholar. If he was considered a Ferenczi scholar, why did he omit any references to Ferenczi in his own work on empathy and working with difficult cases like Miss F. (Rachman, 1989a; see this chapter, Heinz Kohut/the case of Miss F)? When I asked this question of Gedo, he indicated that, in his opinion, Kohut did not always credit others. Gedo's version of Ferenczi's contributions consisted of a focus on his earlier work. Gedo did not include Ferenczi's later work on the analysis of trauma. In fact, the contributions of Ferenczi and Severn were completely excluded. Ignoring or deliberately excluding the Ferenczi/Severn contributions by Gedo, I believe, reinforced the *Todschweigen* experience, as did Kohut's silence about Ferenczi's contributions to the development of clinical empathy and the analysis of difficult cases.

This same era in analytic history produced a book by Bergmann and Hartman, (1976), which was focused on introducing the origins of psychoanalytic technique to a modern audience. The authors suggested that Ferenczi should be considered one of the significant figures in the history of psychoanalysis since they have included six separate articles by him in their collection, more than any other analytic pioneer. Apparently Bergmann seemed to shift in his thinking in his later years, as I have reported in his dramatic contribution to the *Todschweigen* of Ferenczi in contemporary psychoanalysis (see Chapter 7).

Ferenczi Renaissance

The decade of 1970s–1980s saw the beginning of the Ferenczi Renaissance (Rachman, 1997a). Several important publications helped begin the Ferenczi Rennaisance, such as Paul Roazen's (1975) revisionist history of psychoanalysis; Jeffrey M. Masson's (1984) dramatic criticism of Freud's suppression of Ferenczi's work on trauma, and the French publication (Ferenczi, 1985), then, the English translation, of Ferenczi's *Clinical Diary* (Ferenczi, 1988). These publications provided a reevaluation of Ferenczi's ideas and methodology at a time when psychoanalysis had begun to develop important alternatives to Freudian psychology. By the time of the publication of Ferenczi's *Clinical Diary* the Object Relations, Interpersonal Psychoanalysis, Self Psychology, and Relational Psychoanalysis perspectives had provided a more liberal, integrated perspective, which began to include ideas and practices Ferenczi had introduced.

Roazen's research (1975) focused on examining the contributions of the neglected dissidents of psychoanalysis, like Ferenczi, Rank, and Groddeck. Roazen interviewed anyone who had contact with Freud and could provide first-person accounts of personal and clinical interactions as analysands, colleagues, friends, rivals, etc. This work demonstrated the political rivalry that existed between Freud, Jones, and Ferenczi which led to the silencing of Ferenczi's work. What is more, Roazen highlighted Ferenczi as an unappreciated, significant figure in psychoanalysis. Roazen became a psychoanalytic hero for me. It was shortly after I discovered Ferenczi in 1976 that I read Roazen's book and found a psychohistorian of psychoanalysis who verified my thinking about the significance of Ferenczi. In the 1980s, Esther Menaker introduced me to Roazen. He encouraged me to continue my work on Ferenczi and appeared as a book reviewer on my first Ferenczi book (Rachman, 1997a).

Jeffrey M. Masson became a pariah in psychoanalysis when, in his book, *The Assault on Truth*, (Masson, 1984), he questioned Freud's personal courage. He believed that Freud abandoned the seduction hypothesis because he could not stand up to the criticism of the colleagues, the Viennese medical establishment, to whom he presented the hypothesis. Masson like Roazen's work, was a light at the end of the *Todschweigen* tunnel. Masson's personal criticism of Freud is open to question, but his research on Ferenczi became one of the building blocks for the Ferenczi Renaissance (Rachman, 1997a). Unfortunately, Masson suffered the same *Todschweigen* experience as Ferenczi. He has been completely removed from psychoanalysis. What is more, he has also removed himself from psychoanalysis.

In the years since he was fired as the Secretary of the Freud Archives, Masson has involved himself in the study of the emotions of animals and veganism. When I discussed with him my desire to write this volume, he was very interested and told me to keep in touch with him about the project. In addition, several years ago, he had agreed to be a participant in a symposium I was planning on a re-evaluation of The Confusion of Tongues theory and the study and treatment of trauma. Unfortunately, the symposium did not materialize.

Before the publication of Ferenczi's *Clinical Diary*, French and Hungarian psychoanalysts had contributed to the Ferenczi Renaissance. The French analysts, led by Judith Dupont, founded a group, called *Le Coq-Heron* that published a journal, *Confrontation*, which originated in 1969. *Confrontation* authors such as Brande (1972), Covello (1984), Dupont (1984), Saubourin (1984), and Torok (1984) published articles and books, and this group became the literary heirs to the work of Ferenczi and Balint.

The appearance of the long-awaited *Clinical Diary* of Sándor Ferenczi in French (Ferenczi, 1985) and English (Ferenczi, 1988) was one of the most significant events in the Ferenczi Renaissance. The *Diary's* publication turned a light on the darkness that was initiated by the *Todschweigen* experience by traditional analysts. For the first time, contemporary analysts could read for themselves Ferenczi's pioneering ideas and methods, without the negative commentary of Ferenczi's political enemies and critics. The *Clinical Diary* became a rallying point for non-Freudian analysts who were not aware of the origins of their theories and methods of their perspectives. Wolstein (1989), for example, after reading the *Clinical Diary*, realized that his work on countertransference and the Interpersonal Perspectives owed a debt to Ferenczi. The Ferenczi community owes a great debt to Gizella Ferenczi who gave the typed copy of Ferenczi's *Clinical Diary* to his heir apparent Michael Balint, who kept it safe during WWII and then passed it on to Judith Dupont when she became Ferenczi's literary executor. Balint, in an attempt to reduce the *Todschweigen* experience for Ferenczi's work in the analytic community, decided not to publish the *Clinical Diary* in his lifetime. We can thank Judith Dupont as editor of the *Clinical Diary* for all her efforts on the publication of one of the most important books in the history of psychoanalysis.

It is fitting that a group of Hungarian psychoanalysts kept Ferenczi alive in his native country and contributed to the Ferenczi Renaissance (Hermann, 1974; Hidas, 1993; Hynal, 1989; Mészáros, 1993). This group founded the Sándor Ferenczi Society, Budapest, Hungary, and published a journal *Thalassa* from 1990 to 2010, in Hungarian, to maintain interest and scholarship in Ferenczi's work in his country and Europe as well as in Ferenczi's mother tongue. This was to ensure that a *Todschweigen*, which did exist in Hungary regarding Ferenczi's work during the communist occupation, did not happen again. The Ferenczi Society has continued to significantly contribute to the Ferenczi Renaissance by sponsoring International Ferenczi Conferences. Recently, the Sándor Ferenczi Society, led by Judith Mészáros and Carlo Bonomi of the Italian Ferenczi Society; have made a very significant contribution to diminishing the *Todschweigen* of Ferenczi. The Sándor Ferenczi apartment and office, in the Buda Hills, where Ferenczi treated Elizabeth Severn and wrote the *Clinical Diary*, has been purchased by the Ferenczi Society and The International Ferenczi Foundation and named The Ferenczi House. The Archives is the heart and soul of the Ferenczi House, containing the legacy of Ferenczi and The Budapest School of Psychoanalysis in the form of manuscripts, books, photographs, and letters (Mészáros, 2016).

Now there is a series of books which have emerged establishing a new Ferenczi literature. These publications not only demonstrated Ferenczi's influence in the evolution of psychoanalysis, but established a new scholarship about the Freud/Ferenczi relationship. The *Clinical Diary* established an understanding and treatment of trauma (Aron & Harris, 1993; Harris & Kuchuck, 2015; Haynal, 1989; Lorin, 1983; Masson, 1984; Rachman, 1997a, 2003a; Rachman & Klett, 2015; Rudynsky, 2000). The publication of the Freud/Ferenczi correspondence further contributed to the Ferenczi Renaissance by opening up the history of the Freud/Ferenczi relationship as well as the history of the pioneering period of psychoanalysis as seen through the eyes of the founder and his favorite students (Brabant, Falzeder & Giamperi-Deutsch, 1993; Falzeder, Brabant & Giampieri-Deutsch, 1996, 2000).

Although the rehabilitation of Ferenczi has begun, there has been no such important attempt to remove the *Todschweigen* taboo for Severn. Since Masson (1984) began the conversation about Severn, there have been few discussions in the analytic literature about Ferenczi's most recognized and famous analysand (Fortune, 1993, 1996, 2015; Haynal, 2010; Rachman, 2010a, 2012b, 2014a, b, 2015a; Rudnytsky, 2015; Smith, 1998, 1999, 2001). Rehabilitating Severn's reputation and establishing her as a significant figure in psychoanalysis is in its infancy. This volume and previous publications are a long-awaited initial attempt to fuel this process.

25

SEVERN AS A PSYCHOANALYST

The road from mysticism to psychoanalysis

Severn began her clinical career in 1908, about the same time as Ferenczi met Freud. Their meeting began his training to become a psychoanalyst. Severn was a self-taught therapist who used her personal attributes—such as empathy, assertiveness, superior intelligence, and creativity, combined with her intellectual curiosity, varied academic interests, motivation to learn, a strong sense of independence, and a belief in her own capacities—to develop her own clinical training (see Chapter 11).

She was not trained as a mental health professional. During the beginning of the twentieth century both psychiatry and psychoanalysis were in their infancy. The Society of Rings (Grosskurth, 1991) was the original circle of analysts who were Freud's first adherents. They were mostly physicians or formally educated individuals who were part of a European intelligentsia and a coffee house society who shared a similar education, culture and sensibility (Ellis, 2004; Lukacs, 1990). In Vienna and Budapest educated individuals, professionals and businessmen would meet regularly to discuss such topics as psychoanalysis. Severn did not have this important mechanism to stimulate her intellectually, nor did she have cohorts who shared her career ambitions. The fields of psychology and social work did not have a place for training clinical practitioners. Severn carved her own path toward becoming a therapist, originally being attracted to mysticism and spirituality as her intellectual framework (see Chapter 12). Her first two books (Severn, 1913, 1920) illustrate that her initial success as a salesperson was an indication that she had a special capacity and desire to be a therapeutic presence with individuals. Severn developed her therapeutic presence into beginning a clinical practice of therapeutic massage. As she developed her own ideas and methods (Severn, 1913, 1920; Chapter 12) she was able to successfully help a wide variety of individuals with a spectrum of methods.

Severn's interest in psychoanalysis was intellectual, clinical, and personal. She became interested in clinical psychology and psychoanalysis as both fields began to develop in the United States in the first two decades of the twentieth century. Severn was acquainted with the work of the psychologist, William James, and the psychoanalyst, James Jackson Putnam. James and Jackson traveled together to Clark University in 1909, to hear Freud's lectures which introduced psychoanalysis to the United States (Hale, 1971a). James' major work was first published in 1890 (James, 1950), 19 years before Severn began her clinical career as a therapist. Jackson was one of the first American neurologists to become interested in psychoanalysis (Hale, 1971b; Putnam, 1915). After Severn's initial clinical period where she practiced using a spiritual and metaphysical perspective (see Chapter 11), she integrated her brand of eclectic and creative methodology, using her intellectual gifts and a desire to better inform her clinical work with a modern therapeutic perspective. She turned toward psychoanalysis as it began to influence American intellectual thought and provided a comprehensive system to work, in depth, with individuals.

Her pre-analytic period of clinical experience involved many cases referred by physicians who had little psychological sophistication, not being attuned to the emotional difficulties that accompany organic illness. Severn began to read widely in psychology and early Freudian psychoanalysis. She became the recipient of a wide variety of physician-based referrals where the patient's recovery was hampered by emotional factors. For example, there were patients who had successful foot surgery, were deemed cured by their physicians, but could not get out of bed or walk. Severn used her understanding of the emotional factors in human behavior to add to the psychological understanding of her cases with organic illness. In cases of protracted recovery from treatment by a physician, or surgeon, Severn would provide talk therapy, encouraging the patient to become active in their own treatment and employing her intuitive capacity to empathize with the patient's subjective experience. These varied therapeutic measures conveyed a sense of non-possessiveness, erotic-free affection, all of which gave the person motivation and hope they would recover from their illness. Severn shared with Ferenczi the important quality of a therapeutic presence. Her therapeutic presence combined with her intellectual desire to integrate the new science of psychoanalysis. Becoming interested in the psychology of human behavior, as well as the desire to find a method that would cure the deepest level of emotional trauma, moved Severn towards the study and practice of psychoanalysis. In addition, she was unconsciously searching for a cure for her own deep-seated emotional disorder.

Severn's childhood traumas and her three failed analyses: a search for a cure for her trauma disorder

Severn made it very clear in the 1952 interview with Kurt Eissler that undertaking her analysis with Ferenczi was her last chance to work through her crippling emotional disorder as her depression and suicidal thoughts were closing in on her. The difficult analysand was joining forces with the analyst of last resort. This was a noble match of life forces. Severn, although emotionally hampered, never lost her desire to conquer her disorder. Ferenczi joined forces with Severn by never giving up on trying to help Severn confront her demons and find ways to therapeutically overcome them.

Severn's three failed analyses prior to undertaking treatment with Ferenczi clarified what kind of clinical interaction she needed from her analyst. She could also draw upon her own clinical experience in her therapy practice, which featured active, emotionally connected, empathically attuned and innovative interaction. Severn was determined to inform her fourth analyst with the understanding of what didn't work in her previous analyses, and what did work from her own therapeutic work with her patients. However, neither Ferenczi nor Severn were fully prepared for the difficulties that arose in a pioneering analysis of trauma disorder. It must be remembered that it is likely that the Ferenczi/Severn analysis was the first time an attempt was made to conduct an analysis of a psychological disorder, whose origin was based on actual parental abuse of a child, using non-interpretative measures to recover, understand, and work through the trauma.

It was the uncovering of her childhood which led to a more successful analysis with Ferenczi than Severn had had in her three previous analyses. Severn knew there was an unknown dimension in understanding her emotional issues. When Ferenczi was able to understand Severn's Semi-Trance Session approach in retrieving her early traumas, he could join her in this pioneering therapeutic regression technique (see Chapter 22). What Severn learned from the struggle over Ferenczi's acceptance of her method was that a co-created therapeutic experience can be the most valuable. Such collaborative efforts illustrate the fundamental and pioneering perspective of empathy and a two-person perspective, which characterized the Budapest School of Psychoanalysis (Rachman, 2016a).

Severn's training analysis with Ferenczi: clinical contributions to the analysis of trauma

The Ferenczi/Severn analysis was not only a pioneering treatment of a trauma disorder, but a training analysis performed by a senior analyst for an analytic candidate who was undergoing training to be a psychoanalyst. Freud did not have a training in analysis and turned down Jung and Ferenczi, who offered him help. Ferenczi had a brief combined personal/training with Freud. The requirement of a training analysis was formalized by The International Psychoanalytic Association in 1922, encouraged by Ferenczi (Laplance & Pontalis, 1973).

Before the formal admission to an analytic training program and the requirement of a training analysis were firmly established during the 1920s, Freud analyzed his daughter, Anna (Rachman, 2003b, 2006), and Ferenczi and Severn were in a training analysis. Ferenczi considered Severn as a training analysand and a colleague. Although Severn was considered emotionally disturbed, the analytic community respected Severn's intelligence and some had positive feelings about her.

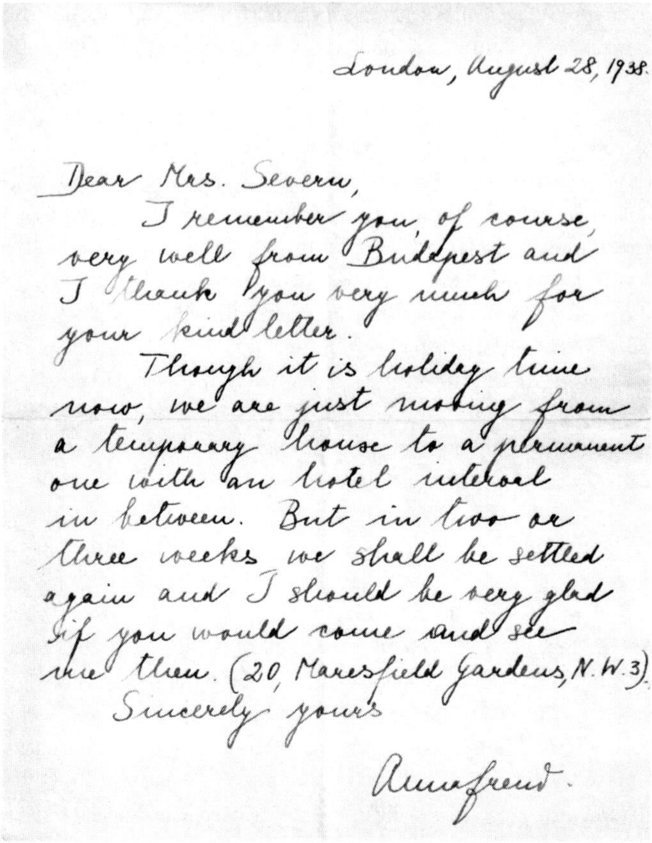

London, August 28, 1938.

Dear Mrs. Severn,
I remember you, of course,
very well from Budapest and
I thank you very much for
your kind letter.
Though it is holiday time
now, we are just moving from
a temporary house to a permanent
one with an hotel interval
in between. But in two or
three weeks we shall be settled
again and I should be very glad
if you would come and see
me then. (20, Maresfield Gardens, N.W.3)
Sincerely yours

Anna Freud.

IMAGE 19 Letter to Mrs. Severn from Anna Freud, London, August 28, 1938

Anna Freud wrote a letter to Severn inviting her to visit their new house as the Freuds resettled in London (Freud, A., 1938; see Image 19). Karen Horney, in the same years after Severn's analysis with Ferenczi was terminated, contacted her to help her daughter who was moving to London (see Image 17, p. 234).

Severn and Ferenczi combined to illustrate that a two-person analytic experience is necessary in order to emotionally understand and treat a trauma disorder. They demonstrated a willingness to deconstruct the traditional analytic encounter into a democratic and mutual interaction, in which, the analysand had a decided voice in conceptualizing and developing methodology for the analysis. Although the Ferenczi/Severn analysis had shortcomings which encouraged dependency and malignant regression, it was a crucible for a paradigm shift in the nature and process of clinical psychoanalysis. The deconstruction of the analytic encounter also involved a dramatic shift in the functioning of the analyst, who became *an empathic presence*, in the here-and-now of the analytic encounter. This shift highlights an emotional encounter where both analyst and analysand are involved in sharing their joint subjectivities. It is through this kind of process that the analyst can better understand the developmental lags that exist in the analysand's internal structures. Through *accurate empathic understanding* the analyst is better equipped to discern the analysand's basic emotional issues and to respond to them from the analysand's perspective. In actuality, the issue of clinical empathy was present in one of Freud's earliest cases, the Case of Dora/Ida Bauer. Freud instinctively knew that Bauer needed empathic understanding, particularly about her mother's emotional neglect of her (Rachman & Mattick, 2009, 2012). It has also been pointed out that Freud was so focused on establishing interpretation as the major clinical interaction of clinical psychoanalysis that he neglected an opportunity to empathize with her sexual trauma with her father's friend who tried to sexually seduce her. It remains a mystery why Freud neglected not only the issue of empathy, but the role the sexual trauma in the origin of psychological disorder and in his own personality development (see Chapter 8). Severn and Ferenczi actually helped focus the issues of empathy and a two-person psychology for psychoanalysis (Rachman, 2016a).

Severn's book, *The Discovery of the Self* (1933): theoretical contributions to a two-person and empathic perspective in psychoanalysis

In the last of three books, Severn published, *The Discovery of the Self* (Severn, 1933), she described the ideas which grew out of her collaboration with Ferenczi during their eight-year clinical experiment in trauma analysis, and her own development, intellectually and clinically as a psychoanalyst. This contribution by Severn deserves to be re-evaluated as we attempt to understand her contributions to the theory and treatment of trauma and the evolution of psychoanalysis toward a relational perspective. I will present data from the book which indicates her psychoanalytic thinking.

Analyst as a human being

A new paradigm for the Severn/Ferenczi perspective involves the analyst as a human being. Severn offered the following:

> I, on the contrary, think that the relation of analyst to patient must be similar to that of his priest to his flock, though perhaps closer in the sense of *being more intimate and human*, and less *distant* and 'other-wordly' than the clerical one is supposed to be … *the analyst must be a better parent – either father or mother – than the original one who was the cause of, or failed to understand, the emotions of the child.*
>
> *(Severn, 1933, p. 63, italics added)*

The paradigm shift in conceptualizing the analyst as a human being parallels Ferenczi's idea of the analyst as a healer (Rachman, 1997a). The personal qualities of the analyst are integrated with the intellectual capacities. This idea of the analyst as a fellow human being interacting with another fellow human being shifts the analysis from one person performing a cure on a patient. Severn is suggesting that the therapeutic dyad consists not of a physician attending to a patient, but two human beings in a bond of collaboration and compassion searching for healing. In healing the analysand, the analyst will be healed.

The paradigm shift from a one-person to a two-person experience in the analytic encounter is stated in Severn's view of analysis:

> Certain it is that unless these two people [analyst and patient] who come together for a common purpose, which is the solving of the difficulties of the patient, can meet on equal ground, plus a lenient, sympathetic and completely unselfish attitude from the analyst no great good can be hoped for.
>
> *(Severn, 1933, p. 61)*

Severn called upon her own analytic experience in her trauma analysis with Ferenczi. It is a rare event that an analyst's perspective is informed not only by their intellect, or clinical experience, but by their personal experience in their own analysis. The Severn/Ferenczi perspective emerged from the mutuality that emerged in their clinical interaction (Ferenczi, 1988). A fundamental change in philosophy arose from the change in the status, power, and control between analyst and analysand. Severn's idea of the analytic relationships echoed Ferenczi's thought in his 1933 paper, the Confusion of Tongues, which she experienced in their clinical interaction:

> Although most patients need to learn many things, the relationship should be anything but a pedagogic, of a teacher and pupil nature. The "I know more than you do" attitude is not successful with a child, invalid or worried person.
>
> *(Ferenczi, 1980k)*

Clinical empathy as a central dimension of the analytic encounter

Ferenczi introduced clinical empathy into psychoanalysis in his 1928 paper (Ferenczi, 1980h, also see Chapter 15), in which he named Severn as a collaborator. Empathy as a significant dimension of clinical psychoanalysis arose out of the struggle Ferenczi endured to make contact with Severn's subjective experience so he could work on her basic emotional issues and search together for meaningful methods to work through them. Severn reached back to Freud's earliest statement, using the German concept of *Einfühling*:

> The patient is a human palpitating being needing endless understanding and "Einfühling," as the Germans say it, a kind of feeling in or identification with him and his problem ... To do this requires not only great liberality of

thought, but great humanness of feeling – not sentimentalism or weeping or commiseration, but the kind of *Pity* that unifies itself with its object in short, in its highest sense – love.

(Severn 1933, pp. 61–62)

Severn realized that to introduce the idea of love as an important, if not essential, ingredient in the analytic relationship was talking blasphemy. In 1933, when her last book was published, psychoanalysis was characterized by Freud's ideas and methods. Severn was in general agreement with the Freudian theoretical principles of psychoanalysis, but not with the intellectual orientation to clinical psychoanalysis (Eissler, 1952). Severn was informed by her own clinical work as well as her clinical experience with Ferenczi. Reconfiguring the tradition of interpretation allowed Severn's analysis with Ferenczi to be the most successful of her four attempts. They believed that the human dimension of the analytic relationship was significant. In particular, the way the analyst relates to the analysand determines not only the structure and process of the analysis, but, more fundamentally, whether the analyst will provide the humanness of an empathic relationship with the analysand.

The love that Severn mentioned in the emphatic contact necessary for a therapeutic relationship in analyzing trauma was maternal affection, not erotic love.

When I speak of love *I do not*, of course, *mean being "in love"* as *this is quite a different thing* and a *very selfish one, to be excluded from the analytic relation of a matter of course*. I mean rather the *love* which is tolerant, *all-merciful and warm, such as a wise mother gives her children*, especially the sick one, as a spontaneous and natural gift. *Only this can bring about a real healing*, but the need of it is unfortunately decried by Psycho-Analysis as a dangerous and weak indulgence.

(Severn, 1933, p. 62, italics added)

Both Severn and Ferenczi believed in the importance of maternal affection. Severn suffered from severe paternal abuse, with apparently little or no intervention by her mother (see Chapter 9). Her own emotional problems forced her to be away from her daughter, Margaret. After she returned from her hospitalization, she and her daughter were very close during the rest of their lives (see Chapter 9). Ferenczi suffered from maternal deprivation, being one of 12 children (Rachman, 1997a). The role of maternal affection and responsiveness in the Ferenczi/Severn perspective was a dramatic shift from the traditional focus on the paternal role in the Oedipal drama. The Severn/Ferenczi perspective emphasized the pre-Oedipal experience of the child and mother. In that experience, they believed, maternal affection and responsivity were crucial. Was Ferenczi influenced in his idea of *cherishing love* (De Forest, 1954), by the following biblical reference?

As a mother comforts her son, so I will comfort you.

(Norton, 2005, Book of Isiah 66:13)

Cherishing love, not erotic love, were the therapeutic qualities of the analyst, that were an important ingredient in the cure that both Severn and Ferenczi introduced. The most significant aspect of the cherishing love quality is the compassion, warmth, and expressed feelings of maternal affection for the analysand. We now have research dates to amplify these theoretical and clinical insights. We now have a study of individuals who were followed from infancy to adulthood on measures of maternal affection and adult stress levels. High levels of affection by mothers in early childhood showed lower levels of overall distress as adults (Maselko, Kubzansky, Lipsett & Buka, 2010).

Based on her clinical experience with Ferenczi, Severn knew that *cherishing love did not lead to a "dangerous and weak indulgence"* (Severn, 1933, p. 62). She had a history of severe abusive behavior with her father. She needed a compassionate, affectionate, empathic parental figure to help her feel understood, safe, and affirmed. The feelings of safety, empathy, and affection led to a joint exploration and working through of the analysand's childhood traumas. As Severn experienced, such empathy was not an indulgence which led to an acting out of sexual behavior, but an uncovering of her unresolved childhood traumas (Ferenczi, 1988; Severn, 1933).

The Confusion of Tongues theory of trauma (Rachman and Klett, 2015), which was developed by Ferenczi with input by Severn, clearly outlined that analysis should be a passion-free experience. The analyst was to be alert to his own as well as the anlaysand's verbal and non-verbal erotic behavior. It is the analyst's task to examine his/her subjective experience to become aware of any sexual countertransference and work it through. Seductive behavior by the analyst re-traumatizes the analysand. The analyst's task is also to discern the manifestations of erotic transference in the analysand's behavior in the here-and-now of the psychoanalytic situation, as well as the origins of it in childhood. When the analyst recognizes the issue of enactment, analyzing the erotic transference can become the uncovering of the childhood trauma (Rachman, Kennedy & Yard, 2005, 2009).

The analyst's therapeutic presence

The reality of a blank screen has never really existed, but nevertheless, revered in traditional psychoanalysis. *An analyst is never a blank screen*, but, a positive or negative force with the analysand. The entire experience of the analyst's personality, behavior, manner of relating, and physical environment of the consultation office as well as non-verbal communications are all part of the therapeutic action of an analytic session (Balint & Balint, 1939). *Every analyst leaves a footprint in the analytic encounter.* It is the kind of footprint that one leaves that can contribute to the analysand's recovery. The idea that the analyst should be invisible or minimally responsive is absurd. What human relationship exists where being minimally involved is helpful? Invisibility or minimal responsiveness do not lead to a positive contribution, since human beings need, want, and thrive on responsiveness.

Modulation of the analyst's response is therapeutic, is necessary so that the analysand does not suffer over-stimulation, being dominated, controlled, or overpowered. Neutrality is experienced as a lack of response or lacking empathy and responsivity, even coldness. Why would an analysand who is suffering from childhood abuse want to continually interact with a passive, neutral observer, analytic surgeon, blank screen, or intellectual interpreter? To remain in analysis with such a stereotype of an analyst, who is playing a role to fulfill a stereotyped, theoretical function, is an exercise in masochism (Larivére, 2016), and can be indicative of an enactment of a childhood trauma (Rachman & Klett, 2015).

Trauma analysis

Severn collaborated with Ferenczi in discerning the possibility of a new category of psychological disturbance, called trauma disorder. At a time when psychoanalysis believed the Oedipal complex was its cornerstone, Severn and Ferenczi were perceived as challenging and personally rejecting Freud. What is more, Freud acted as if Ferenczi, his once adopted son, had deliberately and completely alienated himself from his mentor (Rachman, 1997a). Ferenczi was devastated by Freud's rejection, and some, like Severn, believed Freud's rejection of Ferenczi contributed to his death (Eissler, 1952). This dramatic pronouncement by Severn points to the emotional closeness Ferenczi and Freud shared. Freud's emotional reaction to their relationship reaching the breaking point was his anger and rejection toward Ferenczi.

Severn's analysis with Ferenczi initiated a change in analytic theory and methodology. When actual childhood traumas were perceived as the origins of Severn's severe psychopathology, the data of psychoanalysis was expanded to include the real, actual, and conscious data of the interpersonal interaction of the family, as Ferenczi suggested, along with the unconscious and symbolic data of the Oedipal drama. In this volume, I have suggested that Freud's iconic clinical cases, did not validate his Oedipal theory. Such cases as the Wolf Man, Sergei Panjekeff, can be considered as a case of incest trauma (Rachman & Klett, 2015; see Chapter 8). Freud held his Oedipal theory so tightly that he could not make room for Ferenczi and Severn's alternative theory, The Confusion of Tongues theory of trauma (Ferenczi, 1980k; Rachman & Klett, 2015). Freud misinterpreted the attempt to introduce a theory to expand psychoanalysis to understand and treat trauma disorders as a personal and professional attack (see Chapter 16).

Severn provided her clinical perspective of an analysand whose childhood trauma she analyzed:

> We had to go on, therefore, digging and excavating more lost memories and feelings until *convention* was achieved in the patient's mind as the source of her trouble. Not only were many scenes of childhood recalled, but many were *reenacted* before my eyes, which were very enlightening to her as to the strange manner in which she had developed. Whether this patient ever

recovered sufficiently to marry and be able to enjoy herself as a woman, I do not know, as the treatment was interrupted by external circumstances before it was completed. But I know that she recovered from much suffering and depression and took her place again in her family and society as a normal and reasonably happy person.

(Severn, 1933, p. 93)

On the basis of the discussions of the Ferenczi/Severn analysis in this volume (see Chapters 12–22), as well as Freud's self-analysis (Rachman, 2016c) and the analysis of the Wolf Man/Sergei Pankejeff (see Chapter 8), the necessity to examine the possibility of childhood sexual trauma has been stressed. In Freud's analysis of Ferenczi, there was no trauma analysis. Ferenczi complained that Freud did not delve deep enough to fully analyze him (Ferenczi, 1988). If the Freud/Ferenczi analysis was more thorough, Freud may have been able to discover that his analysand had indeed been the victim of sexual abuse as a child (see Chapter 12). But how could Freud analyze Ferenczi's actual childhood sexual abuse, when he could not analyze his own (Rachman, 2016c)? Freud acknowledged his childhood introduction to sexuality by a nursemaid in his letters to Wilheim Fleiss (Freud, 1954; Rachman, 2016b). But, his self-analysis never analyzed the implications of childhood seduction in the development of his personality and his theory building. If Freud's self-analysis had been more successful, he would have become aware that he was an incest survivor himself. Ferenczi was also unaware of his own childhood sexual trauma. But he had the benefit of his third analysis with Severn (the first with Freud, the second with Groddeck). Severn and Ferenczi's mutual analytic encounter produced a revelation when she helped him turn his negative countertransference reaction toward her into the discovery that the origin of his negative countertransference were his childhood seduction by a nursemaid (Rachman, 2016c). Severn described the necessity of confronting and reliving the childhood trauma:

> [Reliving the trauma] … is an important measure which was worked out between Ferenczi and myself in the course of my own long analysis with him – a development which enables the patient to re-live, as though it were *now*, the traumatic events of his past, aided by the dramatic participation of the analyst … . It is this feeling-quality which has to be recovered and experienced again, in order to bring first, conviction and, it is not really considered enough to recollect these events mentally, but the thing that made them harmful in the first place was, in every case, the *shock*, the psychic reaction to them. This is far more intense and injurious, especially in children, than has ever been realized. The emotion created was of a nature or degree that is incapable of assimilation by the person suffering it, and it is this feeling–quality which has to be recovered and experienced again, in order to bring first, conviction and, secondly, release, through reconstruction.

(Severn, 1933, pp. 93–94)

Severn was presenting a vision for a new analytic perspective, which included a more personal, engaged, and human way of being for the analyst:

> How much sympathy and tact and up-building do these damaged psyches require! To deal in the delicate tissues, which have been stretched and distorted and torn, requires not only a special faculty of identification with the suffer, but a plastic technique capable of galvanizing them into new life and reality. It was to do this that I devised a "Direct Method" for entrance into the unconscious, inducing a temporary trance state, etc., to induce recollection, [This addition to, or alteration in psycho-analytic technique has since been adapted by Ferenczi and is the basis of his so-called "Relaxation" principle (also see Chapters 18 and 22).]
>
> *(Severn, 1933, p. 33)*

Severn was more willing than Ferenczi to clarify and state her alternative to Freudian psychoanalysis, since she was not emotionally tied to Freud's approval as was her mentor:

> The accepted psychoanalytic mode of treatment, which is purely dissecting in nature and which places its reliance chiefly on the mental grasp or "reconstruction" the patient can gain of his past; and a method which having found the trauma or specific cause of the illness, does not scorn to "play mother" or be Good Samaritan to the injured one, which encourages the full reproduction of the emotions and felling-tone of the traumatic period of events *under different and better circumstances*. It takes above all an emotional capacity or "gift" on the part of the analyst, who unless he can do this, is not a true physician to the soul.
>
> *(Severn, p. 95)*

Severn's connection to psychoanalysis was also evident in her continued contact and interest with the Freuds and members of the psychoanalytic community. When Severn moved to London after terminating with Ferenczi, her relationship with Karen Horney was evident when Horney contacted her for help with her daughter, who was moving to London (Horney, 1936; see Image 17). Severn also made contact with a colleague, Bernard Glueck, MD, founder of the Stony Lodge Hospital in Ossining, New York in 1927. He was a prominent forensic psychiatrist and psychoanalyst who Severn contacted when she returned to New York City. In a letter from Europe that he sent to her in 1939, he was responsive to her desire to meet with him (Glueck, 1939). In another interesting letter from an author of a decorating book whom she contacted, she received the following response:

> I was very much interested to hear that you have become a psychoanalyst and possibly one of the reasons why you liked the book was because you

sensed in me that I too have been psychoanalyzed. I went a hour a day for three years to Dr. Smiley Blanton and became enormously interested in the whole subject.

(Draper, 1959)

In part of the artifacts of *The Elizabeth Severn Papers* (Rachman, 2016d), there are three materials which show Severn's continued interest in Freud's ideas and life. The first part of these materials is a letter written by Freud, on the request of a magazine editor, who had written to him to contribute a piece on the persecution of the Jews. Freud responded with a statement of how his life was damaged by the Nazi's persecution of the Jews (Freud, 1938). Severn also collected the notices from *The New York Times* and *The Herald Tribune* announcing the death of Sigmund Freud (Author Unknown, 1939a, 1939b). Also collected was a letter to the Editor, which discussed the controversy over Freud's resistance to leaving Vienna when the Nazis annexed Austria and the persecution of the Jews reached a crescendo. The writer of the comment, Robert Breuer, defended Freud, citing that he left Vienna promptly on June 4, 1938. Ferenczi had urged Freud to leave Austria in 1933, but Freud couldn't entertain leaving his homeland (Rachman, 1997a).

Tribute to Severn: establishment of the Elizabeth Severn Section of the Freud Archives, the Library of Congress

As I researched *The Elizabeth Severn Papers*, I became convinced that Severn's life, clinical career, relationship with Ferenczi, and her own contributions to psychotherapy and psychoanalysis was an unknown treasure. I was convinced that Severn's original negative reputation as an "evil genius" was unjustified. If the designation had any meaning, the "genius" part of the phrase might have been true. As this volume has attempted to demonstrate, Severn as a self-taught student of self-help therapy, psychotherapy, and psychoanalysis was able to develop a successful clinical practice as early as 1908, when Ferenczi first met Freud. She maintained a practice until her death in 1959. She was also able to publish three books during this clinical journey detailing her capacity to both conceptualize the therapeutic process as well as introduce clinical innovation (Severn, 1913, 1920, 1933).

Elizabeth Severn Archives

In 2012, I approached Leonard Bruno, the former Chief of the Scientific Manuscript Division, The Library of Congress, with the possibility of establishing an Elizabeth Severn Section of the Freud Archives. Dr. Bruno was very responsive to this proposal. As I looked over the journey I had taken since first discovering Ferenczi in 1976, I was very pleased to experience the positive response I had received from Nellie Thompson, PhD, the archivist and head of Special Collections at the New York Psychoanalytic Institute, when I asked her to help me store *The Severn Papers* at the New York Psychoanalytic Institute, as well as by her suggestion to contact

The Library of Congress for a permanent home for *The Elizabeth Severn Papers*. I had been accustomed to some form of a negative response from many colleagues regarding Ferenczi. Either they had never heard of him or had a negative story of some clinical acting out. Thompson and Bruno, both scholars outside the Ferenczi community, were open and positive about my interest in Ferenczi and Severn. This was a helpful change from the years I had spent defending Ferenczi to members of the traditional analytic community. It helped me believe that a Severn Archive would be established.

When I approached Len Bruno to establish The Elizabeth Severn Section at The Library of Congress, he said he would contact James Hutson, PhD, head of The Manuscript Division. The three of us had an initial meeting to develop the Severn Archives. In the Fall of 2013, Len Bruno retired from The Library of Congress. In our relationship, he had provided intelligence, enthusiasm, and affirmation and I was concerned that his retirement would jeopardize the establishment of the Severn Archive. As it turned out, there was no reason for concern. I was pleasantly surprised when I was able to continue my efforts at establishing a Severn Archive with James Hutson.

Jim Hutson assumed responsibility for the Severn project for The Library of Congress after Bruno's retirement. He was instrumental in establishing the Severn Section of the Freud Archive, as well as helping me plan and execute the Severn Symposium at The Library of Congress to celebrate the Archive. This symposium was conceived as a way to announce and celebrate the establishment of the Severn Section of the Freud Archives. Originally the symposium was planned to take place on Friday, October 3, 2013 (Rachman, 2014a), but because of the shutdown of the federal government in October 2013, the symposium was rescheduled for Friday, June 20, 2014.

The title presentation of the symposium was, "The 'Evil Genius' of psychoanalysis: Elizabeth Severn, Dr. Sándor Ferenczi's Partner in the Pioneering Study and Treatment of Trauma," delivered by Arnold William Rachman, PhD. The discussants were Lew Aron, PhD, the director of the Postdoctoral Program in Psychoanalysis at New York University, and Joseph D. Lichtenberg, MD, editor-in-chief, Psychoanalytic Inquiry. Aron was invited as a discussant as a leader of the Relational Perspective who had contributed importantly to the Ferenczi literature, as well as to establish Ferenczi's work as a foundation for the Relational Perspective. Lichtenberg, who is one of the leading scholars of the Psychology of the Self Perspective, has a personal interest in Ferenczi as a former analysand of the late Lewis Hill, MD (former Chief, Sheppard Pratt Clinic), who was analyzed by Ferenczi. Through his editorship of the journal *Psychoanalytic Inquiry* Lichtenberg has pioneered the integration of Ferenczi and Severn's work for consideration in the analytic community (Rachman, 1997b, 2014a, 2016d).

The Severn Symposium was well received, and the audience response was lively. There were meaningful exchanges between the speaker and discussants with the audience. This Library of Congress Symposium on the life, ideas, and contributions of Elizabeth Severn was, to my knowledge, the first such scholarly gathering. The video presentation is available from The Library of Congress Webcast (Rachman, 2014a). A shortened published version of the Library of Congress talk is available (Rachman, 2015a). The most comprehensive version of The Library of Congress talk, of course, is the development of the present book.

Donation of The Elizabeth Severn Papers to The Library of Congress

After researching The Elizabeth Severn Papers, the goal was to donate them to The Library of Congress. In the spring of 2008, the first part of the collection was donated to the Manuscript Division of The Library of Congress. At the present time, *The Severn Papers* are in the Severn Section of the Manuscript Collection, which consists of three containers, labeled #MSS85409, containing 1,050 items. The Severn Section is located as part of the Freud Archives in the Madison Building, The Library of Congress, 101 Independence Avenue, S.E., Washington, D.C. When both my research of Severn and the present volume are completed, the remaining Severn materials will be donated to The Library of Congress. When I had talked to Len Bruno about the issues of restrictions to access of The Severn Archive, I had been very aware of the controversies connected to the Freud archives during the period when Jeffrey M. Masson was secretary of the Freud Archives (Malcolm, 1984; see Chapter 7). I had also had contact with Peter Swales, the historian of the first 50 years of Freud's life, who was very frustrated in the unavailability of documents in the Freud Archives. The Masson and Swales issues left me with a clear conclusion: I wanted to create full and unfiltered access to the Severn Archives. Hopefully, this will advance research and advance the truth. Psychoanalysis has a history of suppressing the voice of dissidence through the practice of *Todschweigen* (see Chapter 7). Whatever one's judgment is about Masson's or Swales' motives or methods for criticizing Freud's behavior, their efforts can be seen as trying to lift the taboo in psychoanalysis of analyzing Freud's personal functioning. There is a double standard in traditional psychoanalysis that allows personal condemnation of a dissenting voice, like Ferenczi and Severn (see Chapters 6 and 7). But, when attempts are made to unearth previously unknown or unexplored aspects of Freud's personal functioning they are met with silence or severe criticisms: Masson (1984), criticizing Freud for rejecting Ferenczi for maintaining interest in the seduction theory over the Oedipal complex; Roazen (1975), for establishing in print that Freud analyzed his daughter, Anna; and Peter Swales' (1982) assumption that Freud had a sexual affair with his sister-in-law, Minna Bernays. With these considerations in mind I donated the *Severn Papers* with a stipulation that these materials would be made available as soon as processed *and there would be absolutely no restrictions on the use of the materials*. By the time the Severn Symposium occurred, two analysts who attended the meeting told me that they had researched the Severn Archives prior to the Symposium.

Donation of The Elizabeth Severn Papers to the Sándor Ferenczi Archives, Budapest, Hungary

I had made a duplicate copy of many of the materials in *The Severn Papers* to use in my own research to write the present volume. As I was near to finishing writing the book, I realized that the Severn materials belong at the Ferenczi House, Budapest, Hungary. Judit Mészáros, PhD, the president of the Sándor Ferenczi Society, with the help of Carlo Bonomi, PhD, president of the Associazione Culturale Sándor Ferenczi, Italy, purchased Ferenczi's Villa, located at Budapest, I. ker. Lisznyai utca 11.I.em.4. The apartment of the Villa was the location where Ferenczi saw Severn as an analysand, and wrote two of Ferenczi's most significant works, the Confusion of Tongues paper and *The Clinical Diary*.

The Ferenczi Archives have been established as part of the Ferenczi House/ International Ferenczi Center and Archives, Budapest, Hungary. At the International Sándor Ferenczi Congress in 2010, held in Budapest, Hungary, Judit Mészáros announced that the duplicate copy of *The Elizabeth Severn Papers*, already donated to The Library of Congress, will be sent to the Ferenczi Archives of The Ferenczi House. The donation of the *Severn Papers* was formalized in late 2016. With the donations of the *Severn Papers* to The Library of Congress and the Ferenczi Archives it is hoped that the Ferenczi Community and the larger analytic community will be stimulated to research, understand, and help dissolve the *Todschweigen* process that has silenced the voices of Ferenczi and Severn.

REFERENCES

Abegg, M.P.F. and Urich, E. (2002). *The Dead Sea Scrolls Bible: The oldest known Bible translated for the first time into English*. San Francisco, CA: Harper.

Abraham, K. (1926). Psychoanalytical notes on Coué's method of self-mastery. *International Journal of Psychoanalysis*. 7:2, 190–213.

Adler, E., De Costa, L., Rachman A.W., and Tylin, I. (2013). The Freud/Ferenczi correspondence: a narrative reading. *The Insitute of the Postgraduate Psychoanalytic Society*. November 15, New York City.

Aichorn, A. (1935). *Wayward Youth*. New York: Viking Press.

Alexander, F. and French, T.M. (1980). *Psychoanalytic therapy principle and appreciation*: Nebraska: University of Nebraska Press.

Anonymous (1991). A Ferenczi image.

Aron, L. (1990). One-person and two-person psychologies and the method of psychoanalysis. *Psychoanalytic Psychology* 7: 475–485.

Aron, L. (1992). From Ferenczi to Searles and contemporary relational approaches. *Psychoanalytic Dialogues* 2: 181–190.

Aron, L. and Harris, A. (Eds.) (1993). *The legacy of Sándor Ferenczi*. Hillsdale, NJ: Analytic Press.

Aron, L. and Starr, K.E. (2016). Freud, Ferenczi and the case of Schreber: A mutual enactment of homoerotic longings, homophobia, and internalized anti-semitism. In. A.W. Rachman (Ed.) (2016a). *The Budapest School of Psychoanalysis*. London: Routledge.

(Author Unknown) (1935). A sane asylum. *Fortune Magazine*, p. 124. In A.W. Rachman (Ed.) (2016d). *The acquisition, restoration and donation of The Elizabeth Severn Papers* (Unpublished).

(Author Unknown) (1939a). Dr. Sigmund Freud dies in exile at 83. *The New York Times*. Sunday, September 24. In A.W. Rachman (Ed.) (2016d). *The acquisition, restoration and donation of The Elizabeth Severn Papers* (Unpublished).

(Author Unknown) (1939b). Freud. *Herald Tribune*. September 25. In A.W. Rachman (Ed.) (2016d). *The acquisition, restoration and donation of the Elizabeth Severn Papers* (Unpublished).

(Author Unknown) (1948). Freud to The Editor. *The New York Times*. June, pp. 2 and 4. In A.W. Rachman (Ed.) (2016d). *The acquisition, restoration and donation of the Elizabeth Severn Papers* (Unpublished).

Bacal, H. (2016). The Budapest School's Concept of Supervision: Michael Balint's legacy to the development of psychoanalytic specificity theory. In. A.W. Rachman (Ed.) (2016a). *The Budapest School of Psychoanalysis: the origins of a two-person psychology and empathic perspective*. London: Routledge.

Bacal, H.A. and Carlton, L. (2010). Kohut's last words on analytic cure and how we hear them now – a view from specificity theory. *International Journal of Psychoanalytic Self Psychology* 5: 132–143.

Bacon, K. and Gedo, J.E. (1993). Ferenczi's contributions to psychoanalysis. In L. Aron and A. Harris (Eds.) (1993). *The legacy of Sándor Ferenczi*. Hillsdale, NJ: Analytic Press, pp. 121–139.

Balint, M. (1969a). Draft Introduction. In. J. Dupont (Ed.) (1988). *The Clinical Diary of Sándor Ferenczi*, Cambridge, MA: Harvard University Press, pp. 219–220.

Balint, M. (1969b). Notes to preface by Michael Balint. In. J. Dupont (Ed.) (1988). *The Clinical Diary of Sándor Ferenczi*. Cambridge, MA.: Harvard University Press, pp. 221–222.

Balint, M. (1992/1968). *The basic fault: therapeutic aspects of regression*. Evanston, IL: Northwestern University Press. Paperback Edition (Original edition published in 1968, London, Tavistock).

Balint, A. and Balint, M. (1939) On transference and countertransference. *International Journal of Psychoanalysis* 20: 223–230.

Basch, M.F. (1984). The self–object theory of motivation and the history of psychoanalysis. In. P.F. Stepansky and A. Goldberg (Eds.) (1984). *Kohut's legacy contributions to self psychology*. Hillsdale, NJ: Analytic Press, pp. 3–17.

Basch, M. (1995). *Doing brief psychotherapy*. New York: Basic Books.

Batten, S.V. (2002). Written disclosure on a therapeutic tool. In. L. Vande Creek and T.L. Jackson (Eds.) *Innovations in clinical practice: a source book*, Vol. 20. Sarasota, FL: Professional Resource Press, pp. 257–268.

Beebe, B. (2014). My journey in infant research and psychoanalysis: micro-analysis, a social microscope. *Psychoanalytic Psychology* 31:1, 4–25.

Berger, L. (2009). *A dream of undying fame: how Freud betrayed his mentor and invented psychoanalysis*. New York: Basic Books.

Bergmann, M.S. and Hartman, F.R. (Eds.) (1976). *The evolution of psychoanalytic technique*. New York: Basic Books.

Berrios, G.E. (1982). Tactile hallucinations: conceptual and historical aspects. *Journal of Neurology Neurosurgery & Psychiatry* 45: 285–293.

Bertin, C. (1992). *Marie Bonaparte: A Life*. New Haven, CT: Yale University Press.

Black, D. (1979). Lie down in darkness. *New York Magazine* 12: 48–60.

Binswanger, L. (1975). *Being-in-the-world: selected papers of Ludwig Binswager* (Trans. J. Neddleman). New York: Souvenir Press.

Bjoroy, A., Madigan, S. and Nylund, D. (2015). The practice of therapeutic letter writing in narrative therapy. In B. Douglas, R. Woolfe, S. Strawbridge, E. Kasel, and V. Galbraith (Eds.). *Handbook of Counseling psychology*. 4th Edition. London: Sage Publications.

Blos, P. (1962). *On adolescence: a psychoanalytic interpretation*. New York: The Free Press.

Blum, H. (2013). On the request to lift the restriction on the Eissler/Severn Interview (1952) by Arnold Wm. Rachman. Email.

Bodenheimer, D.A. (2010). A multi-paper examination of non-erotic love within the psychotherapeutic dyad: Doctorate in Social Work (DSW). *Dissertation*, Paper 5, Cherishing love.

Boerstler, R.W. and Kornfeld, H.S. (1995). *Body, mind and spirit*.

Bollas, C. (1987). *The shadow of the object: psychoanalysis of the unthought known*. New York: Columbia University Press.

Boss, M. (1993). *Psychoanalysis and Dasein analysis* (trans. L.E. Lefebre). New York: Basic Books.

Bowlby, J.C. (1988). *A secure base: clinical applications of attachment theory*. London: Routledge.

Boyer, L.B. and Giovacchini, P.L. (1967). *Psychoanalytic treatment of characterological and schizophrenic disorders*. New York: Science House.

Brabant, E., Falzeder, E. and Giampieri-Deutsch, C. (Eds.) (1993). *The correspondence of Sigmund Freud and Sándor Ferenczi, Vl I, 1908–1914*. Cambridge, MA: Harvard University Press.

Brande, I. (1972). *Sándor Ferenczi*. Paris: Payot.

Brennan, B.A. (1988). *Hands of Light: a guide to healing through the human energy field*. New York: Bantam Books.

Brennan, W.B. (2009). Ferenczi's forgotten messenger: the life and work of Izette De Forest. *American Imago*. 06:4, 427–455.

Brennan, W.B. (2009). Personal communication – Providence, Rhode Island, February 20.

Brenner, J.D. (2006). Traumatic stress: effects on the brain. *Dialogues in Clinical Neuroscience* 8:4, 445–46.

Bressler, J. and Starr, K. (2015). *Relational psychoanalysis and psychotherapy, integration and evolving synergy*. London: Routledge.

Breuer, J. (1955) Franklin, Anna O. In S. Freud. (Ed.) (1955). *Standard Edition*: 2 (J. Strachey Ed.). London: Hogarth Press.

Breuer, J. and Freud, S. (1895). *Studies on hysteria. Standard Edition* (Trans. J. Strachey) (in collaboration with Anna Freud). New York: Basic Books, 2000.

Briggs, K. (1976). *An encyclopedia of fairies, hobgoblins, brownies, bogies and other supernatural creatures "Changelings"*. New York: Pantheon Books.

Brooks, C.H. (2015). *The practice of autho-suggestion by the method of Emile Coué*. Cambridge, MA: Patalon Press.

Brunswick, R.M. (1928). A supplement to Freud's "History of an infantile neurosis." In M. Gardiner (Ed.) (1971) *The Wolf-Man by the Wolf-Man*. New York: Basic Books, pp. 263–307.

Brunton, P. (1952). *Spiritual crisis of man*. London: Rider.

Bugenthal, J. (1964). The third force in psychology. *Journal of Humanistic Psychology* 4:1, 19–26.

Burnet, E.M. (1952). Recovery from a long neurosis. *Psychiatry* 15(2).

Butler, W.E. (1998). *How to reach the aura and practice psychometry, telepathy, and clairvoyance*. New York: Destiny Books.

Carlson, S. (1985). A double-blind test of astrology. *Nature* 318: 419–425.

Carter, P. (2015). Big bands drumming and the Whiplash backlash *Jazzwise Magazine*. February 5.

Casement, P. (1985). *On learning from the patient*. London: Routledge.

Cates, P. (1955). Letter to Elizabeth Severn. January 12. In A.W. Rachman (Ed.) (2016d). *The acquisition, restoration and donation of The Elizabeth Severn Papers* (Unpublished).

Charney, D.S. (2004). Psycho-biological mechanism of resilience and vulnerability: implications for successful adaptation to extreme stress. *American Journal of Psychiatry* 161: 2, 195–216.

Choder-Goldman, J. (2015). Trauma and the "Confusion of Tongues" in supervision: interview with Arnold Rachman, PhD. *Psychoanalytic Perspectives* 12:2, 136–142.

Clark, R.W. (1980). *Freud: the man and the cause*. New York: Random House.

Clark, R.W. (1980). Sigmund Freud's sortie to America. *American Heritage*. April/May, pp. 34–43.

Coltera, J.T. and Ross, N. (1967). Freud's psychoanalytic techniques: from the beginning to 1923. In B.B. Wolman (Ed.) (1967) *Psychoanalytic techniques*. New York: Basic Books.

Covello, A. (1984). Lettres de Freud: du scenario de Jones au diagnostic sur Ferenczi. *Confrontation.*

Coué, E. (2006). *Self-mastery through conscious auto-suggestion.* Whitefish, MT: Kessinger Publishing (Originally published in 1922).

Dallam, S.J. (2001). Crisis or creation? A systematic examination of False Memory Syndrome. *Journal of Child Sexual Abuse* 9:34, 9–36.

De Carvalho (1999). Otto Rank. *History of Psychology* 2:2, 132–148.

De Forest, I. (1942). The therapeutic technique of Sándor Ferenczi. *International Journal of Psycho-Analysis* 23:1: 121–139.

De Forest, I. (1954). *The leaven of love: a development of the psychoanalytic theory and technique of Sándor Ferenczi.* New York: Harper & Row.

Dietrich, D.W. and Dietrich, S.P. (Eds.) (1989). *Self Psychology: comparison and contrast.* Hillsdale, NJ: Analytic Press.

Donn, L. (1989). *Freud and Jung: years of friendship, years of loss.* New York: Charles Schibner's Sons.

Draper, D. (1959). Letter from Dorothy Draper to Mrs. Severn, July 31, 115 East 86th Street, New York, NY. In A.W. Rachman (Ed.) (2016b). *The acquisition, restoration and donation of The Elizabeth Severn Papers* (Unpublished).

Drob, S. (1989). Freud and chasidim: redeeming the Jewish soul of psychoanalysis. *The Jewish Review* 3:1, 1–8.

Dufrense, T. (1997). *Freud under analysis: history, theory practice.* Northvale, NJ: Jason Aronson.

Dufrense, T. (2007). Psychoanalysis eats its own: or, the heretical Saint Roazen. *Psychoanalysis and History* 9:1, 93–109.

Dupont, J. (Ed.) (1982a). *Ferenczi/Groddeck Correspondence, (1921–1933).* Paris: Payot.

Dupont, J. (1982b). Letter from J. Dupont to J. M. Masson, November 29. In A.W. Rachman (Ed.) (2016d). *The acquisition, restoration and donation of The Elizabeth Severn Papers* (Unpublished).

Dupont, J. (1984). Entre Freud et Ferenczi: Groddeck. *Confrontation* 12: 33–42.

Dupont, J. (1988). Introduction. In J. Dupont (Ed.). *The Clinical Diary of Sándor Ferenczi.* Cambridge, MA: Harvard University Press.

Ebert, R. (1967). Reflections in a golden eye. *Movie review.* October 7. Roger Ebert.com.

Edwards, I.E.S. (1976). *Treasures of Tutankamun.* New York: Metropolitan Museum of Art.

Eissler, K. (1952). Interview with Dr. Elizabeth Severn, December 20, 1952. Container 121. Sigmund Freud Papers, Sigmund Freud Collection, Manuscript Division, Library of Congress, Washington, DC.

Eissler, K.R. (1953). The effect of the structure of the ego on psychoanalytic technique. *Journal of the American Psycho-Analytic Association* 1: 104–143.

Eissler, K. R. (1965). *Medical Orthodoxy and the future of psychoanalysis.* New York: International Universities Press.

Eissler, K.R. (1971). *Talent and genius: Tausk contra Freud.* New York: Quadrangle Books.

Eissler, K.R. (1983). *Victor Tausk's suicide.* Madison, CT: International Universities Press.

Eissler, K.R. (1985). Notice of information about Elizabeth Severn. *The New York Review of Books.* June 13.

Eissler, K.R. (1990). Letter from Kurt Eissler, M.D. to Arnold Wm. Rachman, Ph.D. In A.W. Rachman (Ed.) (2016d). *The acquisition, restoration and donation of The Elizabeth Severn Papers* (Unpublished).

Elliman, C., Grand, S., Silvan, M., and Elliman, S. (2000). *The modern Freudians.* Northvale, NJ: Jason Aronson.

Ellis, M. (2004). *The coffee house: a cultural history.* London: Weidenfeld & Nicolson.

Erickson, E.H. (1950). *Childhood and society.* New York: W.W. Norton.

Falzeder, E. (2010). Sándor Ferenczi between orthoxy and heterodoxy. *American Imago* 66:4, 395–401.

Falzeder, E., Brabant, E., and Giampieri-Deutsch, P. (Eds.) (1996). *The correspondence of Sigmund Freud and Sándor Ferenczi, Vol II, 1914–1919*. Cambridge, MA: Harvard University Press.

Falzeder, E., Brabant, E. and Giampieri-Deutsch, P. (Eds.) (2000). *The correspondence of Sigmund Freud and Sándor Ferenczi, Vol III, 1920–1933*. Cambridge, MA: Harvard University Press.

Farber, M. (2006). *The foundation of phenomenology: Edmund Husserl and the quest for a rigorous science*. Albany, NY: State University of New York.

Fenichel, O. (1999). *The psychoanalytic theory of neurosis*. London: Routledge.

Ferenczi, S. (1902). *Homosexualitas feminine* (Female homosexuality). *Gyogydszat* 11: 167–168.

Ferenczi, S. (1927). Review of O. Rank's technique of psychoanalysis. *International Journal of Psycho-Analysis* 8: 93–100.

Ferenczi, S. (1934). Trauma in psychoanalysis. *Indian Journal of Psychology* 9: 29–38.

Ferenczi, S. (1950). *First contribution to the theory and technique of psychoanalysis, Vol I*. (E. Jones Ed.). London: Hogarth Press.

Ferenczi, S. (1952). *Further contribution to the theory and technique of psychoanalysis, Vol II*. (J. Rickman Ed.). London: Hogarth Press.

Ferenczi, S. (1955). *Final contributions to the theory and technique of psychoanalysis, Vol III*. (M. Balint Ed.). London: Hogarth Press.

Ferenczi, S. (1980a). On the technique of psycho-analysis In. J. Rickman (Ed.). *Further contributions to the theory and technique of psycho-analysis, Vol II*, pp. 177–189. New York: Bruner/Mazel (Original work published 1919).

Ferenczi, S. (1980b). The further development of the active therapy in psychoanalysis. In. J. Rickman (Ed.). *Further contribution to the theory and technique of psychoanalysis, Vol II*, pp. 198–217. New York. Bruner/Mazel (Original work published 1919).

Ferenczi, S. (1980c). Technical difficulties in the analysis of a case of hysteria including observations on larval forms of onanism and onanistic equivalents. In J. Rickman (Ed.). *Further contributions to the theory and technique of psycho-analysis, Vol II*, pp. 189–197. New York: Bruner/Mazel (Original work published 1919).

Ferenczi, S. (1980d). On influencing of the patient in psycho-analysis. In J. Rickman (Ed.). *Further contributions to the theory and technique of psycho-analysis*, Vol. 2, pp. 235–237. New York: Bruner/Mazel (Original work published 1919).

Ferenczi, S. (1980e). On forced phantasies: activity in the association technique. In J. Rickman (Ed.). *Further contributions to the theory and technique of psychoanalysis, Vol. II*, pp. 68–77. New York: Bruner/Mazel (Original work published 1924).

Ferenczi, S. (1980f). Contributions to the "active" psycho-analytic technique. In J. Rickman (Ed.). *Further contributions to the theory and technique of psycho–analysis, Vol. II*, pp. 217–230. New York: Bruner/Mazel (Original work published 1925).

Ferenczi, S. (1980g). Psycho-analysis of sexual habits. In J. Rickman (Ed.). *Further contributions to the theory and technique of psycho-analysis, Vol. II*, pp. 257–297. New York: Bruner/Mazel (Original work published 1925).

Ferenczi, S. (1980h). The elasticity of psychoanalytic technique. In. M. Balint (Ed.). *Final contributions to the problems and methods of psychoanalysis, Vol. III*, pp. 87–102. New York: Bruner/Mazel (Original work published 1928).

Ferenczi, S. (1980i). The principle of relaxation and neocatharsis. In M. Balint (Ed.). *Final contributions to the problems and methods of, Vol. III*, pp. 108–125. New York: Bruner/Mazel (Original work published 1929).

Ferenczi, M. (1980j). Child analysis in the analysis of adults. In. M. Balint (Ed.). *Final contributions to the problems and methods of psychoanalysis, Vol III*, pp. 126–142. New York: Bruner/Mazel (Original work published 1931).

Ferenczi, S. (1980k). The Confusion of Tongues between adults and children: the language of tenderness and of passion. In. M. Balint (Ed.). *Final contributions to the problems and methods of psychoanalysis, Vol III*, pp. 156–157. New York: Bruner/Mazel (Original work published 1933).

Ferenczi, S. (1985). *Journal Clinique, Janvier – Octobre*. Paris: Payot.

Ferenczi, S. (1988). *The clinical diary of Sándor Ferenczi* (Ed. J. Dupont, trans. M. Balint and N.Z. Jackson). Cambridge, MA. Harvard University Press.

Ferenczi, S. and Rank, O. (1925), *The Development of psychoanalysis*. New York and Washington: Nervous and Mental Disease Publishing Company.

Ferenczi, S. and Groddeck, G. (1982). *Correspondence: 1921–1933* (Ed. J. Dupont). Paris: Payot.

Finkelhor, D, Hotaling, G., Lewis, I.A. and Smith, C. (1990). Sexual abuse in a national survey of adult men and women. *Prevelance, characteristics, and risk factors Child Abuse and Neglect* 14:1: 19 – 28.

Finnegan, P. (2013). Notes on Severn's indications of Multiple Personality Disorder as indicated in Ferenczi's *Clinical Diary (1988)*. November (Unpublished).

Fodor, N. (1961). Sándor Ferenczi's psychic adventures. *International Journal of Parapsychology* 3:13: 48–63.

Fortune, C. (1993). The case of "RN": Sándor Ferenczi's radical experiment in psychoanalysis. In. L. Aron and A. Harris (Eds.). *The legacy of Sándor Ferenczi*. Hillsdale, NJ Analytic Press., pp. 101–120.

Fortune, C. (1996). Mutual analysis: a logical outcome of Sándor Ferenczi's experiments in psychoanalysis. In P.L. Rudnytsky, A. Bokay, and P. Giampieri-Deutsch (Eds.). *Ferenczi's turn in psychoanalysis*. New York: New York University Press, pp. 170–186.

Fortune, C. (2015). Twarting the psychoanalytic detectives: Defending the Severn legacy *American Journal of Psychoanalysis* 75: 19–28.

French, T.M. and Fromm, E. (1986). *Dream interpretation: a new approach* Madison, Conn. International Universities Press.

Freud, A. (1938). Letter from Anna Freud to Elizabeth Severn. London, August 28. In A.W. Rachman (Ed.) (2016d). *Acquisition, restoration, and donation of The Elizabeth Severn Papers* (Unpublished).

Freud, S. (1918). From the history of an infantile neurosis. Reprinted in M. Gardiner (1971) (Ed.). *The Wolf-Man: the double story of Freud's most famous case*. New York: Basic Books, pp. 153–262.

Freud, S. (1933). Sándor Ferenczi: Obit. International Journal of Psycho-Analysis. 14:3: 297– 299.

Freud, S. (1938). A letter from Freud, November 17, 1938. *Time and Tide. A Supplement*, November 26, p. 1649.

Freud, S. (1953). *Fragment of an analysis of a case of hysteria*. Standard Edition Trans. J. Strachey) 7: 3–122 (Original work published 1905, 1901).

Freud, S. (1954). *The origins of psychoanalysis: Letters to Wilhelm Fliess, Drafts and Notes, 1887–1902*. New York: Basic Books.

Freud, S. (1955a). Notes upon a case of obsessional neurosis. In J. Strachey (Ed. and trans.). *Standard Edition, Vol X*, pp. 153–250. London: Hogarth Press (Original work published in 1909).

Freud, S. (1955b). From the history of infantile neurosis: In. J. Strachey (Ed. and trans.). *Standard Edition, Vol X11*, pp. 3–104. London: Hogarth (Original work published 1918).

Freud, S. (1955c). Lines of advance in psycho-analytic therapy. In. J. Strachey (Ed. and trans.). *Standard Edition, Vol. DVII*, pp. 157–168. London: Hogarth (Original work published [1918] 1919).

Freud, S. (1957).The future prospect of psychoanalytic therapy. In J. Strachey (Ed. and trans.). *Standard Edition, Vol. XI*, pp. 139–152. London: Hogarth (Original work published 1910).

Freud, S. (1958a). Psycho-analytic notes on an autobiographical account of a case of paranoia (dementia paranoid). In J. Strachey (trans.) *Standard Edition, Vol XII*, pp. 3–82. London: Hogarth (Originally published 1911).

Freud, S. (1958b). Observations on transference-love. In J. Strachey (ed. and trans.). *Standard Edition, Vol. XII*, pp. 159–171. London: Hogarth (Originally written (1915[1914]).

Freud, S. (1958d). Recommendations to physicians practicing psycho–analysis. In J. Strachey (Ed. and trans.) *Standard Edition, Vol XII*, pp. 109–129. London: Hogarth (Original work published 1912).

Freud, S. (1964). Sándor Ferenczi: Obit In. J. Strachey (Ed. and trans.) *Standard Edition, Vol XXII*, pp. 227–229. London: Hogarth (Original work published 1933).

Freud, S. (1971). From the history of an infantile neurosis. In. M. Gardiner (Ed.). *The Wolf-Man by the Wolf-Man*. New York: Basic Books, pp. 153–262. Reprinted in J. Strachey (Ed.). *The Standard edition of the complete psychological works of Sigmund Freud*, Vol. *XVII*, pp. 7–122. London: Hogarth (Original work published 1918).

Freud, S. (1990). *New introductory lectures on psychoanalysis*. New York: W.W. Norton. (Originally published 1933).

Freyd, J.J. (1996). *Betrayal trauma: the logic of forgetting childhood abuse*: Cambridge, MA: Harvard University Press.

Freyd, J.J. and Birrell, P.J. (2013). *Blind to betrayal: why we fool ourselves we aren't being fooled*. Somerset, NJ: Wiley.

Fromm, E. (1955). Love stood between him and Freud: Review of Izette De Forest *The leaven of love. New York Times*. August 7.

Fromm, E. (1956). *The art of loving*. New York: Harper & Row.

Fromm, E. (1959). *Sigmund Freud's mission*. New York: Harper & Row.

Gardner, M. (1971). *The Wolf-Man by The Wolf-Man*. New York: Basic Books pp. 153–262.

Gardner, M. (1993). *The healing revelations of Mary Baker Eddy*. New York: Prometheus Books.

Gay, P. (1988). *Freud: a life for our time*. New York: Norton.

Gedo, J. (1968). Noch eimnal de Gelehtre Saugling. *Psyche*. 22: 301–319.

Gedo, J. (1976). The wise baby reconsidered. In J.E. Gedo and G.H. Pollock (Eds.). *Freud: the fusion of science and humanism*. New York: International Universities Press, pp. 357–378.

Gedo, J. (1986). *Conceptual issues in psychoanalysis: essays in history and method*. Hillsdale, NJ: Analytic Press.

Gedo, J. (1988). Letter to Arnold Rachman, March, 15.

Gendlin, E. (1962). *The creation of meaning*. Evanston, Ill.: Northwestern University Press.

Ghent, E. (1990). Masochism, submission, surrender 1: masochism as a perversion of surrender. *Contemporary Psychoanalysis* 26: 108: 136.

Gilhooley, D. (2002). Misrepresentation and misleading in the case of Anna O. (Unpublished).

Glueck, B. (1939). Letter from Dr. Bernard Glueck to Dr. Elizabeth Severn. July 28 115 sent to 86th Street, New York City. In A.W. Rachman (Ed.) (2016d). *Acquistion, restoration, and donation of the Elizabeth Severn Papers*. (Unpublished).

Godwin, J. (2007). The Orphic mysteries. In J. Godwin (Ed.) *The golden thread*. Weathon, IL: Quest Books.

Goleman, D. (1988). Psychologists gain entry to institutes. Health Column. *The New York Times*. October 20.

Gottschalk, S. (2006). *Rolling away from the stone: Mary Baker Eddy's challenge to materialism*. Bloomington, IN: Indiana University Press.

Green, M.R. (Ed.) (1964). *Interpersonal psychoanalysis: papers of Clara M.* Thompson: New York: Basic Books.

Groddeck, G. (1928). *The book of the it.* New York: Nervous and Mental Diseases Publishing Company.

Groddeck, G. (1977). *The meaning of illness: selected psychoanalytic writings.* Madison, CT.: International Universities Press.

Grosskurth, P. (1991). *The secret ring: Freud's inner circle and the politics of psychoanalysis.* New York: Addison–Wesley.

Grotjahn, M. (1966). Georg Groddeck 1866–1934: The untamed analyst. In F. Alexander, S. Einstein and M. Grotjahn (Eds.). *Psychoanalytic pioneers.* New York: Basic Books, pp. 308–320.

Grubbich-Simitus, I. (1986). Six letters of Sigmund Freud and Sándor Ferenzi on the interrelationship of psycho–analytic theory and technique. *International Review of Psycho–analysis* 13: 259–277.

Guasto, G. (2015). Orpha l'Irriducibile vs. Thanatos l'Irrestible morte e sopravurvenza nei pensiero di Sándor Ferenczi. In F. Brogogno (Ed.). *Rieggere Ferenczi Oggi contibuti Italinai.* Roma: Berla, pp. 119–139.

Gutheil, T.G. and Gabbard, G.D. (1993). The concept of boundaries in clinical practice: theoretical and risk management dimension. *American Journal of Psychiatry* 150: 188–196.

Hale, N.G. (1971a). *James Jackson Putnam and psychoanalysis: letters between Putnam and Sigmund Frued, Ernest Jones, William James, Sándor Ferenczi and Morton Prince 1877–1917.* Cambridge, MA: Harvard University Press.

Hale, N.G. (1971b). *Freud and the Americans: the beginnings of psychoanalysis in the United States, 1876–1917.* New York: Oxford University Press.

Hampton, C. (2011). *A dangerous method.* Film. D. Oronenberg, Director. Recorded Picture Company Telefilm, Canada. Sony Pictures Classics.

Harris, A. and Kuchuck, S. (2015). *The legacy of Sándor Ferenczi: from ghost to ancestor.* London: Routledge.

Haynal, A. (1989). *Controversies in psychoanalytic method: from Freud and Ferenczi to Michael Balint.* New York: New York University Press.

Haynal, A. (2010). R.N. and the development of trauma *Plenary Presentation International Ferenczi Conference.* May 30 – June 4 Budapest, Hungary.

Haynal A. (2013). Personal communication. Email Monday, May 27, pp. 1–2.

Hermann, I. (1974). L'objectivité de diagnostique de Jones concernant la maladie de Ferenczi. *Revie Francaise de Psychoanalyse* 38:4.

Hickman, L. and Alexander, T. (1998). *The essential Dewey, Vols. 1 and 2.* Bloomington, Indiana, Indiana University Press.

Hidas, G. (1993). Flowing over–transference, countertransference, telepathy: subjective dimensions of the psychoanalytic relationship in Ferenczi's thinking. In L. Aron and A. Harris (Eds.) (1993). *The legacy of Sándor Ferenczi.* Hillsdale, NJ: Analytic Press.

Hoffman, M.T. (2010). *Toward mutual recognition: relational psychoanalysis and the Christian narrative.* London: Routledge.

Horney, K. (1936). Letter from Dr Karen Horney to Dr Elizabeth Severn, May 26, 26 Old Broad Street, London, E.C., England. In A.W. Rachman (Ed.) (2016d). *The acquisition, restoration and donation of the Elizabeth Severn Papers* (Unpublished).

Husserl, E. (1962). *Edmund Husserl, ideas: general introduction to pure phenomenology* (Trans. W.R. Boyce Gibson). New York: MacMillan.

Hutson, J. (2013). Response to Arnold Rachman requesting declassification of the 1952 Eissler/Severn interview. Email. In A.W. Rachman (Ed.) *The acquisition restoration, and donation of the Elizabeth Severn Papers* (Unpublished).

Hutson, J. (2014). Freud archives, containers 112–126 – Eissler Interviews (loc.gov/rr/mss). Email to Arnold Rachman. Wednesday, July 30, 3:33 p.m.). In A.W. Rachman (Ed.) *The acquisition, restoration and donation of The Elizabeth Severn Papers* (Unpublished).

Jackson, C., Davidson, G., Russel, J., and Vanderlycken, W. (1990). Ellen West revisited: the theme of death in eating disorders. *International Journal of Eating, Disorders* 9:5, 529–538.

James, W. (1950). *Principles of psychology*. New York: Dover Publications (Originally published 1890).

Jones, E. (1953). *The life and work of Sigmund Freud. Vol I. The formative years and great discoveries.* New York: Basic Books.

Jones, E. (1955). *The life and work Sigmund Freud. Vol. II. Years of maturity, 1901–1919.* New York: Basic Books.

Jones, E. (1957). *The Life and work of Sigmund Freud. Vol. III. The last phase: 1919–1939.* New York: Basis Books.

Jung, C.G. (2010). *The Red Book.* New York: W.W. Norton & Co.

Kahn, R. (2013). Why Kraeplin was right: brain loss in schizophrenia is related to decline in IW. *International Congress in Schizophrenia Research.* April 21–25, Orlando, Florida.

Kellerman, H. (2009). *Dictionary of Psychopathology.* New York: Columbia University Press.

Kellerman, H. (2013). Personal communication. Email Monday, May 26, 1–3.

Kellerman, H. (2014). Discussion. The evil genius of psychoanalysis: Elizabeth Severn. Invited presentation. Library of Congress, Washington, DC. June 20.

Kerr, J. (1993). *A most dangerous method.* New York: Random House.

Khan, M. (1958). Introduction In D.W. Winnicott (Ed.). *Through pediatrics to psychoanalysis.* New York: Basic Books.

Kohut, H. (1971). *The analysis of the self: a systematic approach to the psychoanalytic treatment of narcissistic personality disorders.* New York: International Universities Press.

Kohut, H. (1977a). *The disorders of the self.* London: Karnac Books.

Kohut, H. (1977b). *The restoration of the self.* New York: International Universities Press.

Kohut, H. (1978). Introspection, empathy, and psychoanalysis: an examination of the relationship between mode of observation and therapy. In P.H. Ornstein (Ed.). *The search for the self.* New York: International Universities Press.

Kohut, J. (1984). *How does psychoanalysis cure?* (A Goldberg and P.E. Stepansky Eds.). Chicago, IL: The University of Chicago Press.

Kreiger, D. (1993). *Accepting your power to heal: the personal practice of therapeutic touch.* Santa Fe, NM: Bear & Company.

Krüll, M. (1986). *Freud and his father.* New York: Norton.

Lamm, M. (2000). *Mourning observances of Shiva and Shoshun.* Middle Village, NY: Jonathan David Publishers.

Langs, R. (1973). *The technique of psychoanalytic psychotherapy, Vol. 1.* New York: Jason Aronson.

Langs, R. (1974). *The technique of psychoanalytic psychotherapy, Vol. 2.* New York: Jason Aronson.

Laplance, J. and Pontalis, B. (1973). *The language of psychoanalysis.* New York: W.W. Norton and Company.

Larviére, M. (2016). From Lacan to Ferenczi. In. A.W. Rachman (Ed.) (2016a). *The Budapest School of psychoanalysis: the origin of a two–person psychology and empathic perspective.* London: Routledge, pp. 58–82.

Launer, J. (2005). Anna O. and the "talking cure." *Oxford Journal of Medicine* 98:b: 465–466.

Launer, J. (2014). *Sex versus survival: the life and ideas of Sabrina Spielrein.* London: Bloomsbury Publishing.

Lewandowski; K.E. (2009). Tactile, olfactory, and gustatory hallucinations in psychotic disorders: a descriptive study. *Annual Academy Medicine* 38:5: 383–385.

Lichtenberg, J. (2016a). Memories of sexual abuse of Elizabeth Severn. Telephone conversation. February 27.

Lichtenberg, J. (2016b). Introduction In A.W. Rachman (Ed.) (2016a). *The Budapest School of Psychoanalysis*. London: Routledge.

Lichtenberg, J. (2016c). *Narrative and resilience*. London: Routledge.

Lieberman, M.A., Miles, M.B., and Yalom, I.D. (1973) *Encounter groups: first facts*. New York: Basic Books.

Lilly, J.C. and Gold, E.J. (2000). *Thanks for the memories: flotation tank talks*. New York: Gateway Books.

Lindgren, C.E. (2000). *Capturing the aura: integrating science technology and metaphysics*. Nevada City, CA: Blue Dolphin Publications.

Lipskis, P. (1980). *Dance masks, the world of Margaret Severn*. Film. Berkeley, CA: University of California, Extension Media Center.

Lipskis, P. (1992). *Portrait of an artist as a young woman*. Documentary film.

Lipskis, P. (1993). Internationally–acclaimed dancer to reappear in Vancover. Press release. Great Productions, Vancouver, B.C., Canada. In A.W. Rachman (Ed.) (2016d). *The acquisition, restoration and donation of the Elizabeth Severn Papers* (Unpublished).

Lipskis, P. (2010). Margaret Severn's spotlight: Personal communication.

Lipskis, P. (2011). Interview about Elizabeth Severn. Vancouver, B.C., Canada In. A.W. Rachman (Ed.) (2016d). *The acquisition, restoration and donation of The Elizabeth Severn Papers* (Unpublished).

Lipskis, P. (2015a). Elizabeth Severn's mother. Recollections by Margaret Severn. Email June 5. In A.W. Rachman (Ed.) (2016d). *The acquisition, restoration and donation of The Elizabeth Severn Papers* (Unpublished).

Lipskis, P. (2015b). Margaret and Elizabeth Severn. Email September 9. In A.W. Rachman (Ed.) (2016d). *The acquisition, restoration and donation of The Elizabeth Severn Papers* (Unpublished).

Lipskis, P. (2015c) E.S. and Leon Dabo. Email. September 25, 13:14. In. A.W. Rachman (Ed.) *The acquisition, restoration and donation of the Elizabeth Severn Papers* (Unpublished).

Lipskis, P. (2016a). Margaret's analysis. Email January 27th. In A.W. Rachman (Ed.) (2016d). *The acquisition of The Elizabeth Severn Papers* (Unpublished).

Lipskis, P. (2016b). C. Fortune's paper on M. Severn. Email. Saturday, February 6. In. A.W. Rachman (Ed.) (2016d). *The acquisition, restoration and donation of The Elizabeth Severn Papers* (Unpublished).

Little, M. (1951). Countertransference and the patient's response to it. *International Journal of Psycho–Analysis* 32: 32–40.

Loftus, E.F. (1993). The reality of repressed memories. *American Psychologist* 48: 518–537.

Logue, M. and Conradi, P. (2010). *The king's speech: how one man saved the British monarchy*. London: Quercus.

Lorand, S. (1946). *The technique of psychoanalysis*. New York: International Universities Press.

Lorand, S. (1966). Sándor Ferenczi, 1873–1933: pioneer of pioneers. In. F. Alexander, S. Eisenstein, and M. Grotjohn (Eds.). *Psychoanalytic pioneers*. New York: Basic Books.

Lorin, C. (1983). *Le jeune Ferenczi: premiers ecrits: 1899–1906*. Paris: Aubier – Montaigne.

Lorin, C. (1997). Discovering the young Ferenczi. In A.W. Rachman (Ed.) (1997b). *The clinical and theoretical contributions of Sándor Ferenczi. Psychoanalytic Inquiry* 17:4.

Lothane, Z. (2003). Tender love and transference: unpublished letters of C.G. Jung and Sabina Spielrein. In C. Covington and C. Wharton (Eds.). *Sabina Spielrein: forgotten pioneer of psychoanalysis*. Hove, London: Brunner–Routledge.

Lothane, Z. (2010). Sándor Ferenczi: the dramatologist of love. *Psychoanalytic Perspective* 7:1, 165–182.

Luckas, J. (1990). *Budapest 1900: a historical portrait of a city and its culture*. New York: Grove Press.

Lysova, M. (2007). Margaret and Elizabeth Severn. Telephone interview, December 7, 10. In A.W. Rachman (Ed.) (2016d). *The acquisition, restoration and donation of The Elizabeth Severn Papers* (Unpublished).

McGrath, W.J. (1991). How Jewish was Freud? *The New York Review of Books*. December 5.

McGrum, W.I. (1946). Letter from W.I. Grum to Elizabeth Severn. Birmingham, England, May 25, 1946. In A.W. Rachman (Ed.) (2016d). *The acquisition, restoration and donation of the Elizabeth Severn Papers* (Unpublished).

McGuire, W. (Ed.) (1974). *The Freud–Jung letters* (Trans. R. Manheim & R.F.C. Hall). Princeton: Princeton University Press.

Macmillan, M. (1991). *Freud evaluated*. New York: Elsever.

Magee, G.A. (2016). *The Cambridge handbook of Western mysticism and esotericism*. Cambridge: Cambridge University Press.

Mahler, S., Pine, M.M. and Bergman, A. (1973). *The psychoanalytical birth of the human infant*. New York: Basic Books.

Mahoney, P.L. (1986). *Freud and the Rat Man*. New Haven, CT: Yale University Press.

Makari, G. (2008). *Revolution in minds: the creation of psychoanalysis*. New York: Harper Perennial.

Malcolm, J. (1981). *Psychoanalysis: the impossible profession*. New York: Alfred A. Knopf.

Malcolm, J. (1984). *In the Freud archives*. New York: Knopf.

Malcolm, J. (2000). The lives they lived: Kurt Eissler, b. 1908; keeper of Freud's secrets. *The New York Times*, January 2.

Mann, T. (1969). *Magic mountain*. (trans. H.T. Lowe–Porter). New York: Vintage Books [also quoted in Kennedy, R. (1995). Zen spirit, Christian spirit. New York: Continium].

Maroda, K. (1992). *The power of countertransference*. New York: John Wiley & Sons.

Maroda, K. (1998). Why mutual analysis failed: The case of Ferenczi and R.N. *Contemporary Psychoanalysis* 34:1: 115–132.

Maselko, J., Kubzansky, L., Lipsett, L., and Buks, S.L. (2010). Mother's affection at 8 months predicts emotional distress in adulthood. *Journal Epidemiology and Community Health*.

Maslow, A. (1962). *Toward a psychology of being*. New York: Van Nostrand.

Masson, J.M. (1984). *The assault on truth: Freud's suppression of the seduction theory*. New York: Farrar, Straus and Giroux.

Masson, J.M. (1986). Letter to Margaret Severn from J.M. Masson May 27. In A.W. Rachman (Ed.) (2016d). *The acquisition, restoration and donation of the Elizabeth Severn Papers* (Unpublished).

Masson, J.M. (1990). *Final analysis: the making and unmaking of a psychoanalyst*. Boston, MA: Addison Wesley.

Masson, J.M. (1993). *My father's guru: a journey through spirituality and disillusion*. New York: Addison–Wesley.

Masson, J. M. (2014). Discussion of Ferenczi and Severn. Email.

May, R. (1958). *Existence: A new dimension in psychiatry and psychology*.

Mead, G.H. (1934). *Mind, self and society*. Chicago, IL: University of Chicago Press.

Menaker, E. (1982). *The freedom to inquire: self–psychological perspectives on women's issues, masochism and the therapeutic relationship*. Northvale, NJ: Jason Aronson.

Menaker, E. (1989). *Appointment in Vienna*. New York: St. Martin's Press.

Menniger, K. (1958). *Theory of psychoanalytic technique*. New York: Basic Books.

Mészáros, J. (1993). Ferenczi's pre–analytic period embedded in the cultural streams of the Fin de Siécle. In L. Aron and Harris, A. (Ed.). *The legacy of Sándor Ferenczi*. Hillsdale, NJ: Analytic Press, pp. 41–51.

Mészáros, J. (2014). Ferenczi's "wise baby" phenomenon and resilience. *International Forum of Psychoanalysis* 23:1, 3–10.

Mészáros, J. (2016). The Ferenczi House as a space for identity formation. In A.W. Rachman (Ed.) (2016a). *The Budapest school of psychoanalysis*. London: Routledge.

Mihacy, I. (1993). *My reminiscences of Sándor Ferenczi: Presentation*. William Alanson White Institute March, New York City.

Miles, G. (1999). *Classical mythology in English literature: a critical anthology*. London: Routledge.

Miller, D. (2005). *Women who hurt themselves: a book of understanding and hope*. New York: Basic Books.

Miller, J.P. (1985). How Kohut worked. *Progress in Self Psychology* 1: 13–30.

Mills, J. (2012). *Conundrums: a critique of contemporary psychoanalysis*. New York: Routledge.

Minder, B. (2001). Sabina Spielrein, Jung's patient at the Burghölzi. *Journal of Analytical Psychology* 46: 43–66.

Mitchell, S.A. (1996). Introduction. Symposium on the "False Memory" controversy. *Psychoanalytic Dialogues* 6:1: 151–153.

Moore, P. (2005). Mysticism, further considerations. In. L. Jones, M. Eliade, and C.J. Adams (Eds.). *Encyclopedia of religion*. New York: MacMillan.

Murray, R. (2013). Schizophrenia does not show progressive clinical deterioration. *International Congress on Schizophrenia Research*. April 21–25, Orlando, Florida.

Narody, I. (1969). *Leon Dabo: American Artist*. Hanover, NH: Ayer Publishing (First published in 1930).

Newman, K. (1992). Abstinence, neutrality, gratifications: new trends, new climates, new implications. *The Annual of Psycho–analysis* 20:131–144. Hillsdale, NJ: Analytic Press.

Norton, D. (Ed.) (2005). *The New Cambridge Paragraph Bible with the Apocrpha*. Cambridge: Cambridge University Press.

Obholzer, K. (1982). *The Wolf Man: sixty years later: conversations with Freud's patient*. London: Routledge & Kegan Paul.

Orstein, P. (1992). Introduction. In M. Balint (Ed.) (1992/1968). *The basic fault. Evanston*, IL: North Western University Press. Paperback.

Owens, L.S. (2015). *Jung in love: the mysterium in liber novus*. Los Angeles, CA: Gnosis Archive Books.

Park, R.L. (2000). *Voodoo science: the road from foolishness to fraud*. New York: Oxford University Press.

Paskausas, R.A. (Ed.) (1993). *The complete correspondence of Sigmund Freud and Ernest Jones, 1908–1939*. Cambridge, MA: Harvard University Press.

Pearce, J. (2009). Paul Roazen, 69, scholar who found flaws in Freud, dies. Obituary: *The New York Times*. November 23.

Pennibaker, J.W., Kiecolt–Glaser, J.K., and Glaser, R. (1988). Disclosure of trauma and immune function: health implications for psychotherapy *Journal of Consulting and Clinical Psychology* 56:239–245.

Peterson, C., Maier, S.F., and Seligman, M.E.P. (1995). *Learned helplessness: a theory for the age of personal control*. New York: Oxford University Press.

Pfeifer, L. (1970). A subjective report of tactile hallucinations in schizophrenia. *Journal of Clinical Psychology* 26:1, 57–60.

Pigman, G.W. (1995). Freud and the history of empathy. *International Journal of Psycho–Analysis* 76: 237.

Putnam, J.J. (1910). Personal impressions of Sigmund Freud: his work with special reference to the recent lectures at Clark University. *The Journal of Abnormal Psychology* 46:6: 373–379.

Putnam, J.J. (1915). *Human motives*. Boston, MA: Little Brown and Co.

Putnam, R.A. (1999). *Cambridge Companion to William James*. Cambridge: Cambridge University Press.

Rachman, A.W. (1967). *A life-saving fantasy* (Unpublished).

Rachman, A.W. (1975). *Identity group psychotherapy with adolescents*. Springfield, IL: Charles C. Thomas.

Rachman, A.W. (1977). Interviews with Dr. Sándor Lorand. New York City (Unpublished).

Rachman, A.W. (1978). The First Encounter Session: Ferenczi's Case of the Female Croation Musician. Presentation: American Group Psychotherapy Association Convention. New Orleans, LA. February.

Rachman, A.W. (1980). Positive termination: sudden, planned, bilateral or unilateral (Unpublished).

Rachman, A.W. (1981). Humanistic analysis in groups. *Psychotherapy: Theory, Research and Practice* 18:4: 457–477.

Rachman, A.W. (1988a). The rule of empathy: Sándor Ferenczi's pioneering contributions to the empathic method in psychoanalysis. *Journal American Academy of Psychoanalysis* 16:1, 1–27.

Rachman, A.W. (1988b). The rule of empathy: Sándor Ferenczi's pioneering contributions to the empathic method in psychoanalysis. *Paper Presentation*. American Association of Psychoanalysis Conference. New York City.

Rachman, A.W. (1989a). Ferenczi's contributions to the evolution of a Self Psychology framework in psychoanalysis. In. D.W. Detrick and S.P. Detrick (Eds.). *Self Psychology: Comparison and Contrast*. Hillsdale, NJ: Analytic Press, pp. 81–100.

Rachman, A.W. (1989b). Sándor Ferenczi: psychoanalysis' fallen angel (Unpublished).

Rachman, A.W. (1991). An analysand's "Aura of Ferenczi." Psychoanalytic session, November 15.

Rachman, A.W. (1993). Ferenczi and sexuality. In. L. Aron and S. Harris (Eds.). *The legacy of Sándor Ferenczi*. Hillsdale, NJ: Analytic Press, pp. 81–100.

Rachman, A.W. (1996). Countertransference analysis and the subjective experience of the analyst (Unpublished).

Rachman, A.W. (1997a). *Sándor Ferenczi: the psycho–therapist of tenderness and passion*. Northvale, NJ: Jason Aronson.

Rachman, A.W. (1997b). The suppression and censorship of Ferenczi's Confusion of Tongues Paper. In A.W. Rachman (Ed.) (1997). *Psychoanalysis' favorite son. The legacy of Sándor Ferenczi. Psychoanalytic Inquiry* 17:4, November.

Rachman, A.W. (1998). Ferenczi's "relaxation–principle" and the contemporary clinical practice of psychoanalysis. *American Journal of Psychoanalysis* 58:1, 63–81.

Rachman, A.W. (1999a). Death by silence (*Todschweigen*): the traditional method of dealing with dissidents in psychoanalysis. In R. Prince (Ed.). *The death of psychoanalysis: suicide, murder or rumor greatly exaggerated*. Northvale, NJ: Jason Aronson, pp. 154–164.

Rachman, A.W. (2000a). Ferenczi's Confusion of Tongues theory and the analysis of the incest trauma. *Psychoanalytic Social Work*. 7:1: 27–53.

Rachman, A.W. (2000b). Issues of power, control and status: from Ferenczi to Foucault. *Journal of Eastern Group Psychotherapy* 7:1: 121–144.

Rachman, A.W. (2003a). *Psychotherapy of difficult cases: flexibility and responsiveness in clinical practice*. Madison, CT: Psychosocial Press.

Rachman, A.W. (2003b). Freud's analysis of his daughter Anna: a Confusion of Tongues. In A. Roland B. Ulanov, and C. Babre (Eds.). *Creative dissent: psychoanalysis in evolution*. Westport, CT: Preager, pp. 59–71.

Rachman, A.W. (2003c). Bill of sale. The Elizabeth Severn Papers and the transfer of copyrights. Signed by Arnold W. Rachman and Peter Lipskis (Literary Executor, Margaret Severn Estate). In A.W. Rachman (Ed.) (2016d). *The acquisition, restoration and donation of the Elizabeth Severn Papers. A lost legacy of psychoanalysis* (Unpublished).

Rachman, A.W. (2004a). Beyond neutrality: the creative function of analyst self–disclosure in the psychoanalytic situation. In J. Reppen, M.A. Schulman, and J.Tucker (Eds.). *Way Beyond Freud: Postmodern psychoanalysis evaluated*. London: Open Gate Press.

Rachman, A.W. (2004b). A Confusion of Tongues in supervision (Unpublished).

Rachman, A.W. (2006). From phenomenology and humanistic psychotherapy to the Budapest School of Psychoanalysis to Relational Psychoanalysis. Invited Address. Postgraduate Psychoanalytic Society. New York City, December.

Rachman, A.W. (2007a). Sándor Ferenczi's contributions to the evolution of psychoanalysis. *Psychoanalytic Psychology* 24:1, 74–96.

Rachman, A.W. (2007b). The road to creative dissidents. Sándor Ferenczi's clinical journey and the evolution of psychoanalysis. Invited address, Postgraduate Psychoanalytic Society – Friday evening series, "Learning From Our Past," New York City.

Rachman, A.W. (2010a). An "in vitro" study of intersubjectivity: the analysis of Mrs Elizabeth Severn with Dr Sándor Ferenczi. *Presentation: International Forum of Psychoanalysis*. Athens, Greece.

Rachman, A.W. (2010b). The origins of a relational perspective in the ideas of Sándor Ferenczi and the Budapest School of Psychoanalysis. *Psychoanalytic Perspectives*. 7:1, 43–60.

Rachman, A.W. (2012a). The analysis of the incest trauma: From the Seduction Hypothesis to the Confusion of Tongues theory of trauma. Symposium. The Institute of the Postgraduate Psychoanalytic Society. The Hungarian House. New York City. Saturday, November 17.

Rachman, A.W. (2012b). The Confusion of Tongues between Sándor Ferenczi and Elizabeth Severn. Plenary Presentation. The International Sándor Ferenczi Conference, "Faces of Trauma." Budapest, Hungary, Saturday, June 3.

Rachman, A.W. (2012c). The relational dimension in psychoanalysis: from Ferenczi to Mitchell. *Presentation*. The Czech Psychoanalytic Society. Prague, The Czech Republic, Saturday, May 26.

Rachman, A.W. (2013). Arnold William Rachman's discussion with Professor Martin Bergmann. Freud/Ferenczi Narrative. Presentation. New York City. November 13.

Rachman, A.W. (2014a). The "evil genius" of psychoanalysis: Elizabeth Severn, Dr. Sándor Ferenczi's partner in the pioneering study of trauma, The Library of Congress, Washington, DC, June 2. Webcast–www.loc.gov.

Rachman, A.W. (2014b). Sándor Ferenczi's analysis with Elizabeth Severn: "Wild analysis" or pioneering treatment of the incest trauma. In A.W. Rachman (Ed.). *Sándor Ferenczi's contributions to the evolution of the theory and technique in psychoanalysis. Psychoanalytic Inquiry*, 34:2, March, pp. 145–168.

Rachman, A.W. (2014c). My personal analysis: a "tender mother experience" with Betty Feldman, MS, MSW (Unpublished).

Rachman, A.W. (2014d). Sándor Ferenczi as the bridge: my journey from phenomenology and humanistic psychotherapy to relational analysis. In A.W. Rachman (Ed.). *Sándor Ferenczi's contributions to the evolution of theory and technique in psychoanalysis. Psychoanalytic Inquiry* 34:2.

Rachman, A.W. (Ed.) (2014e). *Sándor Ferenczi and the evolution of psychoanalysis: innovations in theory and technique. Psychoanalytic Inquiry* 34:2. February – March.

Rachman, A.W. (2015a). Elizabeth Severn: Sándor Ferenczi's analysand and collaborator in the study and treatment of trauma. In A. Harris and S. Kuchuck (Eds.). *The legacy of Sándor Ferenczi: Vol II from Ghost to Ancestor*. London: Routledge, pp. 111–126.

Rachman, A.W. (2015b). Elizabeth Severn: from initiative, self–taught therapist, to psychoanalyst and Sándor Ferenczi's mutual analytic partner. Presentation. The Sándor Ferenczi Center at The New School of Social Research, NYC., September 19, 2015.

Rachman, A.W. (2015c). Co–creating the termination process in psychoanalysis (Unpublished).

Rachman, A.W. (Ed.) (2016a). *The Budapest School of Psychoanalysis: the Origin of a two-person psychology and empathic perspective* London: Routledge.

Rachman, A.W. (2016b). Psychoanalysis' neglect of the incest trauma: the Confusion of Tongues between psychoanalysis and society. In A.W. Rachman (Ed.) (2016a). *The Budapest School of Psychoanalysis*. London: Routledge, pp. 164–181.

Rachman, A.W. (2016c). Confusion of Tongues Trauma in child abduction: revising the Stockholm Syndrome. In A.W. Rachman (Ed.) (2016a). *The Budapest School of Psychoanalyst* London: Routledge, pp. 182–208.

Rachman, A.W. (2016d). *The acquisition, restoration and donation of the Elizabeth Severn Papers: A lost legacy of psychoanalysis* (Unpublished).

Rachman, A.W. (2016e). Elizabeth Severn's horoscope. In A.W. Rachman (Ed.) (2016d). *The acquisition, restoration and donation of The Elizabeth Severn Papers* (Unpublished).

Rachman, A.W. and Hutton, L. (2006). Clinical flexibility in psychoanalytic situation: "the elasticity principle." *Psychoanalytic Social Work* 13:1, 21–42.

Rachman, A.W., Kennedy, R. and Yard, M. (2005). Erotic transference and the relationship to childhood sexual seduction: perversion in the psychoanalytic situation. *International Forum of Psychoanalysis* 14:3/4: 183–187.

Rachman, A.W., Kennedy, R.E. and Yard, M.A. (2009). Erotic transference and its relationship to childhood seduction. *Psychoanalytic Social Work* 16: 12–30.

Rachman, A.W. and Klett, S. (2015). *Analysis of the incest trauma: retrieval, recovery and renewal*. London: Karnac.

Rachman, A.W. and Mattick, P. (2009). *Freud's Confusion of Tongues with Dora: the need for empathy not interpretation* (Unpublished manuscript).

Rachman, A.W. and Mattick, P. (2012). The Confusion of Tongues in the psychoanalytic relationship. *Psychoanal Social Work* 19:1–2, 167–190.

Rank, O. (1978). *Will therapy*. New York: W.W. Norton & Co. (Original publication 1936).

Rank, O. (1994). *The trauma of birth*. New York: Dover Publications. (Original publication 1924).

Rank, O. (1996). *A psychology of difference: the American Lectures, 1924–1938* (R. Kramer Ed.). Princeton: Princeton University Press.

Raso, R.C. (2005). Which way in psychoanalysis? The problem of suggestion in the postmodern world. Psychoanalytic Psychology 22: 382–394.

Rentoul, R.W. (2010). *Ferenczi's language of tenderness: working with disturbance from the earliest years*. New York: Jason Aronson.

Richards, A.D. (2010). *The Jewish world of Sigmund Freud: essays on cultural roots and the problem of religions*. Jefferson, NC: McFarland & Co.

Righter, J. (2015). My analysis with Elizabeth Severn. Presentation. Elizabeth Severn Symposium. The Sándor Ferenczi Center at the New School for Social Research, New York City. Saturday, September 20.

Roazen, P. (1969). *Brother animal: the story of Freud and Tausk*. New York: New York University Press.

Roazen, P. (1975). *Freud and his followers*. New York: Alfred A. Knopf.

Roazen, P. (1988). Personal communication. April.

Rochon, M. (1920). Letter from Mathilde Rochon to Elizabeth Severn. November 29, 1920. Washington, DC. In A.W. Rachman (Ed.) (2016d). *The acquisition, restoration and donation of the Elizabeth Severn Papers* (Unpublished).

Rogers, C.R. (1942). *Counseling and psychotherapy*. Boston, MA: Houghton Mifflin.

Rogers, C.R. (1951). *Client–centered therapy: its current practice, implications and theory.* Boston, MA: Houghton Mifflin.

Rogers, C.R. (1957). The necessary and sufficient conditions of therapeutic personality change. *Journal of Consulting Psychology* 21: 95–103.

Rogers, C.R. (1959). A theory of therapy, personality, and interpersonal relationships as developed in the client–centered framework. In S. Koch (Ed.). *Psychology: A study of science, Vol. 3*, New York: McGraw-Hill, pp. 184–256.

Rogers, C.R. (1961). *On becoming a person: a therapist's view of psychotherapy.* Boston, MA: Houghton Mifflin Co.

Rogers, C.R. (1967) *On becoming a person: a therapist's view of psychotherapy.* Boston: Houghton Mifflin.

Rogers, C.R. (1970). *Encounter groups.* New York: Harper & Row.

Rogers, C.R. (1975). Empathetic: an unappreciated way of being. *The Counselling Psychologist* 5:2, 2–10.

Rogers, C.R. (1980). *A way of being.* Boston, MA: Houghton Mufflin.

Rogers, C.R. (1986). Person-Centered Psychotherapy. Experiental workshop. American Psychological Association Conference, Philadelphia, PA.

Rosa, L., Rosa, E., Sarner, L. and Barrett, S. (1998). A close look at therapeutic touch. *Journal American Medical Association* 279:13: 1005–10.

Ross, A. (1967). *Pagan Celtic Britain* London: Routledge & Kegan Paul.

Rothenberg, A. and Hausman, C.R. (1976). *The creativity question*: Durham, NC: Duke University Press.

Rudnytsky, P.L. (2000). *Ferenczi's turn in psychoanalysis.* New York: New York University Press.

Rudnytsky, P.L. (2015). The other side of the story: Severn on Ferenczi and mutual analysis. In A. Harris and S. Kuchuck (Eds.). *The legacy of Sándor Ferenczi: from ghost to ancestor* London: Routledge, pp. 134–149.

Sauborin, P. (1984). *Ferenczi, Paladin et Grand Vizir Secret.* Paris: Editions Universities.

Saughnessey, E. (1918). Letters to Elizabeth Severn. October 2, December 11 and 18, 1918. In A.W. Rachman (Ed.) (2016d). *The acquisition, restoration and donation of the Elizabeth Severn Papers: A lost legacy of psychoanalysis* (Unpublished).

Schcoldann, J. (2011). On periodical depression and their pathogens by Carl Lange (1886). *History of psychiatry* 22: 108–130.

Schreber, D.P. (1955). *Memoirs of my nervous illness* (Trans. I. Macalpane and R.A. Hunter). New York: New York Review of Books.

Schutz, W.C. (1973). *Elements of encounter.* Big Sur, CA: Joy Press.

Scott, M. (1995). Party planned for dancer's dancer. *The Vancouver Sun.* Thursday, August 10th.

Searles, H. (1973). Concerning therapeutic symbiosis. *The Annual of Psychoanalysis* 1: 247–262. New York: International Universities Press.

Searles, H.F. (1979). *Countertransference and related subjects.* New York: International Universities Press.

See Saw Films (2010). *The King's Speech.* UK Film Council. Bedlam Productions. Released January 6, 2010, Telluride Film Festival.

Severn, E. (1913). *Psychotherapy: its doctrine and practice.* London: Rider.

Severn, E. (1916). "Dictated in a Subjective or Trance State." Friday morning, January 14. In A.W. Rachman (Ed.) (2016d). *The acquisition, restoration and donation of The Elizabeth Severn Papers: a lost legacy of psychoanalysis* (Unpublished).

Severn, E. (1920). *The psychology of behavior.* New York: Dodd, Mead and Company.

Severn, E. (1933). *The discovery of the self: A study in psychological cure.* London: Rider & Co.

Severn, E. (2013). *Elizabeth Severn Papers.* Library of Congress. Manuscript Division. ID No.: MSS85409, 3 containers.

Severn, M. (1916). Letter from Margaret to Elizabeth Severn. April 13. In. A.W. Rachman (Ed.) (2016d). *The acquisition, restoration and donation of the Elizabeth Severn Papers* (Unpublished).

Severn, M. (1923). Letter from Margaret Severn to Elizabeth Severn, September 20, Memphis, Tennessee. In A.W. Rachman (Ed.) (2016d). *The acquisition, restoration and donation of the Elizabeth Severn Papers* (Unpublished).

Severn, M. (1924). Letter from Margaret to Elizabeth Severn. January 30. Train to Denver, Colorado. In A.W. Rachman (Ed.) (2016d). *The acquisition, restoration and donation of the Elizabeth Severn Papers* (Unpublished).

Severn, M. (1932). Letter from Margaret Severn to Elizabeth Severn. December 1, Paris. In A.W. Rachman (Ed.) (2016d). *The acquisition, restoration and donation of the Elizabeth Severn Papers* (Unpublished).

Severn, M. (1933). Letter from Margaret Severn to Elizabeth Severn. January 21, Paris. In A.W. Rachman (Ed.) (2016d). *The acquisition, restoration and donation of the Elizabeth Severn Papers* (Unpublished).

Severn, M. (1937). Letter from Margaret to Elizabeth Severn. June 16, 1937, Czecholovakia. In A.W. Rachman (Ed.) (2016d). *The acquisition, restoration and donation of The Elizabeth Severn Papers* (Unpublished).

Severn, M. (1986). Letter from Margaret Severn to J.M. Masson, May 1. In A.W. Rachman (Ed.) (2016d). *The acquisition, restoration and donation of the Elizabeth Severn Papers* (Unpublished).

Severn, M. (1988). The letters between Margaret and Elizabeth Severn. The Dance Chronicle Papers, (5)*MGZMD156, Jerome Robbins Dance Division, The New York Library for the Performing Arts. 40 Lincoln Center Plaza, New York, New York 0023–7498.

Severn, M. (1989). *Spotlight: letters to my mother* (Unpublished). New York: The New York Library for The Performing Arts.

Severn, M. (not dated). Letter to Barbara Williams. Vancouver, B.C. In A.W. Rachman (Ed.) (2016d). *The acquisition, restoration and donation of the Elizabeth Severn Papers* (Unpublished).

Severn, M. (not dated). Letter from Margaret Severn to Barbara Williams. Vancouver, B.C., Canada. In A.W. Rachman (Ed.) (2016d). *The acquisition, restoration, and donation of the Elizabeth Severn Papers* (Unpublished).

Shapiro, S.A. (1993). Clara Thompson, Ferenczi's messenger with half a message. In L. Aron and A. Harris (1993). (Eds.). *The legacy of Sándor Ferenczi* Hillsdale, NJ: Analytic Press, pp. 167.

Smith, N.A. (1998). "Orpha reviving": toward an honorable recognition of Elizabeth Severn. *International Forum of Psychoanalysis* 7(4): 241–246.

Smith, N.A. (1999). From Oedipus to Orpha: revisiting Ferenczi and Severn's landmark case. *The American Journal of Psychoanalysis* 59: 345–366.

Smith, N.A. (2001). Angels in the architecture: Contemporary case of orphic functioning. *Journal of American Academy of Psychoanalysis* 29: 575–583.

Smyth, J.M. and Helen, R. (2003): Focused expressive writing as self–help for stress and trauma. *Journal of Clinical Psychology* 59: 227–235.

Snyder, H.N. (2000). *Sexual assault of young children as reported to law enforcement victim, incident and offender characteristics.* Bureau of Justice Statistics, July NCJ 182990.

Spence, D. (1982). *Narrative truth and historical truth.* New York: N.W. Norton & Co.

Stanton, M. (1991). *Sándor Ferenczi: reconsidering active intervention.* Northvale, NJ: Jason Aronson.

Stanton, A.L. and Danoff–Bury (2002). Emotional expressions, expressive writing, and cancer. In. S.J. Lepore and M. Sinyth (Eds.). *The writing cure: how expressive writing promotes health and emotional well-being.* Washington, DC: American Psychological Association, pp. 31–51.

Stewart, H. (1993). Clinical aspects of malignant regression. In L. Aron and A. Harris (Eds.). *The legacy of Sándor Ferenczi*. Hillsdale, NJ: Analytic Press, pp. 249–264.

Stolorow, R. (1976). Psychoanalytic reflections on client centered therapy in the light of modern conceptions of narcissism. *Psychotherapy: Theory, Research and Practice* 13: 26–29.

Stolorow, R. Brandschaft, B., and Atwood, G. (1983). Inter–subjectivity in psychoanalytic treatment, with special reference to archaic states. *Bulletin of the Menniger Clinic* 47: 117–128.

Stone, L. (1954). The widening scope of indications for psychoanalysis. *Journal of the American Psychoanalytic Association* 29: 89–118.

Stone, L. (1981). Notes on the non–interpretative elements in the psychoanalytic situation and process. *Journal of the American Psychoanalytic Association* 29: 89–118.

Strozier, C.B. (2001a). Gentle into that good night. In C.B. Strozier (Ed.). *Heinz Kohut: The making of a psychoanalyst*. New York: Farrar, Strauss & Giroux, p. 377.

Strozier, C.B. (20016b). *Heinz Kohut: The making of a psychoanalyst*. New York: Farrar, Strauss and Giroux.

Sullivan, H.S. (1947). *Conceptions of modern psychiatry*. Washington, DC: William A. White Psychiatric Foundation.

Sullivan, H.S. (1953). *The interpersonal theory of psychiatry*. New York: Norton.

Swales, P. (1982). Freud, Minna, Bernays and the conquest of Rome. New light on the origins of psychoanalysis. *New American Review* 1: 1–73.

Swales, P. (1985). Letter to the editor. *The New York Review of Books*. October 24.

Swisher, C.C. III; Curtis, G. H., and Levin, R. (2000). *Java Man: how two geologists changed our understanding of human evolution*. Chicago, IL: University of Chicago Press.

Taylor, J.B. (2006). *My stroke of insight: a brain scientist's personal journey*. New York: Viking Press.

Terman, D. (1988). Optimum frustration, structuralization and the therapeutic process. In A. Goldberg (Ed.) *Learning from Kohut: Progress in self psychology*, Vol. 4. Hillsdale, NJ: Analytic Press, pp. 113–125.

Thompson, C.M. (1942). The therapeutic technique of Sándor Ferenczi. *International Journal of Psycho–Analysis* 23: 120–134.

Thompson, C.M. (1943). The therapeutic technique of Sándor Ferenczi: a comment. *International Journal of Psycho-Analysis* 16: 64, 66.

Thompson, C.M. (1944). Ferenczi's contribution to psychoanalysis. *Psychiatry* 7: 245–252.

Thompson, C.M. (1950). *Psychoanalysis evolution and development, a review of theory and therapy*. New York: Hermitage House.

Thompson, C.M. (1964). Ferenczi's relaxation method. In M.R. Geen (Ed.). *Interpersonal psychoanalysis: papers of Clara M. Thompson*. New York: Basic Books.

Tillich, P. (1952). *The courage to be*. New Haven, CT: York University Press.

Torok, M. (1984). La correspondence Ferenczi – Freud. La vie de la littre dans l'historie de la psychoanalyse. *Confrontation* 12: 79–100.

Van der Kolk, B.A., McFarlane, A.C., and Weisaeth, L. (Eds.) (1996). *Traumatic Stress: the effects of overwhelming experience on mind, body and society*. New York: Guilford Press.

Wallington, J. (date unknown). Elizabeth Severn's horoscope. In A.W. Rachman (Ed.) (2016a). *The acquisition, restoration, and donation of the Elizabeth Severn Papers* (Unpublished).

Warrier, V., Cohen–Baron, S. and Chakrabart, B. (2013). Genetic variation in GABRB3 is associated with Asperger syndrome and multiple endophenotypes relevant to autism. *Molecular Autism* 4: 48, December.

Werner, E.E. (1971). *The children of Kauai: a longitudinal study from the prenatal period to age ten*. Honolulu: University of Hawaii Press.

Wikipedia (2013). Terotoma: Retrieved May 21.

Wikipedia (2015). Mythopoeia: Retrieved January 27.

Winnicott, D.W. (1949). Hate in the countertransference. *International Journal of Psychoanalysis* 30: 69–75.

Winnicott, D.W. (1958a). Metapsychological and clinical aspects of regression within the psychoanalytic setup. In. D.W. Winnicott (Ed.). *Collected Papers.* London: Tavistock, pp. 278–294 (original publication in 1954).

Winnicott, D.W. (1958b). *Collected Papers.* London: Tavistock.

Winnicott, D.W. (1960). Countertransference. *British Journal of Medial Psychology* 33: 17–21.

Wolberg, L. (1967). *The technique of psychotherapy, Vols. 1 and 2.* New York: Grune & Stratton.

Wolstein, B. (1959). *Countertransference.* New York: Grune & Stratton.

Wolstein, B. (Ed.) (1988). *Essential papers on countertransference.* New York: New York University Press.

Wolstein, B. (1989). Ferenczi, Freud, and the origins of American interpersonal relations. *Contemporary Psychoanalysis* 25: 672–685.

Wolstein, B. (1992). Sándor Ferenczi and American Interpersonal Relations. In. L. Aron, L. and A. Harris (Eds.). *The legacy of Sándor Ferenczi.* Hillsdale, NJ: Analytic Press, pp. 175–183.

Yalom, I. (1974). *A little closer: a twice told therapy.* New York: Basic Books.

Youcha, I. (2014). Discussion about Ferenczi and Severn. Email, July 5. In. A.W. Rachman (Ed.) (2016d). *The acquisition, restoration and donation of The Elizabeth Severn Papers* (Unpublished).

Young–Breuhl, E. (1988). *Anna Freud: a biography* New York: Summit Books.

Young–Breuhl, E. (1992). Anna Freud's analysis with her father. Telephone conversation.

Zalta, E.N. (1995) (Ed.). *The Stanford encyclopedia of philosophy.* Palto Alto, CA: Stanford University Press.

Zuar, O. (2001). Out–of–office experience: when crossing office boundaries and engaging in duel relationships are clinically beneficial and ethically sound. *The Independent Practictioner* 2:1, 96–100.

INDEX

childhood sexual abuse: historical <vsi>. narrative truth on 241–2; repressed memories reality and 240–1; *see also* sexuality
childhood sexual trauma 54, 84, 143–5, 155, 172–4, 188, 222, 281, 298
childhood trauma 21, 36, 52, 53, 60, 66, 86, 89, 109, 110, 114, 117, 137–40, 143, 148, 152, 157–8, 163–4, 166–7, 171–6, 185–8, 193, 194, 196, 206, 207, 214, 224, 227, 237, 238, 241, 247, 248, 250–5, 267, 276, 279, 281, 290–1, 296
Chilispin, F. 105
"chimney sweeping" (Anna O./Bertha Pappenheim) 198, 199, 244, 245, 273
Christian science 120, 129, 261
client-centered psychotherapy *see* person-centered psychotherapy
clinical detachment 56
Clinical Diary (Ferenczi) 20–2, 43, 45, 51, 52, 88–9, 93, 106, 109, 114, 129, 137, 138, 142, 144, 148, 166, 170, 171, 175, 177, 185, 188, 193, 196, 220–4, 238, 247, 283, 286–7, 303; "R.N." as Elizabeth Severn in 24–6
clinical hypocrisy 176–7
clinical in-vitro experiment in intersubjectivity: Ferenczi's struggle to accept Severn's analysis of his functioning and 165–6; negative countertransference therapeutic impasse and 163–4; Severn's diagnosis of Ferenczi's antipathy and 164–5; Severn/Ferenczi analysis and 163; shared subjectivities contribution in analytic encounter and 168–9
clinical psychoanalysis 13, 36, 73, 74, 84, 86, 87, 148, 165, 175, 199, 201, 202, 209, 211, 211, 215, 250, 253, 292, 294–5
Conference of the American Psychoanalytic Association 18
Confrontation (French journal) 287
"Confusion of Tongues, The" (Ferenczi) 96, 141, 218–20, 294, 303
Confusion of Tongues trauma 3–14, 20–3, 36, 39, 40, 42, 52, 61, 67–9, 77, 78, 83, 87, 170–2, 180, 193, 209, 216, 224, 238, 252, 256–7, 268, 284, 285, 287, 296, 297; childhood trauma identification and retrieval and 172; clinical empathy and 173; clinical hypocrisy and 176–7; countertransference analysis and 175–6; psychoanalytic situation re-traumatization and 173–5; from

suppression to inspiration 177; therapeutic need fulfillment and 173
Coué, E. 27, 120, 128
Counseling and Psychotherapy Research Center 191
countertransference analysis 52, 138–45, 155, 163–4, 168–9, 175–6, 185–8, 210, 211, 222, 244, 246–8, 250, 252, 253, 282, 298; negative 158, 159, 191; and self-disclosure 56
creativity 6, 7, 10, 16, 17, 31, 36, 61, 73, 98, 117, 119, 123, 155, 203, 239, 289, 290

Dabo, L. 92
Dance Masks (Lipski) 105
de Costa, L. 19
de Forest, I. 29, 48, 49, 218, 284–5
DeMille, A. 105
denial 60, 68, 137, 221
dependence and dysfunction 54
depression 45, 75, 82, 84, 86, 117, 128, 137, 142, 157, 166, 173, 184, 188, 206, 219, 221, 225, 254, 270, 271, 275, 290, 298
Deutsch, H. 37, 57
Development of Psychoanalysis (Ferenczi and Rank) 201, 202
Dewey, J. 2
direct suggestion 121–3
Discovery of the Self: A Study in Psychological Cure, The (Severn) 28, 128, 229, 235, 284, 293
Dupont, J. 24, 25, 29, 31, 51, 103, 196–7, 219, 287

Eddy, B. 27, 120
"Effect of the Structure of the Ego on Psychoanalytic Technique, The" (Eissler) 36
Einfühling (empathy) 294
Eissler, K. 50, 54, 55, 72, 89, 106–7, 110, 111, 113–15, 120, 131, 149, 150, 184, 187, 220, 230, 235, 238, 280, 283, 290; discovering Severn 40; Freud Archives and 36–8; and Freudian psychoanalysis 35–6; interview with Severn 41–3; Masson and 38–40; Swales' response to 40–1
"Elasticity of Psychoanalytic Technique, The" (Ferenczi) 85, 156
"Elizabeth Severn, The Evil Genius of Psychoanalysis" (Rachman) 34
Elizabeth Severn Archives 300–2
Elizabeth Severn Papers, The 41, 53, 108, 116, 246, 263, 300–2; donation to

University of Chicago 3; Counseling and
Psychotherapy Research Center 16;
Counseling Center 13

Vienna Medical Society 39
Vienna Psychoanalytic Institute 8, 57, 58

Wallington, J. 263–4
Weil, K. 105
West, E. 275–6
Whiplash (film) 9
Whistler, J. A. M. 92
Whitney, H. H. 92
William Alanson White Institute 6–7,
16–17, 252

Wilshire, M. 93–4
Winnicott, D. W. 37, 49, 118, 150, 256,
258–9
Wolberg, L. 7
Wolf-Man by the Wolf-Man, The
(Gardner) 78
Wolf Man Sixty Years, The (Obholzer) 78
Wolstein, B. 196
Wright, E. 103

Young-Breuhl, E. 62–3
Young Ferenczi's First Writings
(Lorin) 31

Zimring, F. 3

Taylor & Francis eBooks

Helping you to choose the right eBooks for your Library

Add Routledge titles to your library's digital collection today. Taylor and Francis ebooks contains over 50,000 titles in the Humanities, Social Sciences, Behavioural Sciences, Built Environment and Law.

Choose from a range of subject packages or create your own!

Benefits for you

- » Free MARC records
- » COUNTER-compliant usage statistics
- » Flexible purchase and pricing options
- » All titles DRM-free.

Benefits for your user

- » Off-site, anytime access via Athens or referring URL
- » Print or copy pages or chapters
- » Full content search
- » Bookmark, highlight and annotate text
- » Access to thousands of pages of quality research at the click of a button.

eCollections – Choose from over 30 subject eCollections, including:

Archaeology	Language Learning
Architecture	Law
Asian Studies	Literature
Business & Management	Media & Communication
Classical Studies	Middle East Studies
Construction	Music
Creative & Media Arts	Philosophy
Criminology & Criminal Justice	Planning
Economics	Politics
Education	Psychology & Mental Health
Energy	Religion
Engineering	Security
English Language & Linguistics	Social Work
Environment & Sustainability	Sociology
Geography	Sport
Health Studies	Theatre & Performance
History	Tourism, Hospitality & Events

For more information, pricing enquiries or to order a free trial, please contact your local sales team: www.tandfebooks.com/page/sales